Hawaii Remembered

Postcards from Paradise

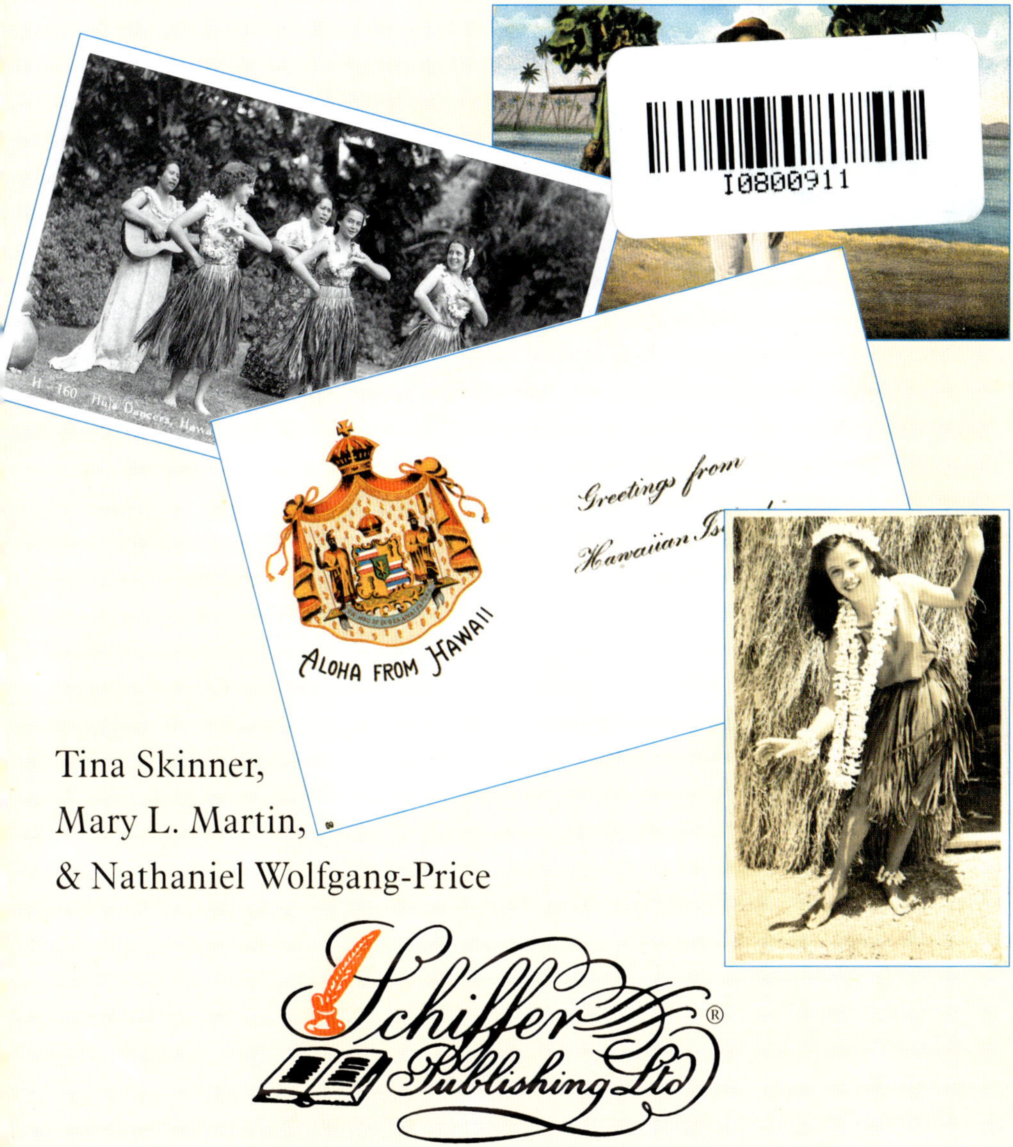

Tina Skinner,
Mary L. Martin,
& Nathaniel Wolfgang-Price

Schiffer® Publishing Ltd
4880 Lower Valley Road, Atglen, PA 19310 USA

Skinner, Tina.
Hawaii remembered : postcards from paradise / by Tina Skinner, Mary L. Martin & Nathaniel Wolfgang-Price.
p. cm.
ISBN 0-7643-2219-2 (pbk.)
1. Hawaii—Pictorial works. 2. Hawaii—Social life and customs—Pictorial works. 3. Natural history—Hawaii—Pictorial works. 4. Hawaii—History—Pictorial works. I. Martin, Mary L., 1936- II. Wolfgang-Price, Nathaniel. III. Title.

DU621.5.S58 2004
996.9'0022'2—dc22
2004031070

Designed by Mark David Bowyer
Type set in Casablanca Antique/Aldine721 Lt BT

ISBN: 0-7643-2219-2
Printed in China
1 2 3 4

Published by Schiffer Publishing Ltd.
4880 Lower Valley Road
Atglen, PA 19310
Phone: (610) 593-1777; Fax: (610) 593-2002
E-mail: Info@schifferbooks.com

In Europe, Schiffer books are distributed by
Bushwood Books
6 Marksbury Ave.
Kew Gardens
Surrey TW9 4JF England
Phone: 44 (0) 20 8392-8585; Fax: 44 (0) 20 8392-9876
E-mail: info@bushwoodbooks.co.uk
Free postage in the U.K., Europe; air mail at cost.

Contents

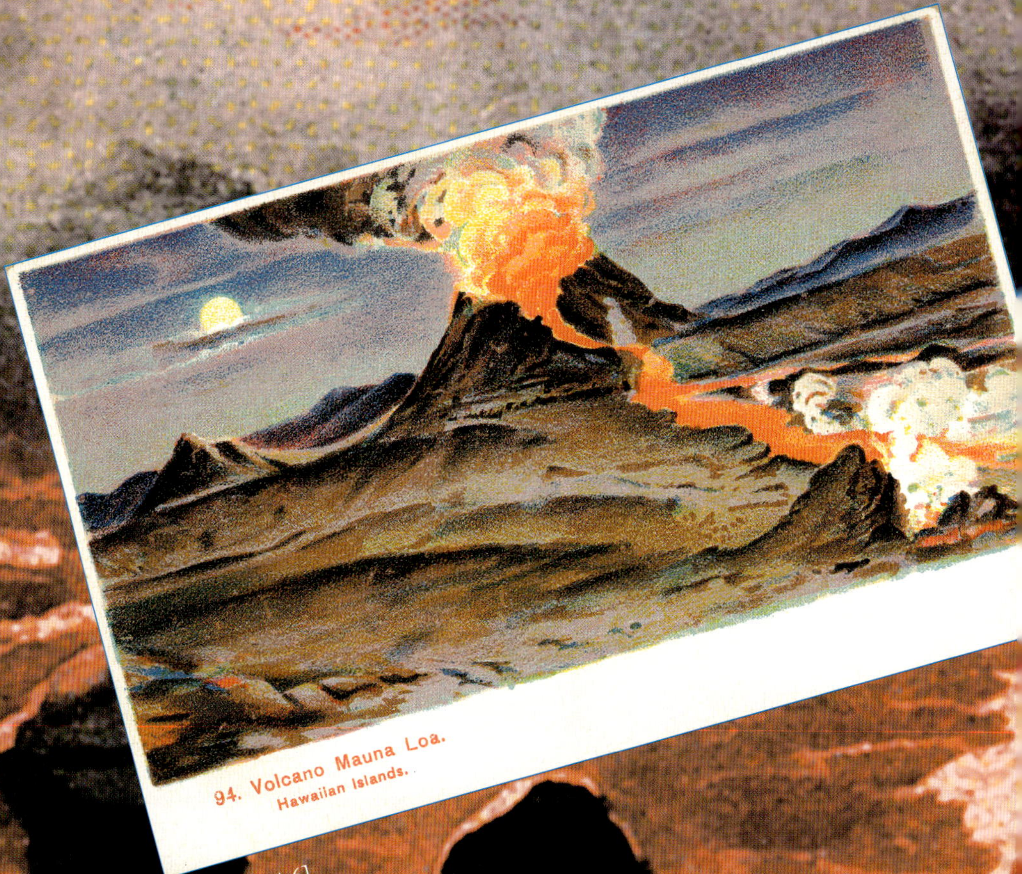

[c. 1900, $4-6]

[c. 1900-1915, $8-10]

Land of Volcanos

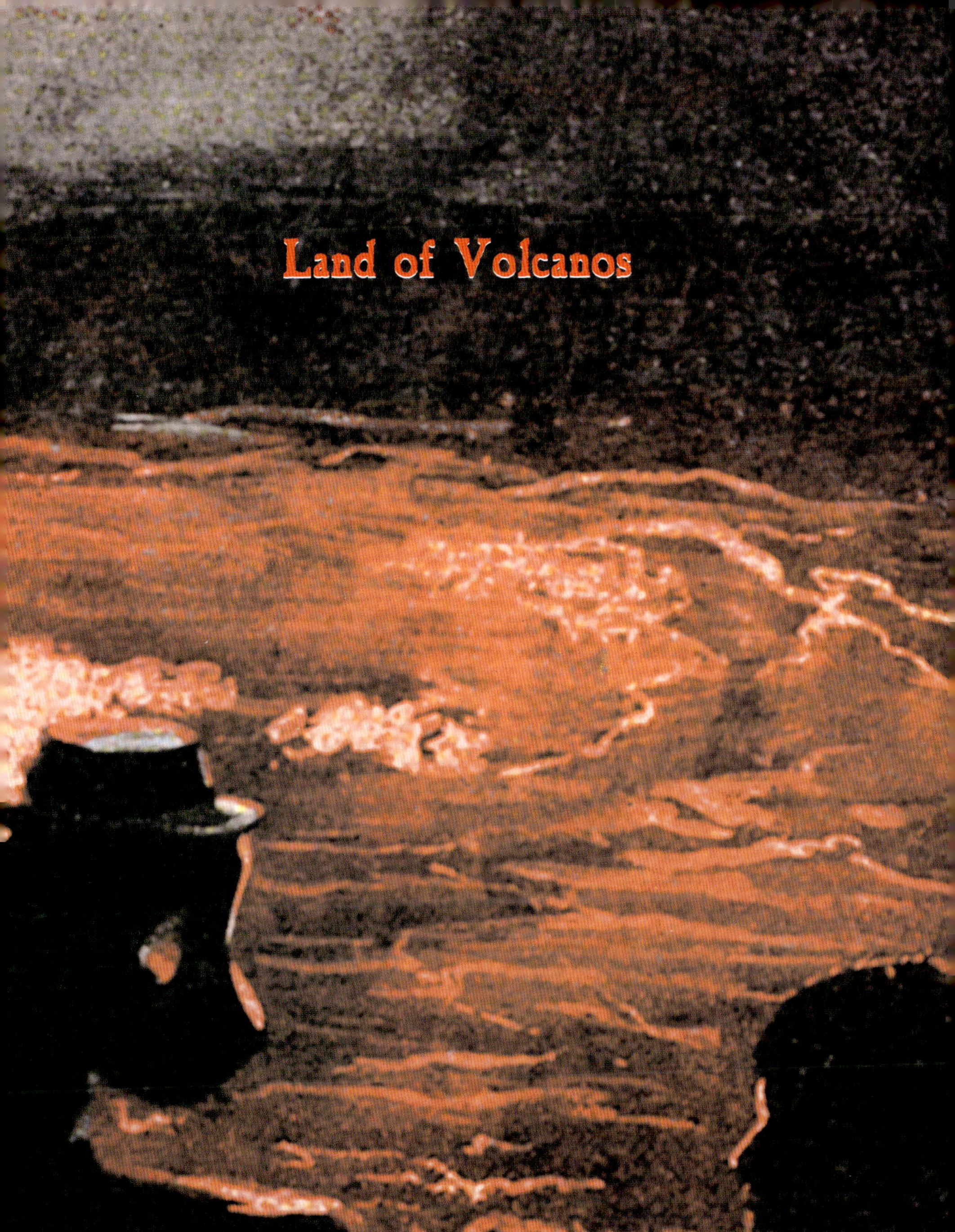

In the beginning there was fire hot enough to melt rock, abundant enough to erupt up through the floor of the Pacific and form a chain of peaks that came to be known as the Hawaiian Islands. The eruptions continue today, with hot lava constantly oozing forth to expand the tiny state. The power of this phenomena inspired worship of the volcano goddess Pele among the natives, and has drawn tourists from around the world who edge close to experience the heat and tempt the fates.

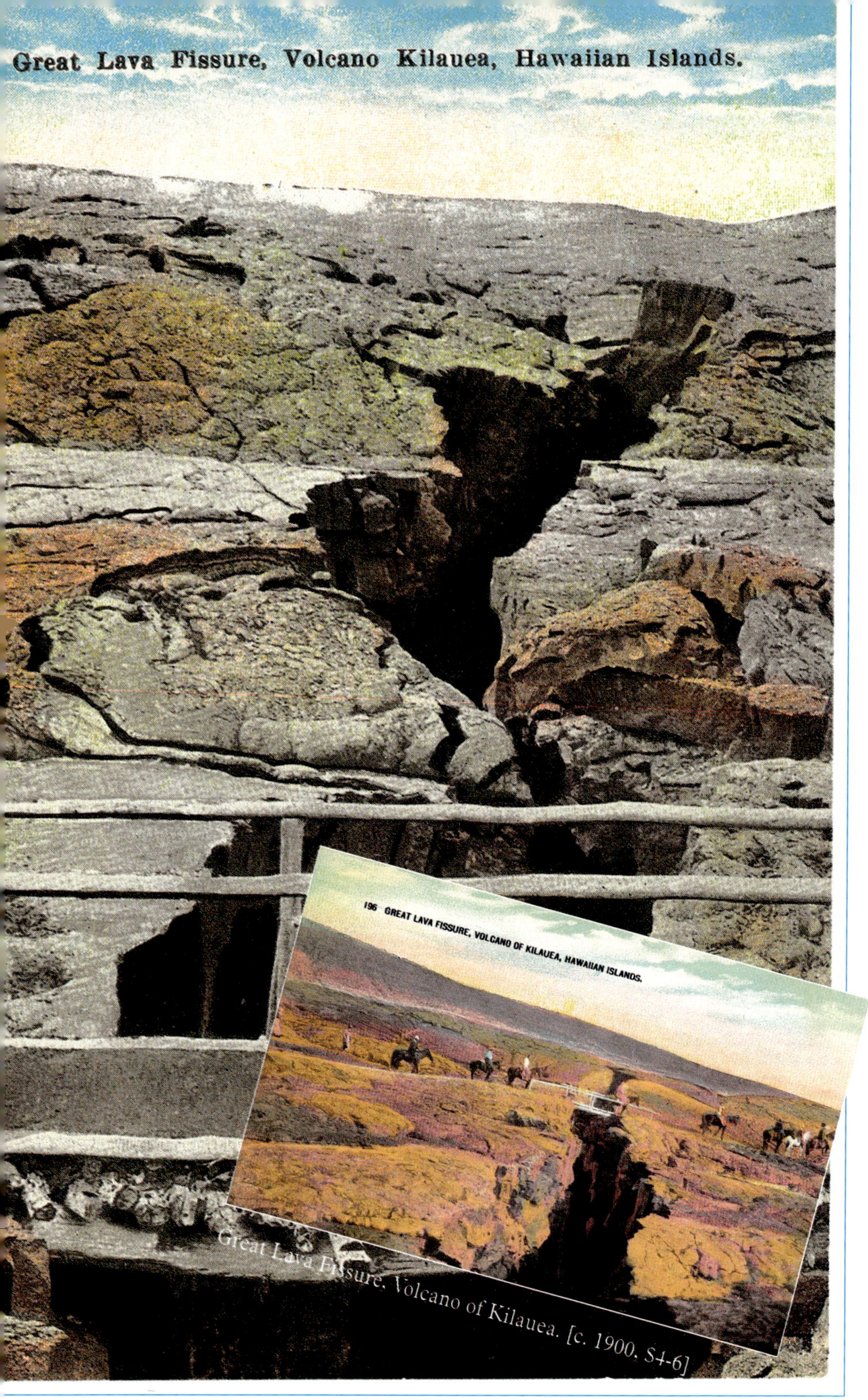

Great Lava Fissure, Volcano of Kilauea. [c. 1900, $4-6]

[c. 1900-15, $8-12]

Kilauea

The main attraction at the turn of the century, from 1823-1924, was an active lava lake within Kilauea caldera that rose and fell and sometimes overflowed. Despite the obvious danger, both tourists and scientists flocked to Kilauea, and two hotels were established to provide services – the Volcano House (1866-present) and the Crater Hotel (1911-1921). The visitors toured lava fields and caves, soaked in sulphur baths created in natural vapor cracks, and ventured close enough to molten lava to singe postcards to send home to friends and family.

Arriving first on horseback, by 1911 roads were servicing the steady traffic from Hilo to Kilauea's summit area thirty miles away. This high summit, 4,000 feet above sea level, afforded a pleasingly cool climate, yet another attraction.

Much of the area belonged to the estate of Bernice Pauahi Bishop, a princess and the last survivor of the royal Kamehameha line. This was leased to the Volcano House and the Hawaiian Volcano Research Association, which built the Hawaiian Volcano Observatory. The area eventually became a national park, being named Hawaii Volcanoes National Park in 1961.

Kilauea is but a bulge on Mauna Loa, the largest volcano on Earth with an estimated volume of 9,600 cubic miles, half of the area of the Island of Hawaii. Mauna Loa began to form nearly a million years ago. Mauna Loa is one of the most active volcanoes on Earth, erupting more than thirty times since its first documented historical eruption in 1843. In 1924 the crater exploded, increasing in size from 1700 feet in diameter and 300 feet deep, to 3000 feet in diameter and 1300 feet deep. It has continued to reshape itself repeatedly.

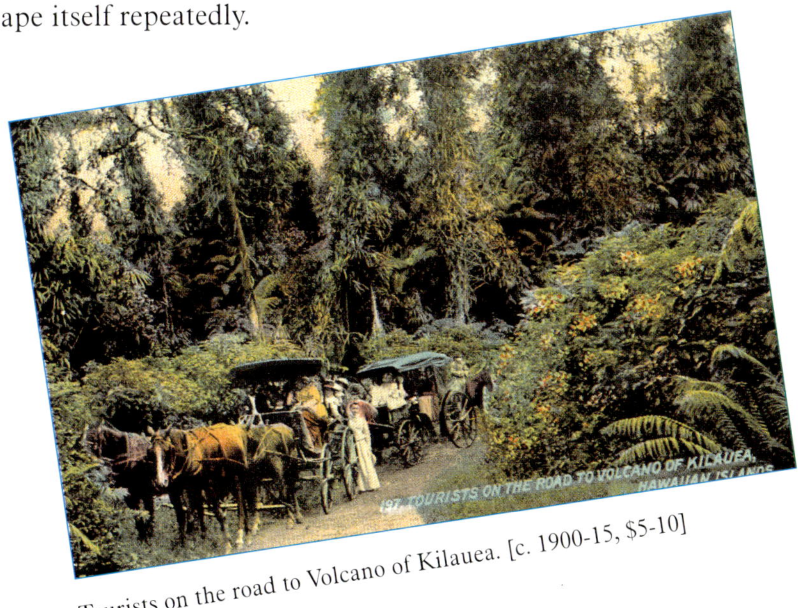

Tourists on the road to Volcano of Kilauea. [c. 1900-15, $5-10]

The danger is ever present on Mauna Loa, and the attraction of this has hardly ebbed. "The Polynesian discoverers of Hawaii developed a respect for the destructive potential of Mauna Loa and learned to coexist with volcanic activity over millennia," wrote J. P. Lockwood and J. M. Rhodes in *Periodico di Mineralogia*, a paper presented in Rome at the 1995 Decade Volcano Symposium. "...the growth of Hawaii's tourist industry has produced large developments along the coast [and] ...recent immigrants tend to deny the potential for disaster, and regard eruptive activity as potentially "entertaining."

Tourists traveling over vast lava fields, Volcano Kilauea. [c. 1900, $4-6]

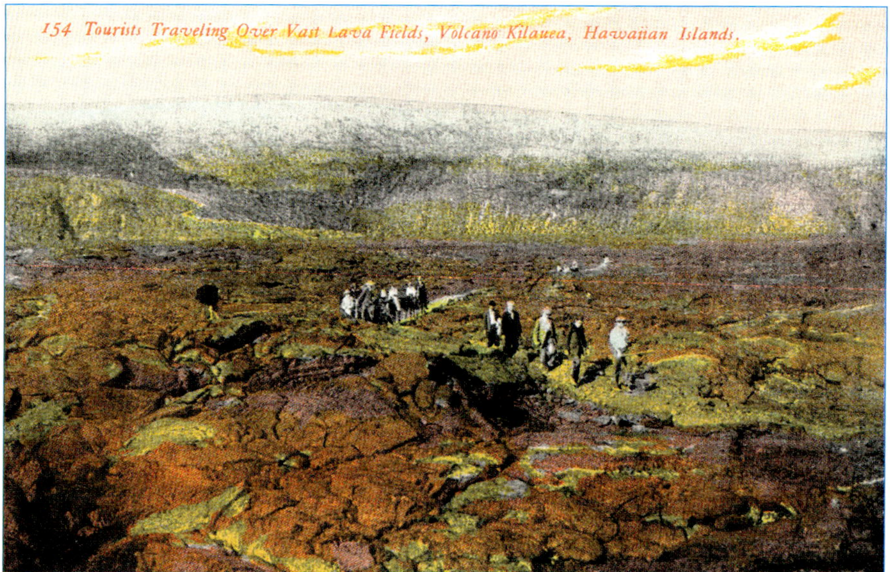

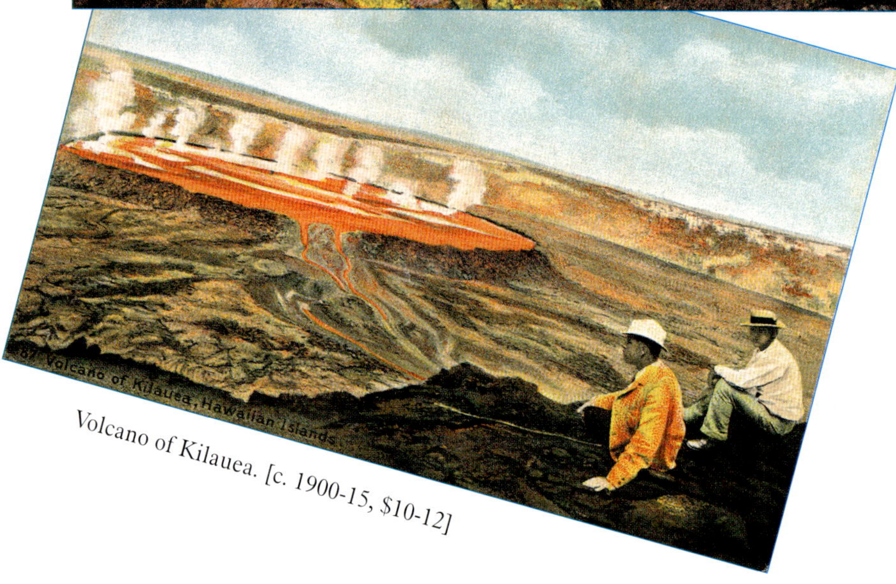

Volcano of Kilauea. [c. 1900-15, $10-12]

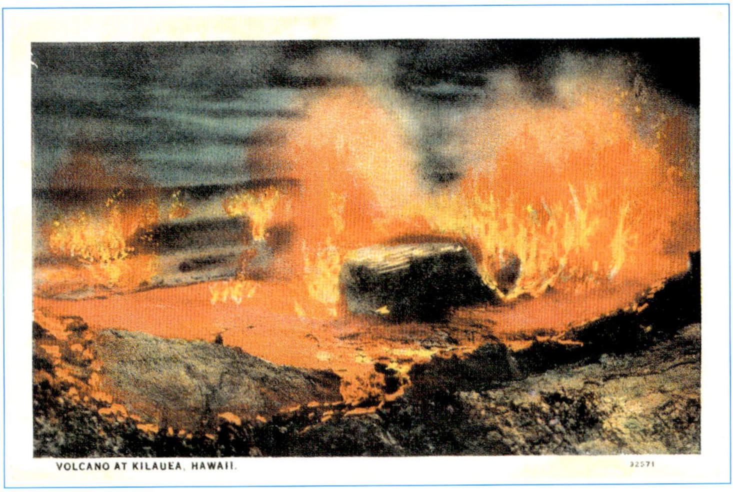

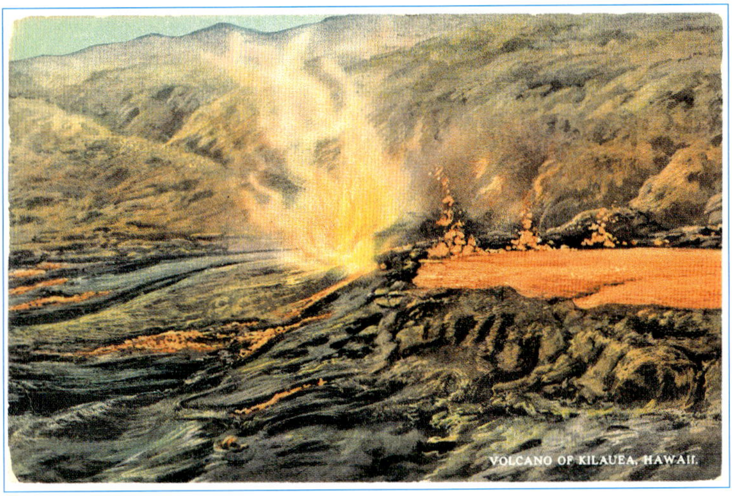

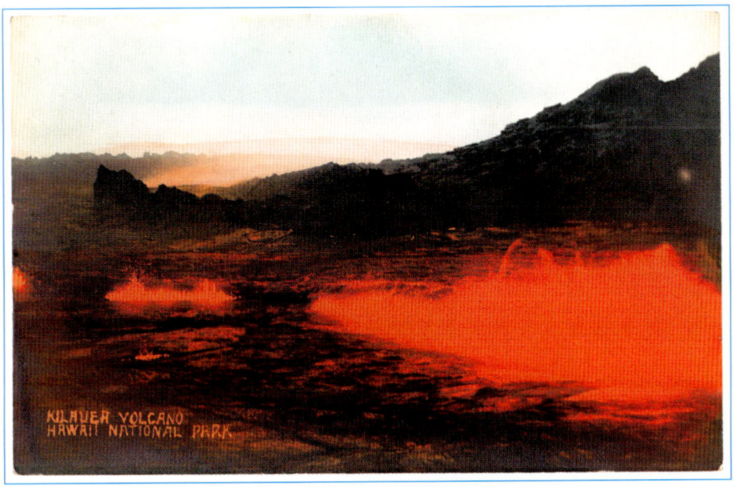

Fiery views of Kilauea. [Top: c. 1940 $4, Center: c. 1900-15, $9-11, Bottom: c. 1900-20, $9]

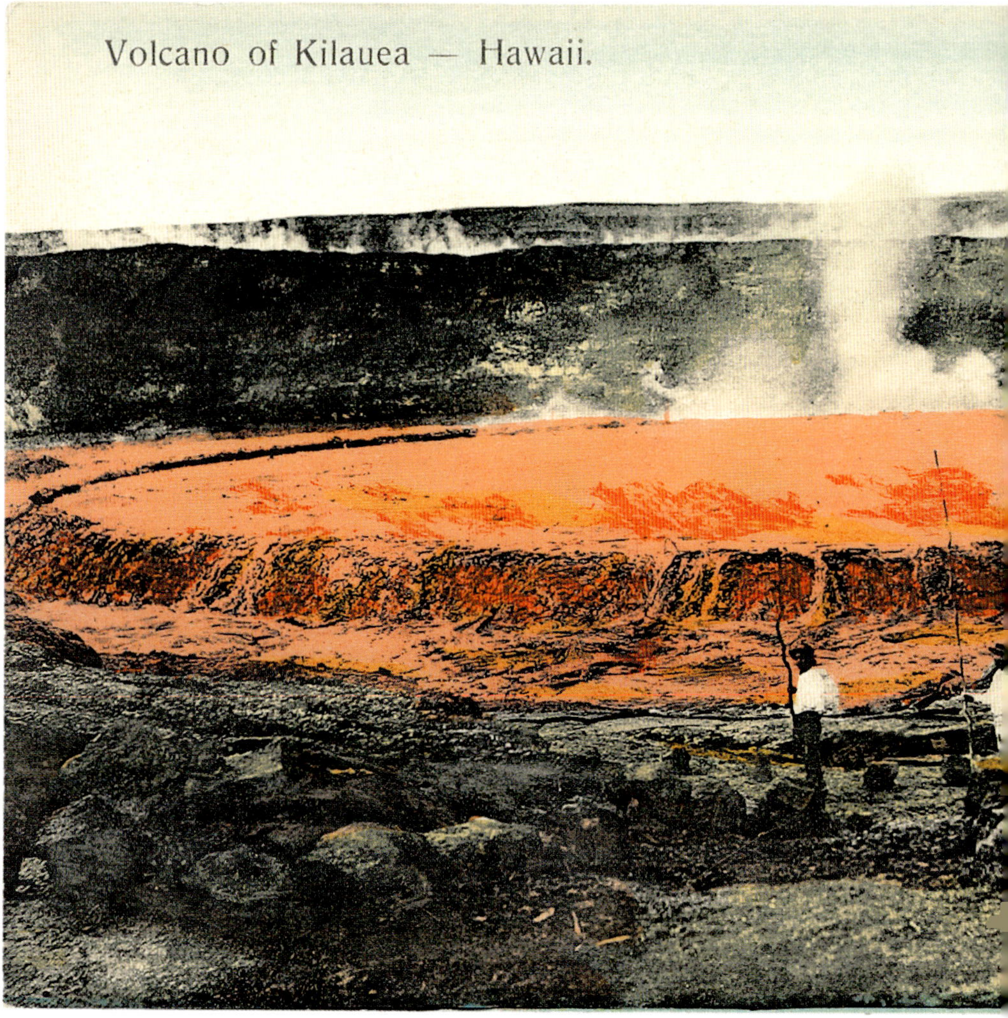

"Tourists casually crowd the edge of Kilauea's fiery caldera. Above, the caldera bubbles over while men carrying sticks walk closer to poke at the lava." [$7-10 each]

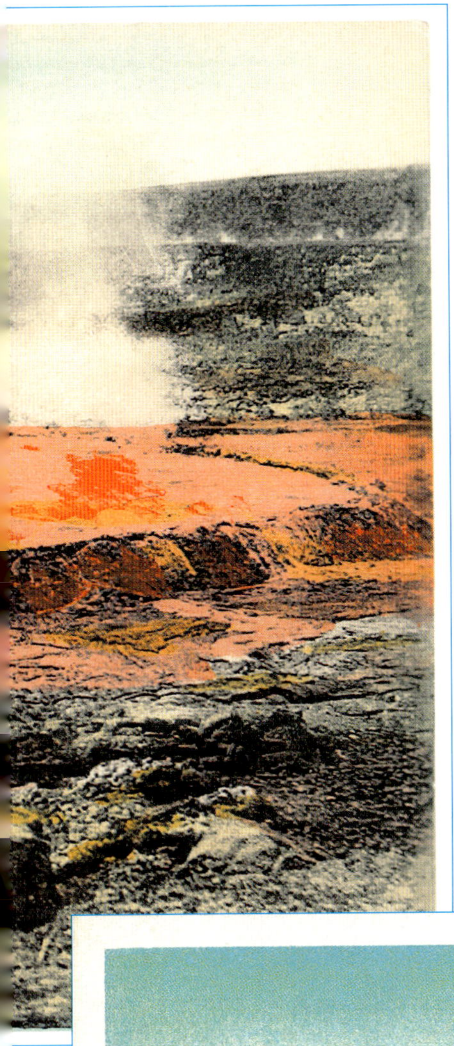

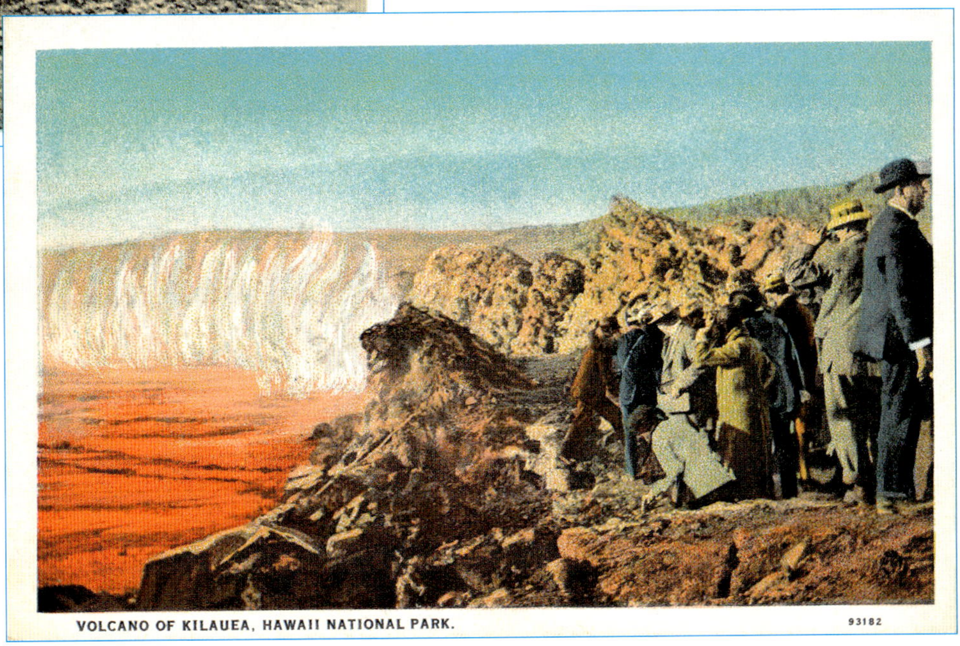

VOLCANO OF KILAUEA, HAWAII NATIONAL PARK. 93182

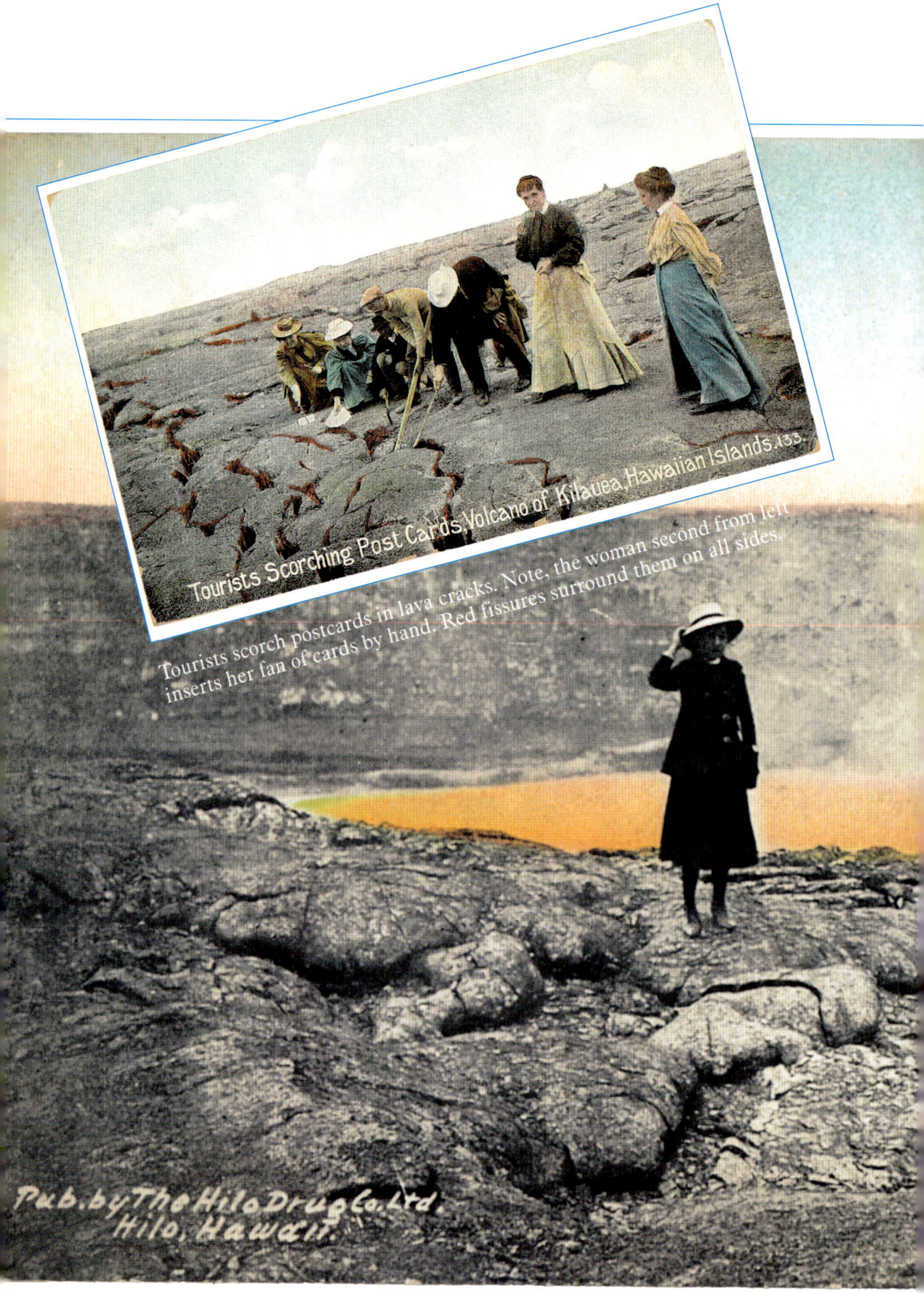

Tourists scorch postcards in lava cracks. Note, the woman second from left inserts her fan of cards by hand. Red fissures surround them on all sides.

A child and two men pose, the crater behind them. [Canceled 1910, $9-12]

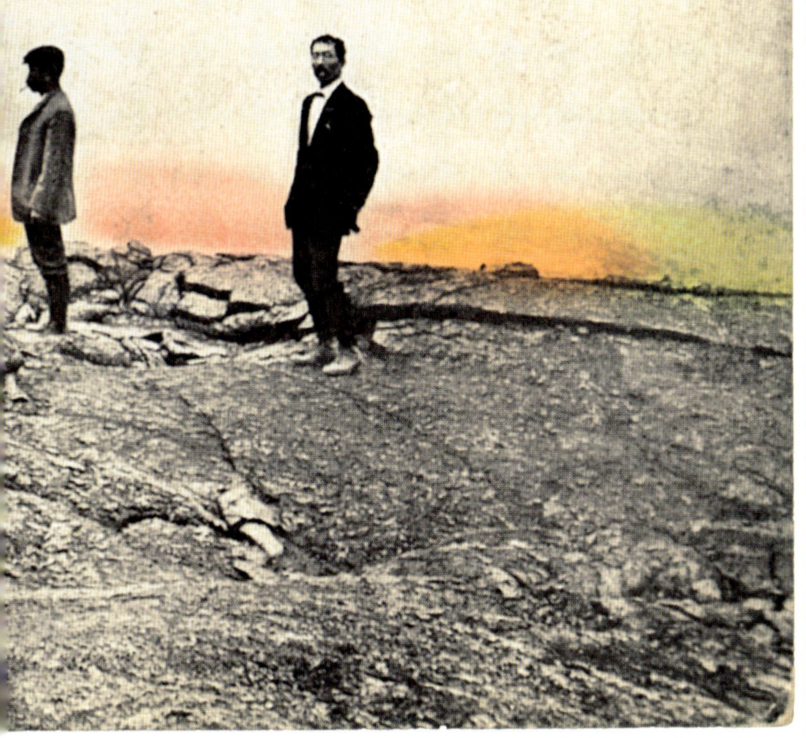

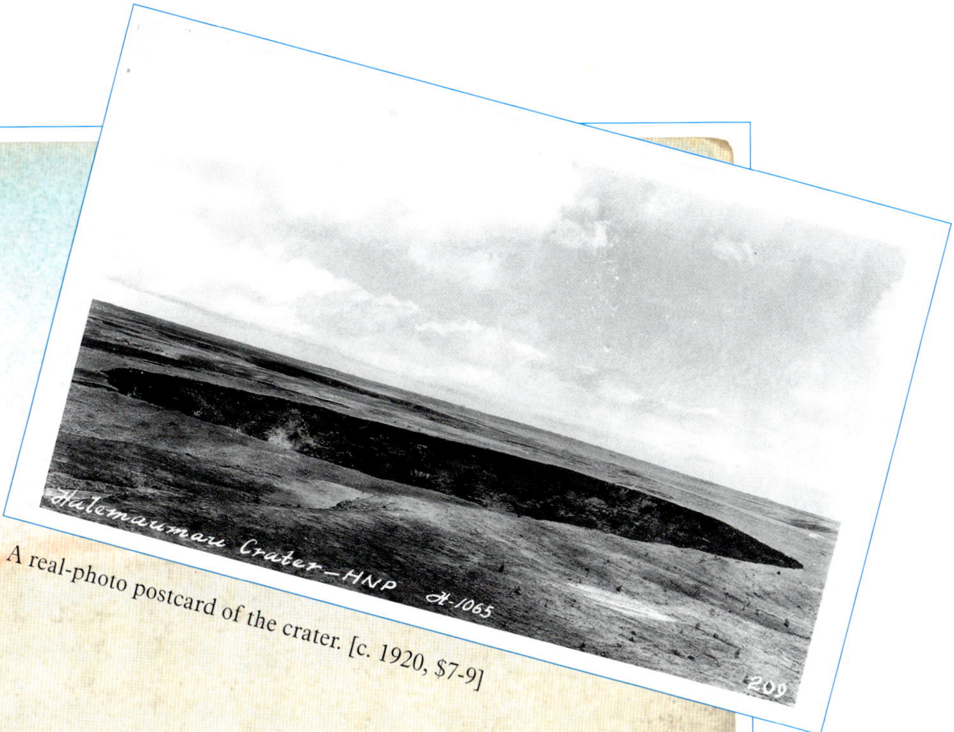

A real-photo postcard of the crater. [c. 1920, $7-9]

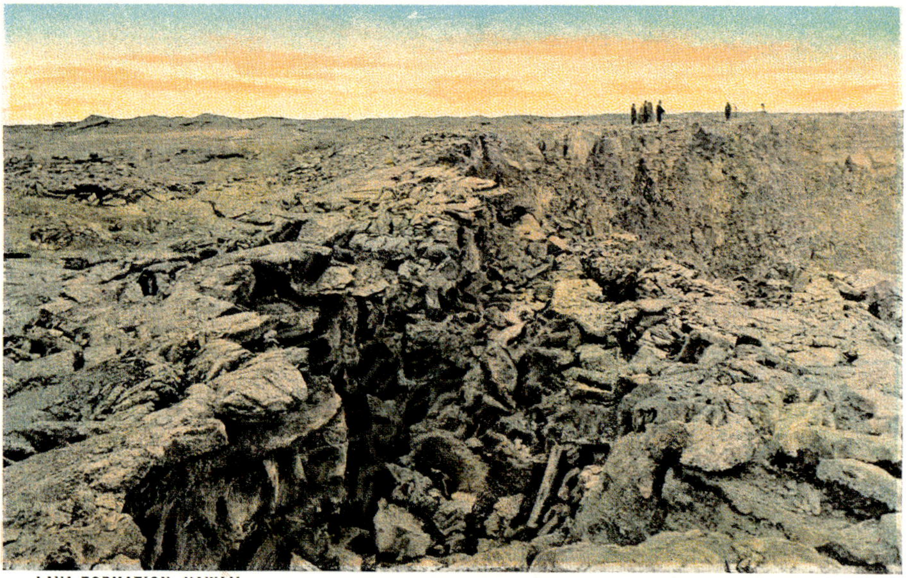

A small party of tourists illustrates the vast stretches of lava around Kilaue – covering an area of eight miles, 2,650 acres at the time this card was produced. [c. pre-1920, $6-8]

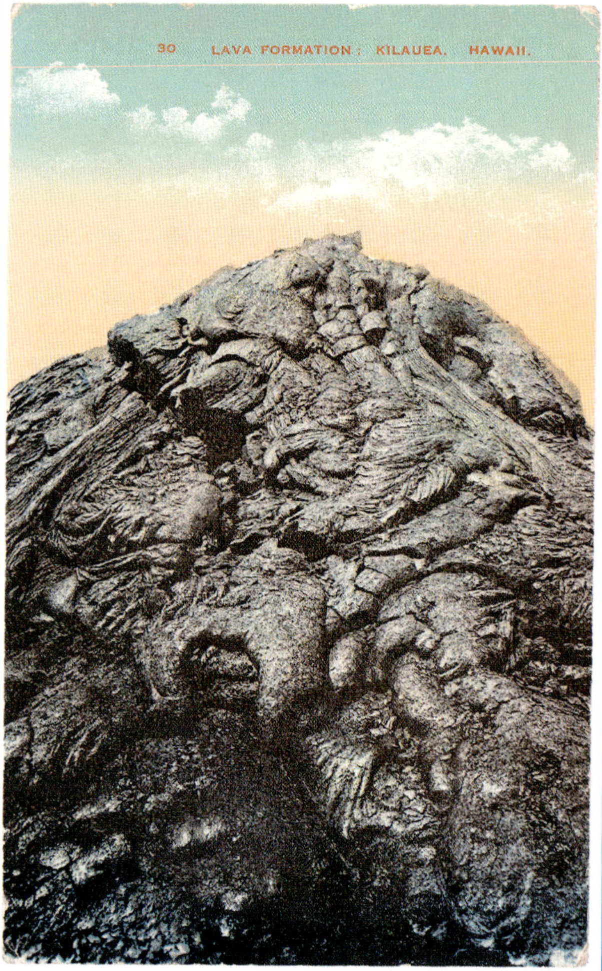

This knoll of lava is twice the height of a man, and has been broken by the settling of the floor of the crater. [Canceled 1911, $6-8]

"Am glad you beat us to it and saw the crater, you can form a little idea of what we did see. Just received your first steamer letter today."
—1911

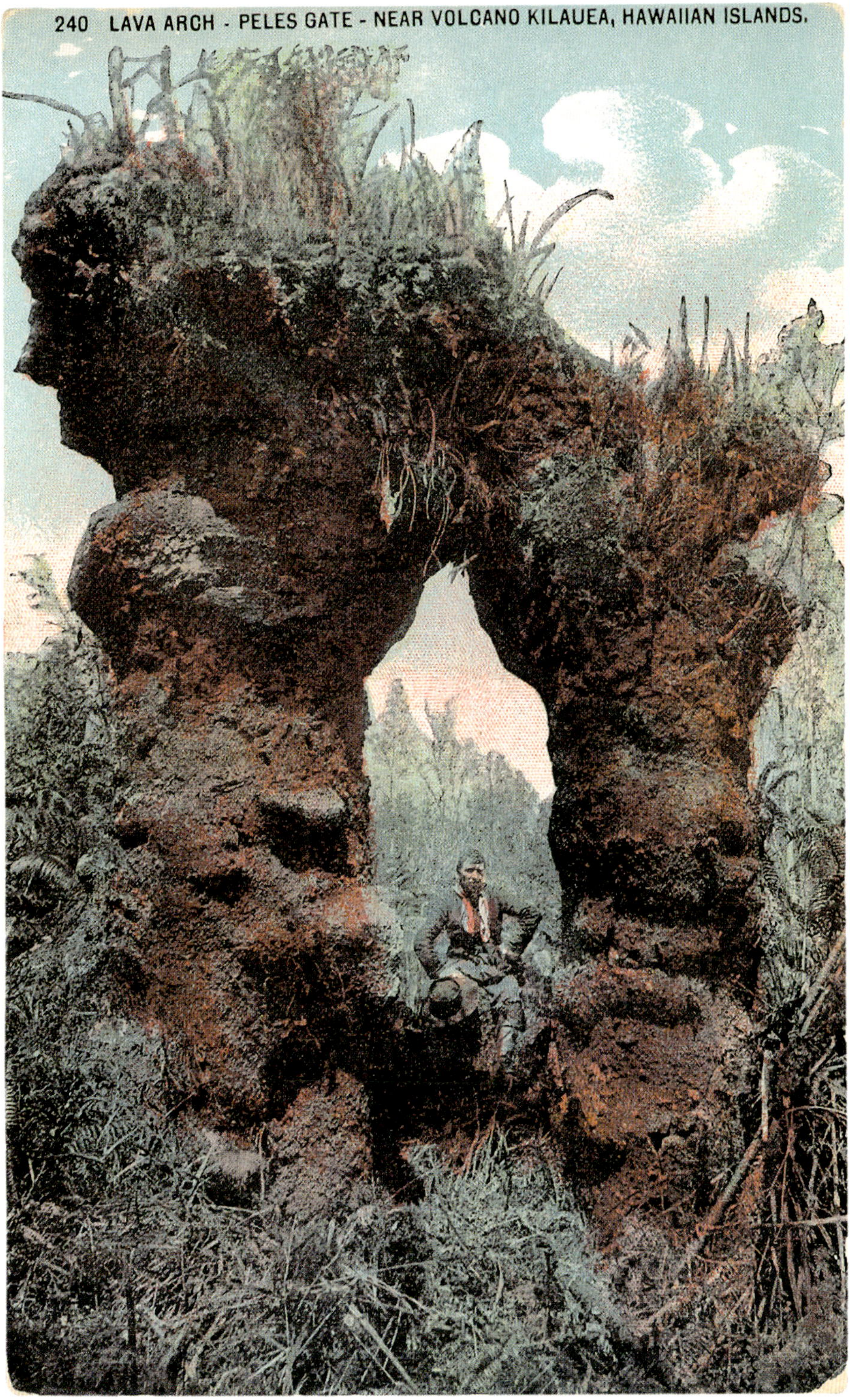

The Lava Arch called Pele's Gate near Kilauea. [pre-1915, $8-10]

Tourists exploring hot lava caves on Kilauea. Back of card: "Kilauea … has been visited by many thousands of persons in comfort and safety, and never disappoints." [canceled 1917, $8-10]

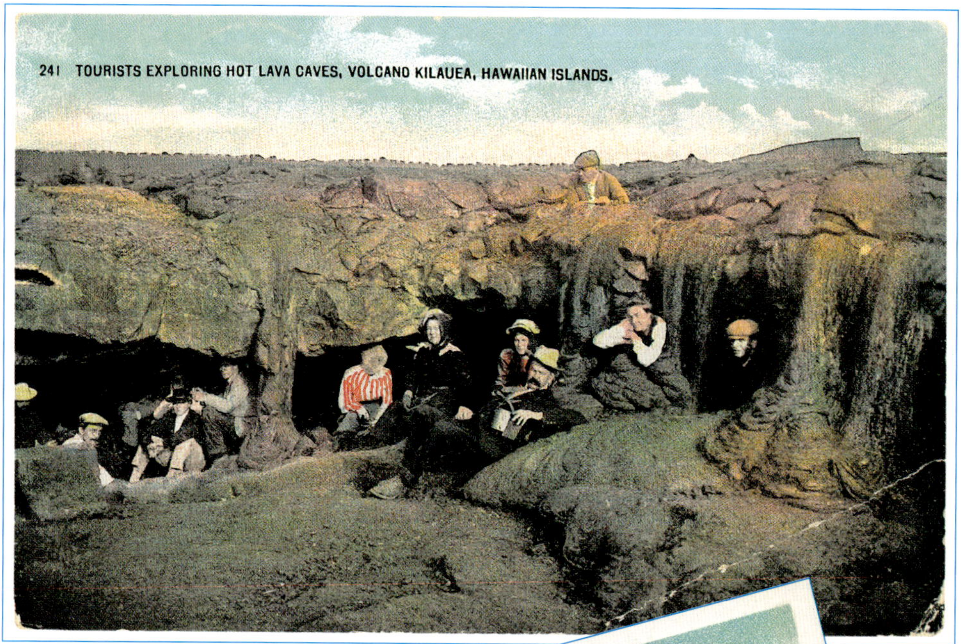

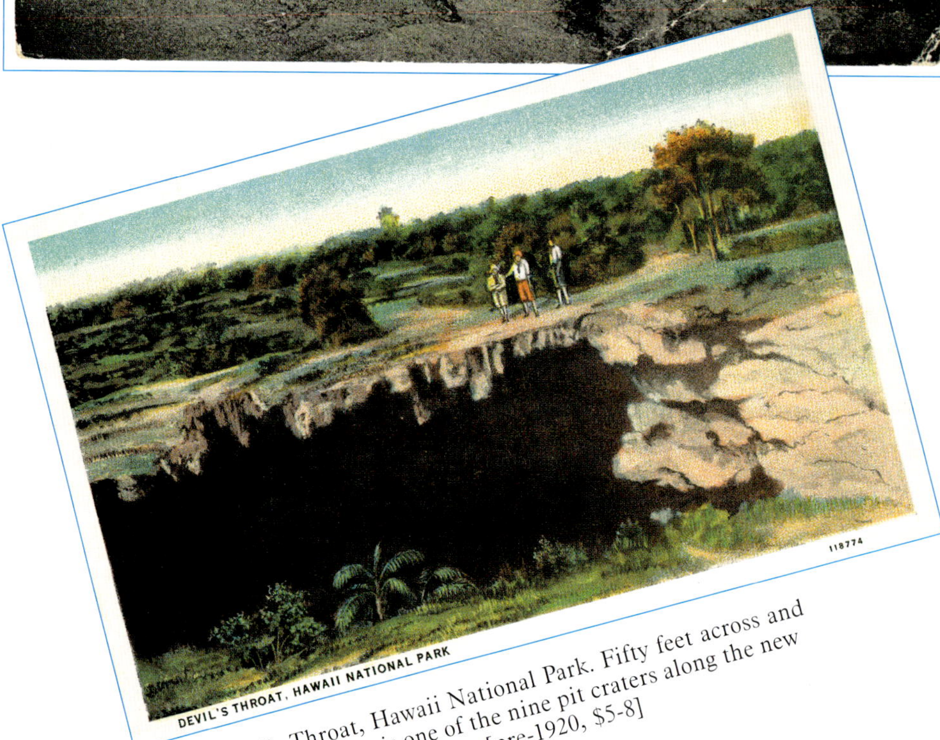

Devil's Throat, Hawaii National Park. Fifty feet across and 250 feet deep, it is one of the nine pit craters along the new Chain Craters park road. [pre-1920, $5-8]

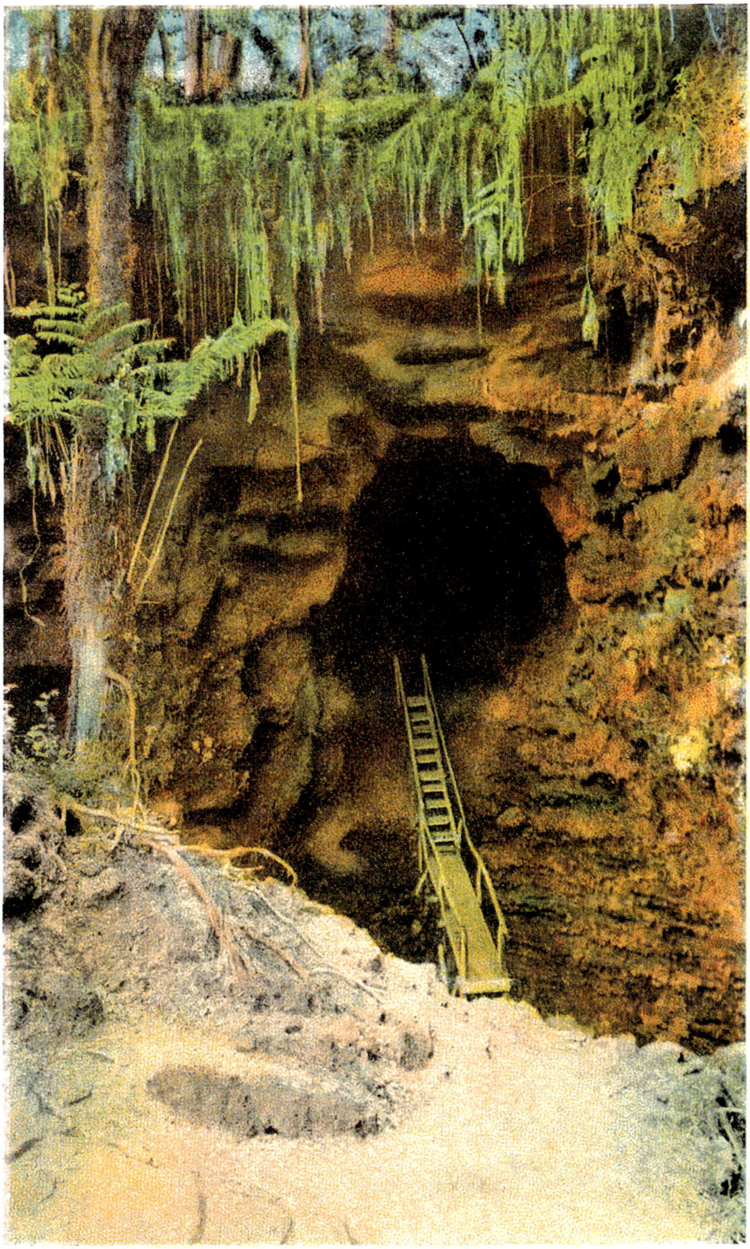

LAVA TUBE, HAWAII. 93187

From the back: "A large lava tube of very recent construction. A descent may be made into this and will well repay the slight effort involved. Many interesting formations upon the roof and walls will be observed. The tunnel should not be entered without flashlights." [Canceled 1929, $2-4]

"Better take your next vacation here. It's a wondrous place."
—1929

Diamond Head

Named by a band of English sailors who thought they'd found treasure, this extinct volcano merely offered calcite crystals embedded in its rocks. That initial disappointment hasn't kept this tuff crater from becoming Hawai'i's best-known landmark, though. Le'ahi Peak stands 761 feet above sea level and affords a spectacular, 360-degree lookout over O'ahu and Waikiki and Honolulu.

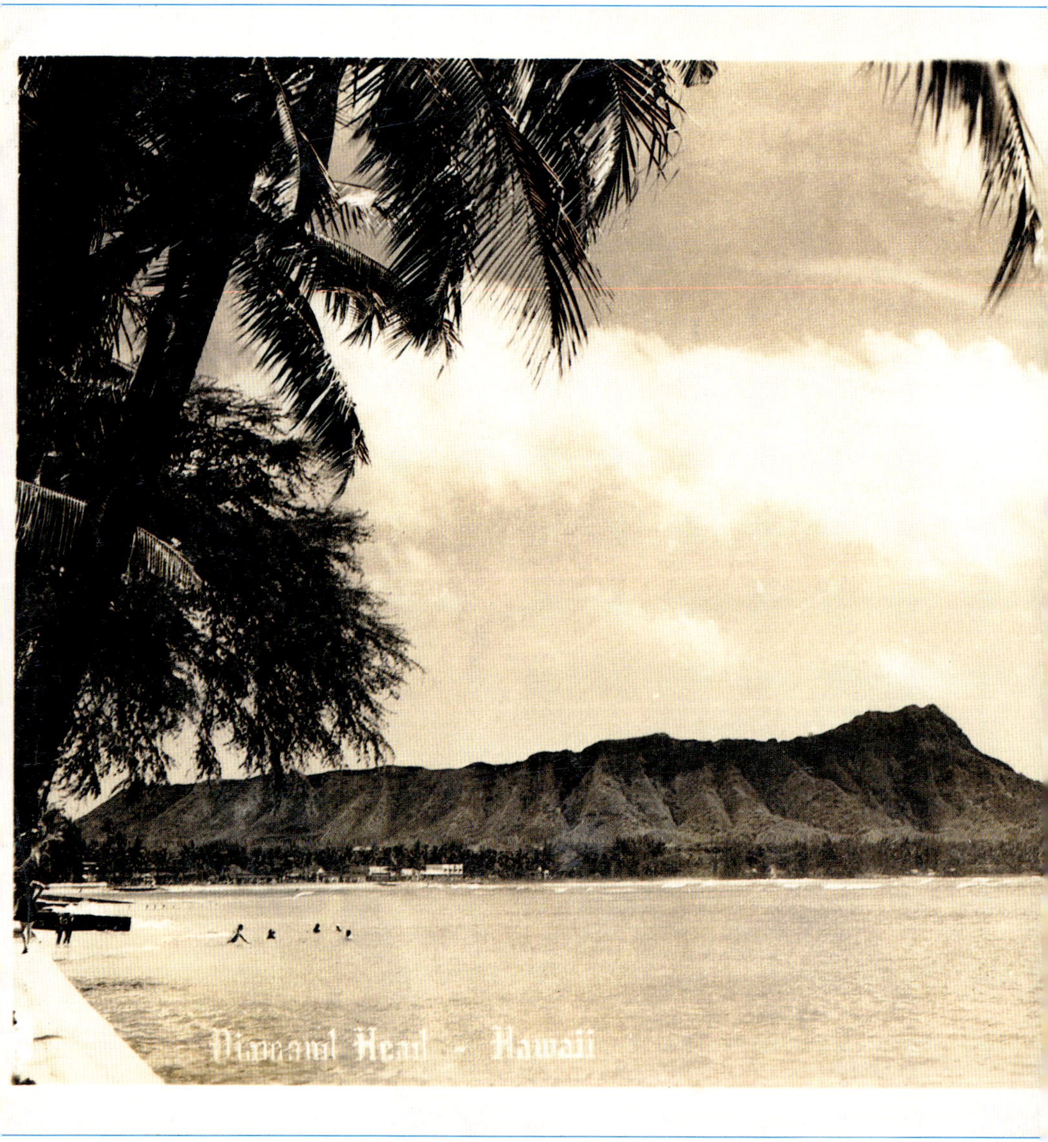

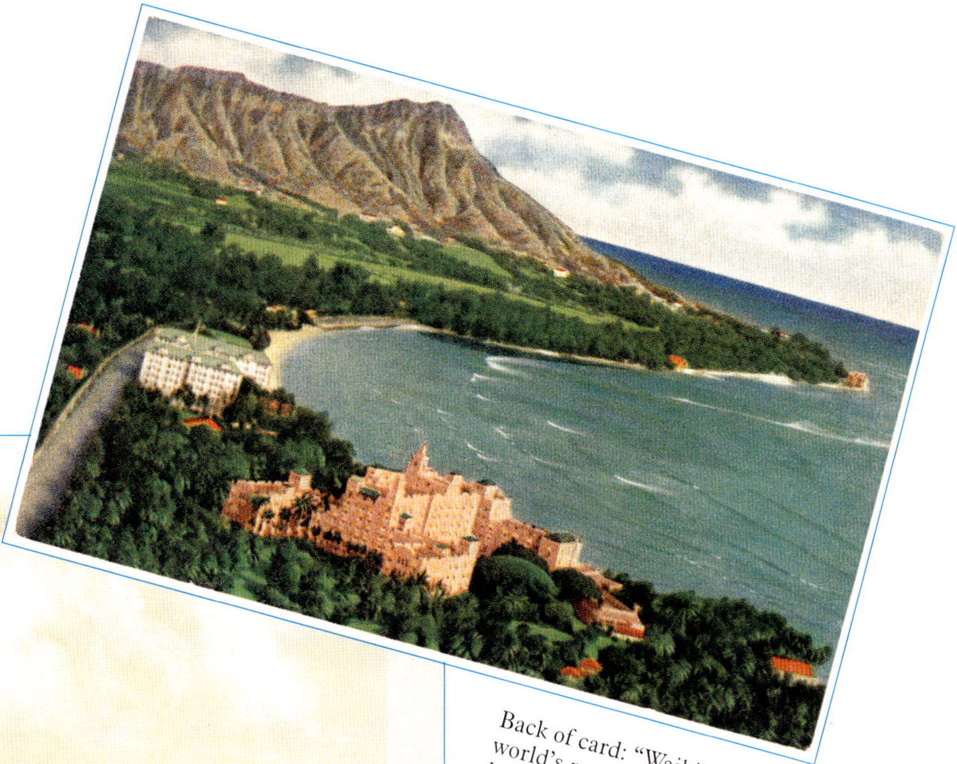

Back of card: "Waikiki: the world's most famous and best-loved beach …Stately Diamond Head rises in the distance." [c. 1925, $6-9]

Real photo postcard. [c.1925, $6-8]

A Brief History of the Islands

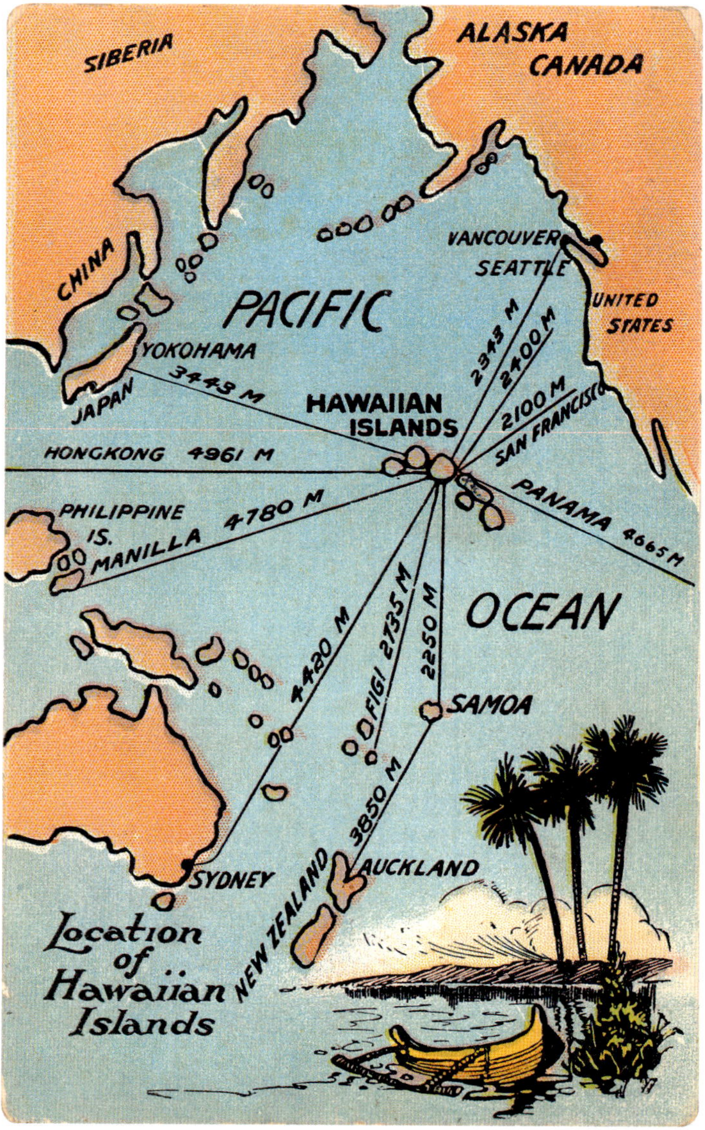

From back of card: "Hawaii lies …about 2,100 miles S.W. of San Francisco. There are eight inhabited islands…The population of Hawaii is about 192,000 and that of Honolulu about 60,000." [pre-1915, $10-12]

Polynesians are believed to have been the first to find and settle the Hawaiian Islands, navigating the Pacific in canoes. These amazing seafarers brought with them the provisions that formed the basis of agriculture and their diet on the new volcanic islands – including cocoanuts, sugarcane, and taro.

It is estimated that the native population had reached anywhere from 400,000 to 1 million people by the time British explorer Captain James Cook "discovered" the islands and used it as a wintering station during his explorations. Following Cook's tragic fallout with the Hawaiians in 1778-1779, Kamehameha I (the Great) of the Island of Hawaii consolidated his power there and then went on to conquer Maui, Oahu, and Kauai – unifying the islands in 1810.

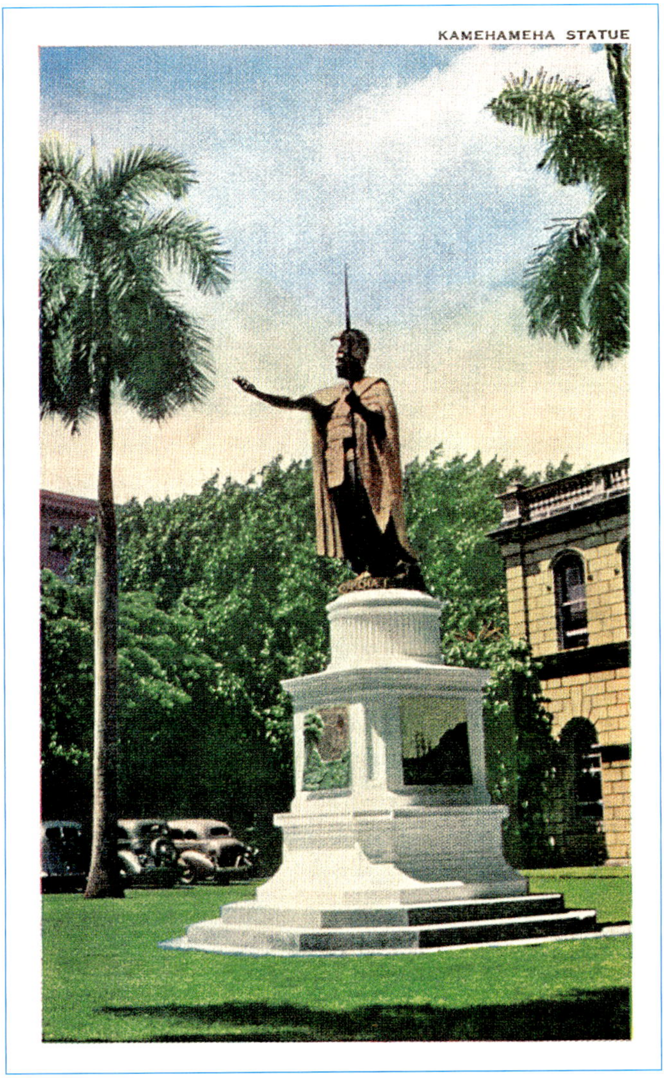

From back of card: "King Kamehameha was one of the greatest kings of Hawaii, and a great warrior, beloved by all. He established the first Hawaiian Monarchy." [c. 1930s, $5-7]

During the next eighty-three years, Hawaii transitioned from a feudal society into an independent hereditary monarchy, recognized by other nations around the world.

In 1820, American missionaries arrived and changed Hawaii, virtually overnight. Hawaiians embraced reading and writing, quickly attaining an impressive rate of literacy. By 1840, Kamehameha III introduced the first Hawaiian Constitution, establishing a House of Nobles and an elected House of Representatives, and the nation was transformed from a hereditary despotic government based on divine right to a Constitutional monarchy with an elected legislature. Subsequent constitutions followed, including an attempt by Queen Lili'uokalani to pass a constitution that would have expanded her powers, but instead got her overthrown. The (Great) Mahele of 1848 divided the land between the King the people, permitting private land ownership for the first time. Not surprisingly, few common people benefited from this.

Many of the new landholdings were subsequently sold or transferred to European and American planters. Plantation owners found territorial

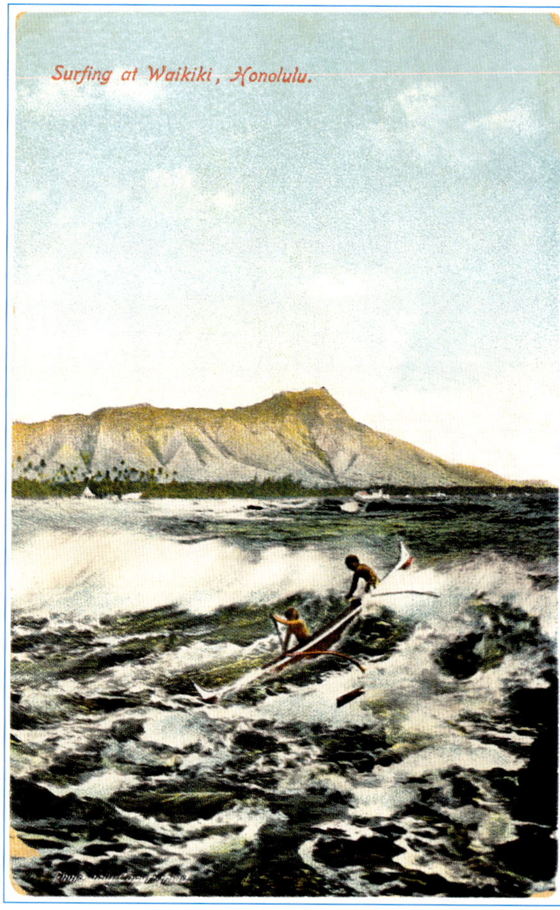

Outrigger canoes are believed to have brought the first Polynesians to the island. [Postmarked 1909, $6-8]

status quite convenient for their operations in Hawaii. It allowed them to import cheap foreign labor, then prohibited in the United States. The first contract laborers were brought from Japan in 1885 to work the sugar plantations. The descendants of the imported laborers eventually advanced their interest in statehood, leading the campaign that ended in 1959 when President Dwight Eisenhower signed the Admission Act, which made Hawaii the 50th state of the Union.

An unexpected outgrowth of the 1978 Hawaii State Constitutional Convention was what some call the "Hawaiian renaissance." Since the late 1970s, there has been a movement among Ethnic Hawaiians to revive their ancestral language and culture. Some consider the U.S government to be an occupying power, and mourn the demise of the Hawaiian monarchy. In 1993, President Clinton signed a congressional resolution apologizing for U.S. actions leading to the overthrow of the Kingdom of Hawaii.

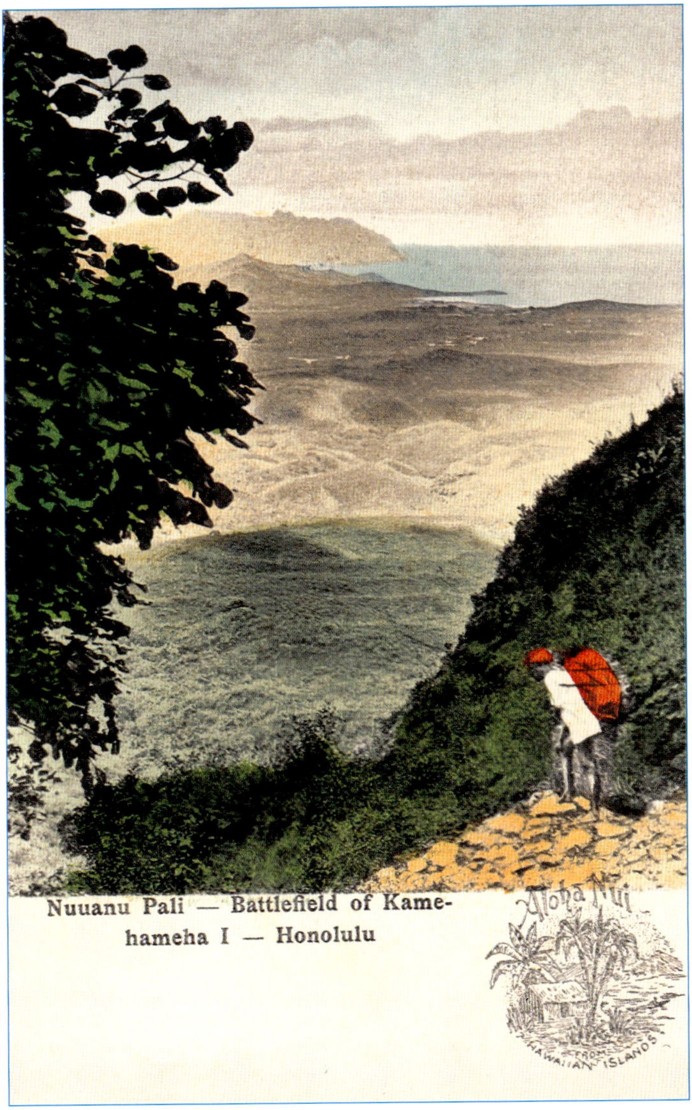

Nuuanu Pali, battlefield of Kamehameha I in Honolulu. [Postmarked 1909, $15-35]

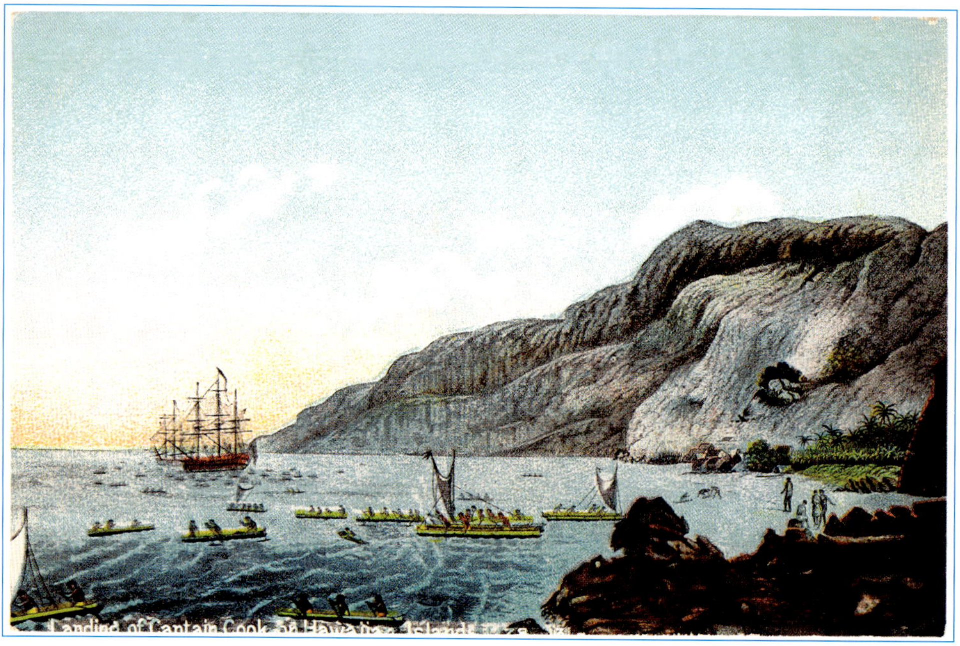

A painting portraying the landing of Captain Cook on the Hawaiian Islands. [pre-1915, $9-12]

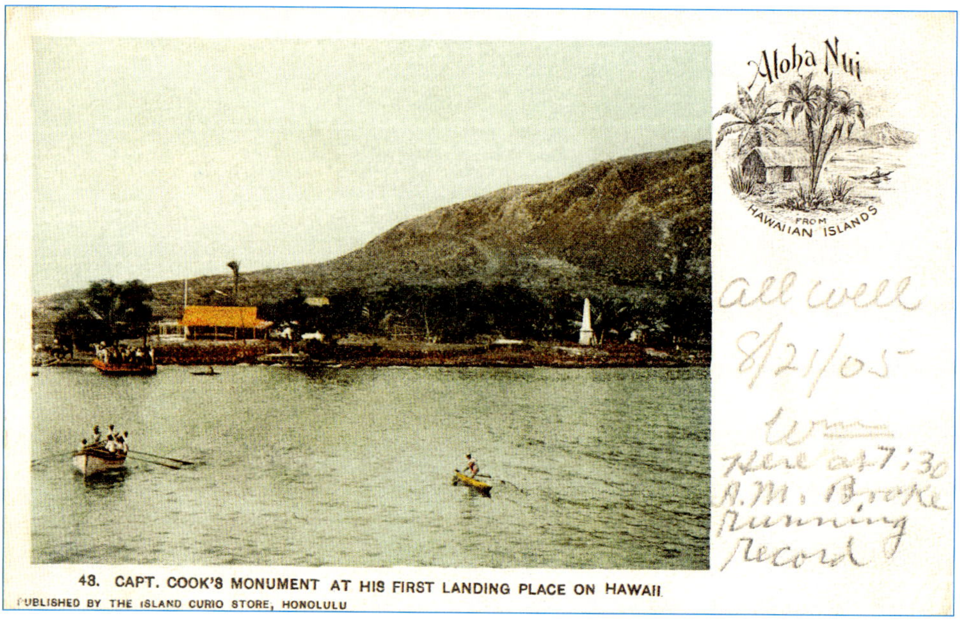

Monument at Captain Cook's first landing place. [canceled 1905, $15-35]

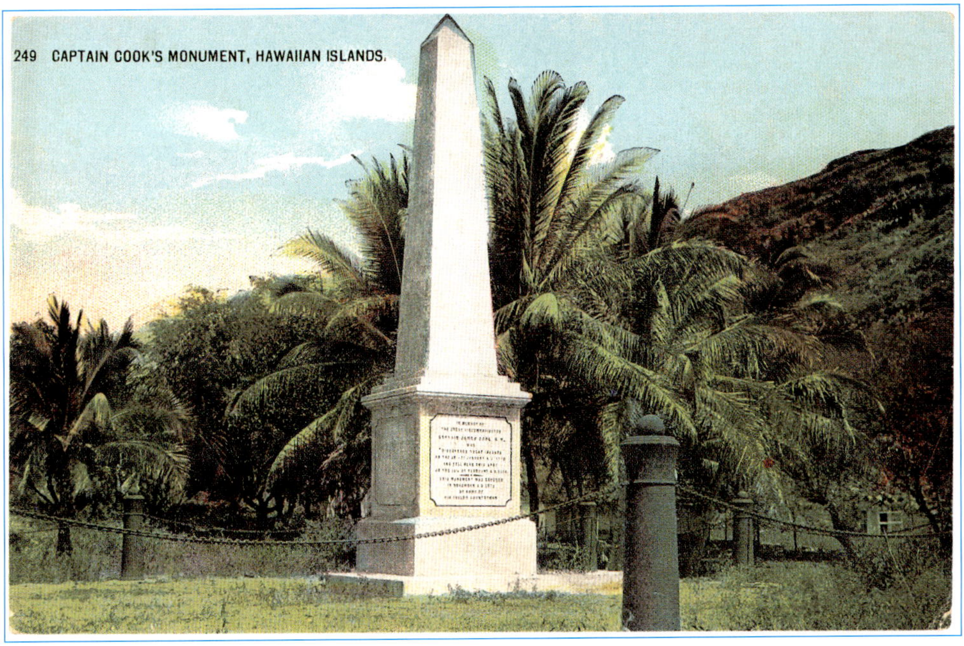

From the back: "Civilization was introduced to the Hawaiian Islands by Captain Cook's discovery in 1778. The aboriginal people were Polynesians, the first coming from Tahiti as early as A.D. 500… The ancient Hawaiians were barbarians, but never cannibals. Till Kamehameha's subjugation of all the islands, at the dawn of the nineteenth century, feudal government prevailed." [pre-1915, $6-8]

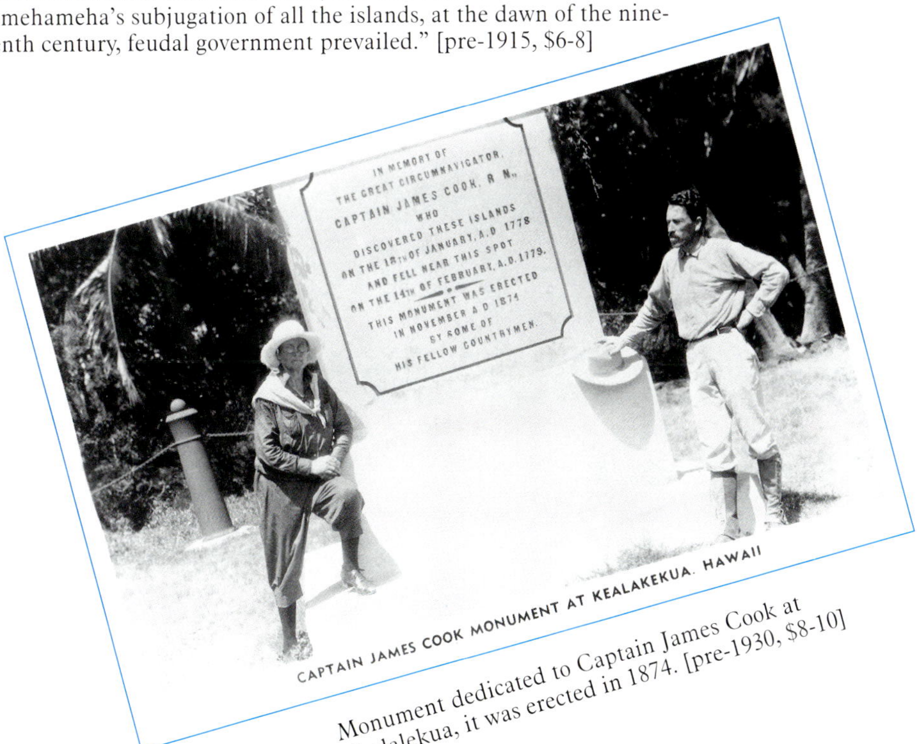

Monument dedicated to Captain James Cook at Kealalekua, it was erected in 1874. [pre-1930, $8-10]

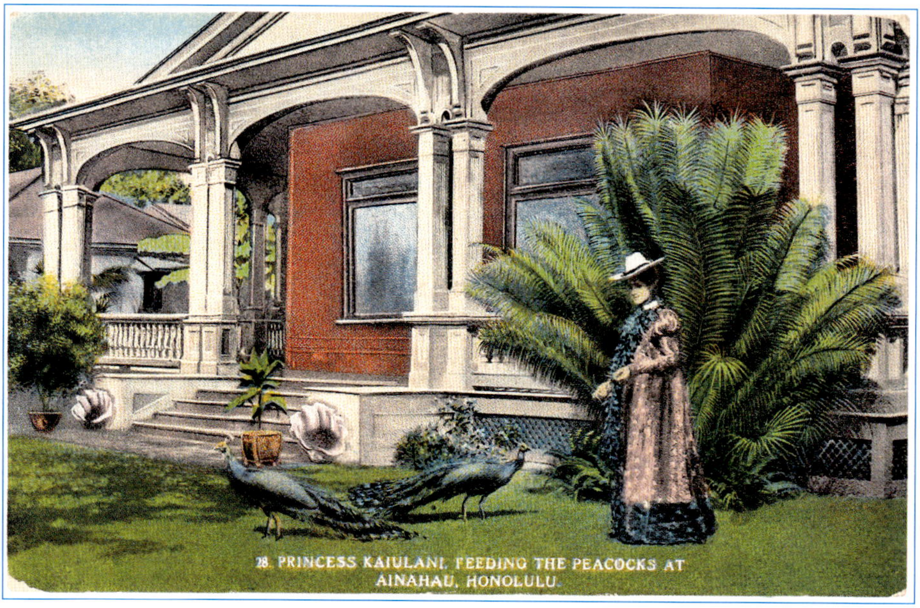

From the back: "The pathetic career of the beautiful Princess Kaiulani, daughter of Princess Likelike who was heir apparent of the last Queen of Hawaii, Liliuokalani, is at once romantic and interesting. Her home at Ainehau, Waikiki near Honolulu is now the park given to the city by her father in memory of this beautiful Princess who, mourned by all, died late in 1800. [pre-1915, $9-12]

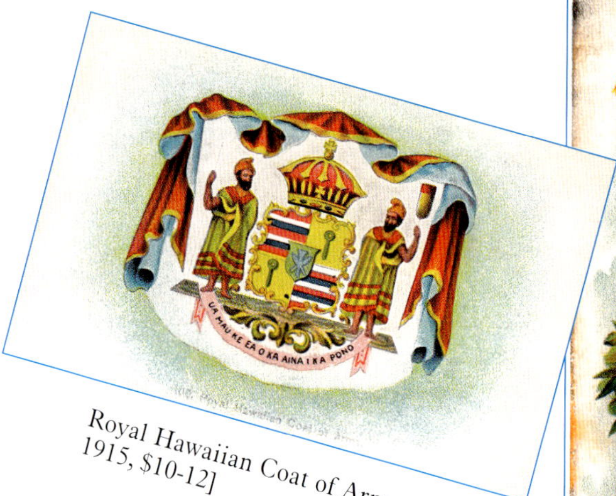

Royal Hawaiian Coat of Arms. [pre-1915, $10-12]

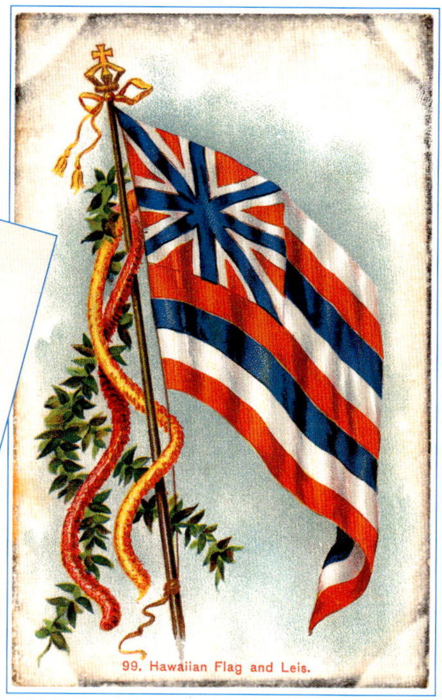

Hawaiian flag and leis. [pre-1915, $10-15]

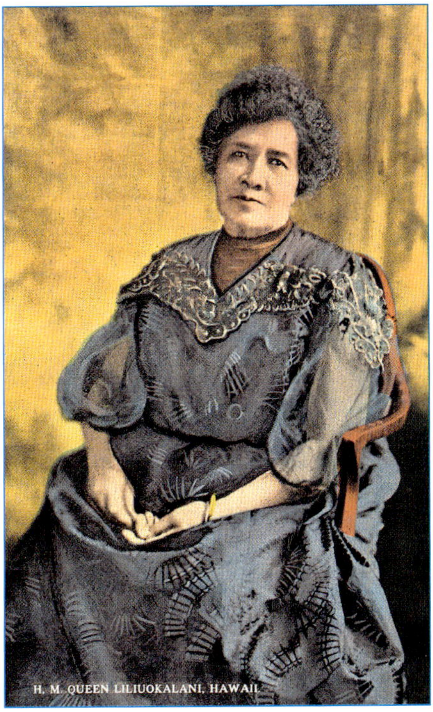

From the back: "H.M. Queen Liliuokalani exceeded [sic] to the crown in 1891, and was desposed [sic] in 1893. In 1895 there was an insurrection for her restoration and during that year she was confined for nine months in her former Palace; during which time she formally denounced all her claims for the throne. Liliuokalani now resides at Washington Palace, and receives a large annuity from the island government. She is a woman of gracious presence and greatly beloved by all her subjects." [pre-1915, $12-20]

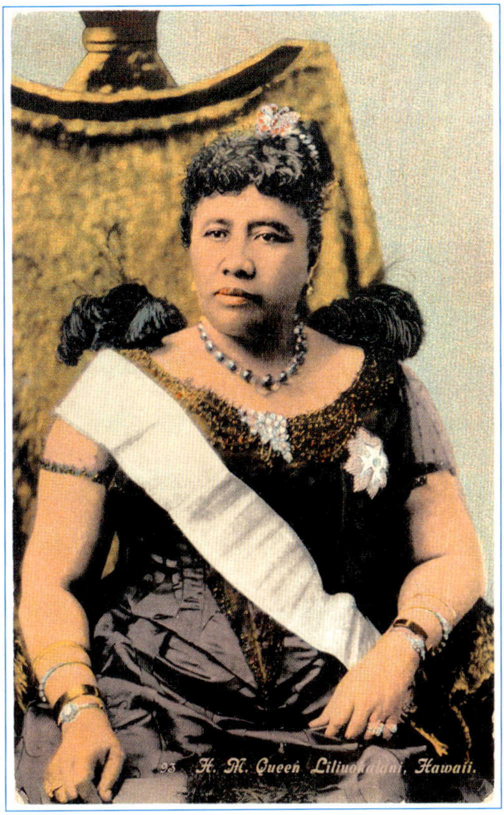

H.M. Queen Liliuokalani. [pre-1915, $12-20]

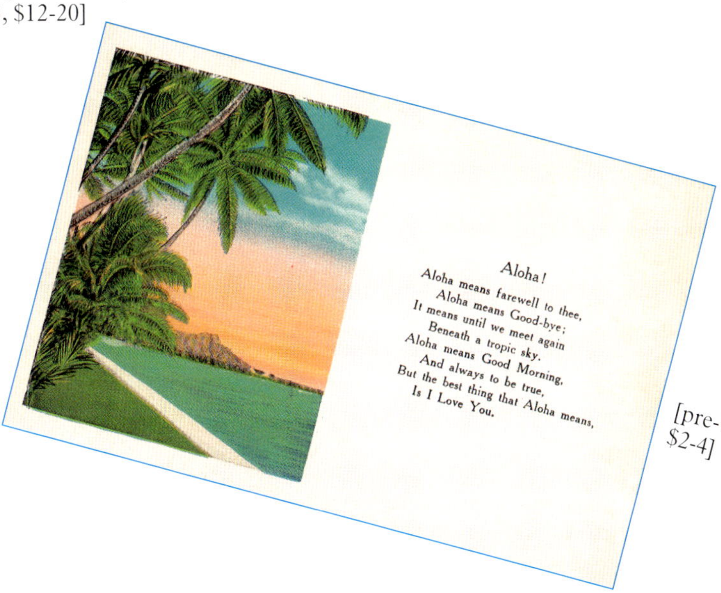

[pre-1940, $2-4]

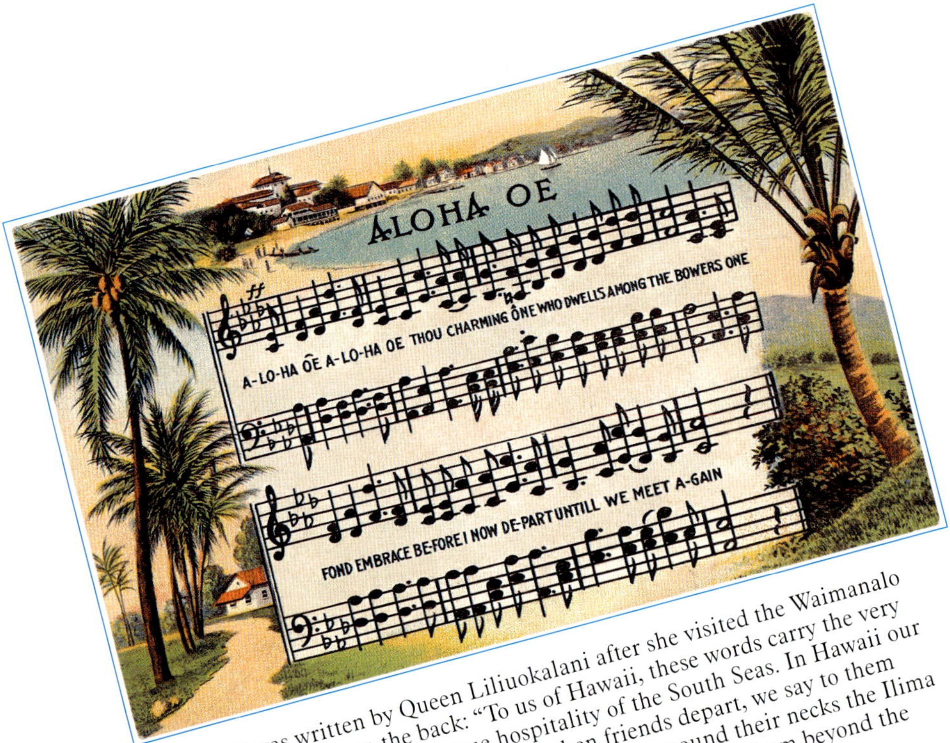

"Aloha Oe" was written by Queen Liliuokalani after she visited the Waimanalo Sugar Plantation. From the back: "To us of Hawaii, these words carry the very breath of romance and picturesque hospitality of the South Seas. In Hawaii our welcome is the "Aloha" of greeting, and when friends depart, we say to them again "Aloha" – this time as a farewell – and twine around their necks the Ilima Lei, that the fragrance of our true devotion may abide with them beyond the parting of our ways. [pre-1915, $10-15]

Right:
From the back: "Many of the plantations ship their output of sugar by means of these wire cables, which are quicker than the ordinary shore boats landing many thousands of bags per hour." [pre-1915, $10-15]

Landing Passengers,
Island of Hawaii.

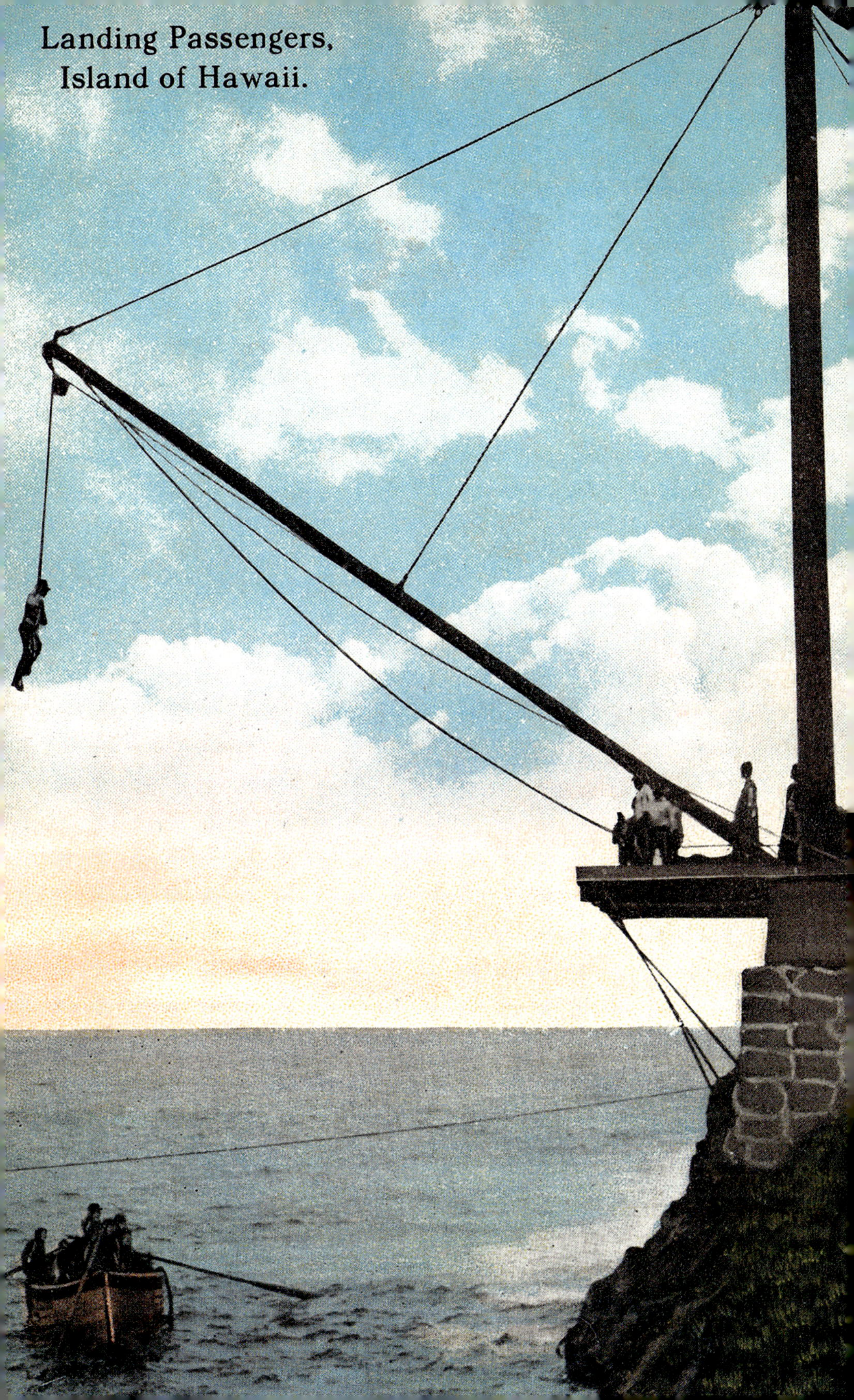

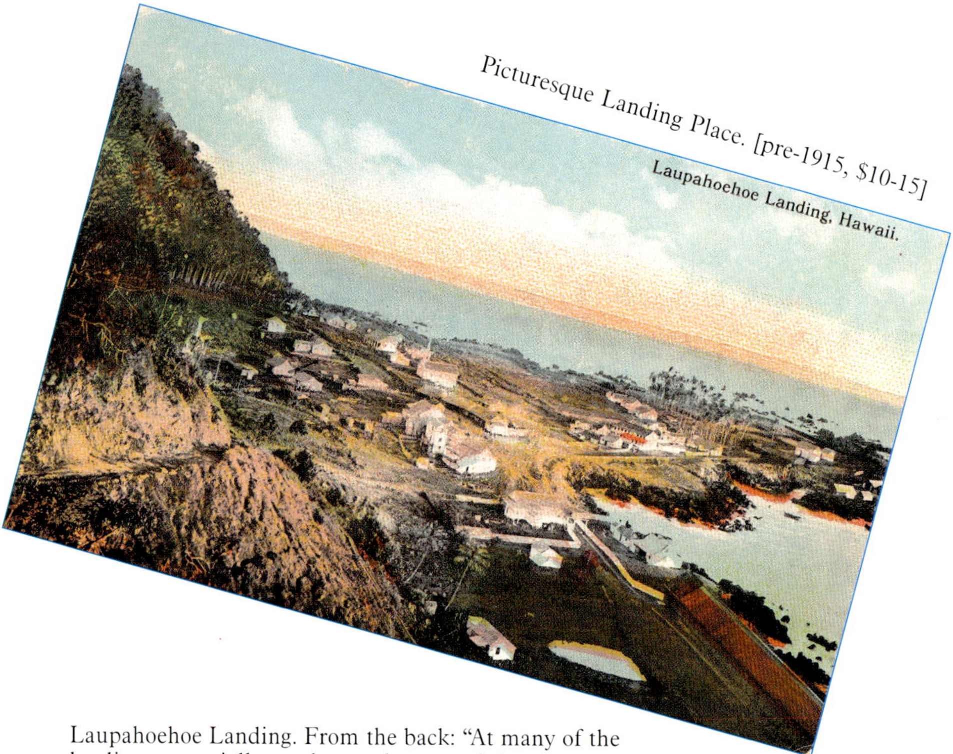

Picturesque Landing Place. [pre-1915, $10-15]

Laupahoehoe Landing. From the back: "At many of the landings, especially on the north coast of the Hawaiian Islands there exists such a high surf that landing is only to be had with the greatest difficulty. Immense wire cable are stretched far out to sea and carries [sic] both freight and passengers from the coasting steamers." [canceled 1914, $12-15]

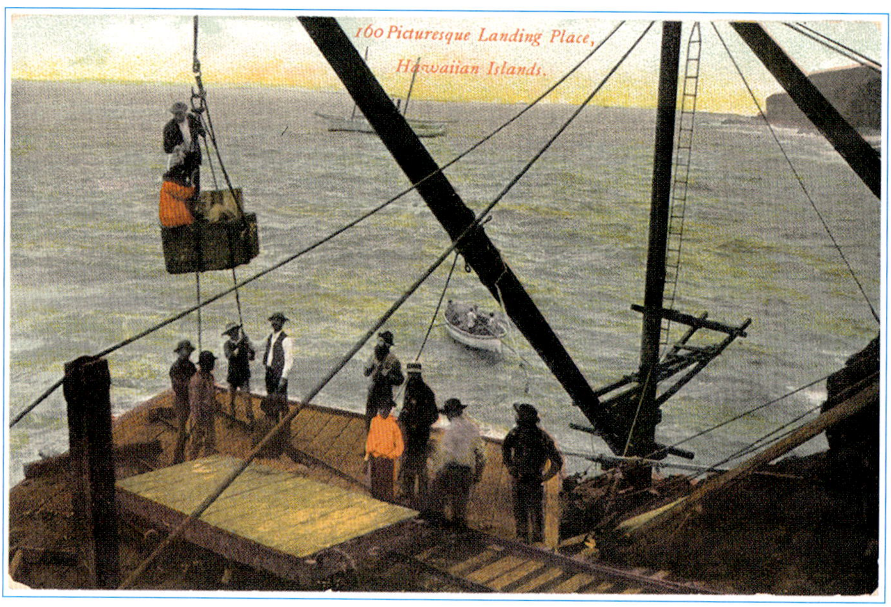

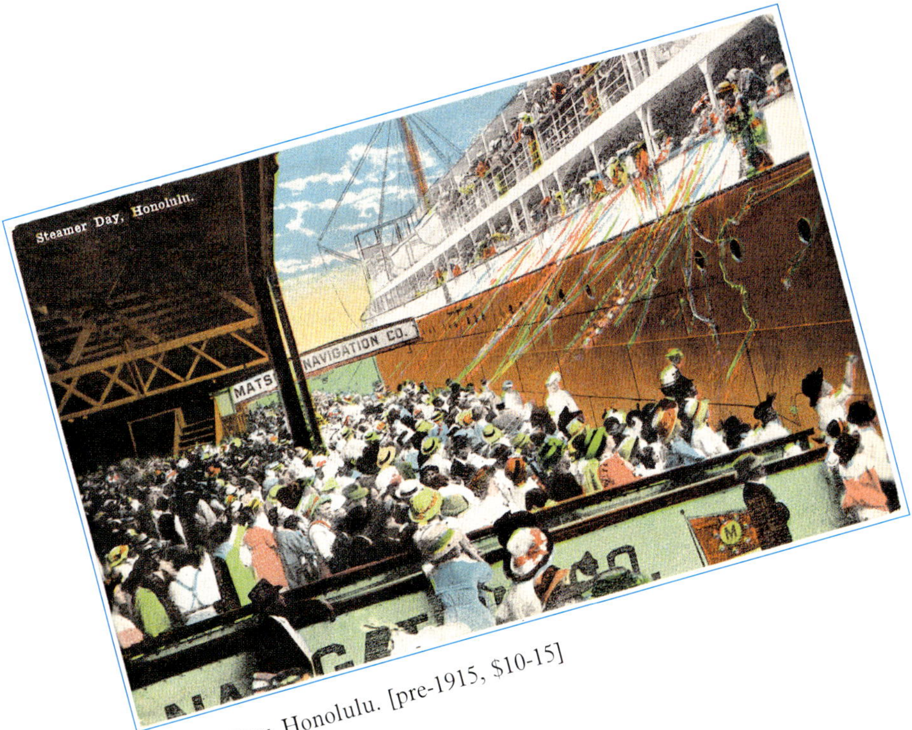

Steamer Day, Honolulu. [pre-1915, $10-15]

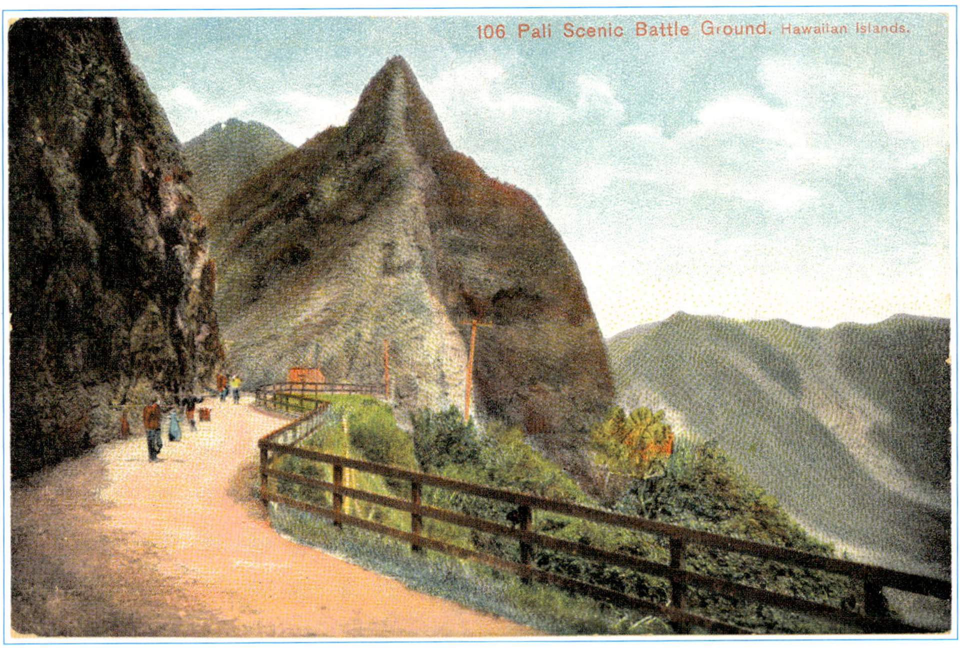

Nuuanu Pali, about six miles from Honolulu, became a world renowned scenic spot, the place where Kamehameha the Great hurled the defending Oahu warriors to their death in 1795, bringing all the Hawaiian Islands together under one rule. [pre-1915, $8-10]

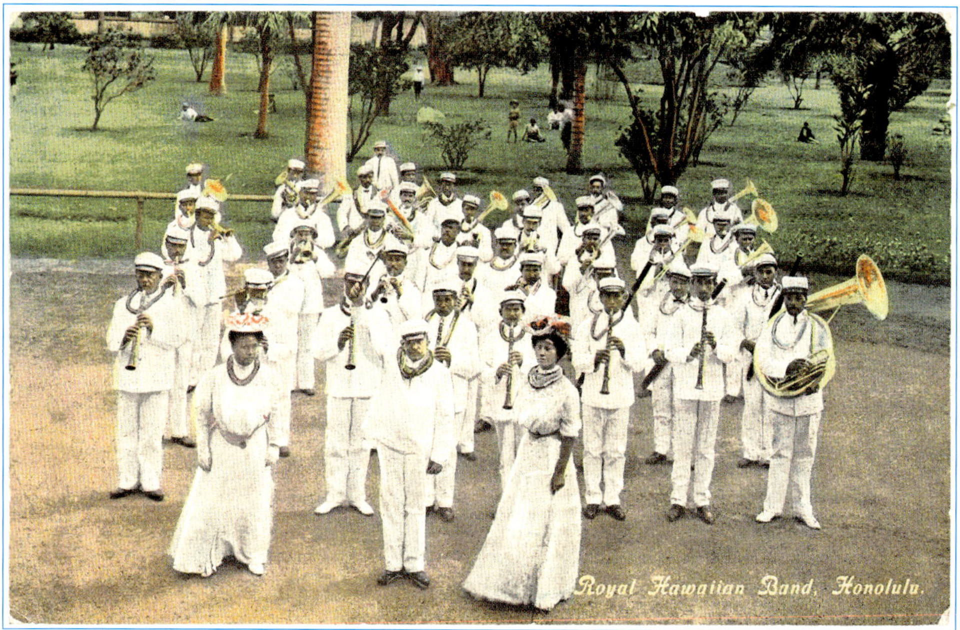

The Royal Hawaiian Band. [pre-1915, $12-18]

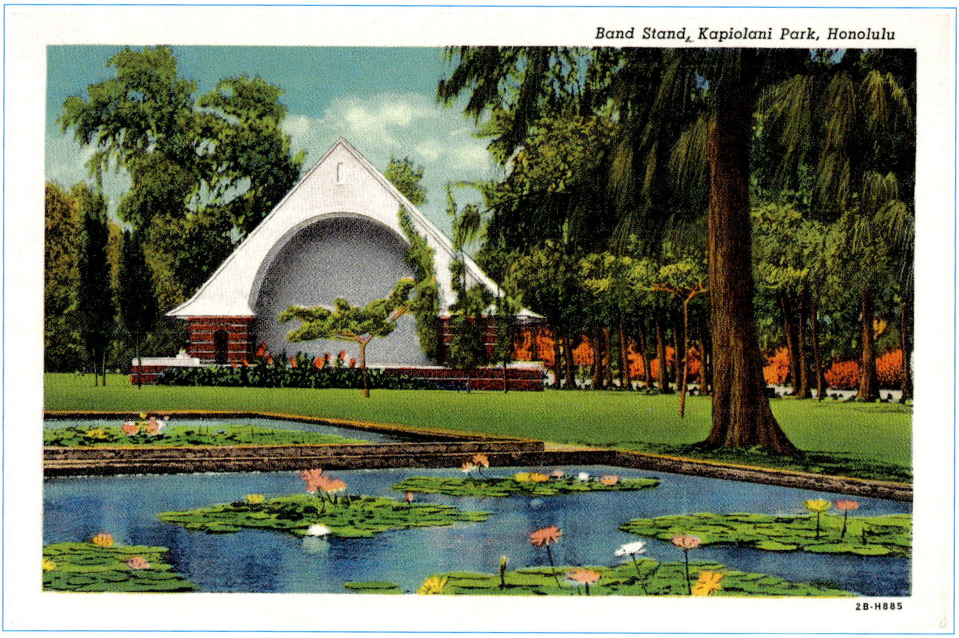

The bandstand in Honolulu's Kapiolani Park. [pre-1940, $2-3]

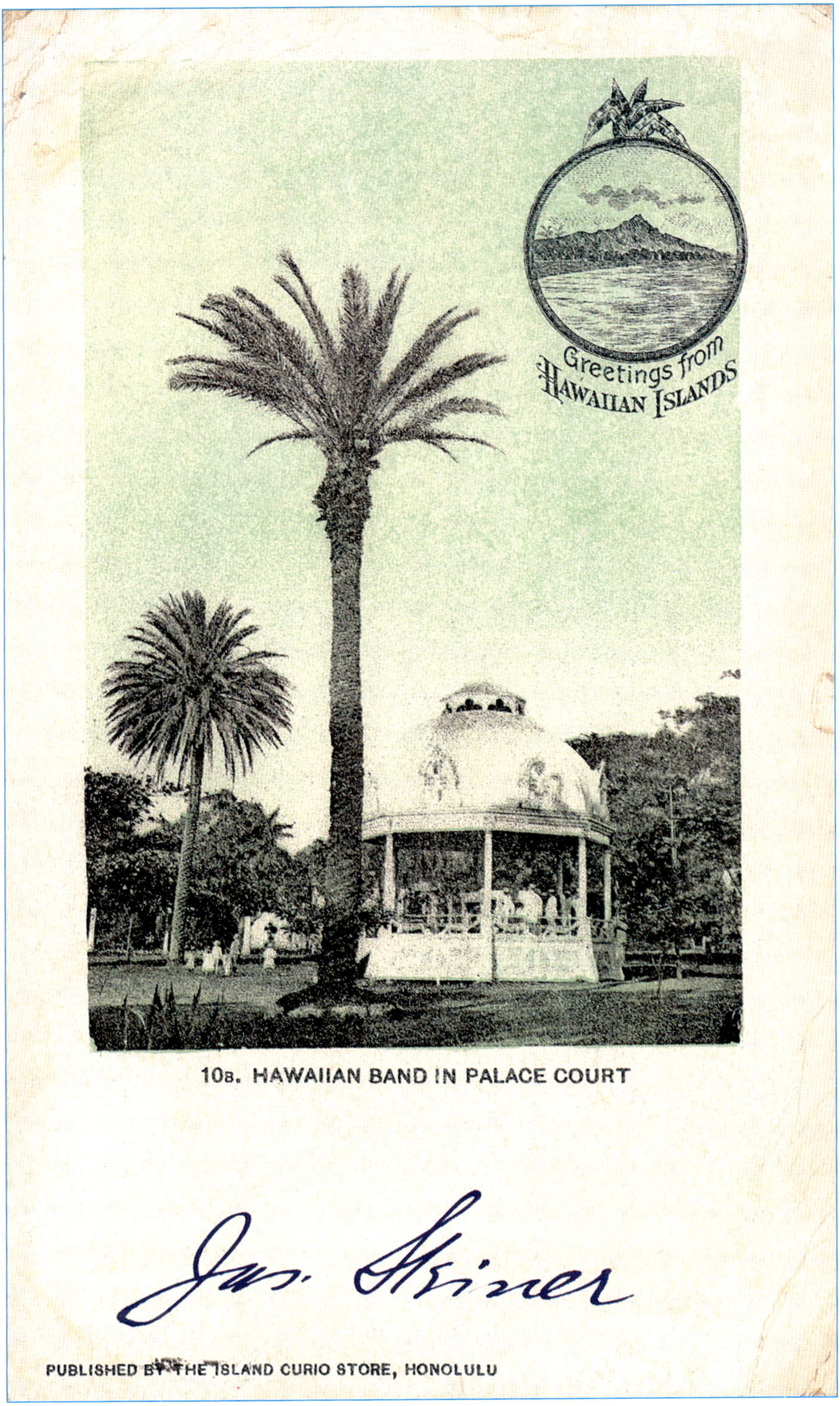

Hawaiian Band in Palace Court. [canceled 1905, $16-20]

Natural Amenities

A view of the coastline near Keanae on Maui. [pre-1915, $6-9]

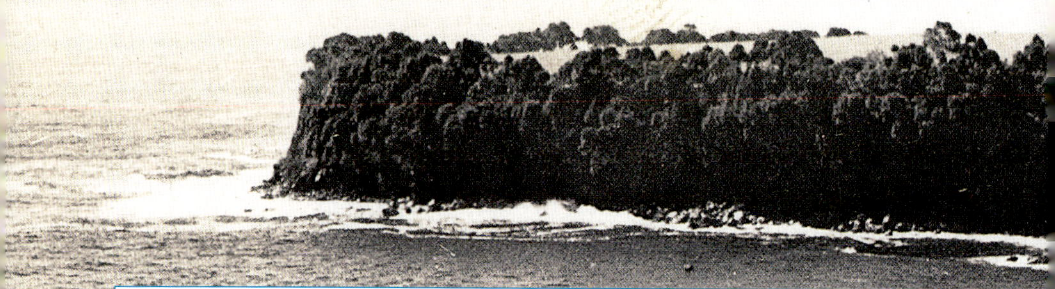

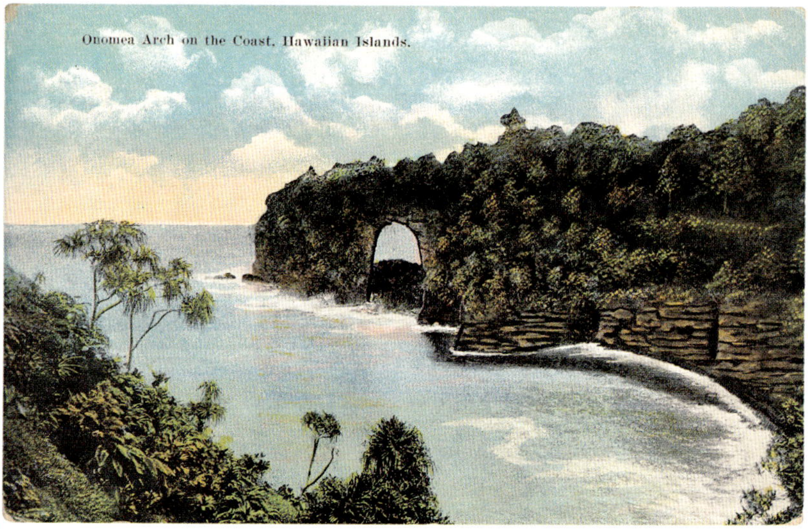

Legend says that the formation of Onomea Arch was the result of a battle fought between Pele and her archenemy the snow-goddess Poliahu. [pre-1915, $6-9]

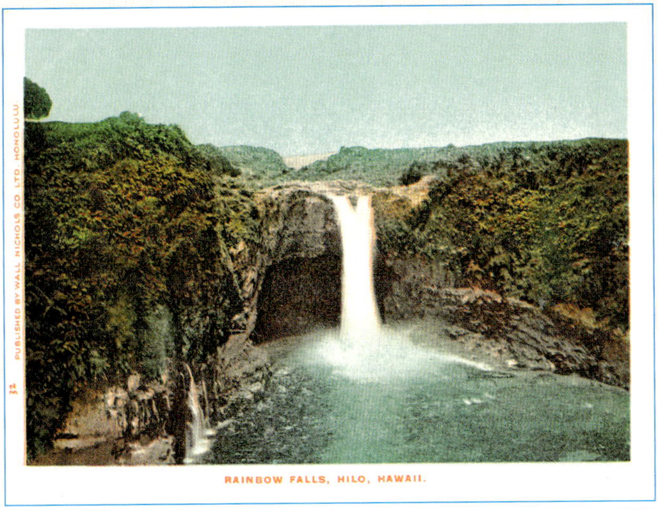

According to legend, the cave underneath Rainbow falls is the home of the Hina, the guardian of the underworld and the goddess of arts and crafts. [pre-1915, $6-9]

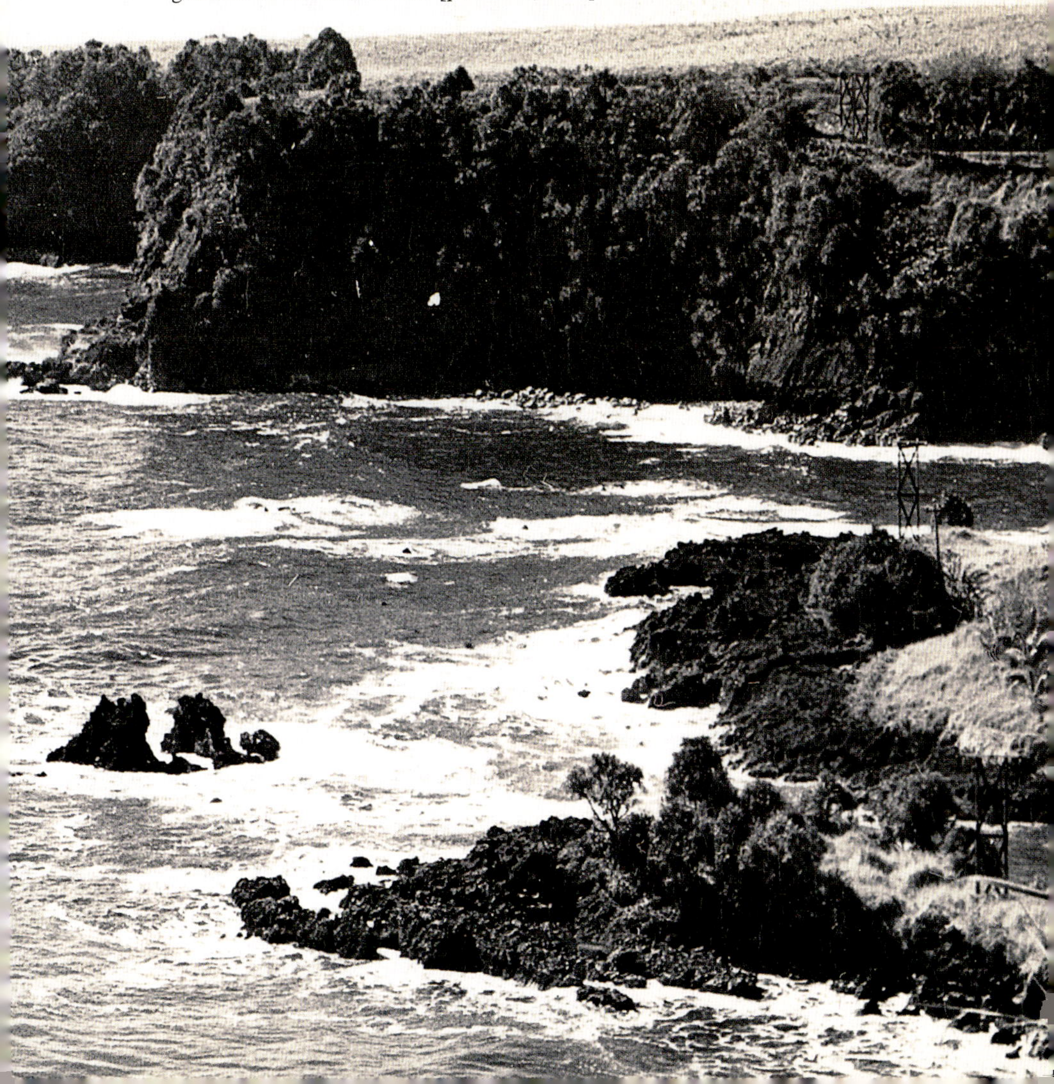

Beach Scenes

Woe the resort that doesn't have a beach, or some major body of water, to attract the vacationer. Hawaii, of course, has water in abundance. It is surrounded by far horizons of Pacific Ocean, the surf-high waves teeming below the surface with colorful fish and sea turtles.

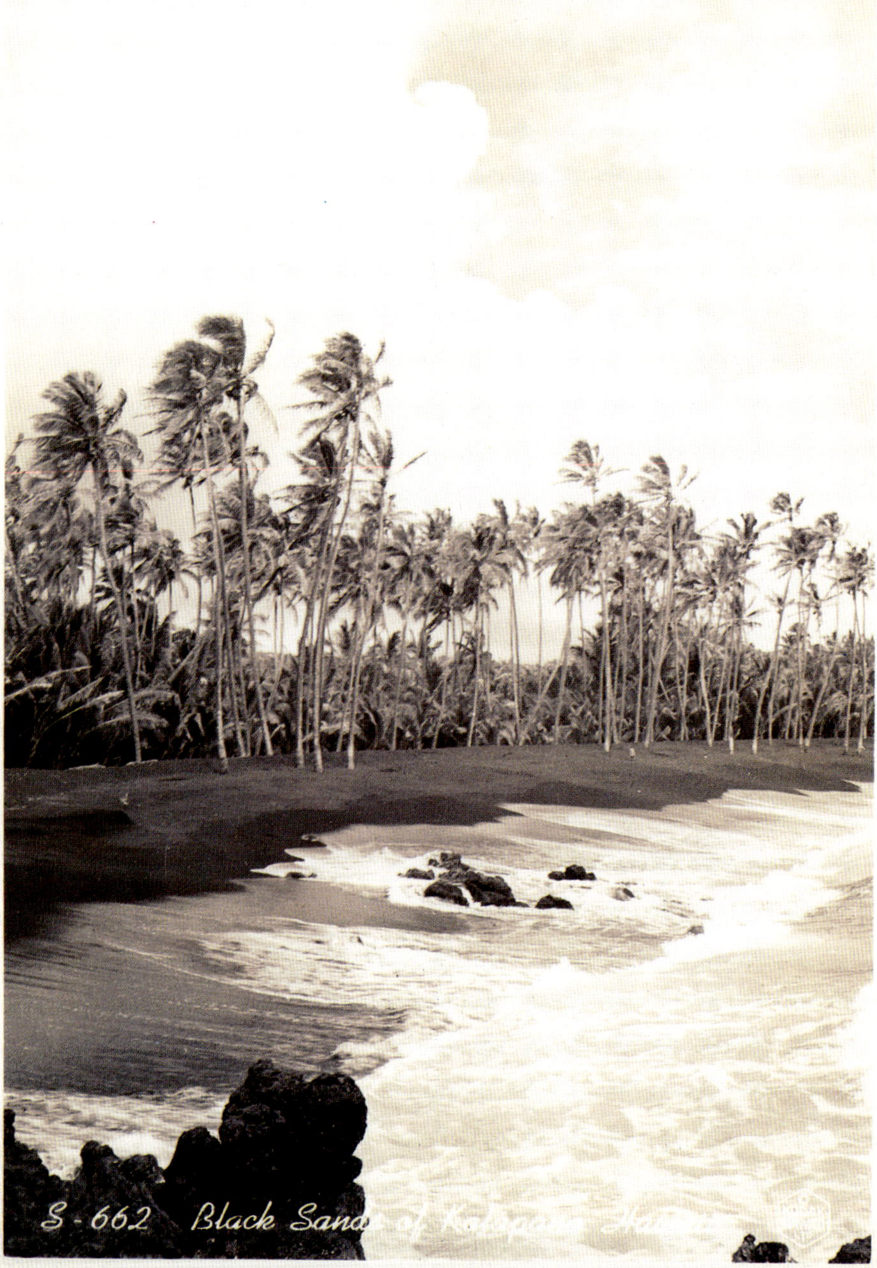

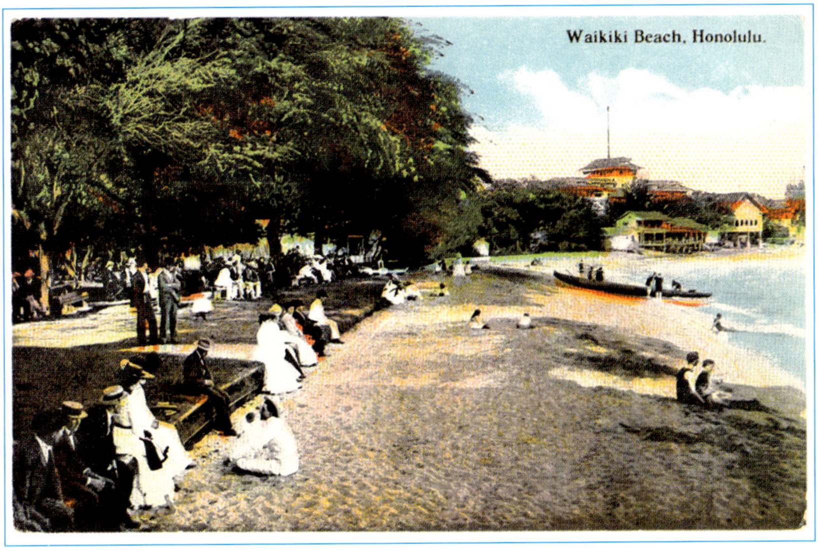

Tourists crowd the beach at Waikiki. [pre-1915, $8-10]

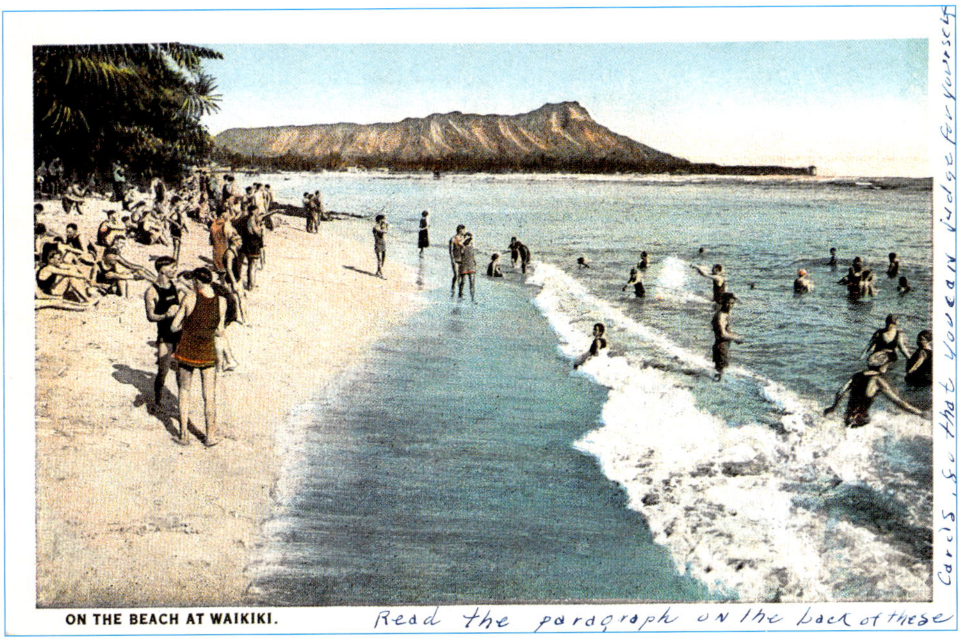

From the back: "Waikiki Beach …has the reputation of being the most beautiful beach in all the world, where bathing can safely be indulged in by day and by night, there being no danger whatever from deep water or undertow. Here may be seen the famous surf riders of Honolulu." [pre-1930, $6-9]

Left:
The black sand on these beaches is a result of volcanic eruptions. [pre-1915, $3-6]

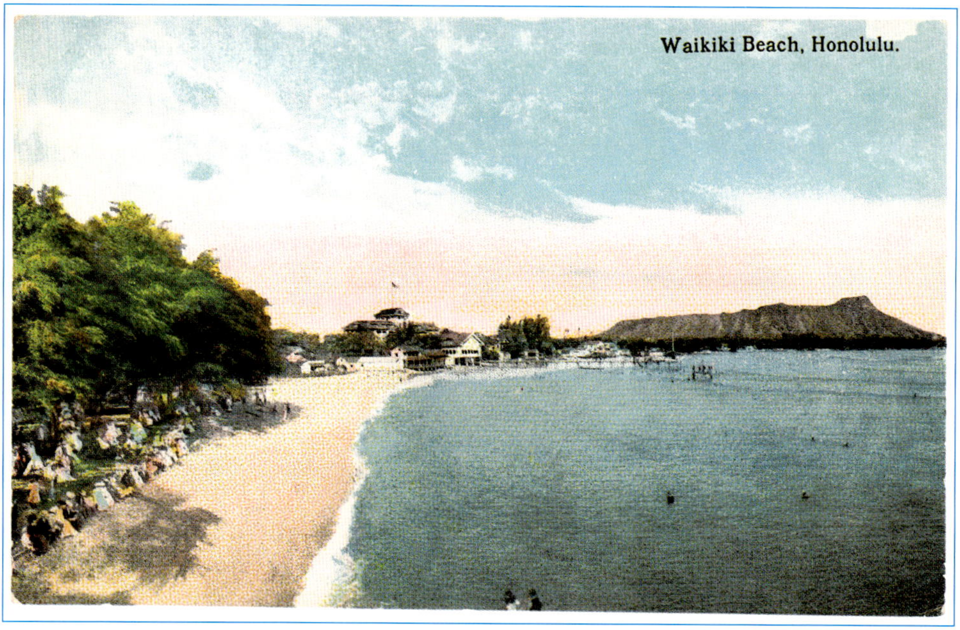

From the back: "At all hours of the day bathers and surf riders can be seen in the surf. Canoes can be seen dashing in the green waves as they come rolling in from the Pacific filled with laughing natives and tourists." [Postmarked 1907, $8-10]

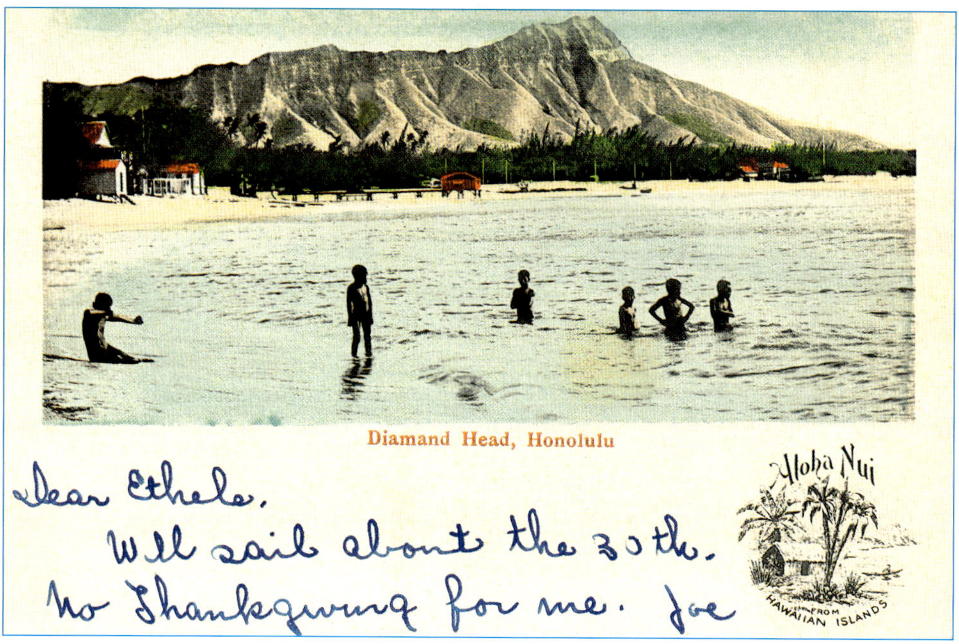

Children splash in the ocean off of Waikiki underneath the shadow of Diamond Head. [canceled 1907, $20-35]

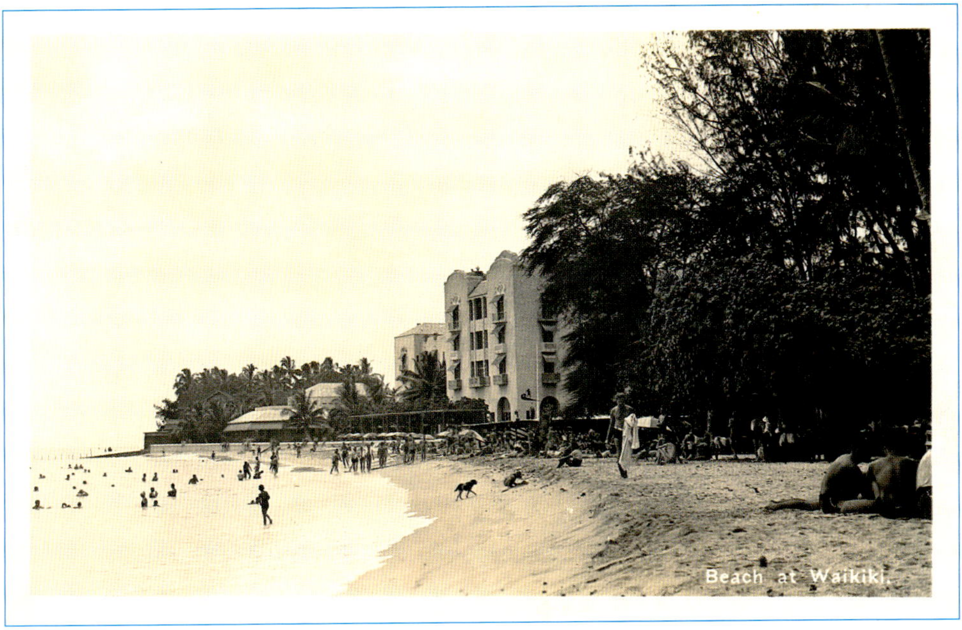

The beach in front of the Royal Hawaiian Hotel. [canceled 1933, $10-15]

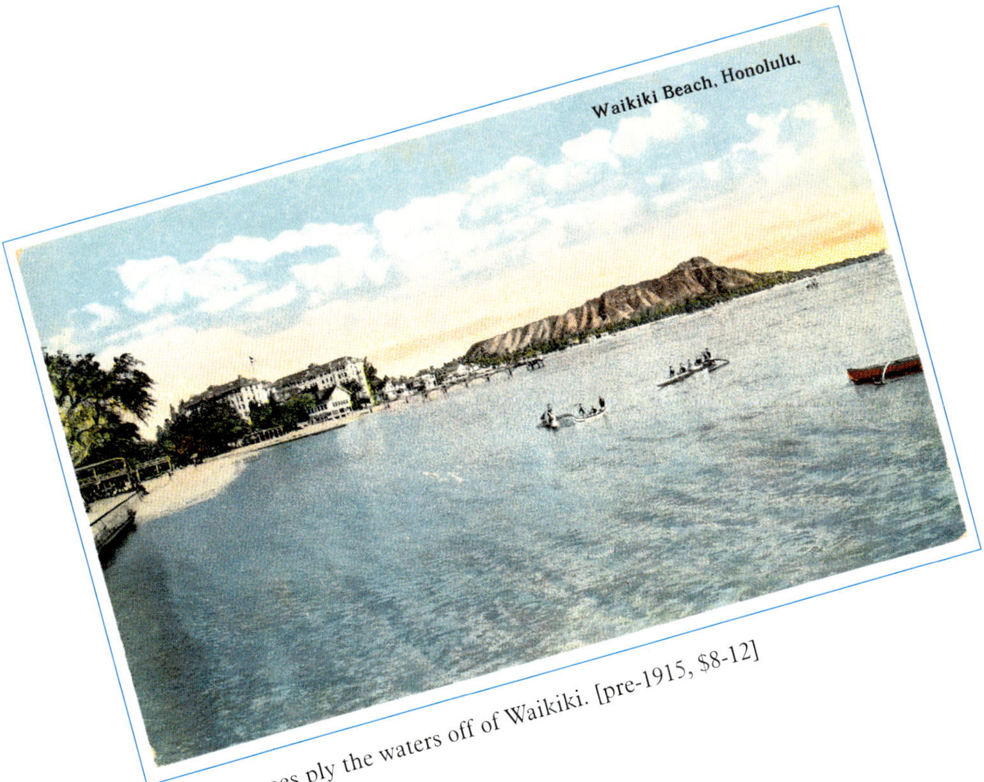

Canoes ply the waters off of Waikiki. [pre-1915, $8-12]

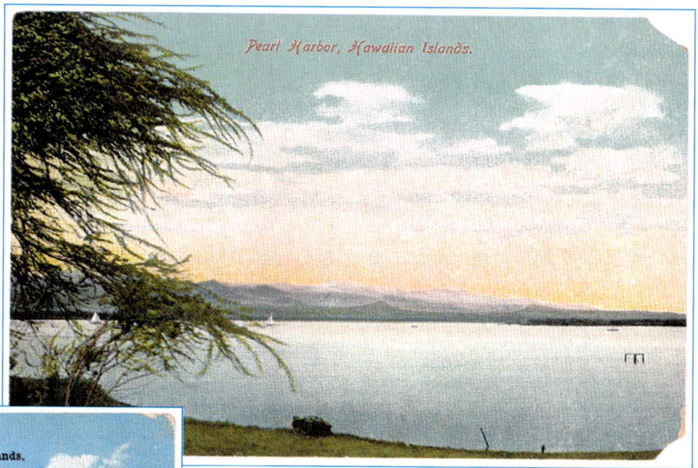

A few boats dot the waters of Pearl Harbor. This harbor would eventually become the location of a United States Naval Base. [pre-1915, $3-5]

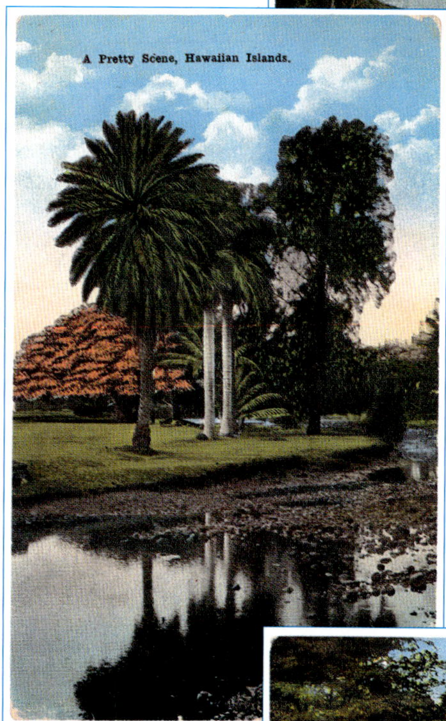

[pre-1915, $2-5]

"This red tree is the Poinciana …the red is a brilliant scarlet. The green leaves on some of the trees …are like beautiful fine ferns. This picture was taken in Moanalua Park, the most beautiful park here."
—1914

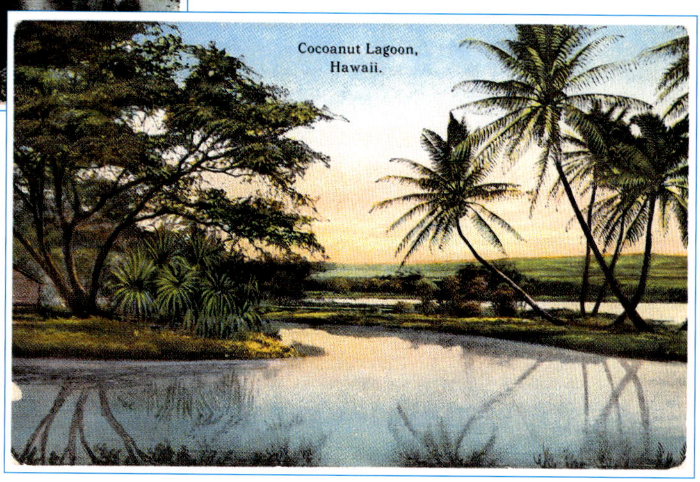

A cocoanut lagoon. [pre-1915, $2-5]

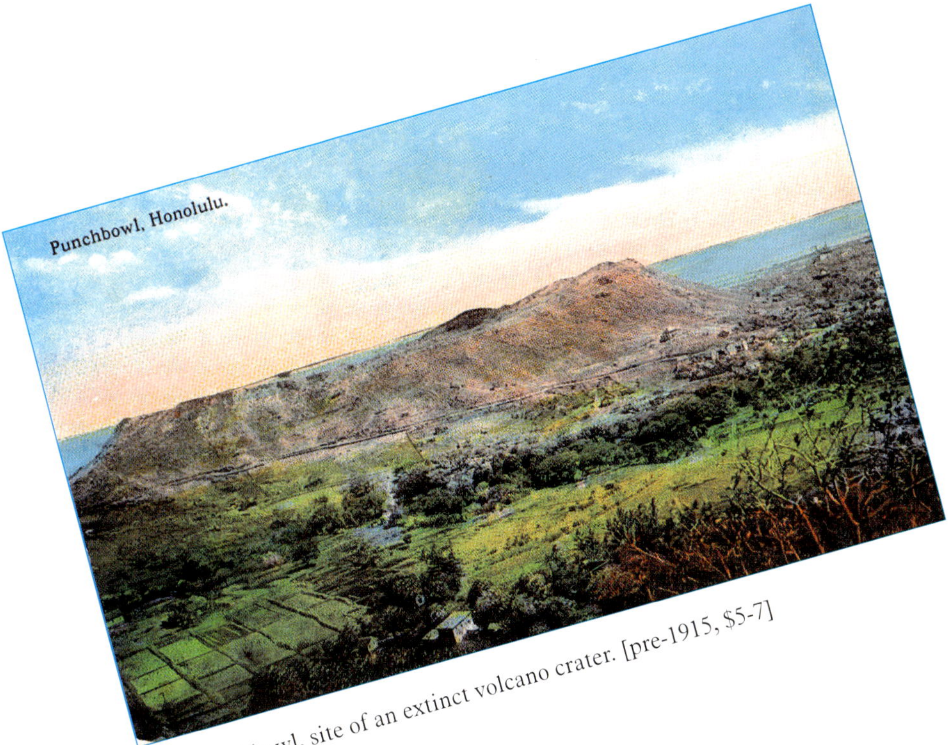

The Punchbowl, site of an extinct volcano crater. [pre-1915, $5-7]

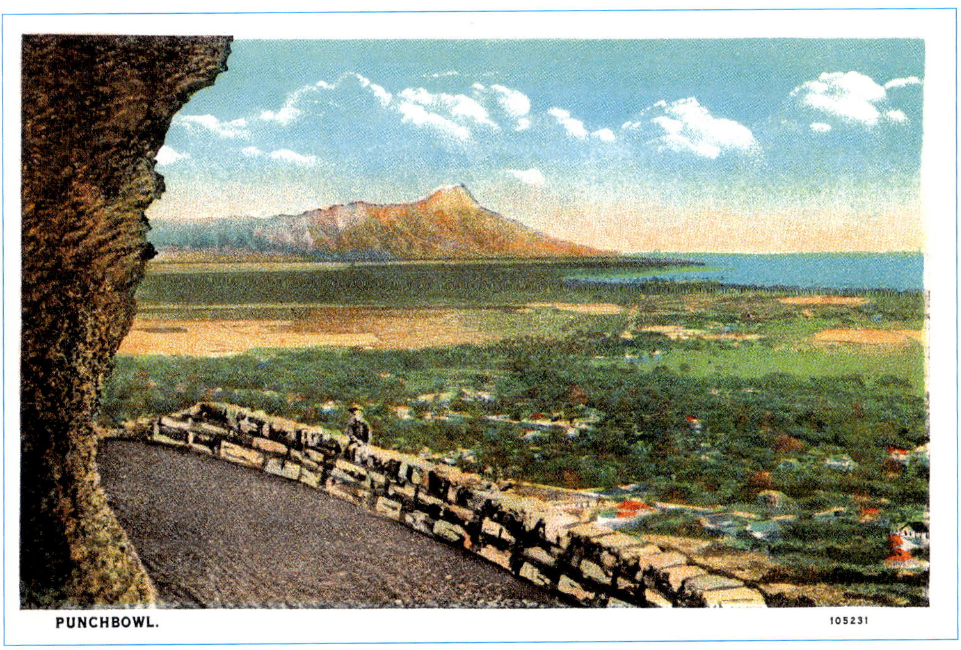

The Punchbowl. [pre-1940, $2-4]

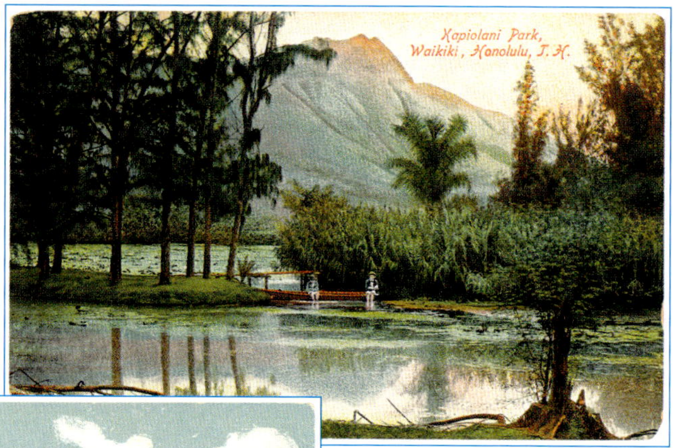

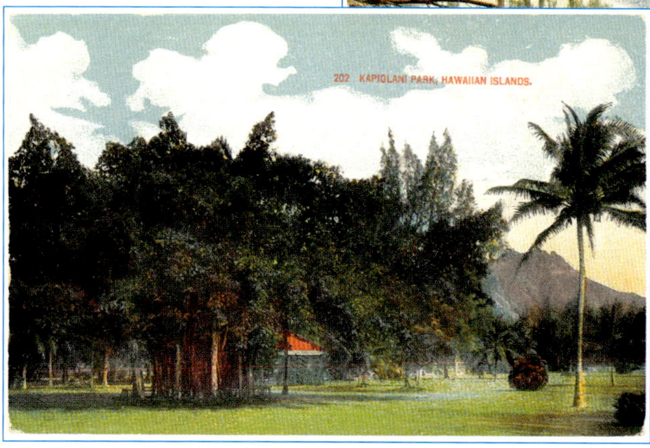

King Kalakaua created Kapiolani Park in the 1870s. It is home to places of interest like Diamond Head and the Honolulu Zoo. [pre-1915, $4-7]

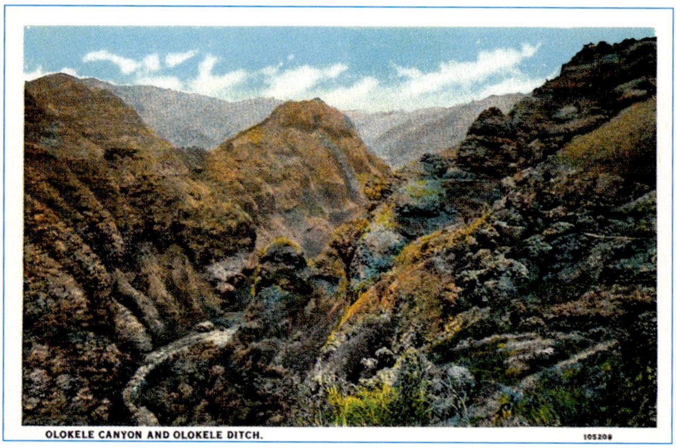

From the back: "Olokele Canyon and Olokele Ditch: Much more easily accessible than and quite as impressive as Waimea. A fine road has been constructed suitable for automobiles, beyond the section camp, commanding many of the grandest views. Beyond this point an excellent bridle path extends to the irrigation system intake, in the very heart of the mountains." [pre-1920, $2-5]

Waterfalls

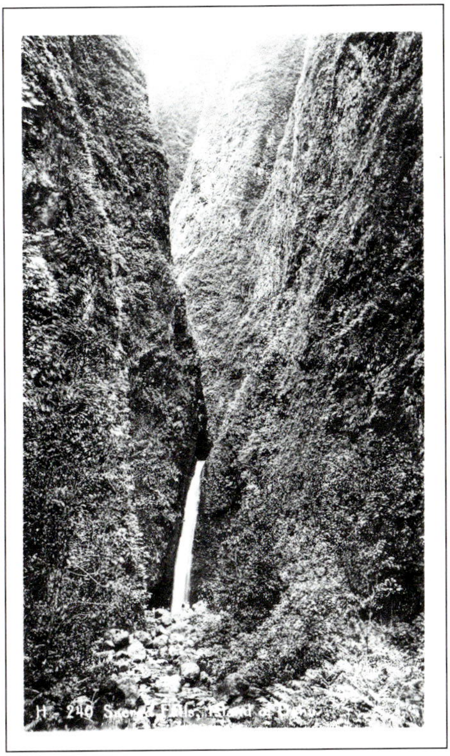

Sacred Falls. [pre-1920, $4-7]

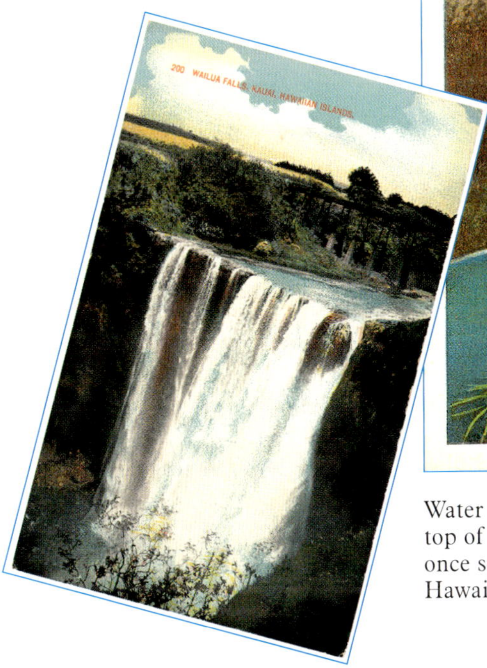

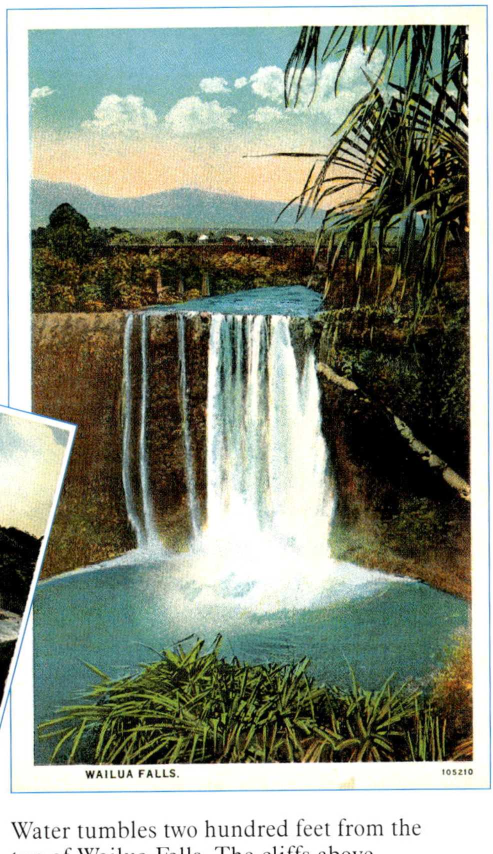

Water tumbles two hundred feet from the top of Wailua Falls. The cliffs above once served as a diving platform for Hawaiian Royalty. [pre-1920, $3-5]

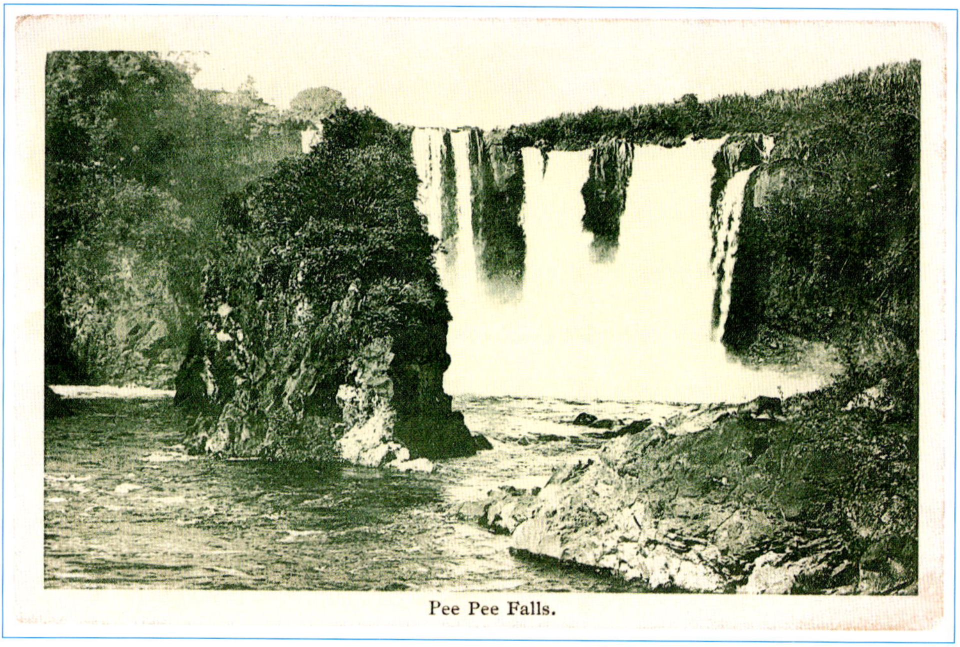

A magnificent view of Pee Pee Falls. [pre-1920, $3-6]

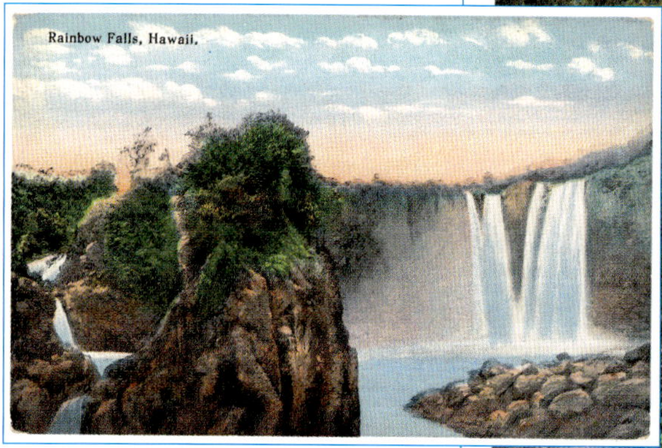

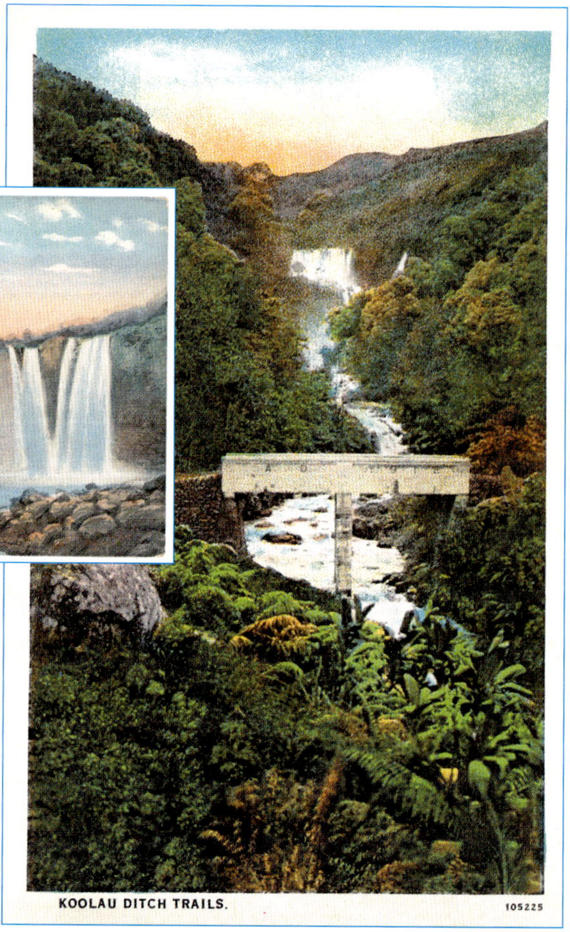

Visitors on horseback pause before they cross a bridge on the Koolau Ditch Trails. These trails could be hiked in one day. Rainbow Falls is located only a few miles from downtown Hilo, making it extremely accessible to the average tourist. [pre-1915, $3-5 ea.]

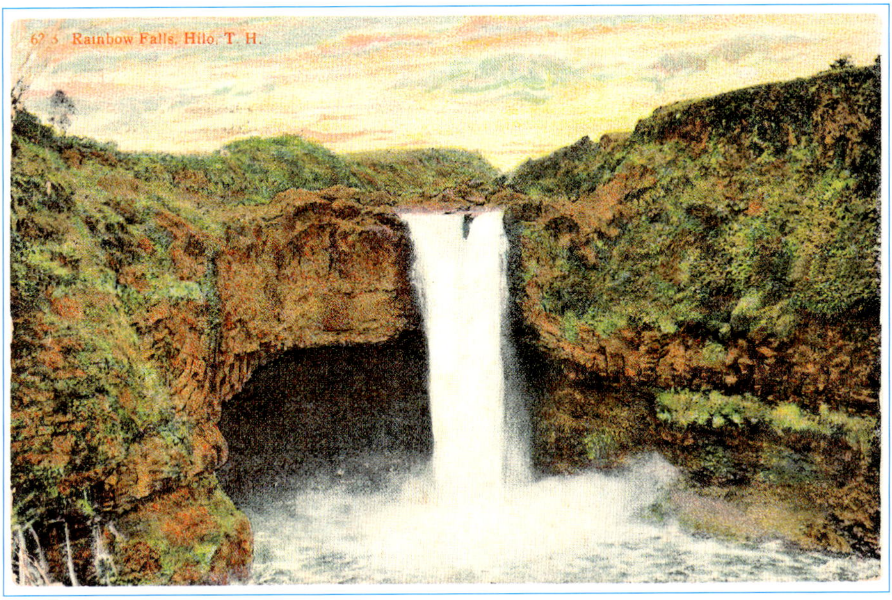

[canceled 1921, $5-8]

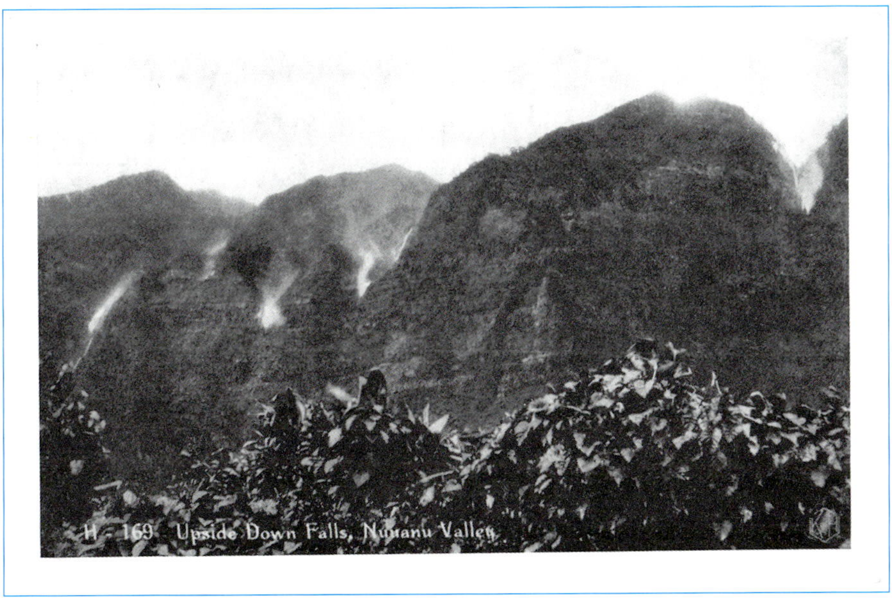

The Upside Down Falls, one of the many examples of the natural beauty found in Nuuanu Valley State Park. [pre-1930, $3-5]

The Flowers

Hawaii is so lush with blooms that the natives have long plucked them for their daily attire. When one thinks about Hawaii, the hibiscus and colorful leis necklaces come foremost to mind. Visitors in search of fragrance and beauty are never disappointed. And this fact has been well documented in postcards sent ‘round the world.

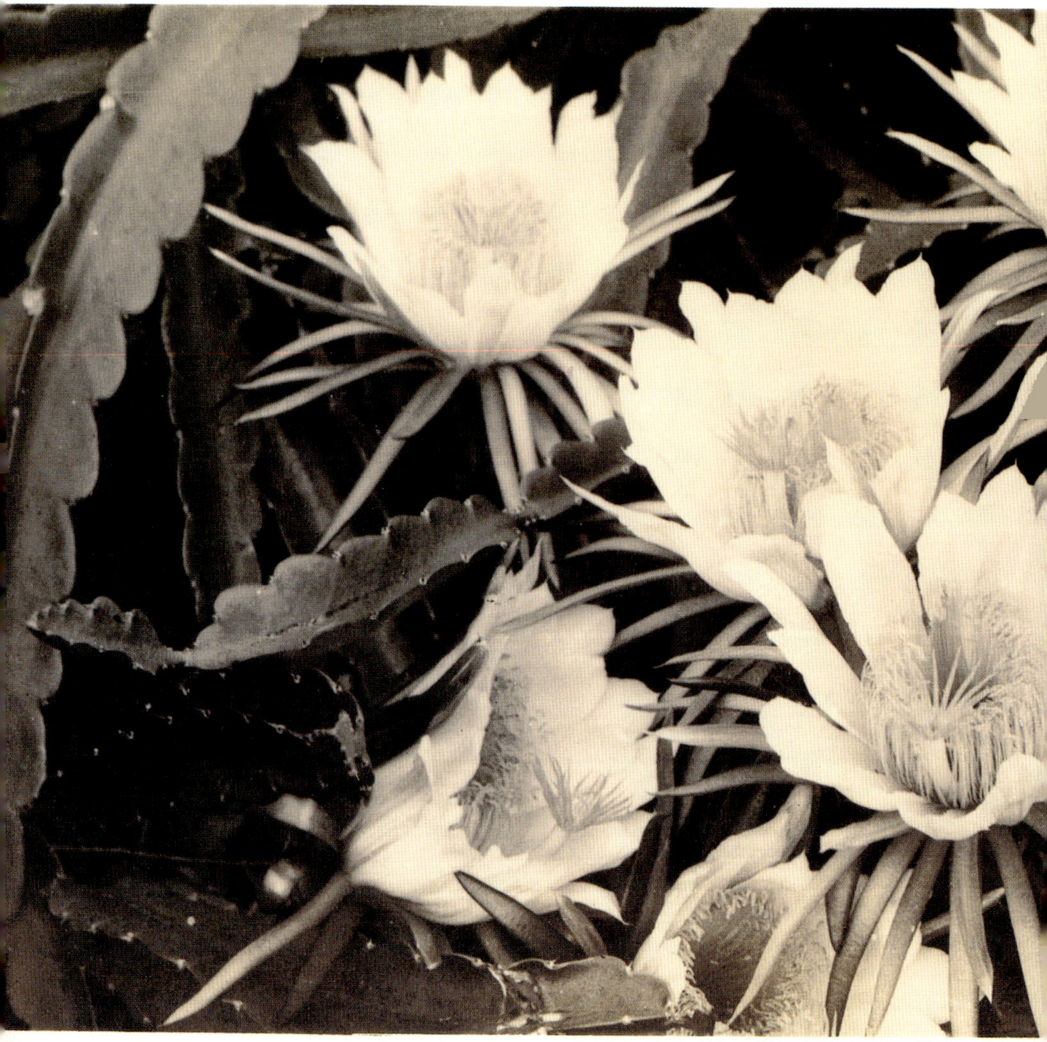

NIGHT BLOOMING CEREU FLO

[pre-1940, $2-4]

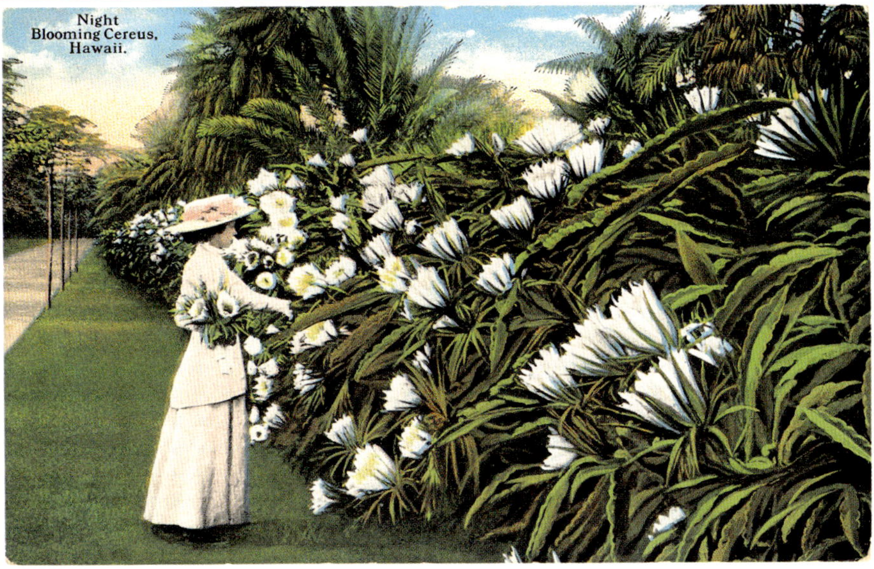

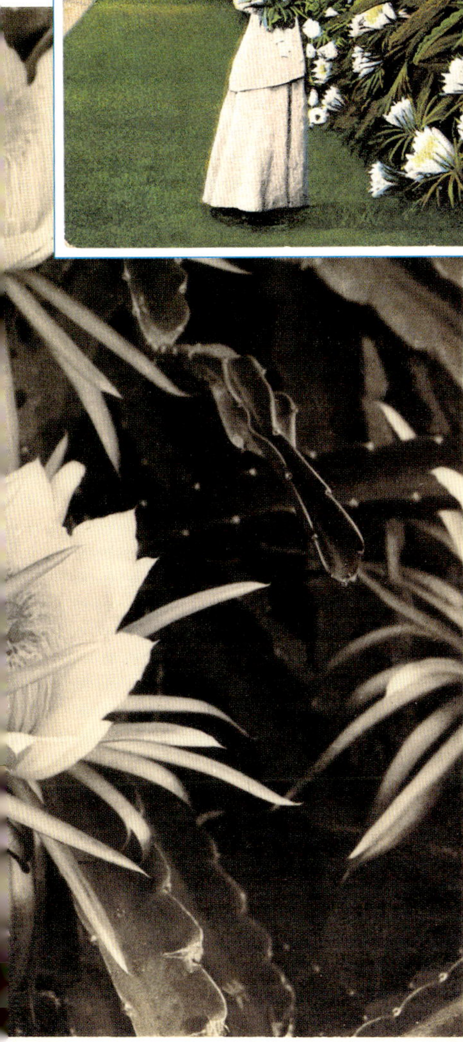

From the back: "The night blooming cereus is to be seen in season all over Hawaii. It is especially prominent on the walls surrounding Oahu College, Honolulu, where its fragrance-laden white blossoms perfume the air." [pre-1920, $3-5]

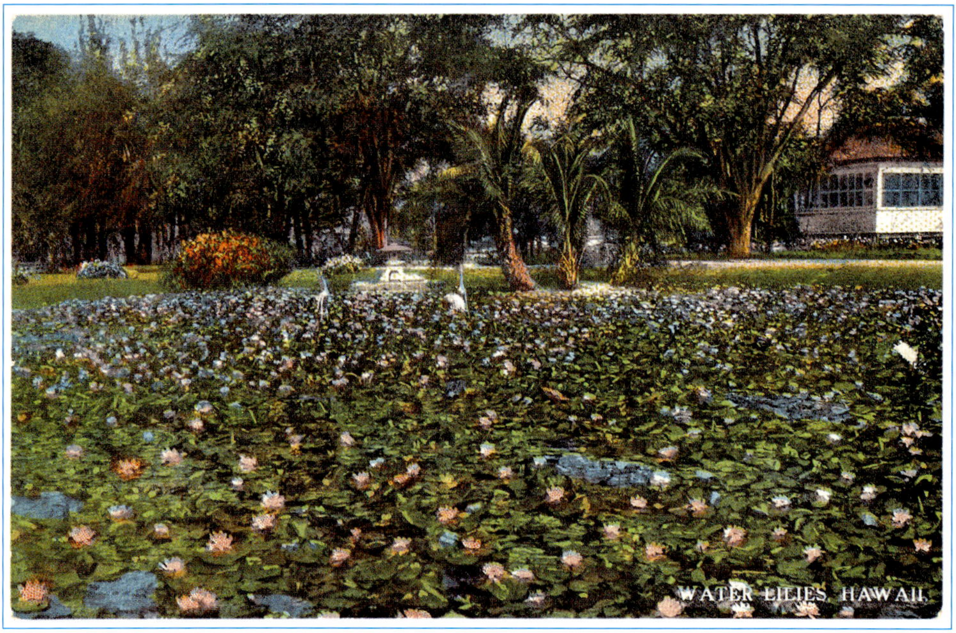

From the back: "The water lilies or Nymphaeas of Hawaii are royally gorgeous, diversified in coloring and admired by all visitors to the islands. The exquisite aquatic plants are always blooming producing a most chaste and beautiful flower and are grown in all the public parks about Honolulu." [pre-1915, $3-5]

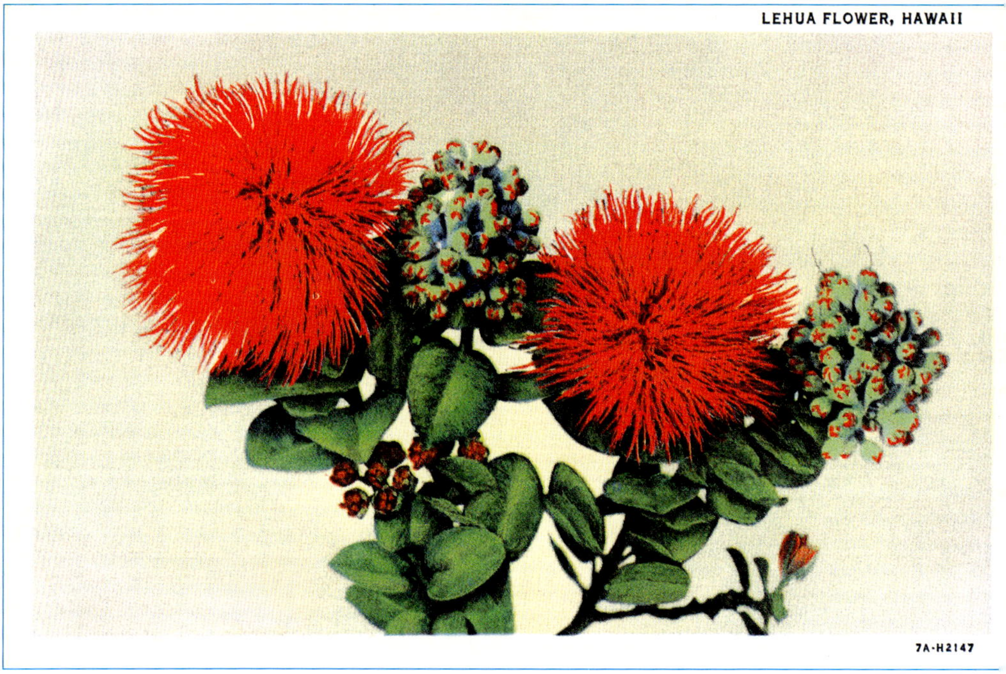

The lehua flower is one of the most abundant plants found in the Hawaiian Islands. [pre-1940, $1-3]

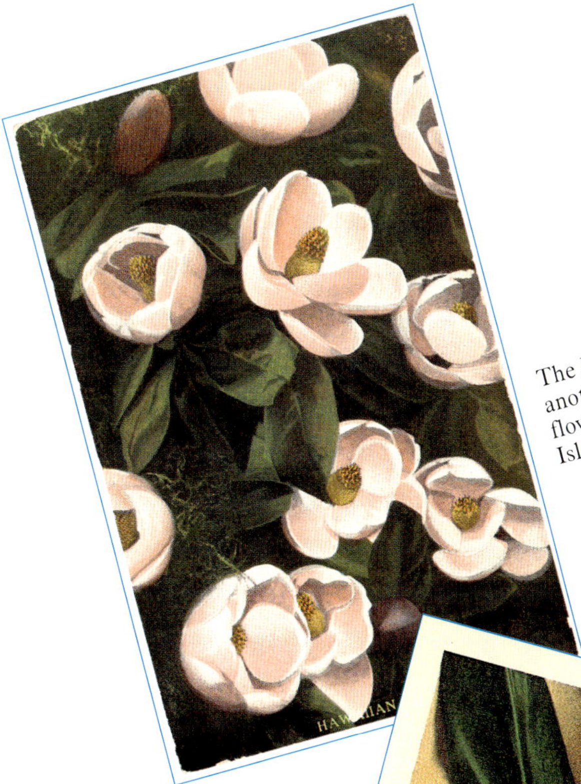

The Hawaiian Magnolia flower, another one of the beautiful flowers that grow in the Hawaiian Islands. [pre-1915, $1-3]

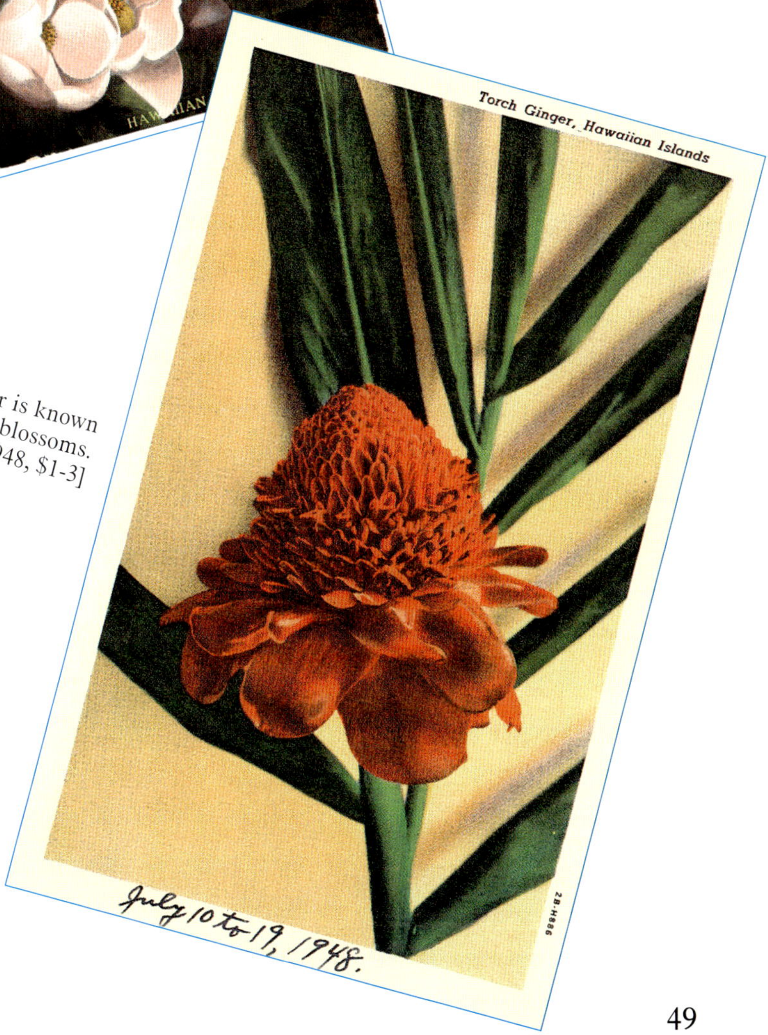

Torch ginger is known for its fragrant blossoms. [Dated 1948, $1-3]

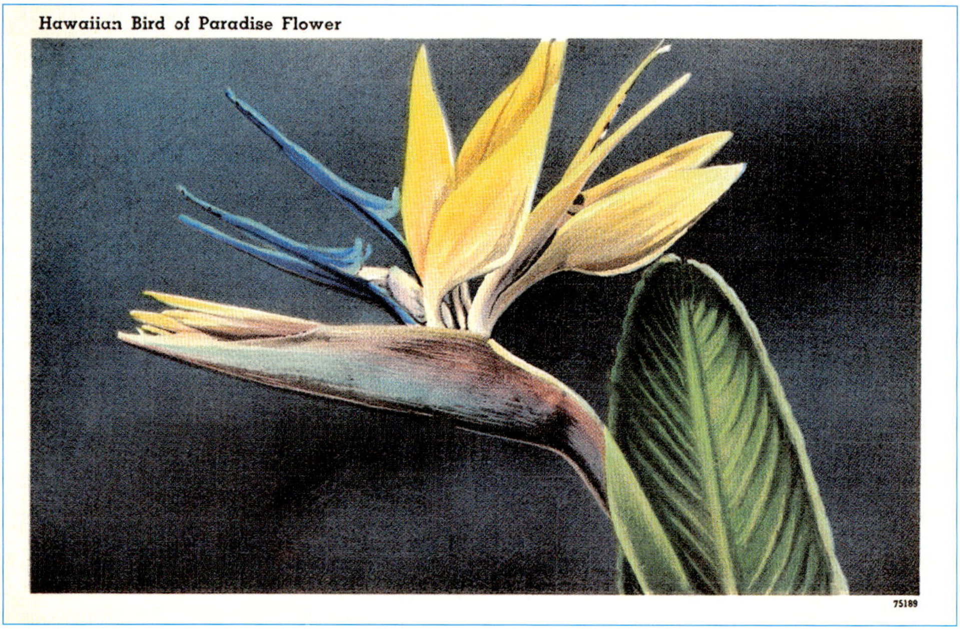

The Hawaiian Bird of Paradise Flower is brightly colored just like the bird that is its namesake. [pre-1940, $1-3]

[pre-1920, $2-3]

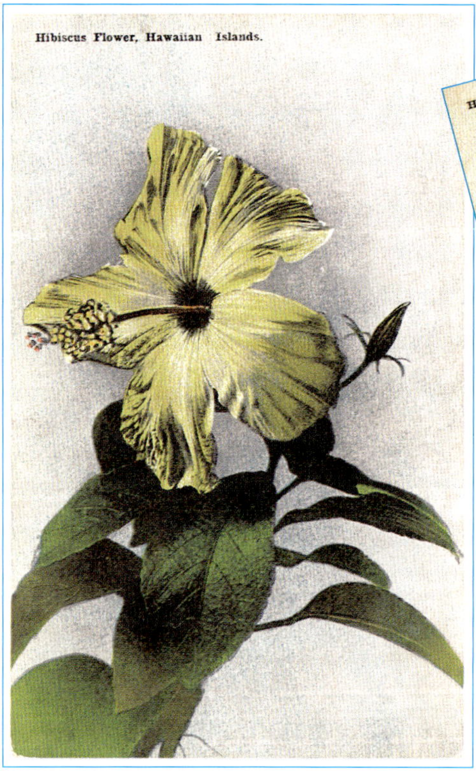

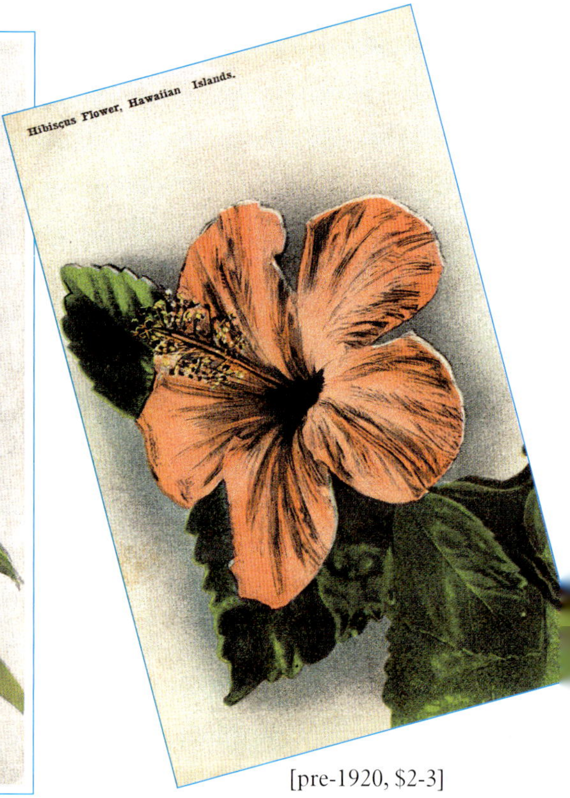

[pre-1920, $2-3]

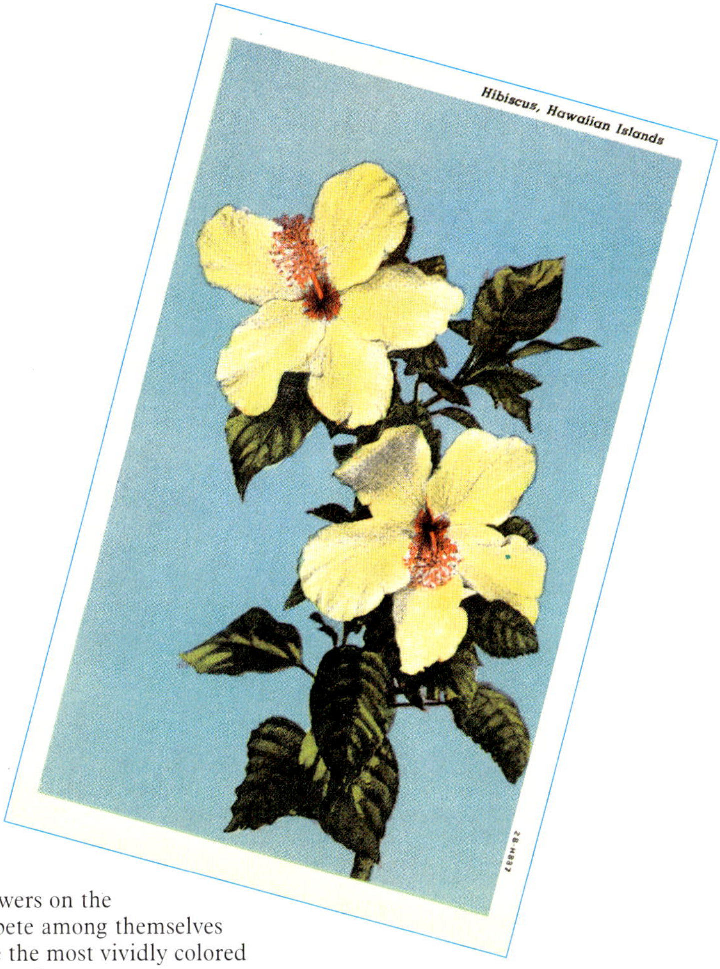

Both pages:
The Hibiscus was first introduced to the Hawaiian Islands in 1855. The Tropical Hibiscus frequently produces seedpods and often cross-breeds with other Hibiscus varieties. Growers on the Hawaiian Islands compete among themselves to see who can produce the most vividly colored blooms. [pre-1940, $1-3 ea.]

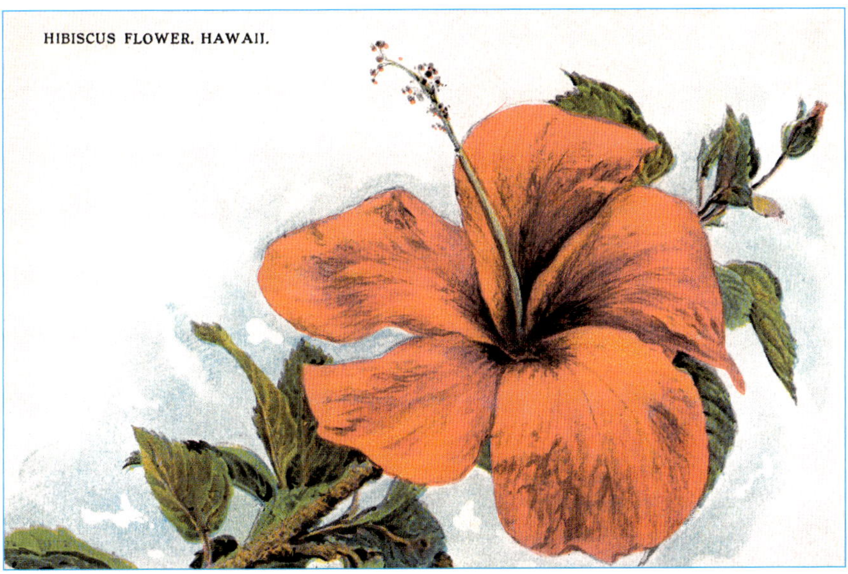

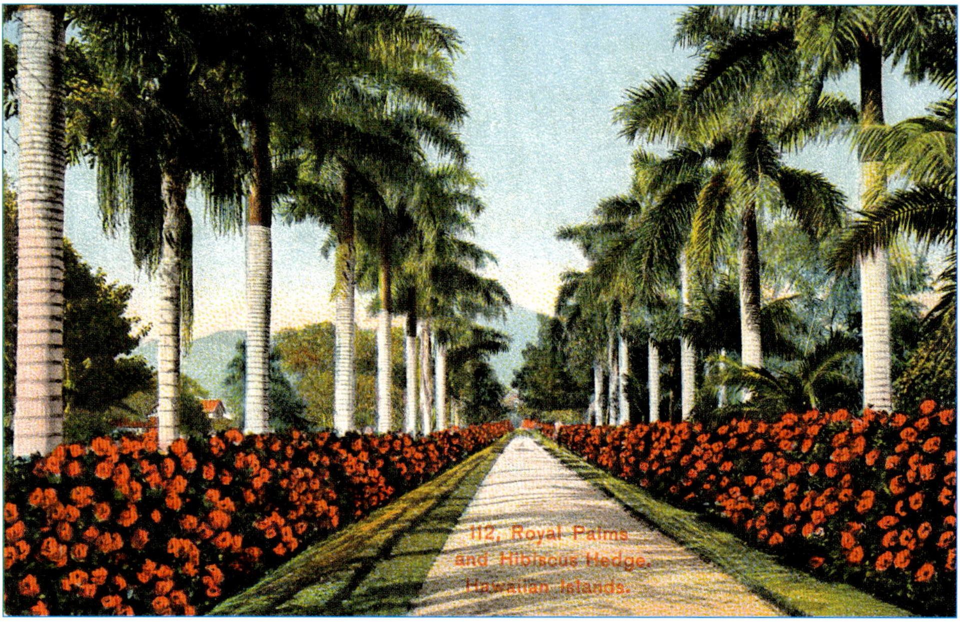

Royal palms tower over Hibiscus hedges. [pre-1915, $2-5]

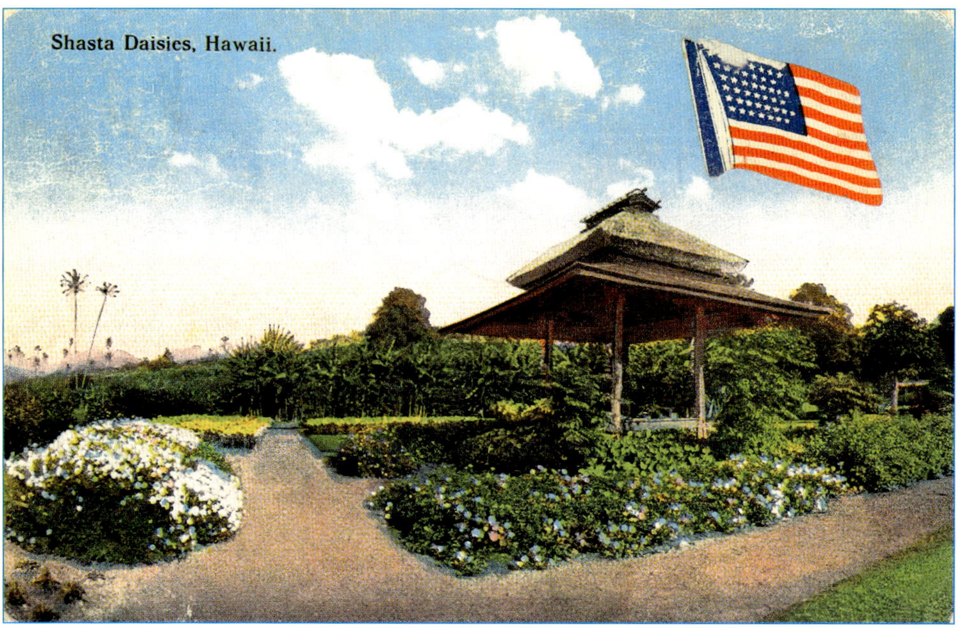

Shasta Daisies. [canceled 1917, $5-7]

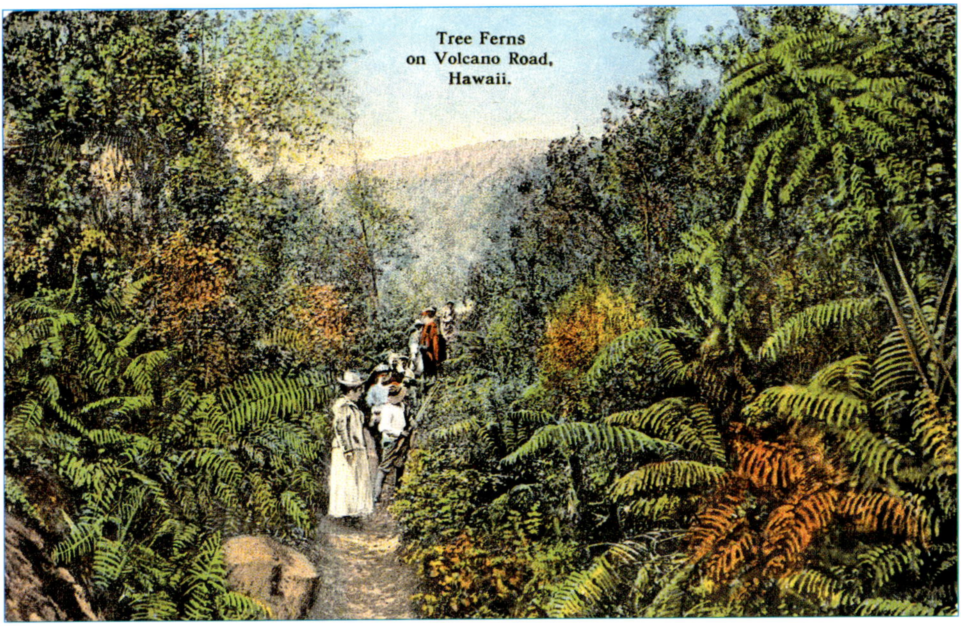

Ferns grow throughout the Islands; some varieties can grow to the size of small trees. [pre-1915, $5-7]

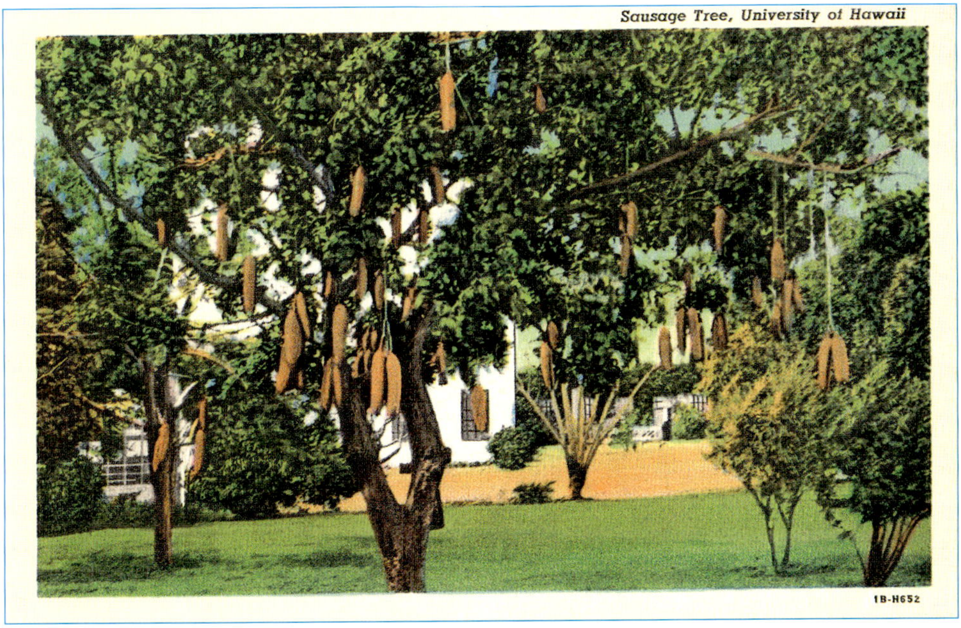

The Sausage Tree, named for the distinct shape of the fruit it bears. [pre-1940, $1-3]

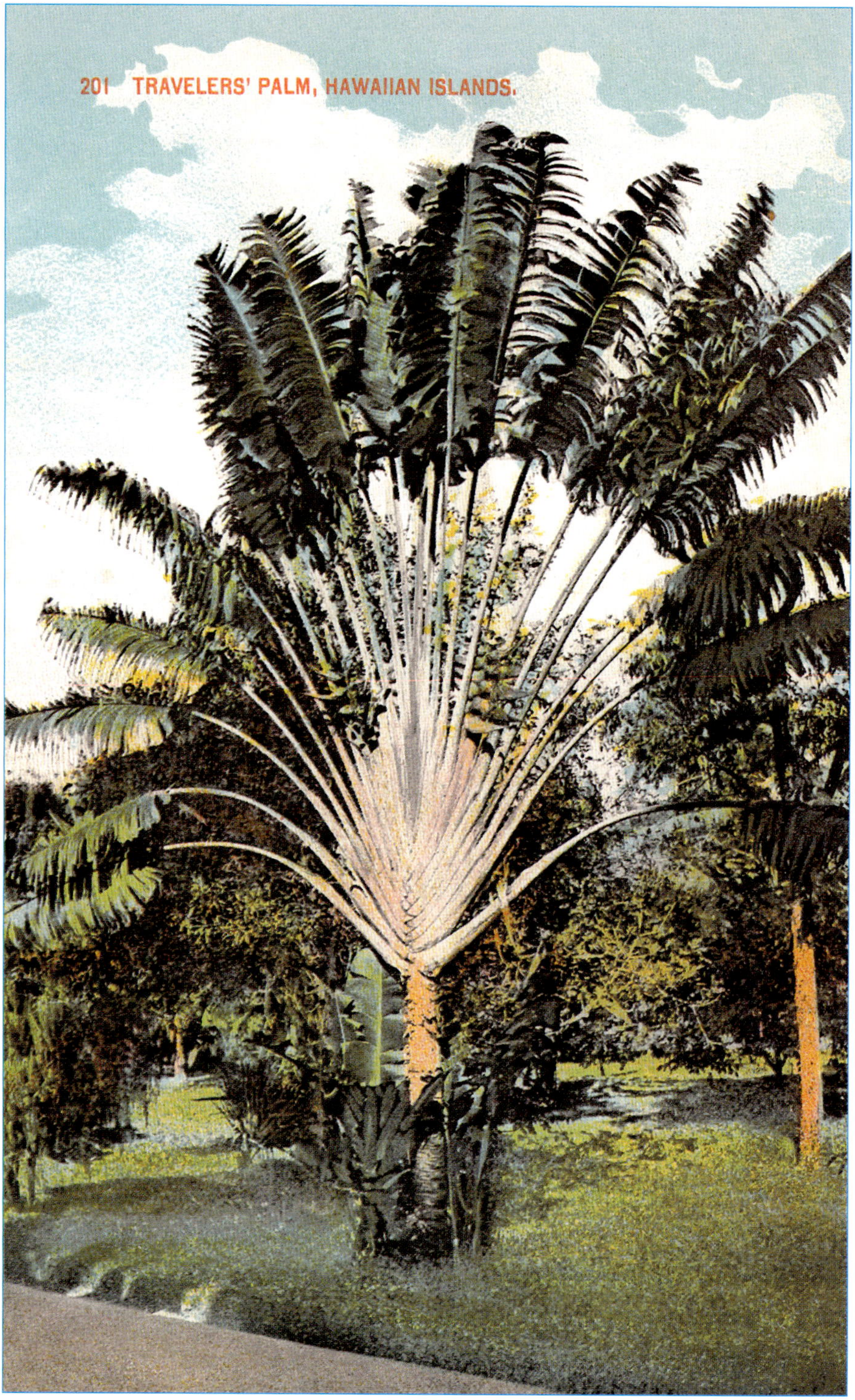

The Traveler's Palm receives its name from the water it stores in its stems, which are useful to a thirsty traveler. [pre-1915, $5-7]

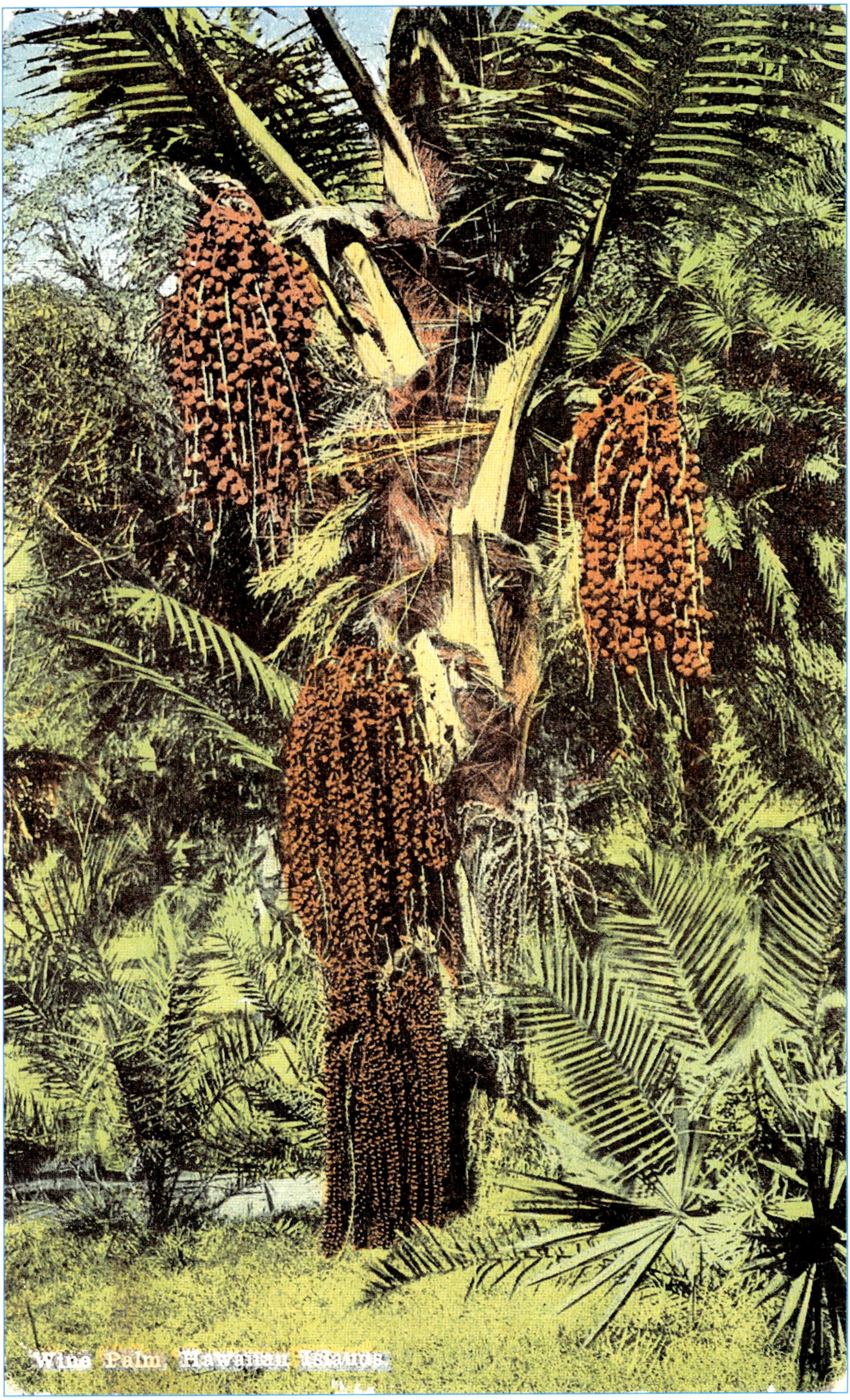

Wine Palms produce sap that could be extracted and made into wine. Unfortunately the extraction of the sap kills the tree. [pre-1915, $4-7]

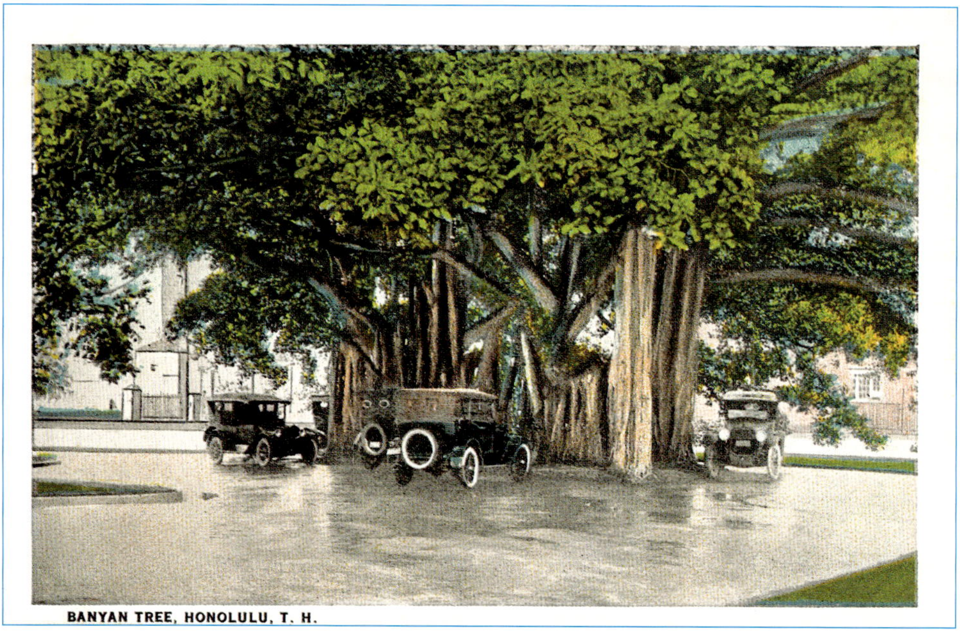

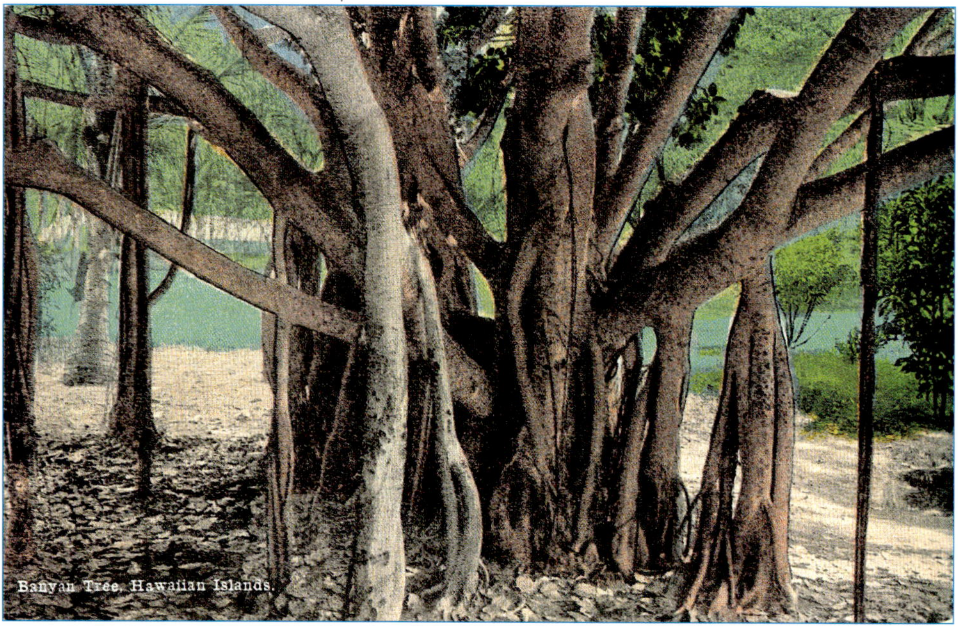

The Banyan Tree is also called the "Upsidedown Tree" because the branches resemble roots. Its air roots grow from the branches and eventually attain the ground. The tree shown with the cars stood at the famous old Palace grounds near Hotel Street in Honolulu. [Top: pre-1920, $6-8. Bottom: pre-1915, $2-3]

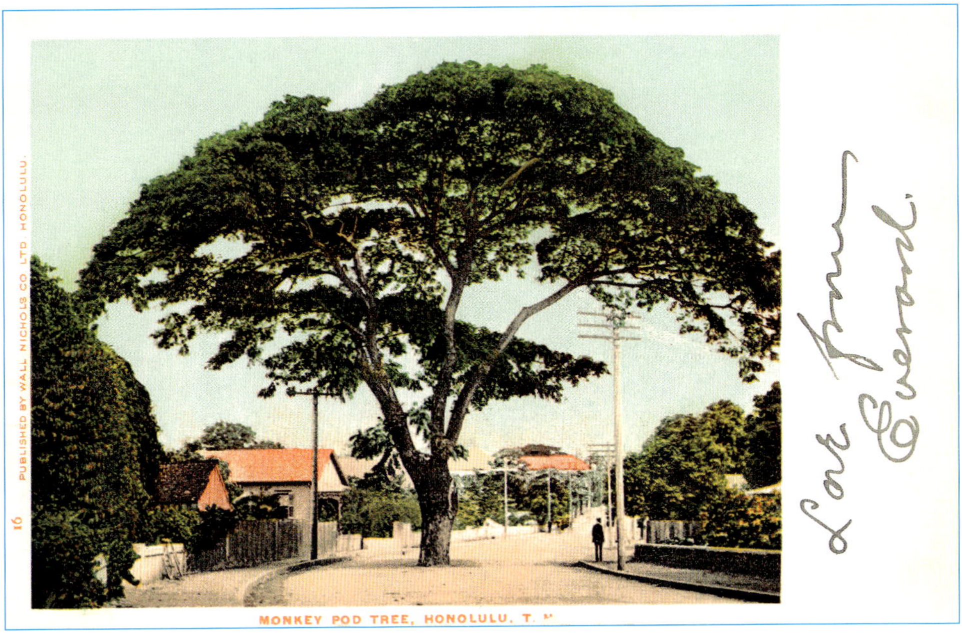

The Monkey Pod Tree is valued for the hardwood it produces. [cancelled 1907, $5-8]

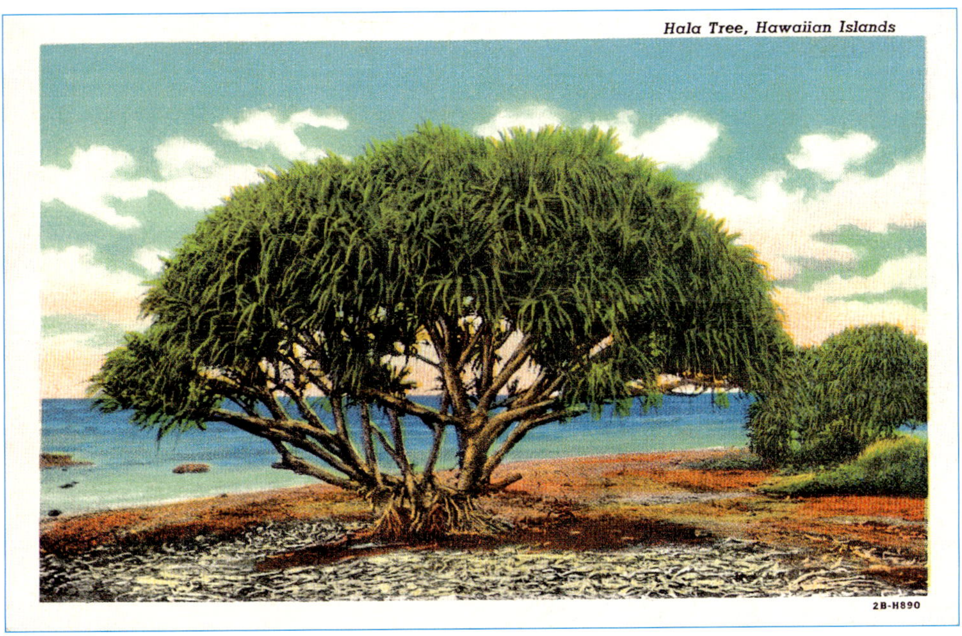

The Hala Tree was very useful to Hawaiian natives, who made mats and clothes from the leaves. [pre-1940, $1-3]

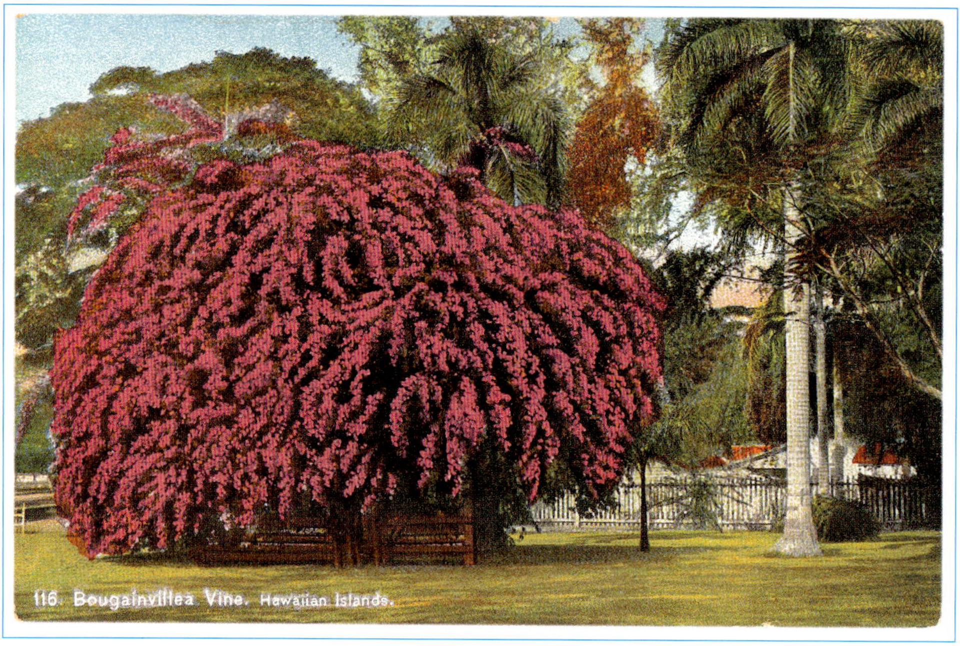

Bougainvillea Vine produces the best color when exposed to a lot of direct sunlight and does well in places like Hawaii. [pre-1915, $2-5]

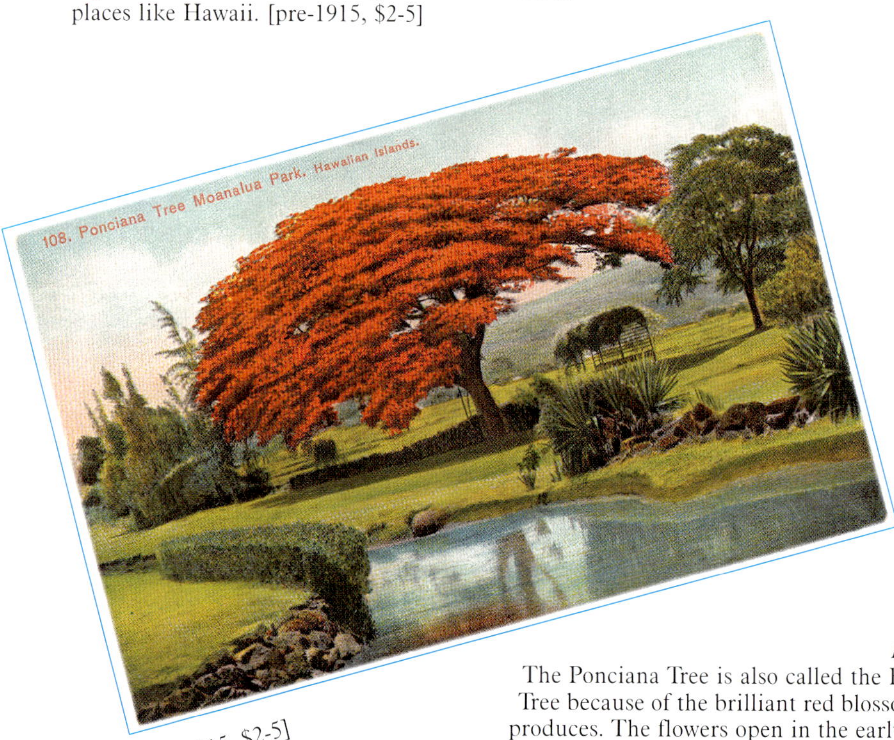

[pre-1915, $2-5]

Right:
The Ponciana Tree is also called the Flame Tree because of the brilliant red blossoms it produces. The flowers open in the early part of the summer and last for four to six weeks. It can only be grown in frost-free tropical climates. [pre-1915, $2-5]

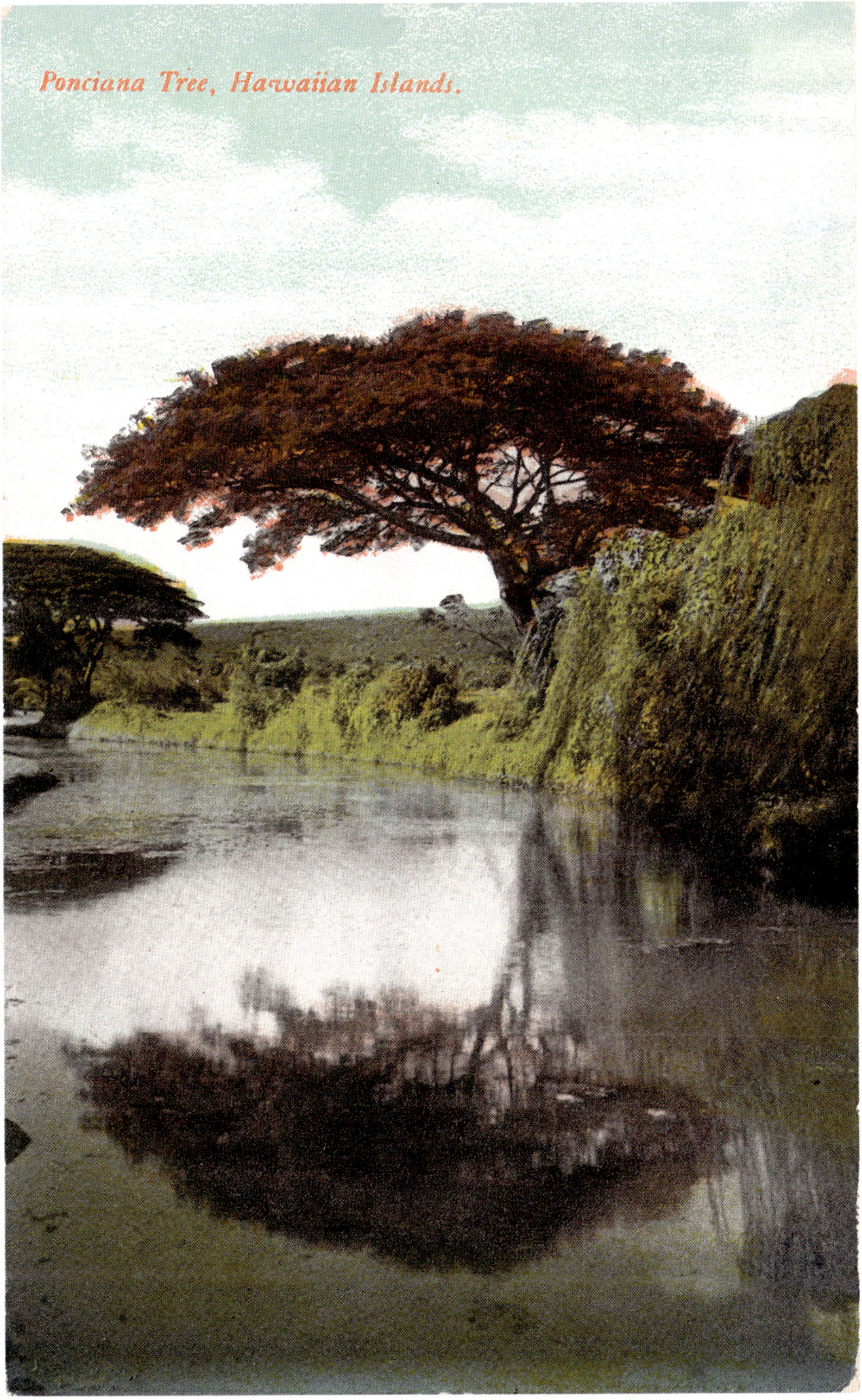
Ponciana Tree, Hawaiian Islands.

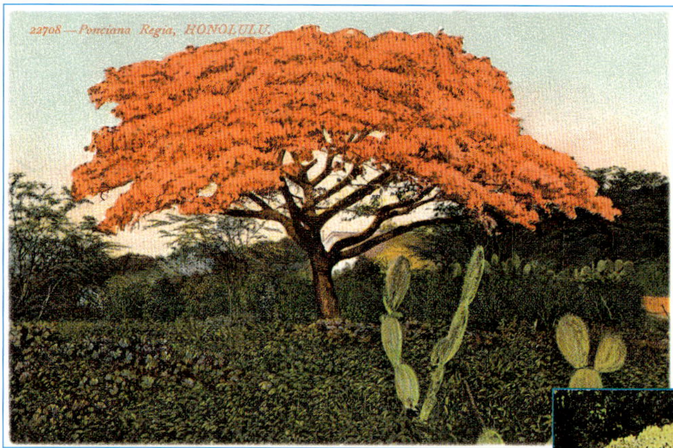

[pre-1915, $2-4]

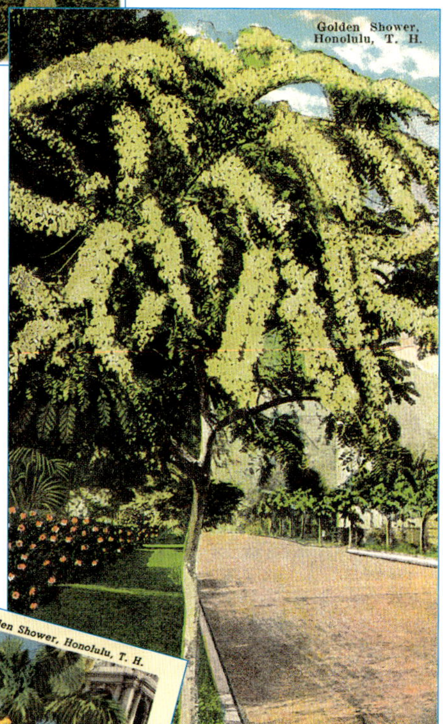

[pre-1915, $2-4]

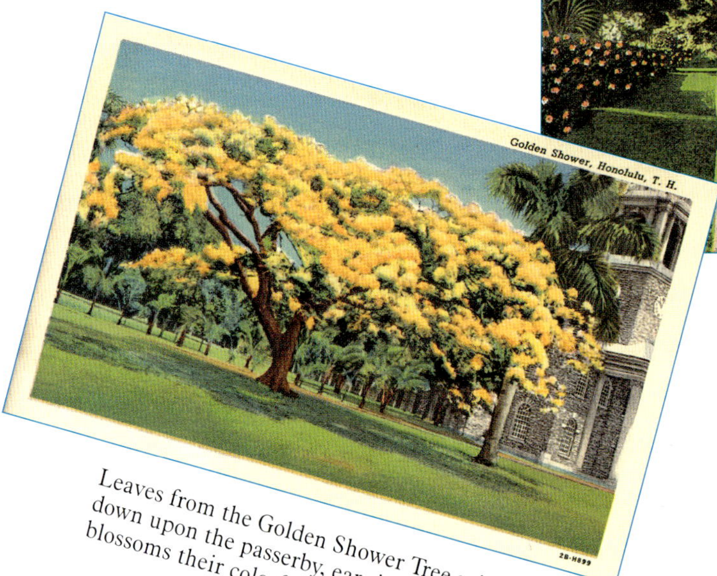

Leaves from the Golden Shower Tree rain gently down upon the passerby, earning these golden blossoms their colorful name. [pre-1940, $1-3]

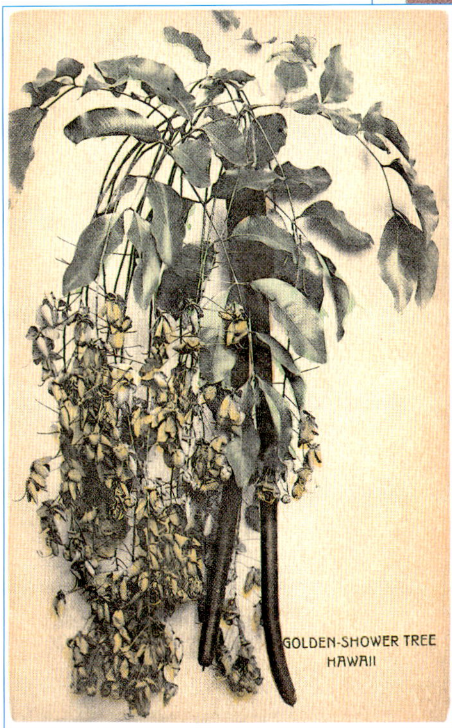

[pre-1915, $1-3]

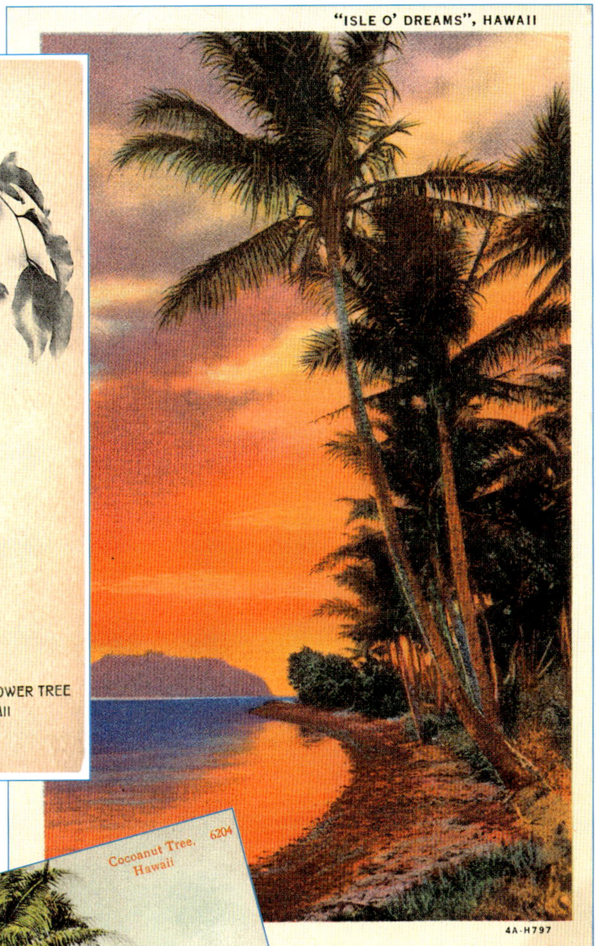

Palm trees – quintessentially Hawaiian. [pre-1940, $1-3]

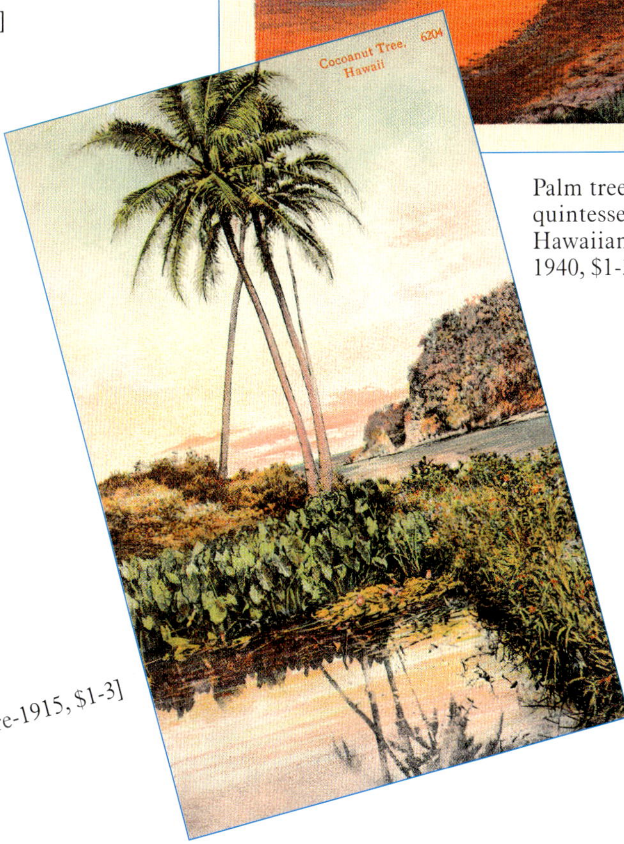

[pre-1915, $1-3]

[pre-1915, $4-7]

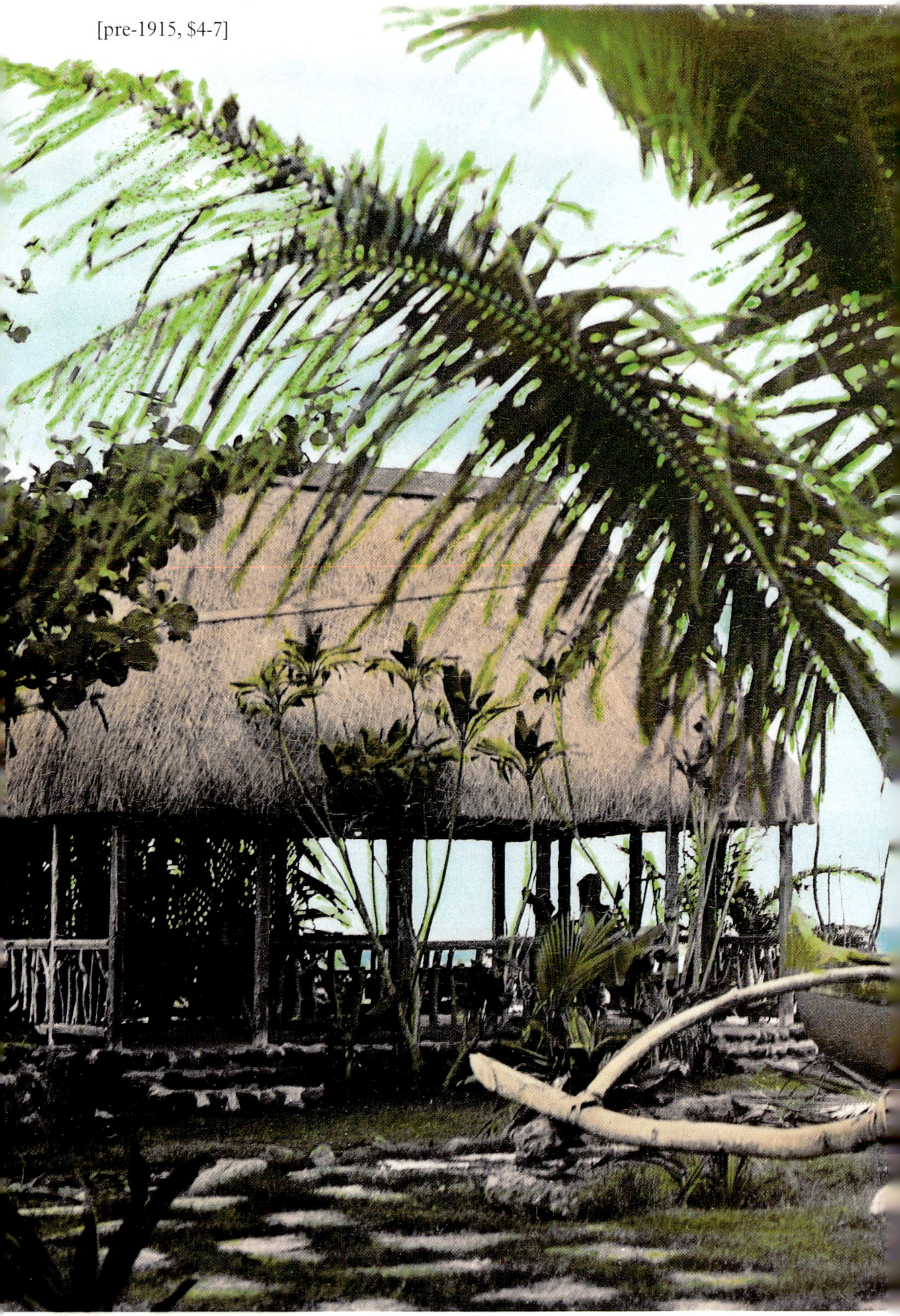

Native Life

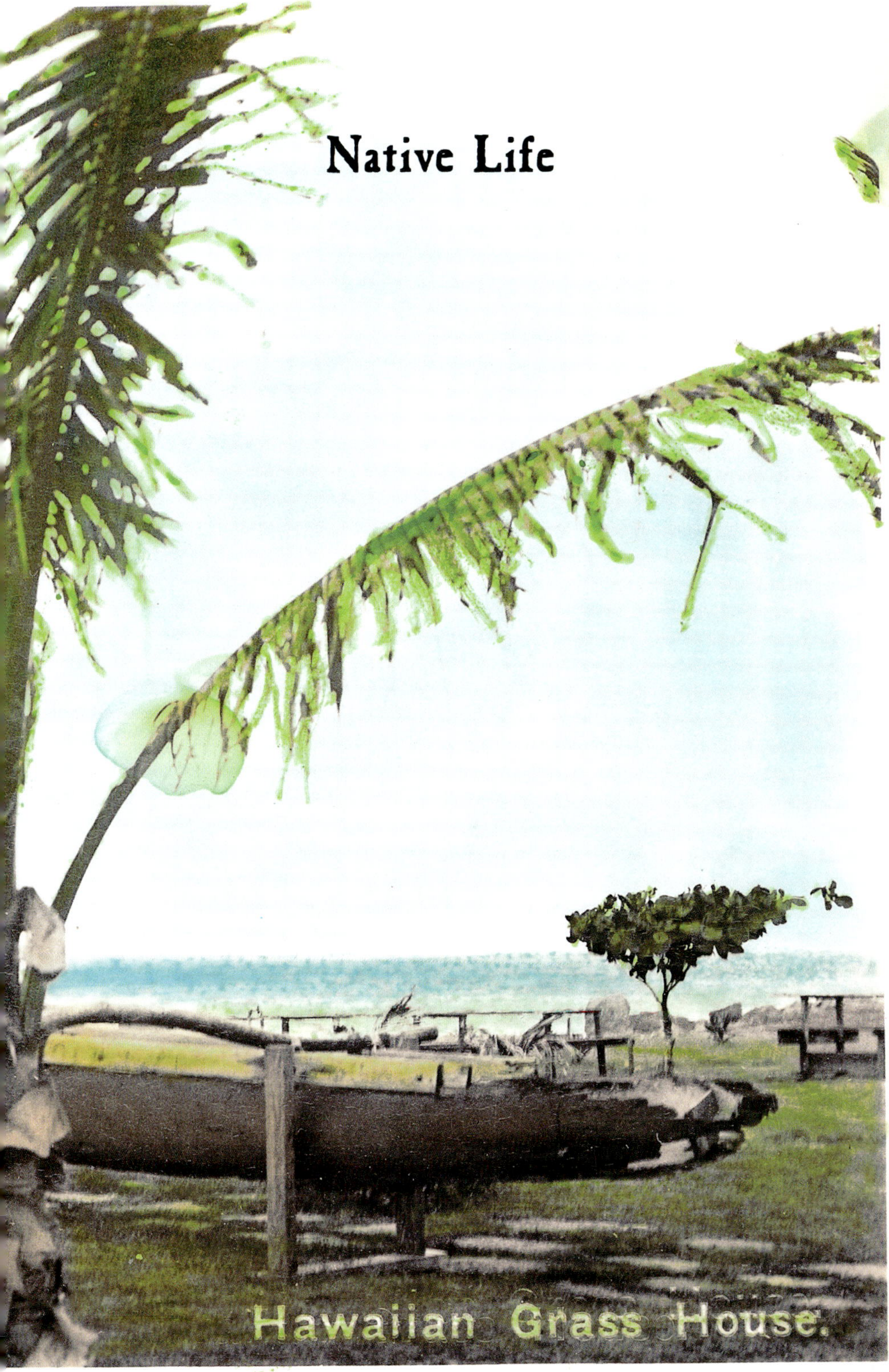

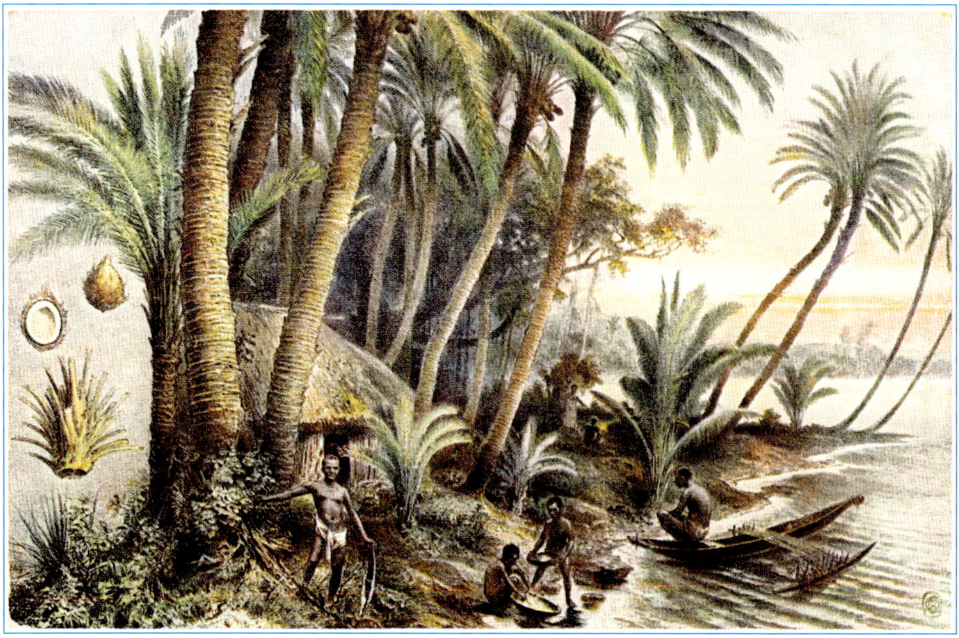

A painting depicts the idyllic paradise life, cocoanuts falling from the tree. [Postmarked 1908, $6-10]

"Honolula [sic] is a paradice [sic]. Wish you could see it. Why don't you ever write to me."
—1908

The Thatched Hut

Most of the people in a Hawaiian village lived in single room huts called *hale noho*.

These huts were made with wood and bamboo frames and thatched with pili grass. Inside the walls were covered with leaves and the floors with woven mats. These mats were woven from leaves, and sleeping mats were fashioned from the stems of the makaloa sedge.

Weaving was always done by women and was done in the *hale ulana,* the village weaving house. There was no furniture, so everyone had to sit and sleep on the floor. These huts were designed to fit an entire extended family. The family slept in the hut in order of importance, with the most important person being closest to the door. They slept on beds made of grass, which were covered with woven mats.

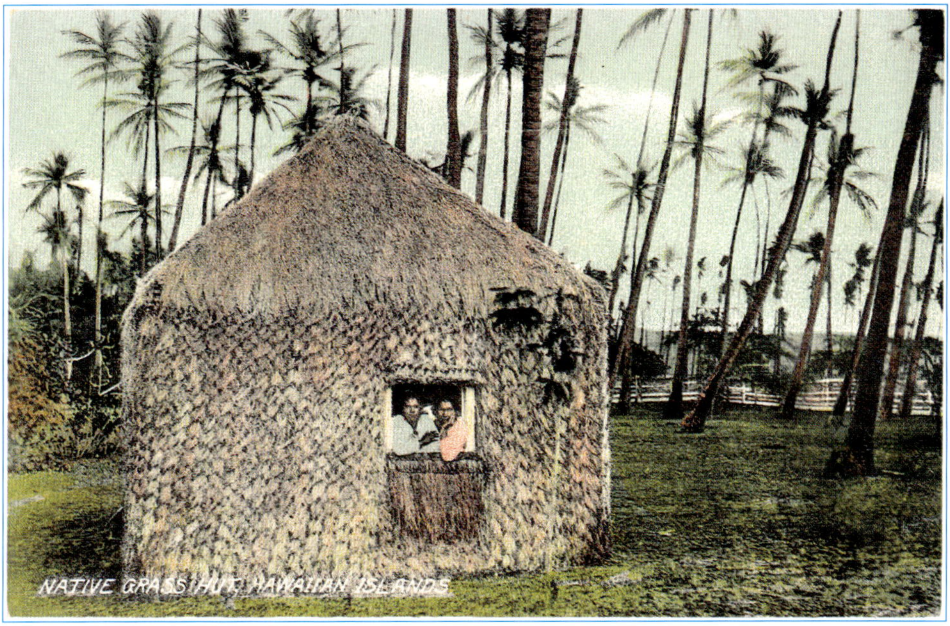

Two women peer from a conical grass hut. [pre-1915, $6-9]

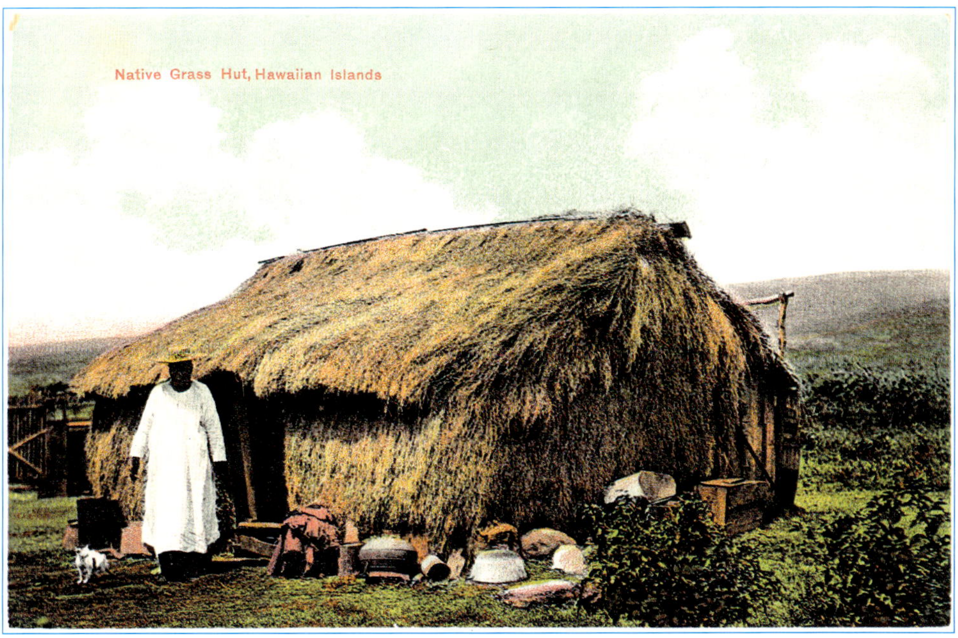

A woman in Western-inspired holoku dress steps outside her abode. [pre-1915, $6-9]

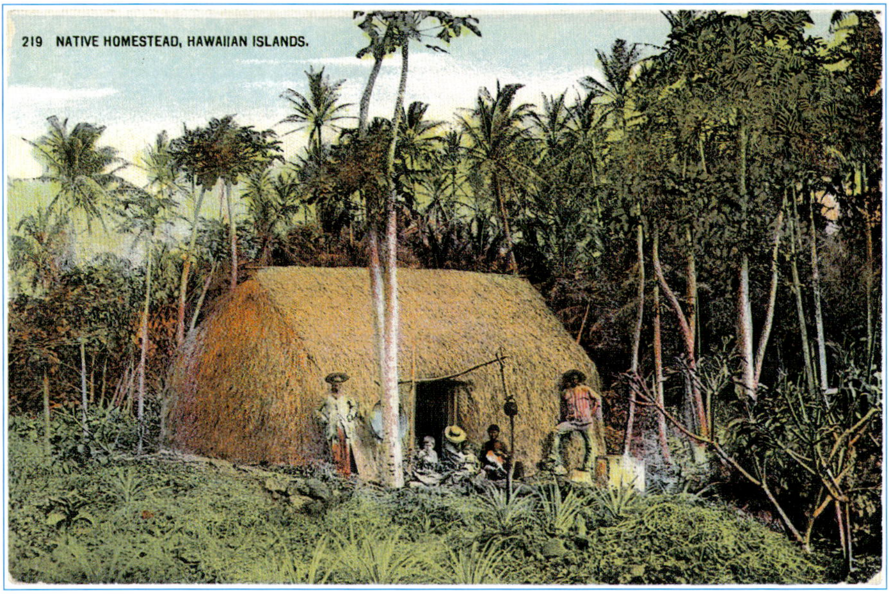

From the back: "A primitive Hawaiian Home. Very few of the primitive homes are still extant. They were but grass huts, situated on the mountain side, amid picturesque, topical surrounds, and are now replaced by frame cottages. The native has few wants beyond his simple food and clothing." [pre-1915, $6-9]

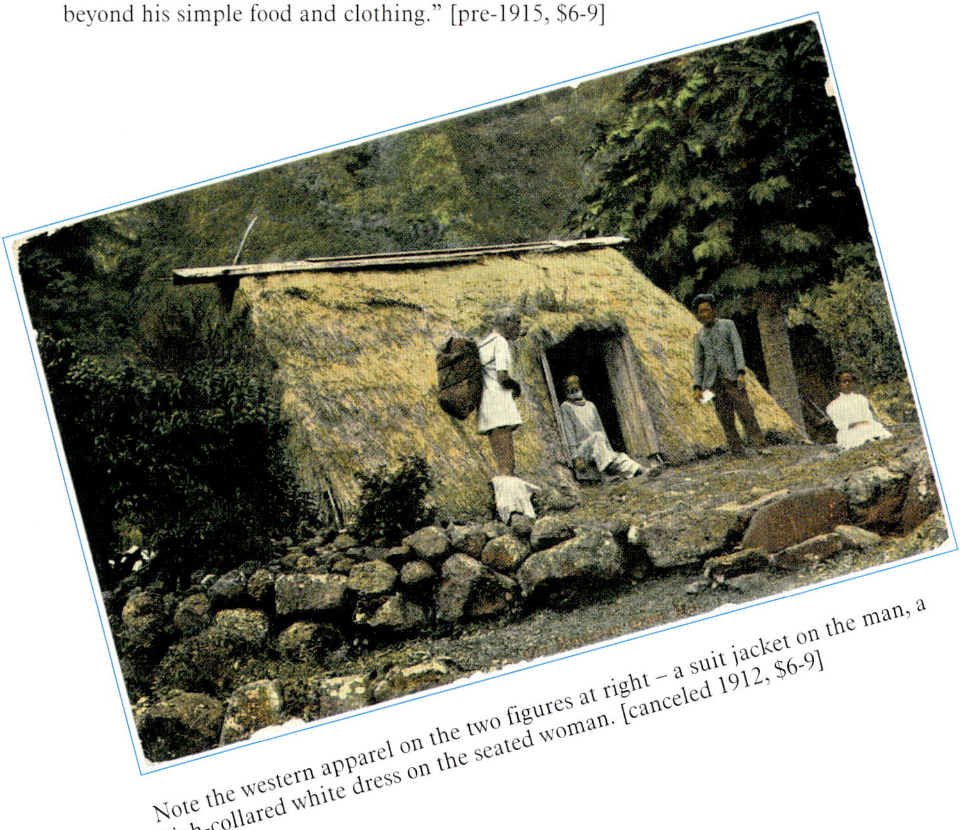

Note the western apparel on the two figures at right – a suit jacket on the man, a high-collared white dress on the seated woman. [canceled 1912, $6-9]

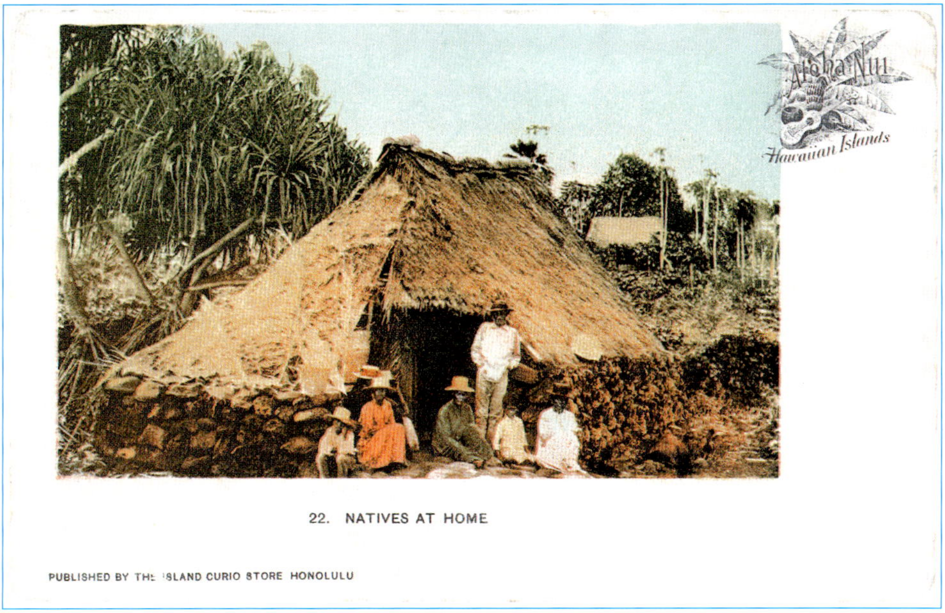

A family gathers at the entrance to their humble home, cocoanut husks stacked waist high as walls. [canceled 1903, $20-40]

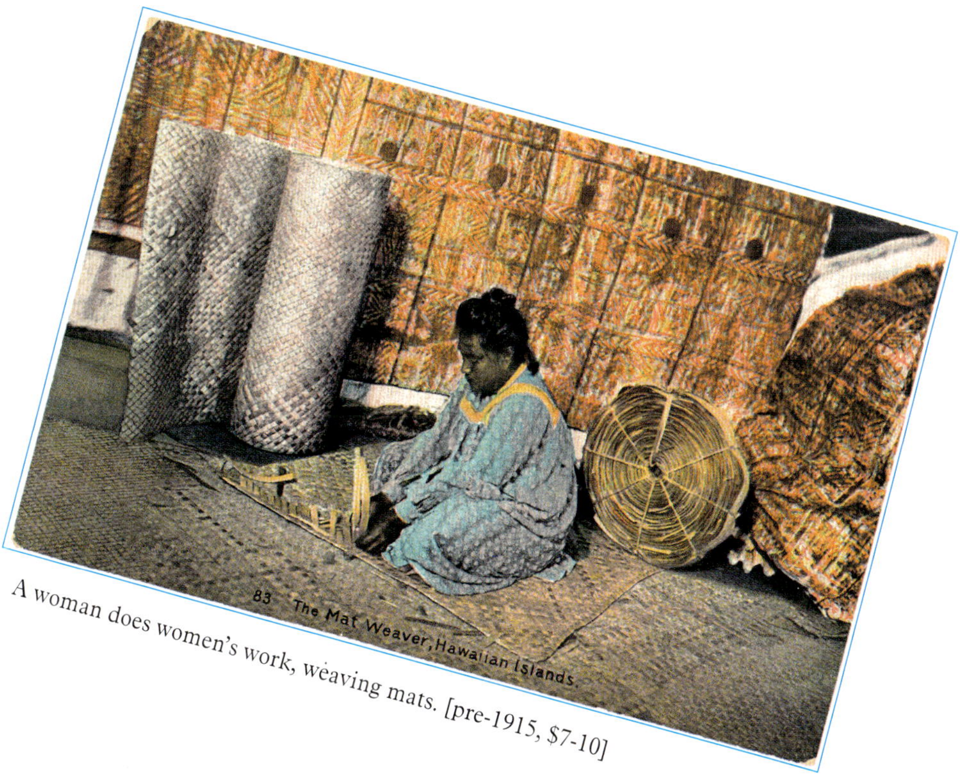

A woman does women's work, weaving mats. [pre-1915, $7-10]

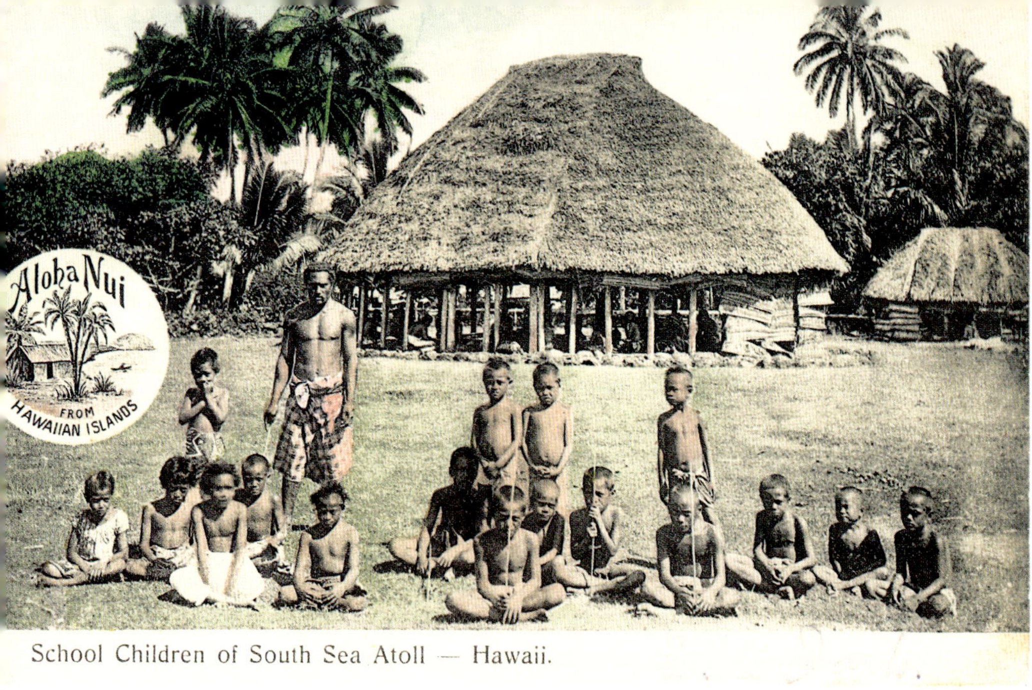

School children of South Sea Atoll, Hawaii. [Canceled 1908, $25-45]

Native Dress

Ordinary Hawaiians worn loincloths and skirts made from tapa cloth. Tapa was made from bark, with the bark of the mulberry producing the best variety of cloth. The bark was stripped from the tree and soaked in saltwater for seven days until it was soft. It was then beaten into strips and left to dry in the sun. The strips were soaked again, beaten to break up the fibers, and then beaten again into a material similar to felt. Finally the cloth was hit with a paddle carved with a pattern. It was set out to dry one last time and then spread over moss and left exposed to dew in order to bleach it.

Garments made of feathers were worn by chieftains and other important men. Important women were identified not by their clothing, but by various ornaments worn and carried on their persons. A necklace called a *lei niha palaoa*, made from braided human hair and decorated with a curved whale's tooth was hung on her neck. Also around her neck or on her head she wore a *lei hulu* made from feathers, and carried a wand of feathers to complete her ornamentation. After the arrival of Christian Missionaries from Europe, both men and women bowed to Western influence and began to cover themselves with more clothing, though they kept many of the ornamentations.

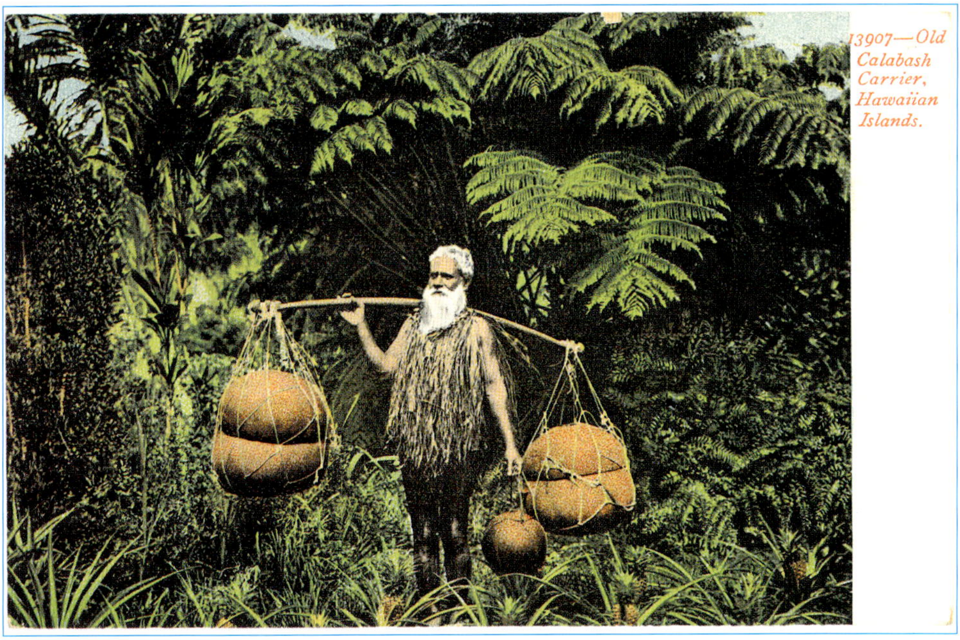

A calabash carrier in a Hawaiian fern forest. [pre-1915, $8-12]

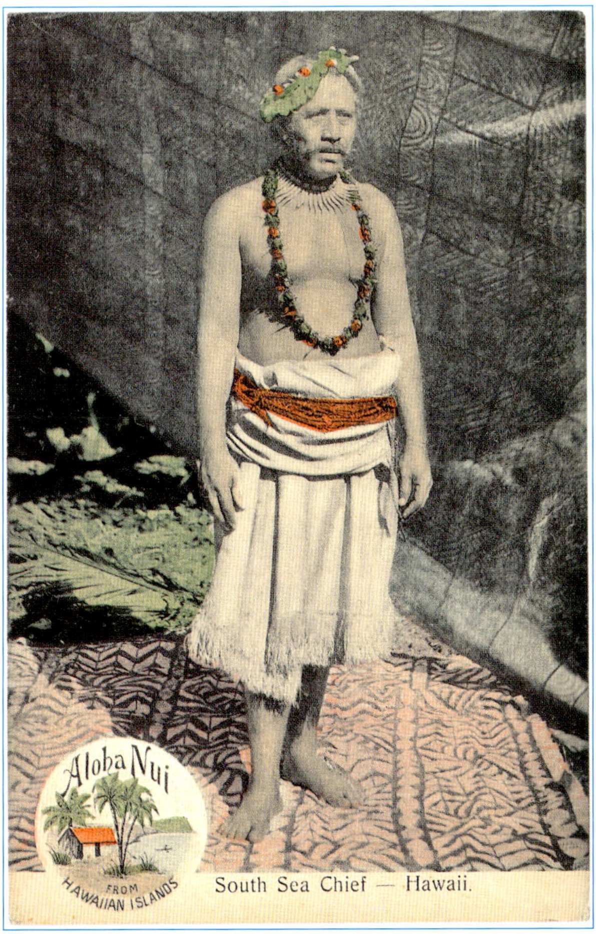

Tapas cloth forms a wonderful background for the portrait of a chief. [pre-1915, $25-45]

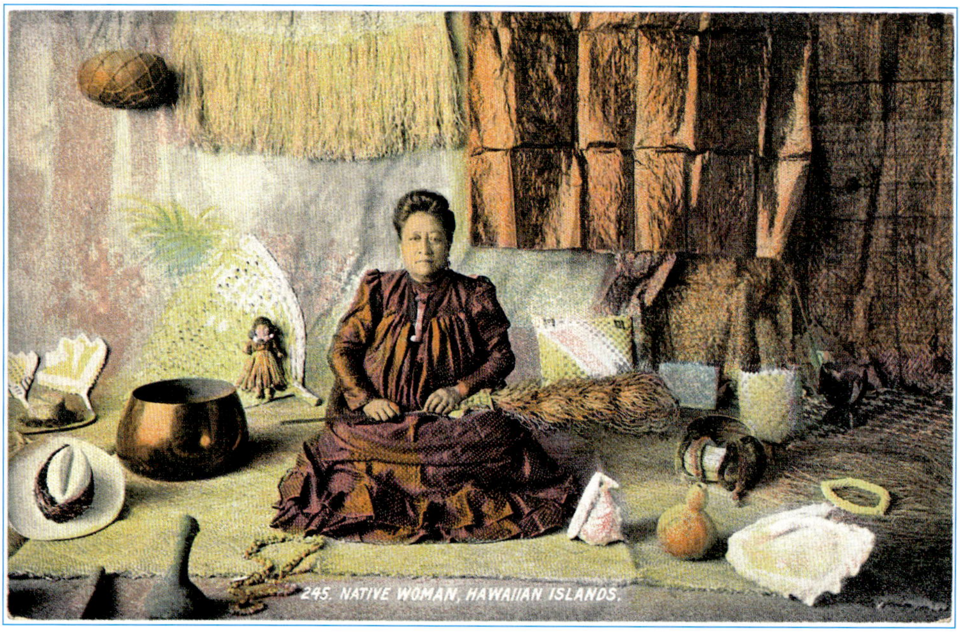

From the back: "A Hawaiian lady in native costume, the *Holuku*; around her neck a chiefess' necklace, the *Leipalaoa*, holding a *kahili* as mark of rank. Surrounded by articles of Hawaiian home industry." [pre-1915, $10-16]

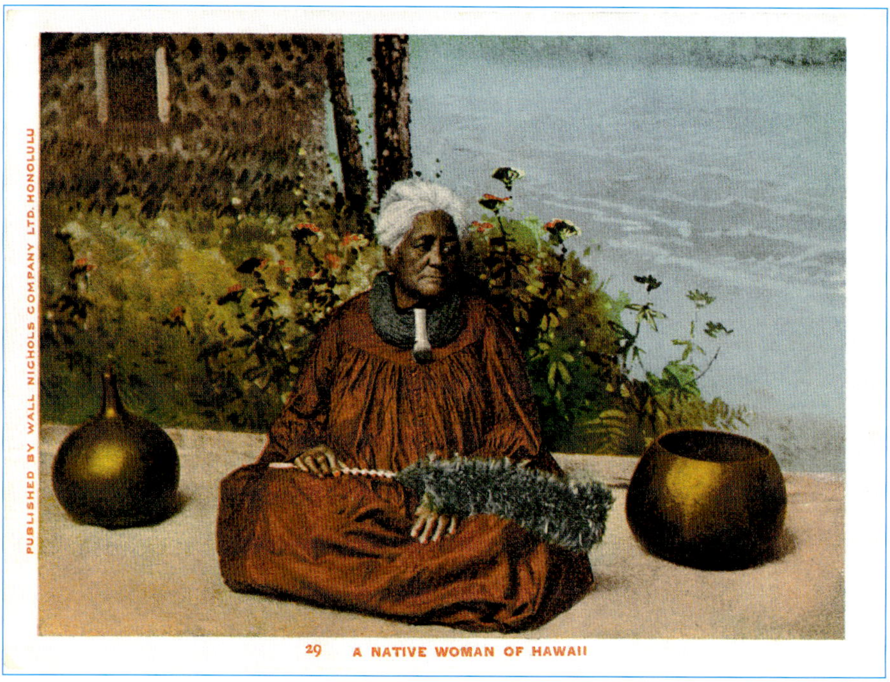

[pre-1920, $6-10]

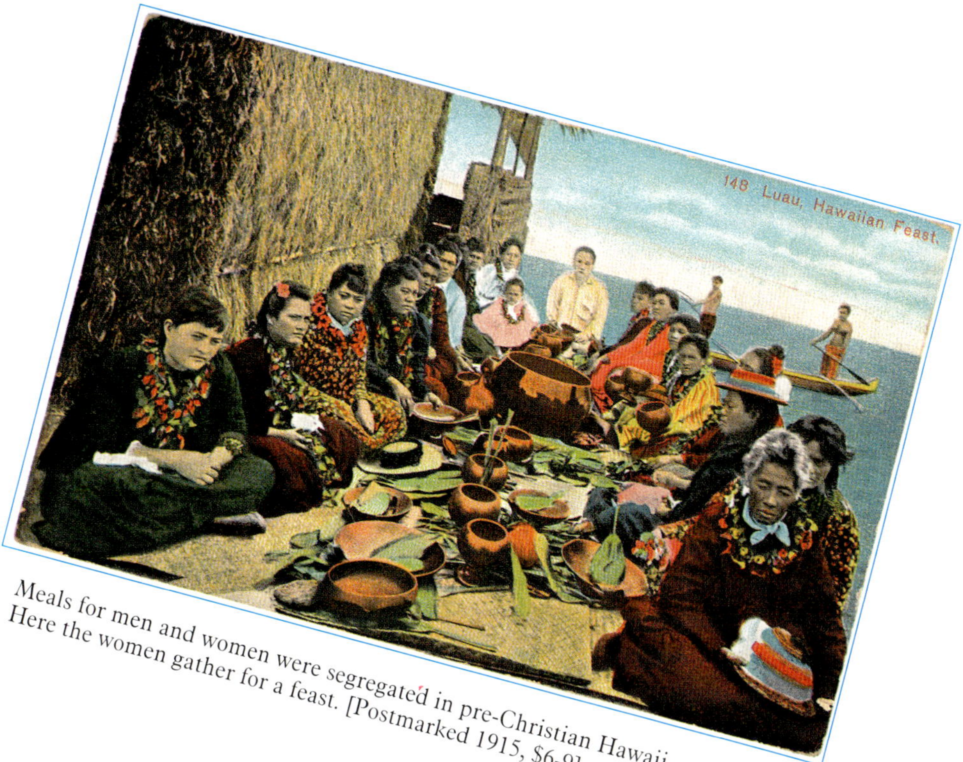

Meals for men and women were segregated in pre-Christian Hawaii. Here the women gather for a feast. [Postmarked 1915, $6-9]

Villagers gather for a portrait. [pre-1915, $8-12]

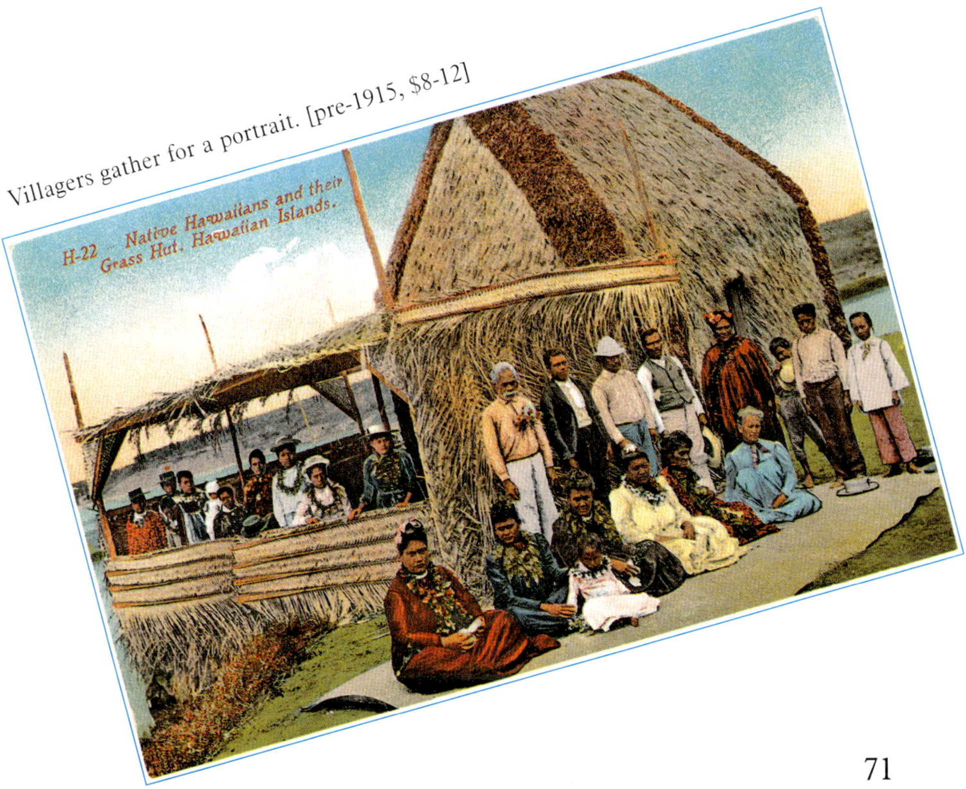

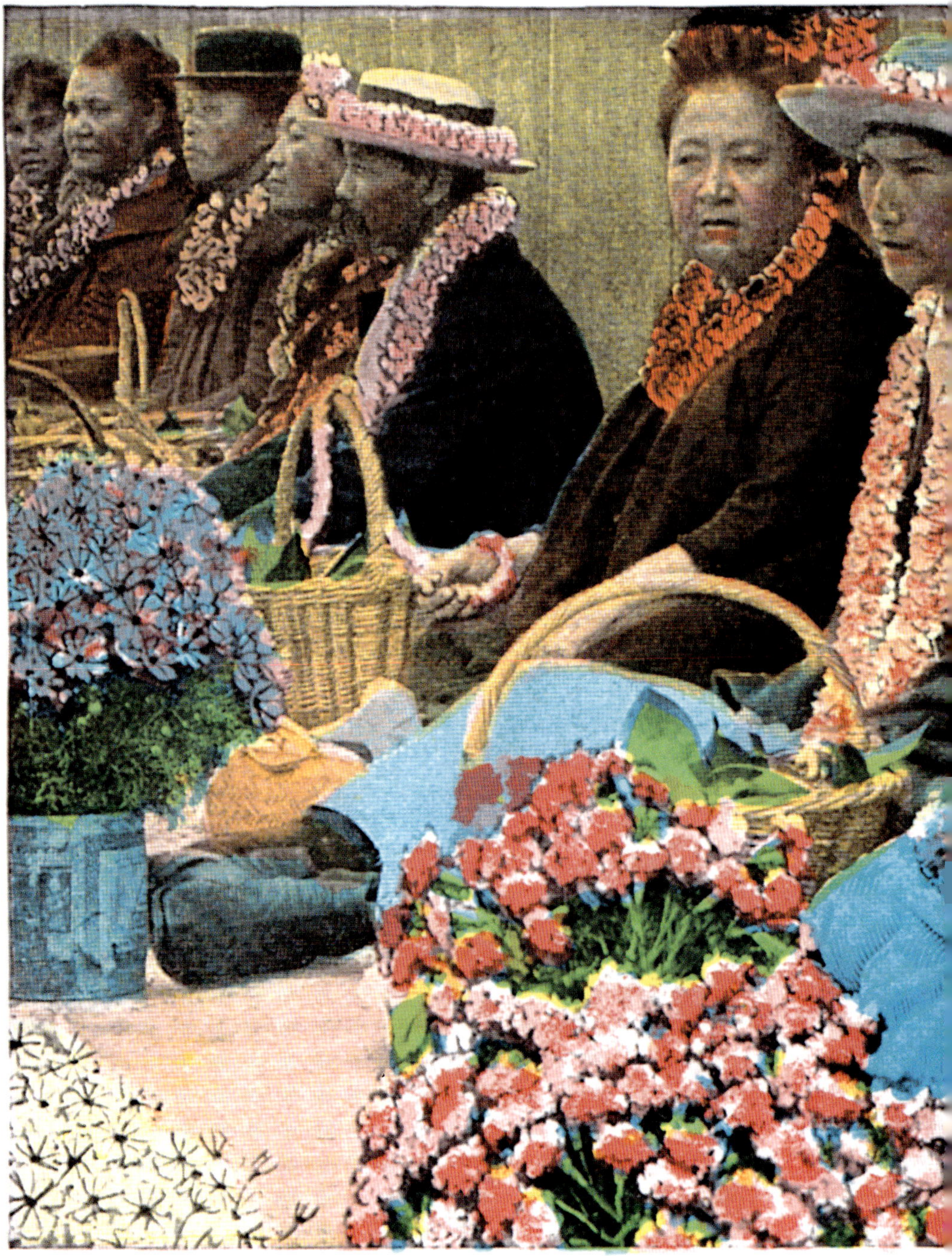

"These are the Hawaiian Lei makers and sellers, but here are plenty of men too, who crowd the docks and beg you to buy. Unfortunate the guest who lands or leaves without gifts of lovely, fragrant leis."
—1948

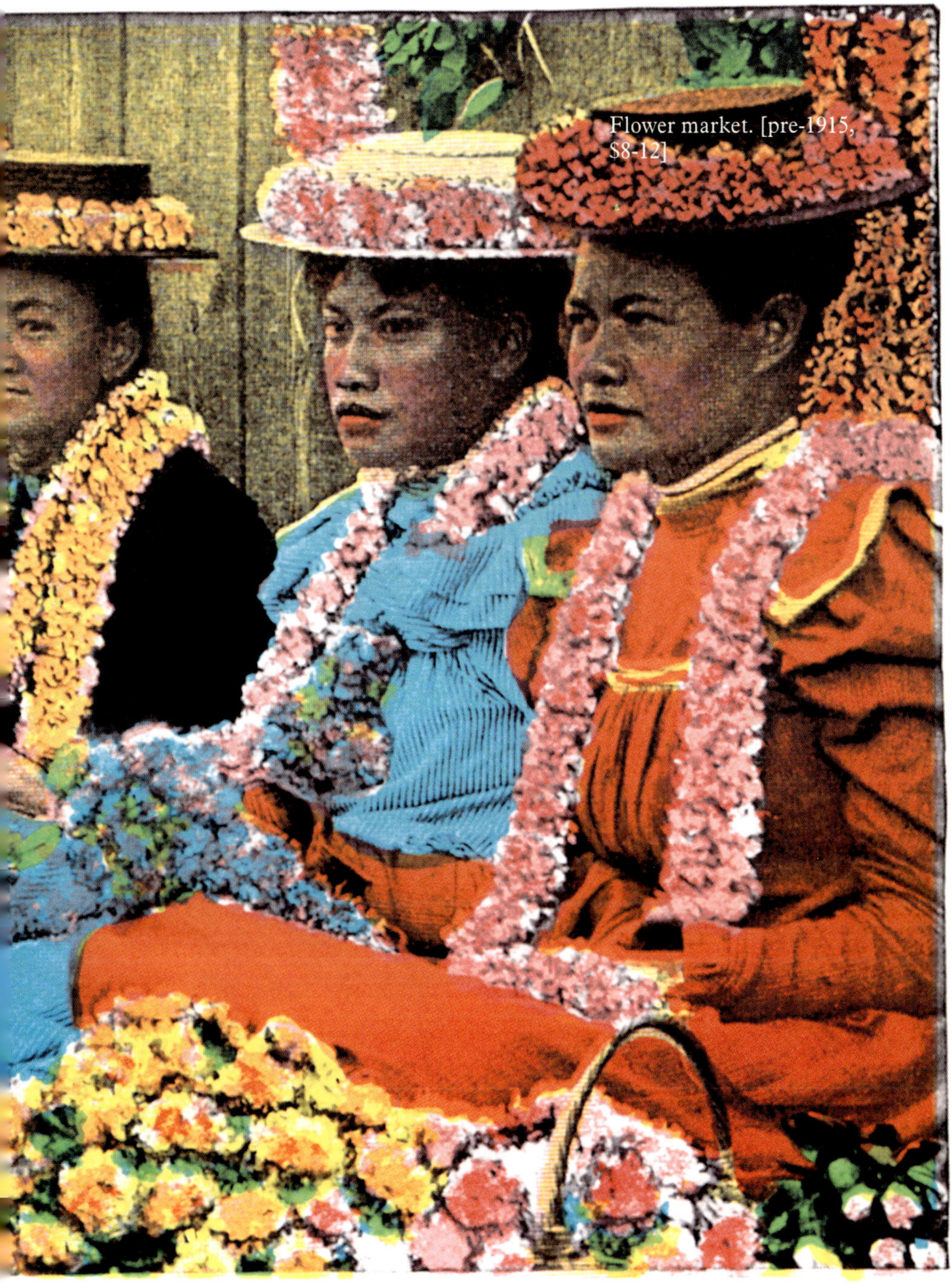

Flower market. [pre-1915, $8-12]

The Lei of the Land

Perhaps the most well known aspect of Hawaiian culture is the lei. No visit to Hawaii is complete without one. Traditionally leis were used to mark special occasions in an individual's life. Leis, which can be worn by both men and women, served to mark events ranging from a person's birth to his death, and were worn during a variety of religious ceremonies.

Each kind of lei can be identified by the individual flowers and leaves, and by the scent the flowers give off. Each flower and leaf carries its own symbolic meaning. Particular scents, flowers, and leaves were used to denote particular occasions. A lei made of maile leaf, for example, was used in ceremonies dedicated to the gods of hula. The plumeria lei is given to tourists when they arrive on the Islands and is therefore the lei that is the most familiar to anyone not acquainted with the old traditions.

These and other leis were crafted by hand and sold by independent vendors throughout the various ports of entry into the Hawaiian islands. The wearing, giving, and selling of leis continues as one of Hawaii's prominent and beloved traditions.

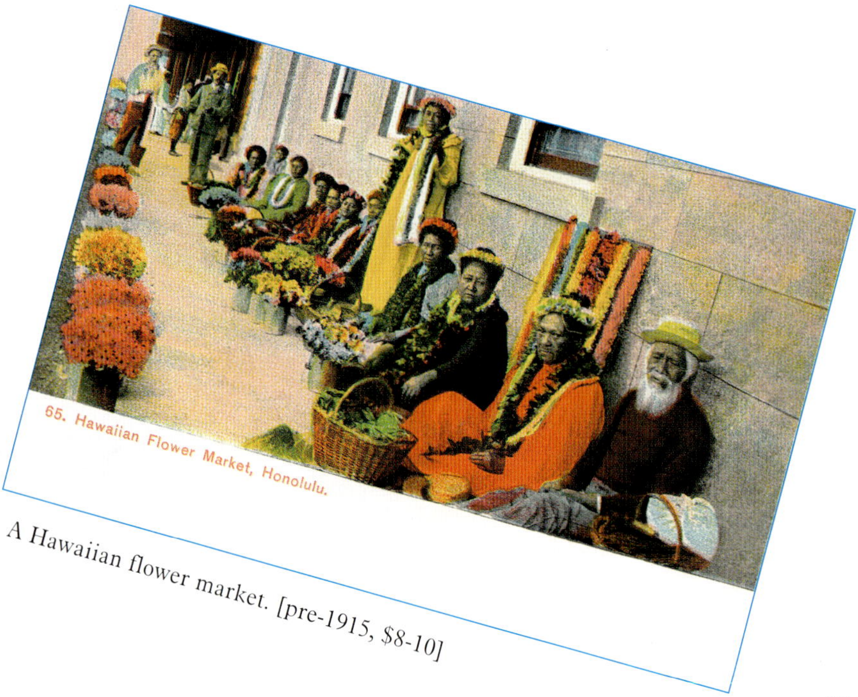

A Hawaiian flower market. [pre-1915, $8-10]

Right:
On the back: "The Royal Hula-hula dancing girls were a feature of olden days in Hawaii. The Hula-hula is acting out by gestures and movements the ideas expressed by the songs which accompany them. The time is marked by striking on gourds or hokeo and in some instances these dances are in honor of the Gods or chief as the alaapa-apa. The professional hula dancers are devotees of the Goddess Laka. The dancers are generally women, though children are sometimes engaged in the less objectionable dances and the men act as buffoons in between the acts." [pre-1915, $15-18]

Hula and Performing Arts

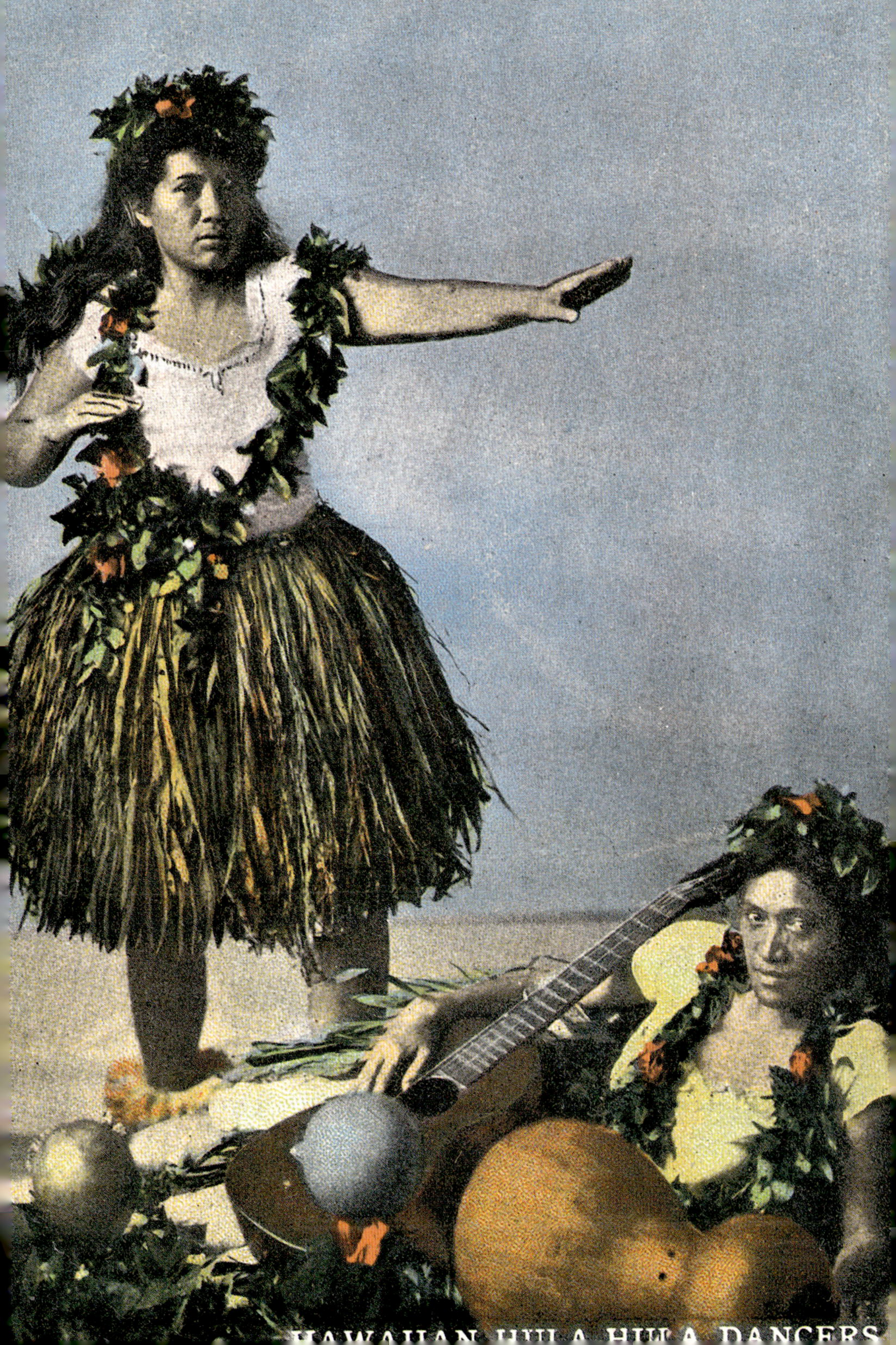

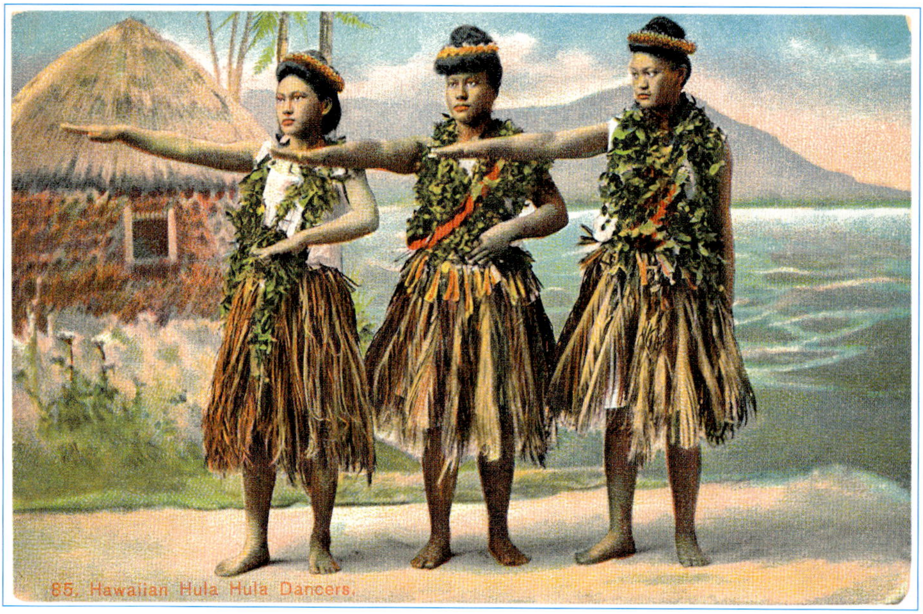

[pre-1915, $15-18]

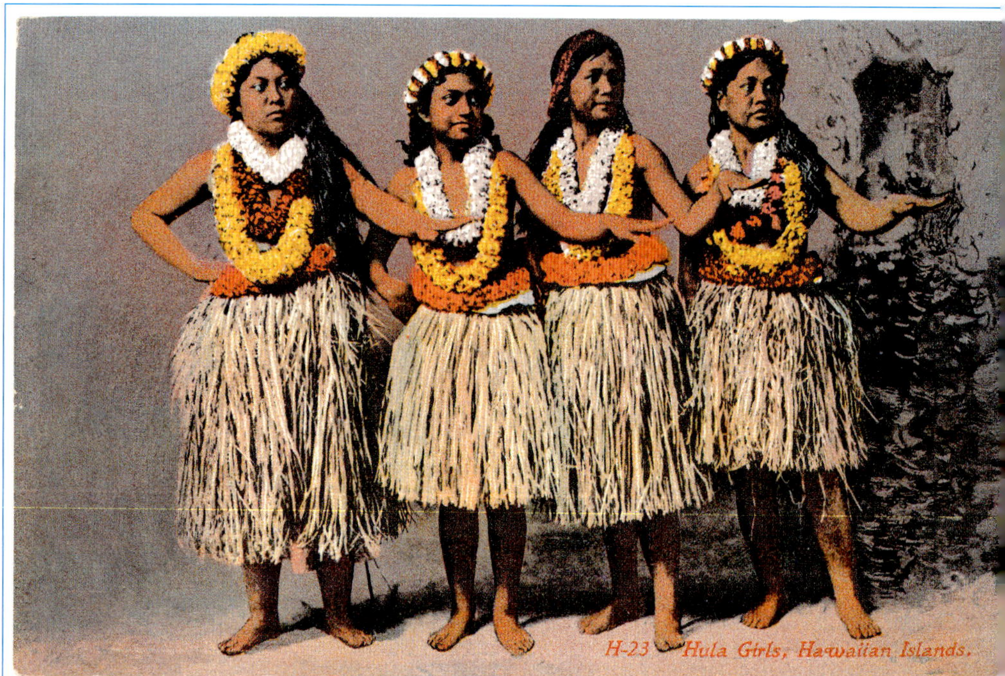

[Postmarked 1916, $15-20]

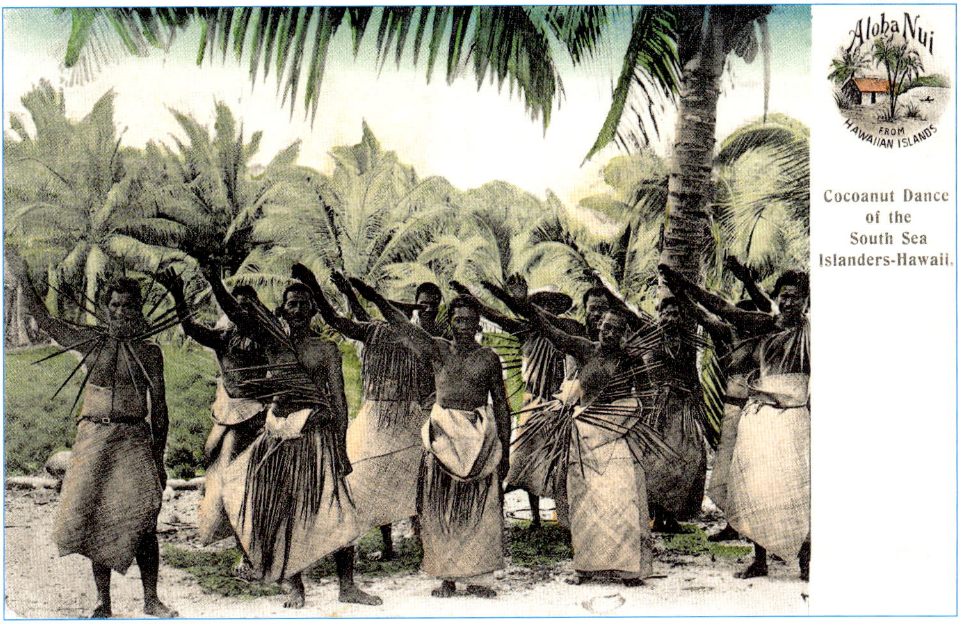

Men perform the Cocoanut Dance. [Postmarked 1908, $25-45]

The original Polynesian settlers developed their own unique dance on the islands. Legend attributes its origins to hi'iaka, who danced to appease her fiery sibling, the volcano goddess Pele. This story still provides the basis for many contemporary dances. Before the Europeans spread their influence on the island, the dance traditions were closely integrated with religious practices of the Hawaiian people.

The term *hula* refers to movement and gestures. These are performed with *mele* (poetry), the most important component as it contains the verbal records of cultural information ranging from prayer to historical records to songs that praise the land and establish romantic motifs.

American Protestant missionaries in the early 1800s convinced converted chiefs to denounce the hula as heathen practice, and it had to be practiced and taught clandestinely through the mid-nineteenth century. King David Kalakaua, who reigned from 1874-1891, encouraged a revival of the practice despite objections from christianized Hawaiians and non-Hawaiians. Hawaiian poetry, chanted vocal performance, dance movements, and costumes were then merged to create a new form of performance art, the *hula ku'i* (*ku'i* means "to combine old and new").

Hollywood later added interest to the art form, with hula igniting the attention of tourists and film audiences. Concessions to non-Hawaiian audiences included English-language lyrics, less allusive pictorial gestures, and sex appeal added by emphasized hip movements, removing the hula from its former religious context.

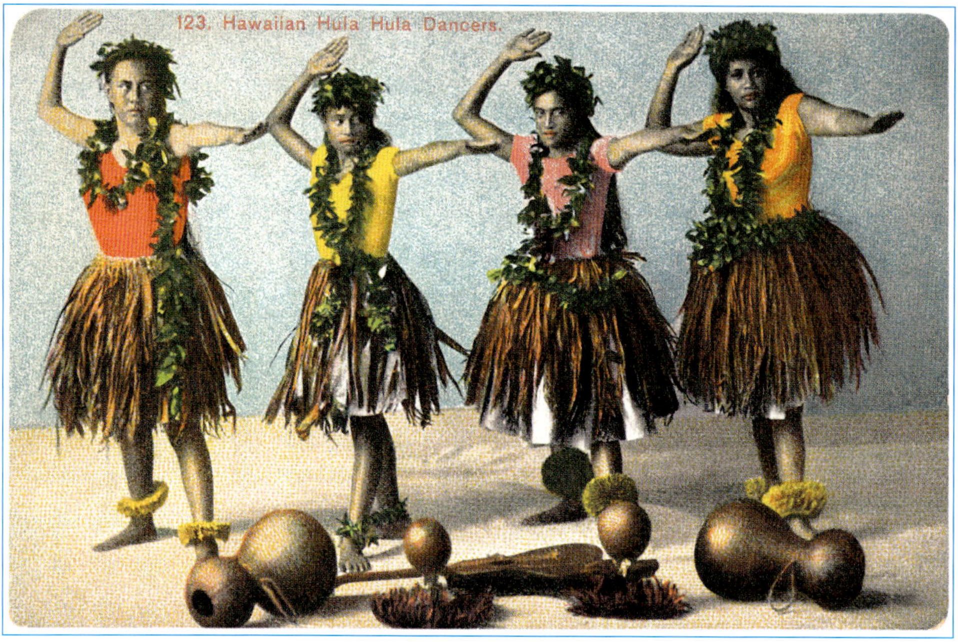

The *ipu* (a gourd) was the indigenous instrument most closely associated with hula. [pre-1915, $12-18]

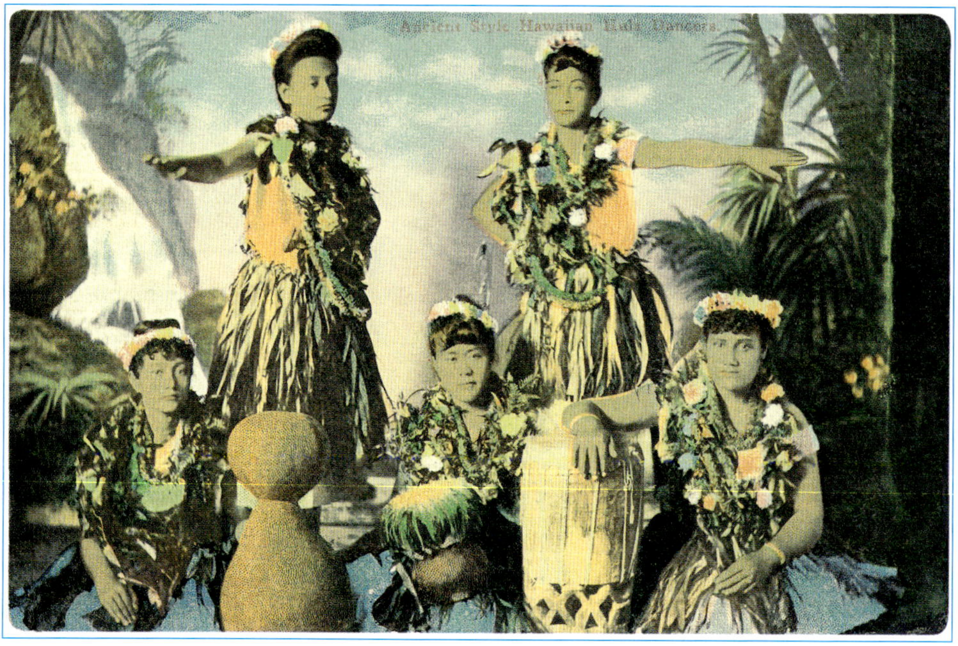

Drummers performed oral chants accompanied by dancers in the traditional storytelling/worship ceremonies of hula. [pre-1915, $12-18]

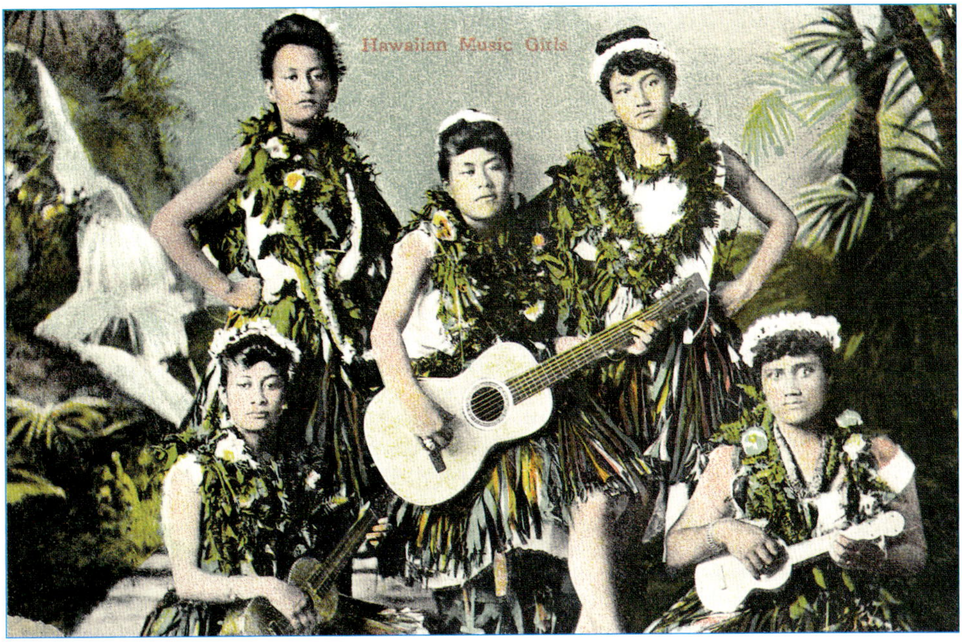

Guitars and ukeleles were introduced to Hawaii by westerners. [pre-1915, $15-18]

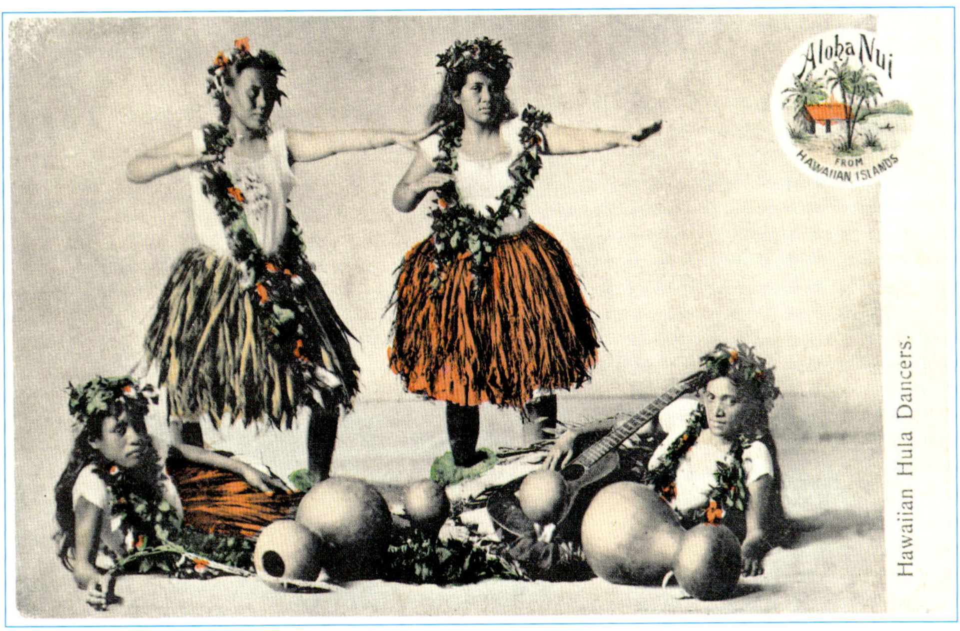

While hand and arm gestures interpret the text, named foot motifs are continuously executed by the dancers. [pre-1915, $25-45]

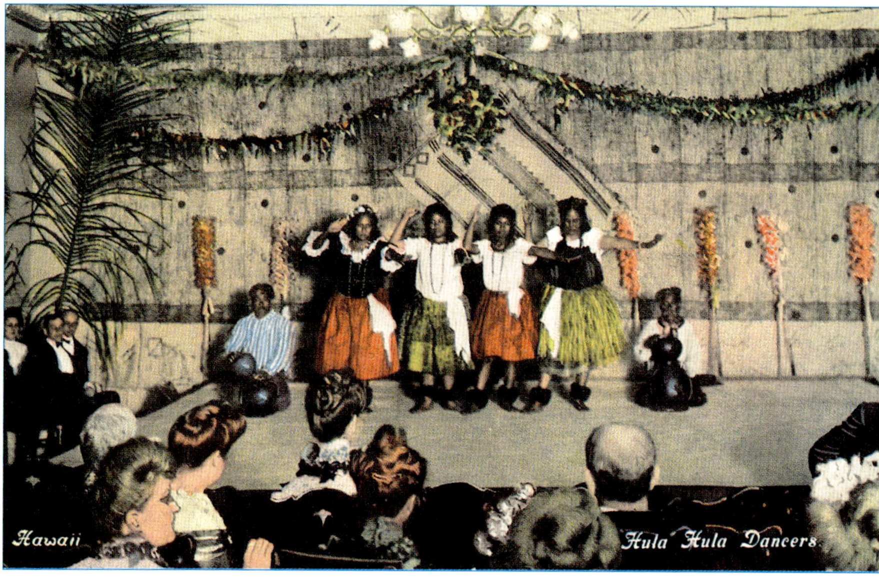

[canceled 1917, $15-20]

This is a very poor picture of some professional dancers. It grows very tiresome, not very pretty, a little disgusting at times.
–1917

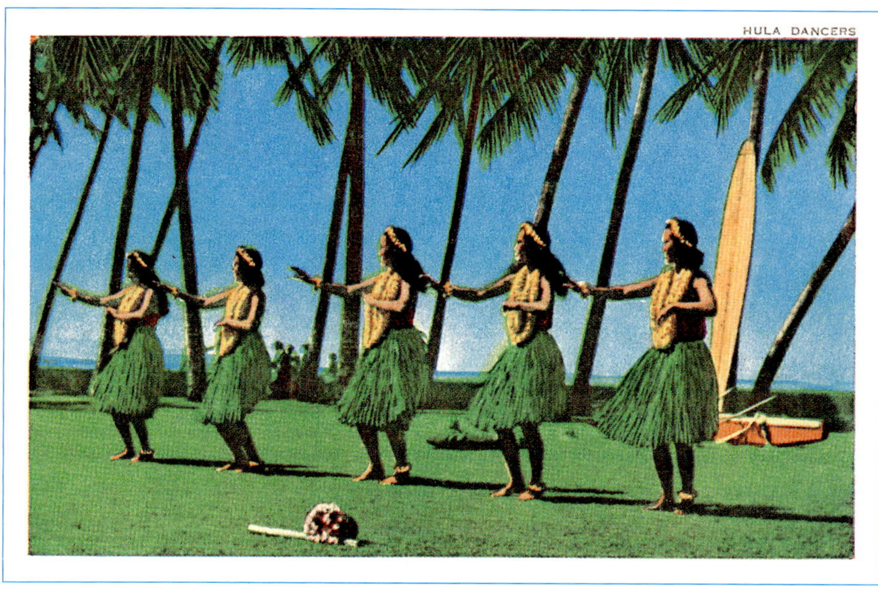

On the back: "The real Hawaiian hula as it is danced... is a graceful interpretive dance telling the legends and stories of Old Hawaii. Skirts woven from the green leaves of the ti plant are usually worn by the Island dancers." [canceled 1945, $3-7]

"A whole story can be told by these dancers in one dance. They move their hips, eyes and hands in certain ways and each way tells part of the story. The dance is a very graceful one."
–1945

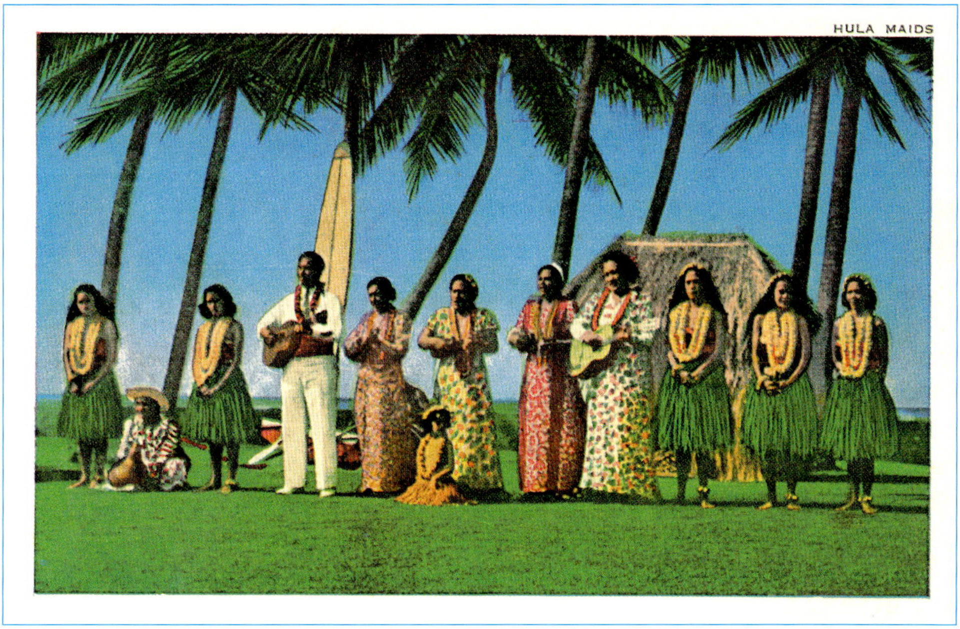

On the back: "Hawaii's native dance is an interpretive form of dancing, which delights everyone who visits Hawaii." [pre-1915, $6-10]

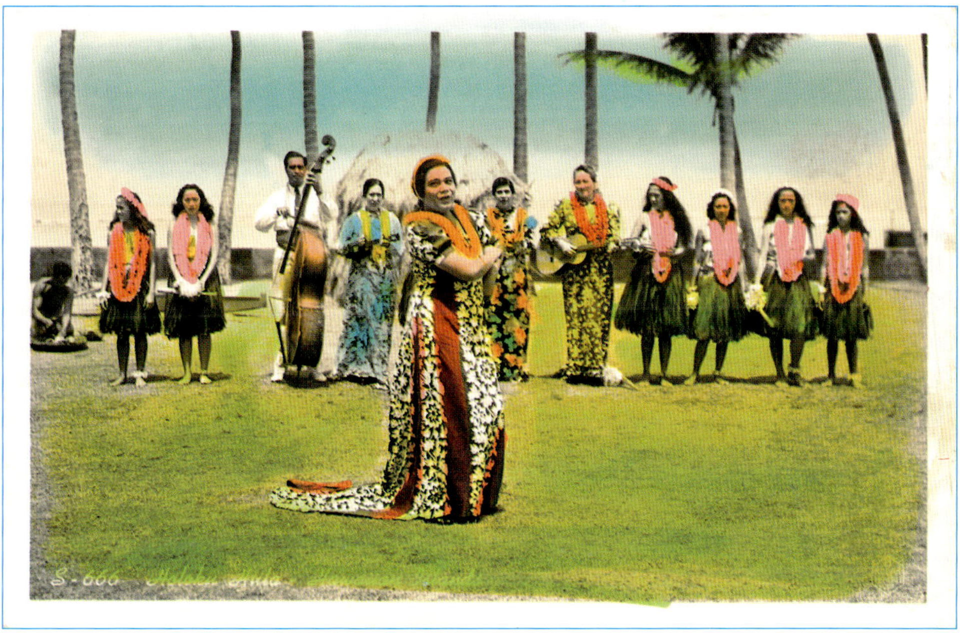

[pre-1920, $7-12]

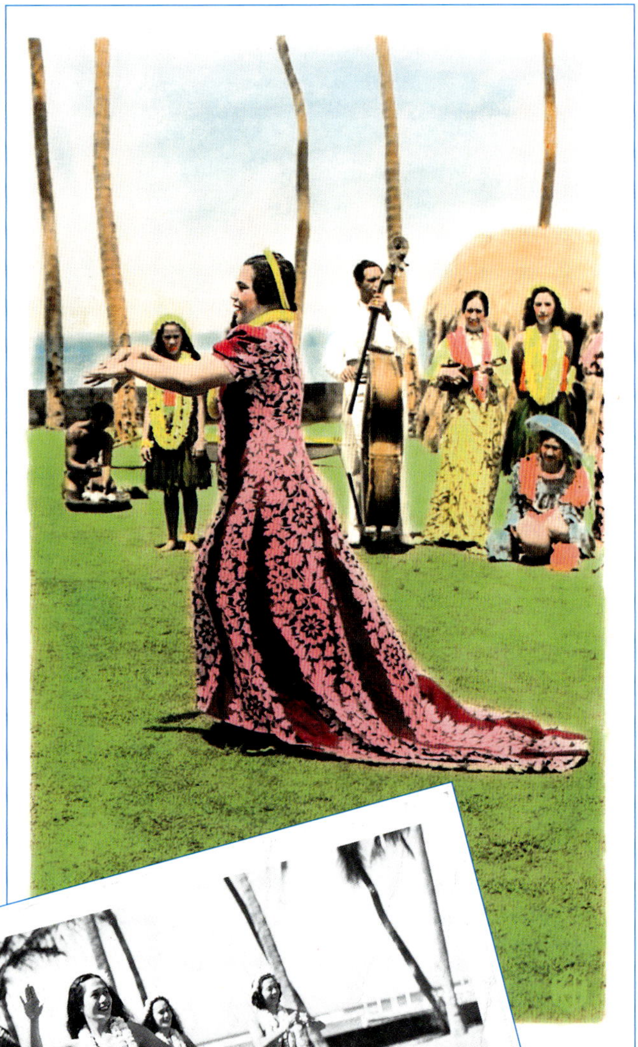

[pre-1915, $9-15]

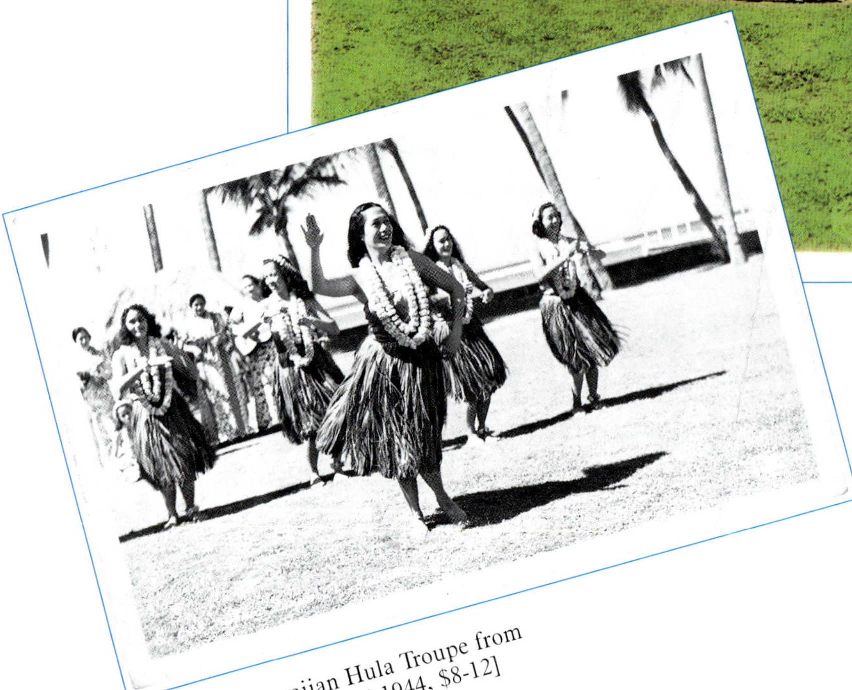

The Royal Hawaiian Hula Troupe from Honolulu. [Postmarked 1944, $8-12]

[pre-1930, $10-12]

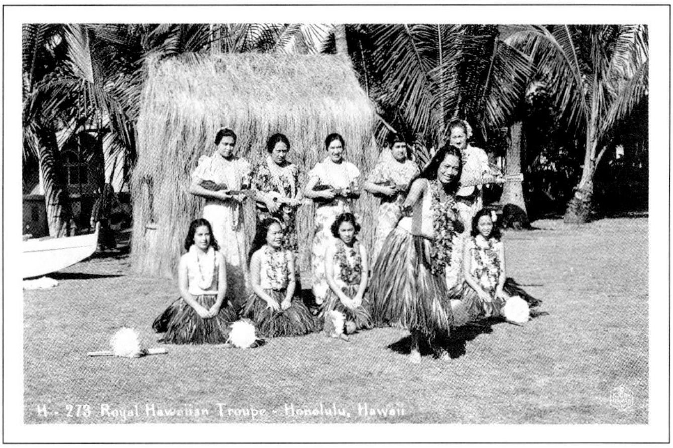

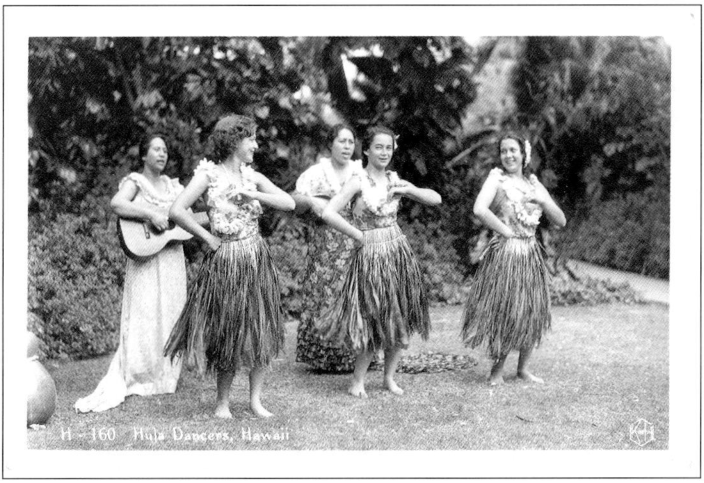

[pre-1930, $10-12]

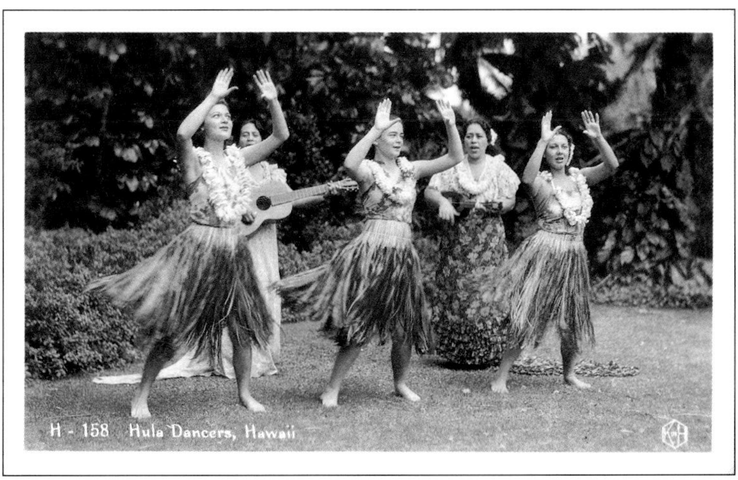

[pre-1930, $10-12]

Island Girls

There's an idyllic notion in the West of the "Island girl," an exotic, happy, beautiful being who epitomizes the lure of tropical paradise, and the temptation to stay. Hawaiian women have spent many decades upon this pedestal. The following missives were sent out worldwide to help perpetuate the attractive stereotype.

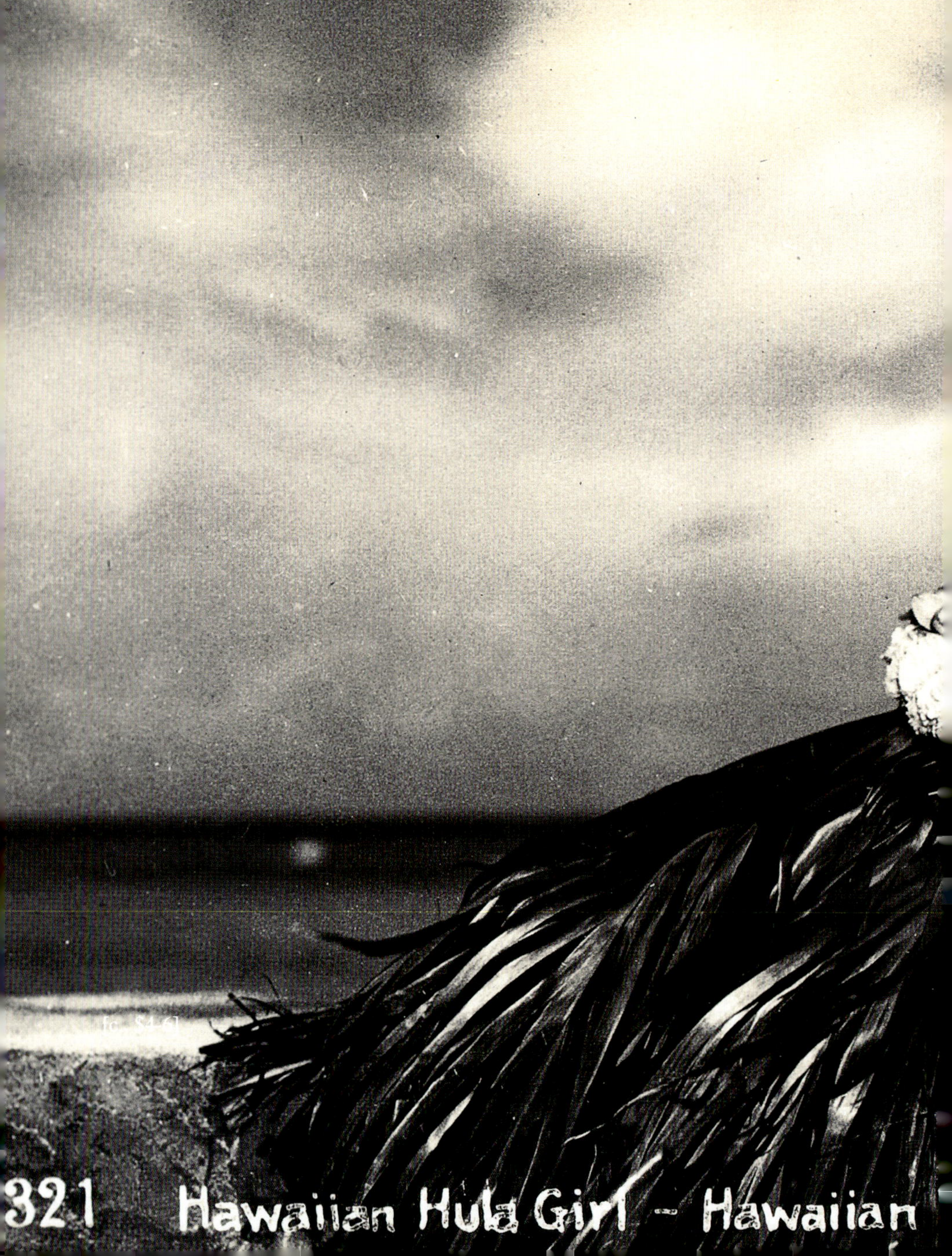

[c. $4-6]

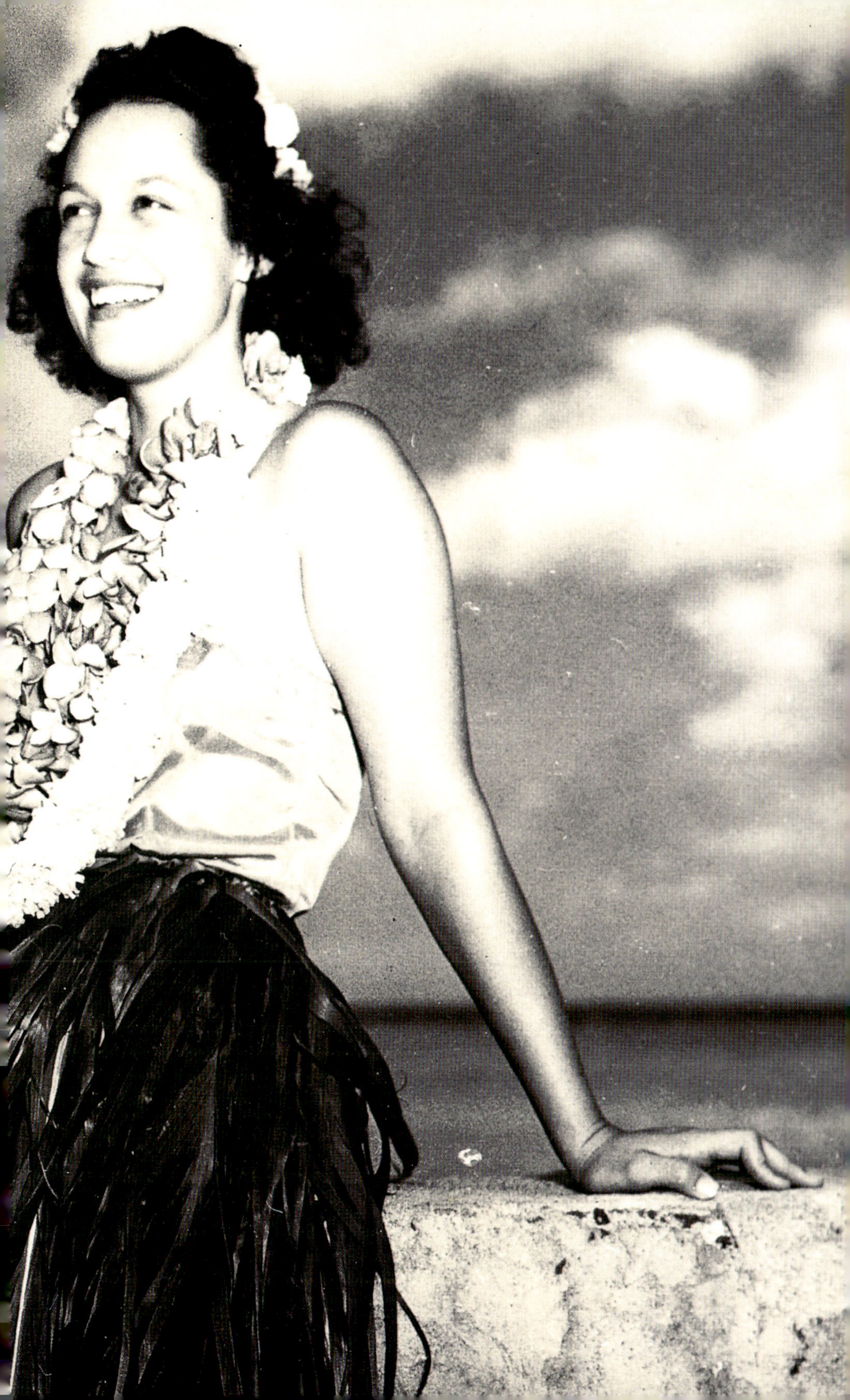

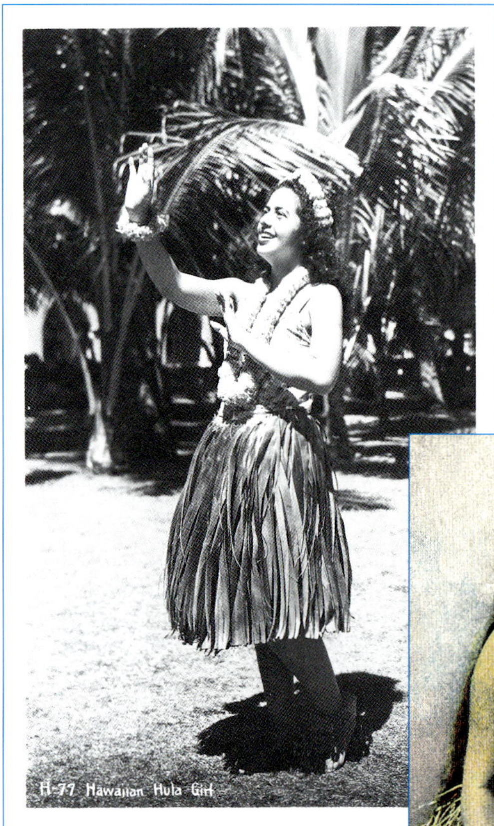

[pre-1940, $6-10]

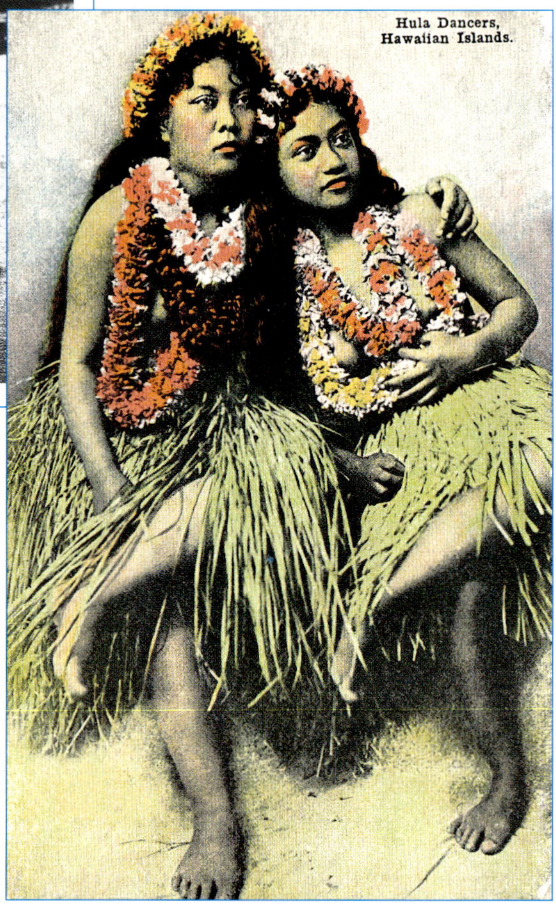

[canceled 1929, $15-20]

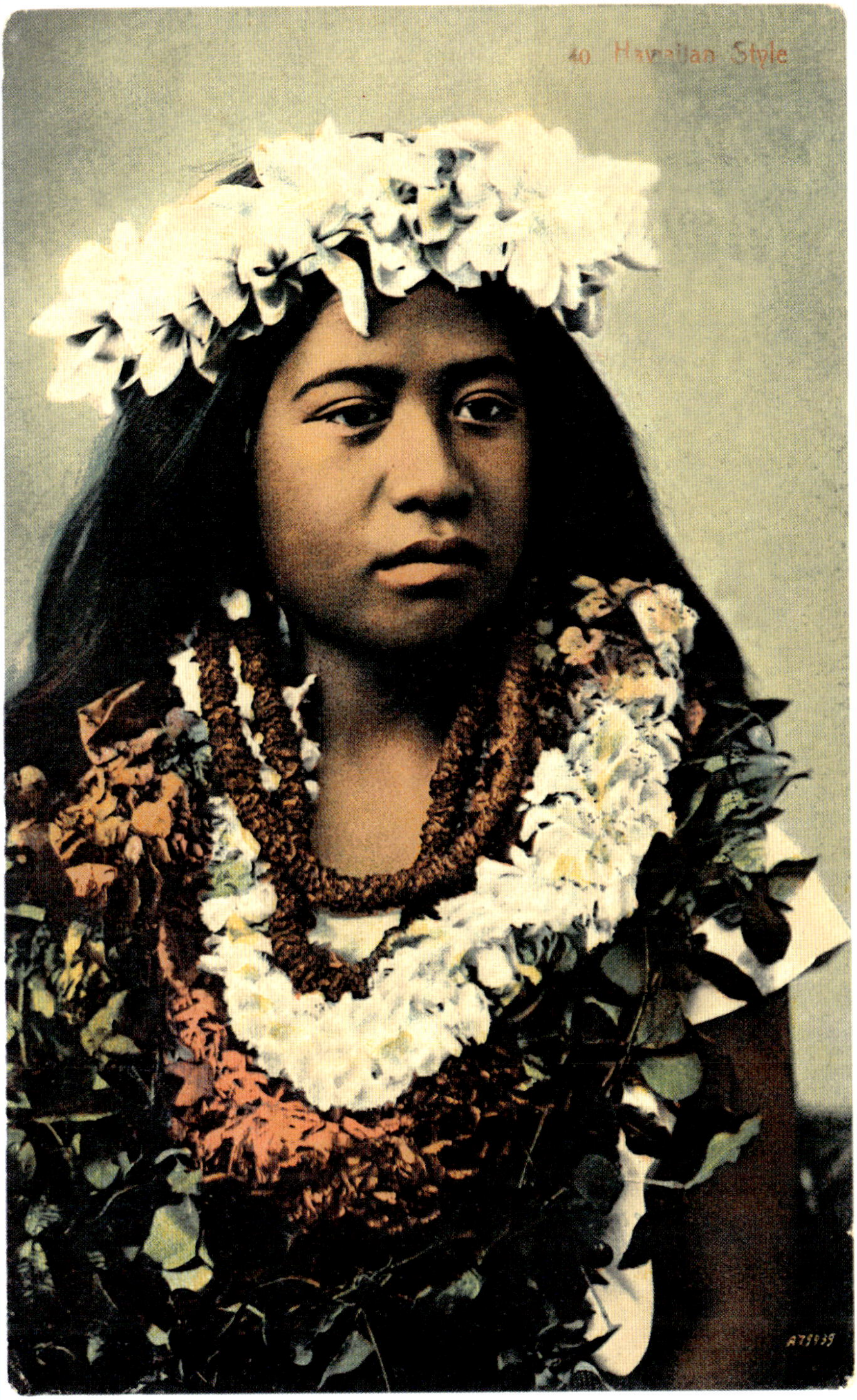

[canceled 1910, $15-20]

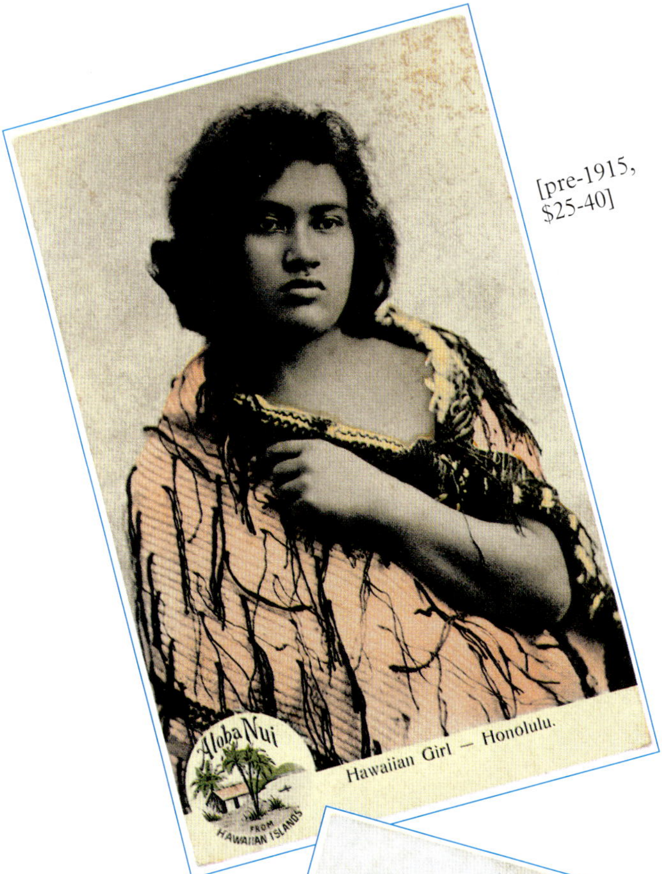

[pre-1915, $25-40]

Right:
On the back: "Each with a beautiful lei or wreath about her neck, the flower girls of Hawaii vend their own perfumed pua or roses in the markets and on the street corners of the city of Honolulu and other places on the islands. The Hawaiians are great lovers of flowers and bedeck their hair with carnations and lehua." [pre-1915, $15-20]

"These people love the flowers and sunshine, and we too find it delightful."
—1906

"This is the way the native girls of Hawaiian Islands look. How do you like them?"
—1911

"Say, this is the kind of girl that are [sic] keeping me away from home. I guess I will never leave here."
—1908

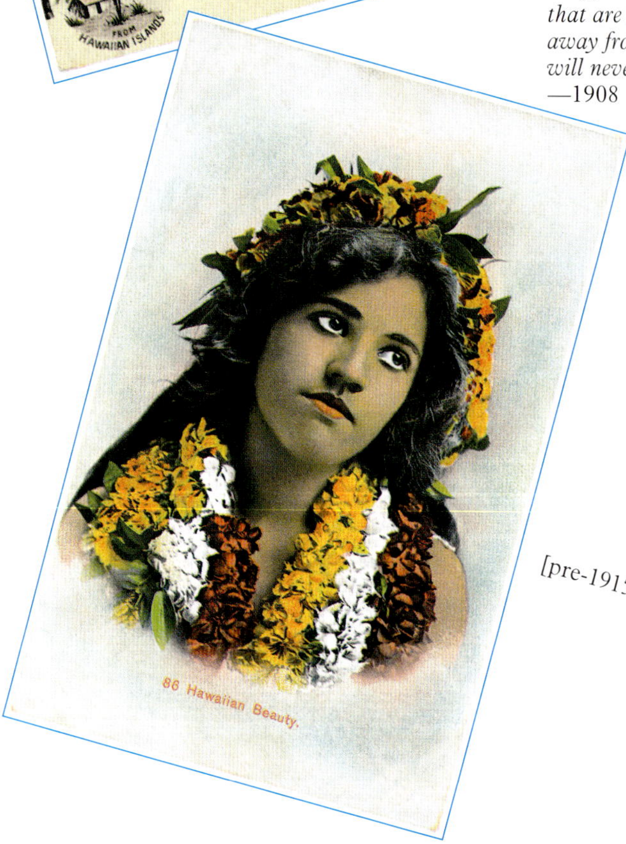

[pre-1915, $12-18]

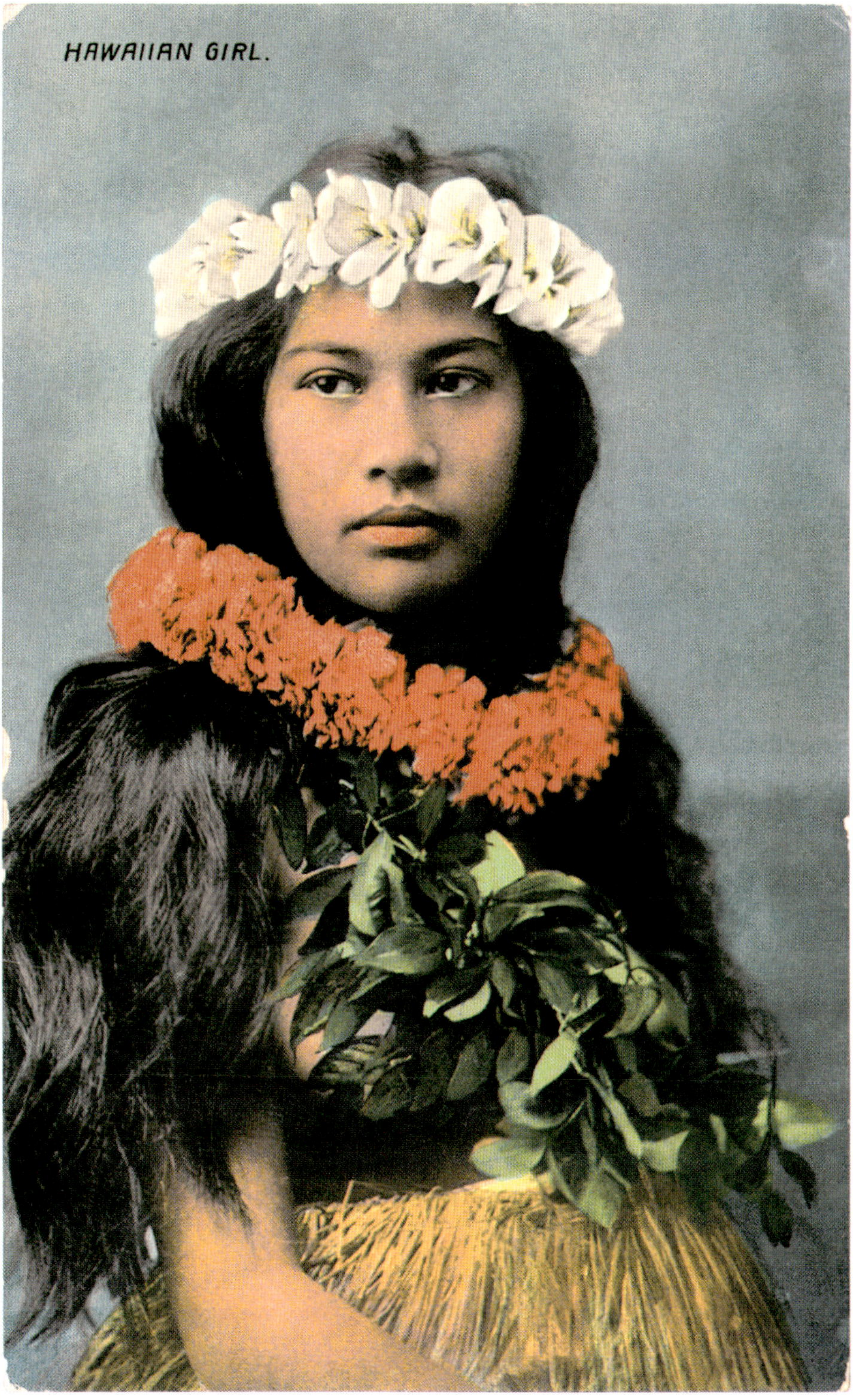

[pre-1915, $15-20]

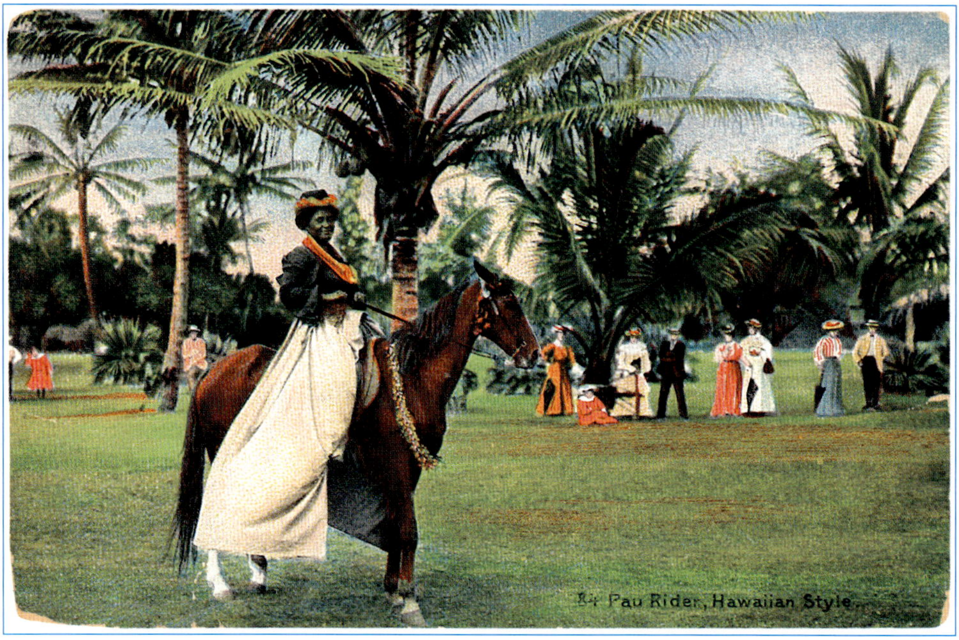

[pre-1915, $12-15]

"This is the way they ride here."
–1912

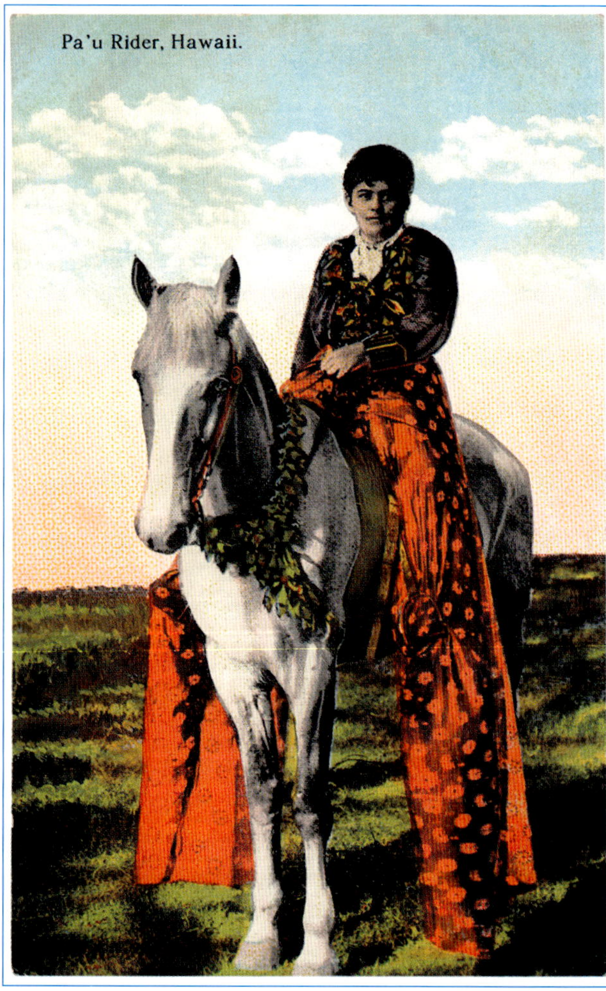

Pa'u Rider. On the back: "Hawaiian girls all wear a divided skirt of pa-u when riding. The sidesaddle is practically unknown in Hawaii. The pa-u or skirt is made so that when the rider advances along the road it streams out, forming a picturesque sight. The Hawaiians both men and women are experts on horseback, and some of the champion cowboys of the world live in Hawaii."
[pre-1915, $12-15]

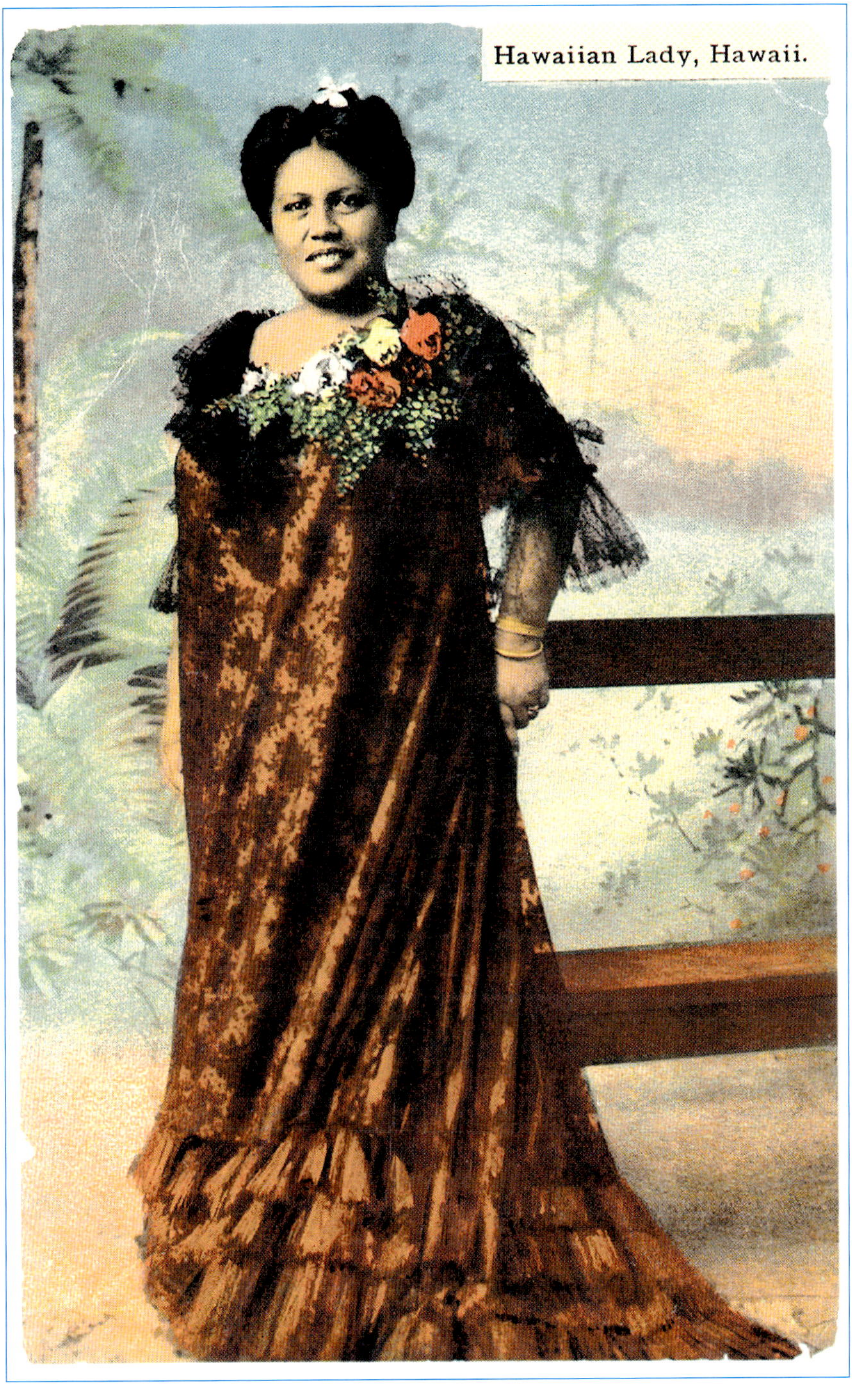

On the back: "The women of Hawaii wear a garment called the holoku which is very becoming; also ornaments of ivory made into brooches and bracelets. They wear leis or wreathes of flowers in their hair. All are smiling and happy, cultivated, refined, and finely educated. They are greatly sought for as wives by foreigners as they are not only a handsome race, but robust and healthy." [pre-1915, $15-20]

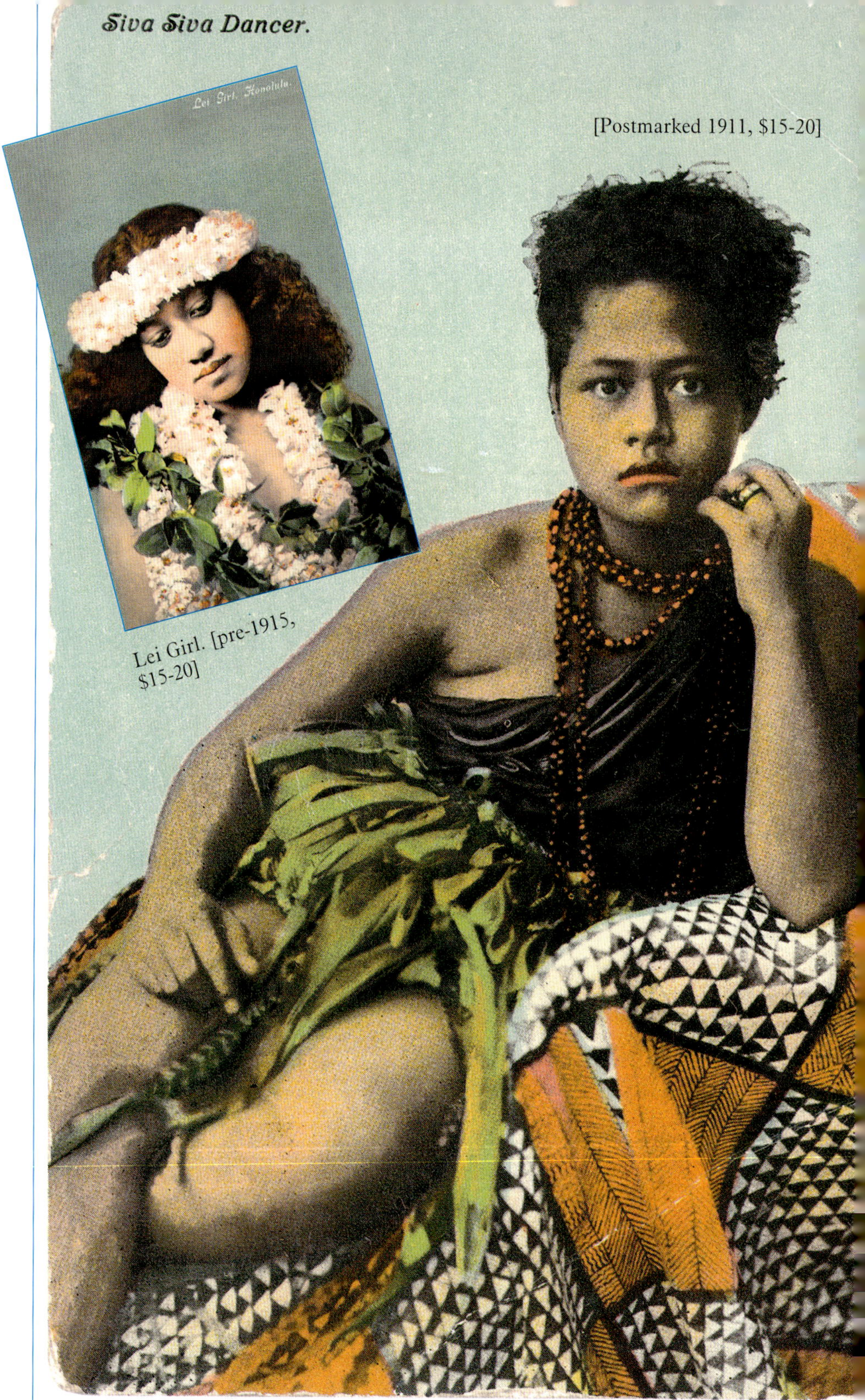

[Postmarked 1911, $15-20]

Lei Girl. [pre-1915, $15-20]

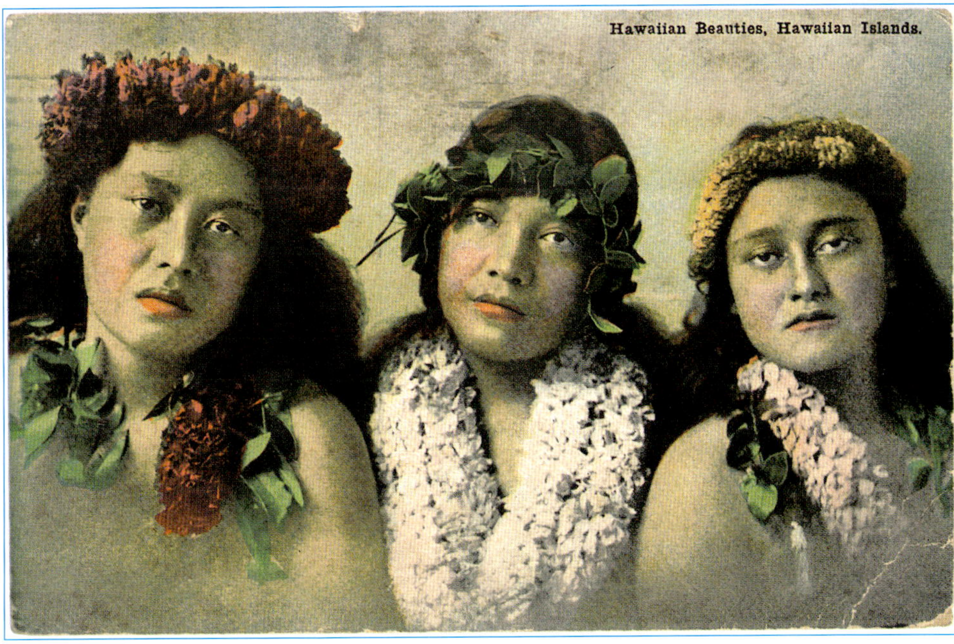

Hawaiian Beauties, looking angelic. [Postmarked 1923, $12-18]

"Perhaps you remember some of these faces. Yet the picture doesn't do them justice."
—1923

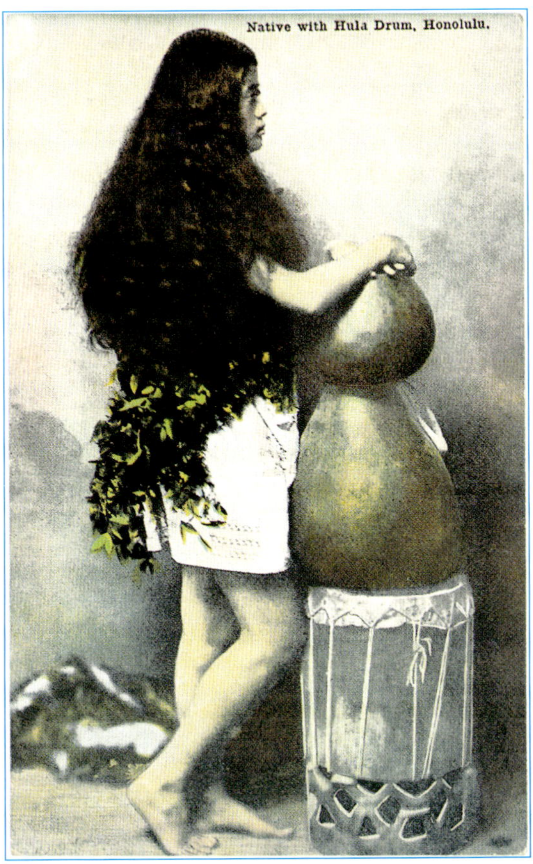

Native with Hula Drum. [pre-1915, $12-15]

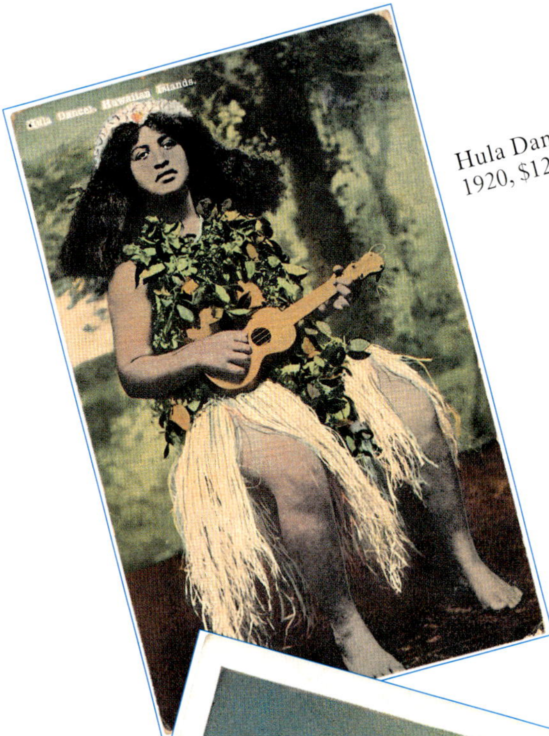

Hula Dancer. [Postmarked 1920, $12-18]

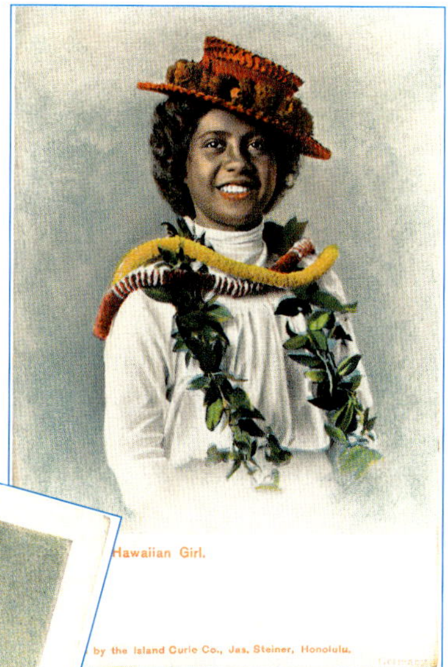

Happy Hawaiian Girl. [pre-1915, $13-18]

"From this you can see what I come over here for!"
—1929

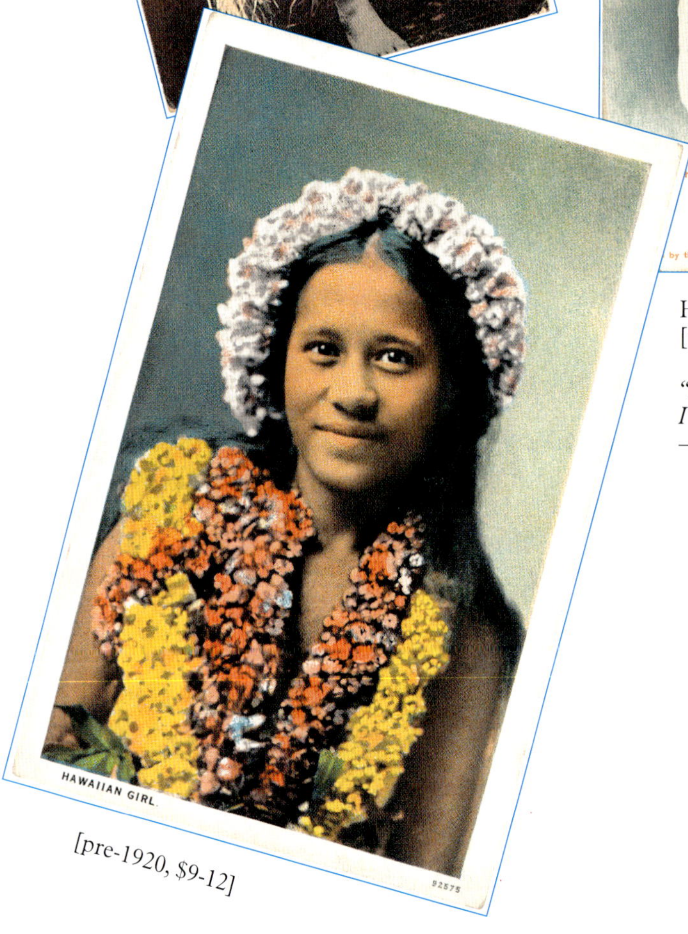

[pre-1920, $9-12]

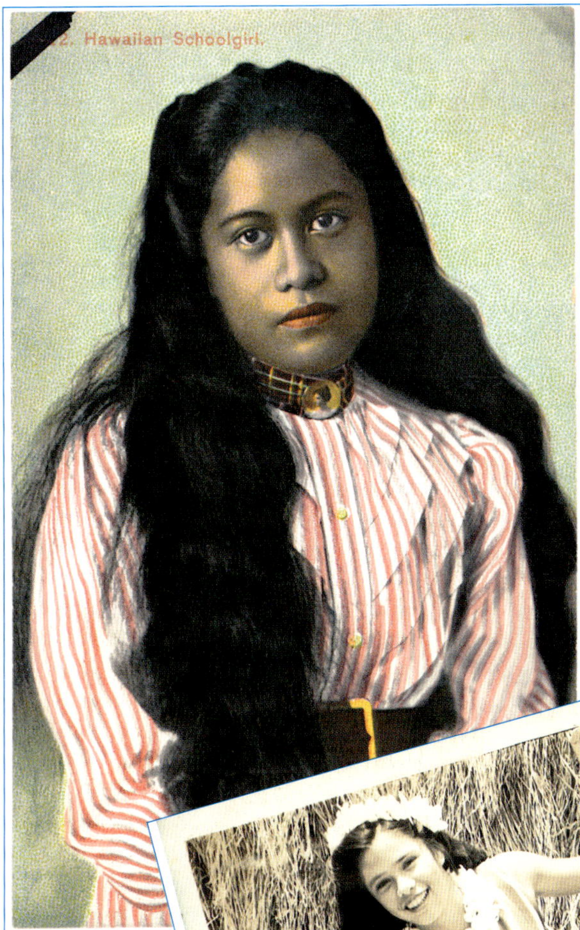

[pre-1915, $15-18]

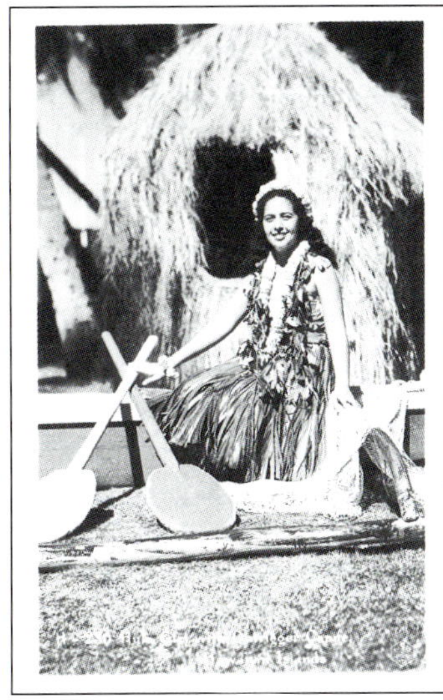

[pre-1930, $6-8]

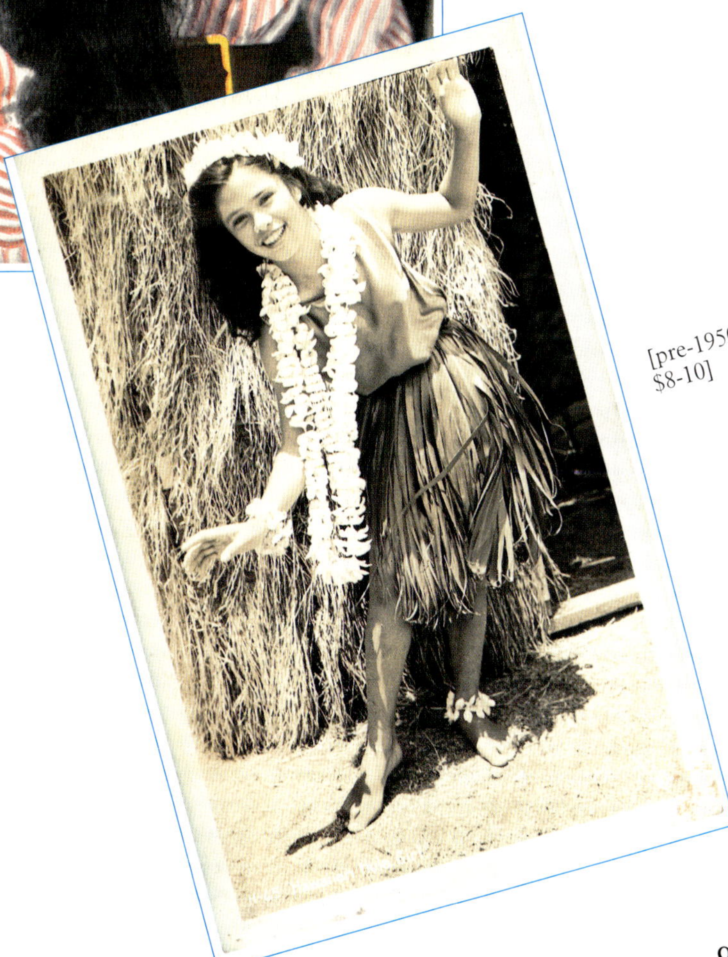

[pre-1950, $8-10]

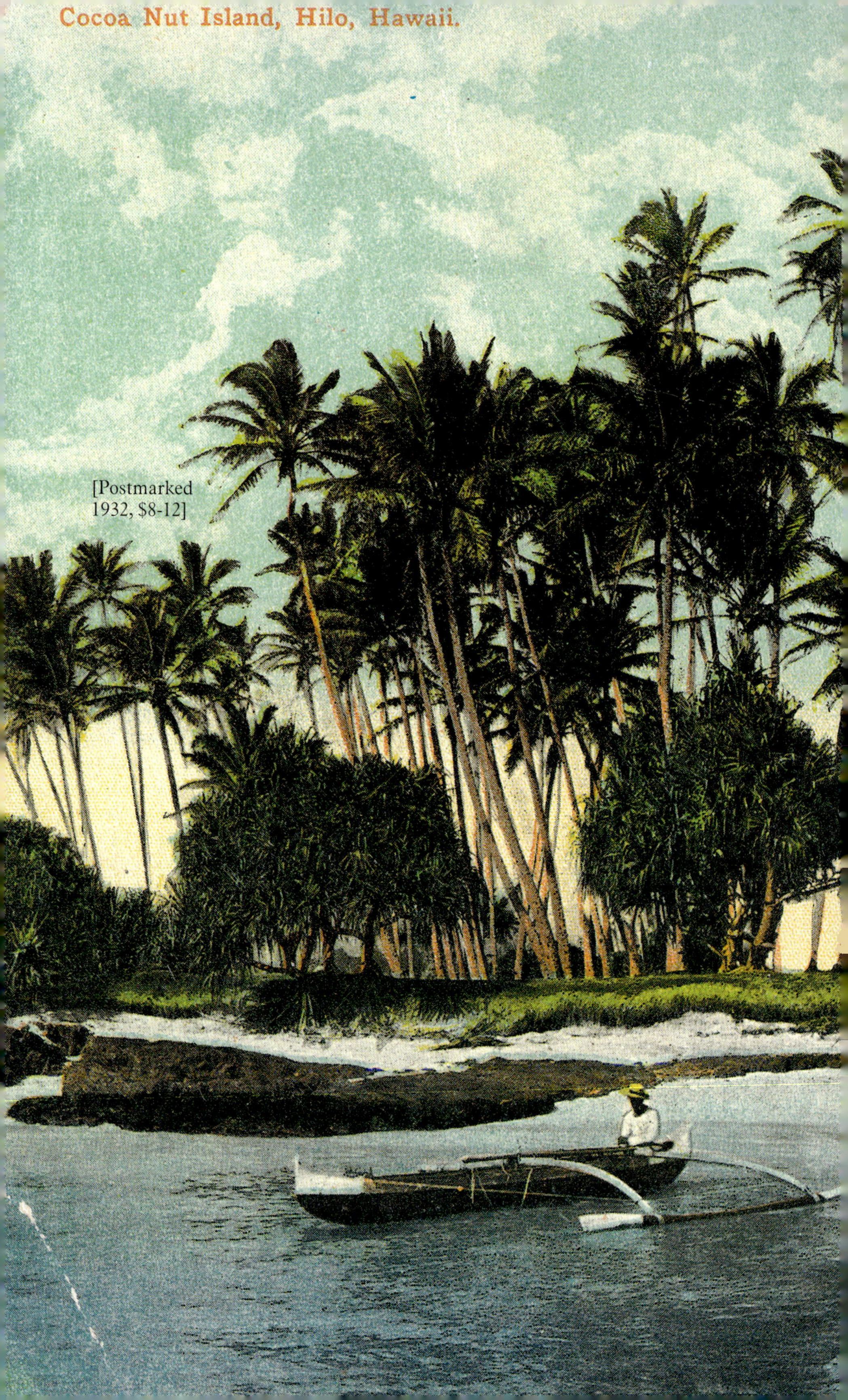

[Postmarked 1932, $8-12]

Outrigger Canoes

Outrigger canoes are attributed to the spread of coastal culture in the Pacific rim region, dating back as far as 30,000 years ago. Outrigger canoes were traditionally built from the trunks of tropical mahogany trees.

The Polynesians who settled Hawaii navigated there using their memory of ocean currents, sea life, and the nighttime sky. And in these boats they brought not only themselves and their fishing skills, but also the domesticated animals and plants to form the basis of their new agrarian lives.

Their skill with these paddled boats has been admired for decades, and is now imitated in outrigger canoe racing events around the world.

The Outrigger Club on the Beach at Waikiki. Members there frequently engage in canoeing and surf riding. [pre-1915, $8-10]

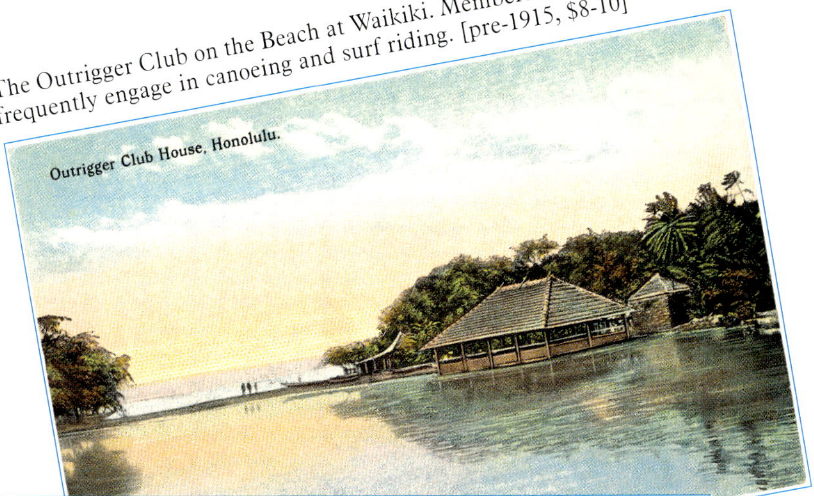

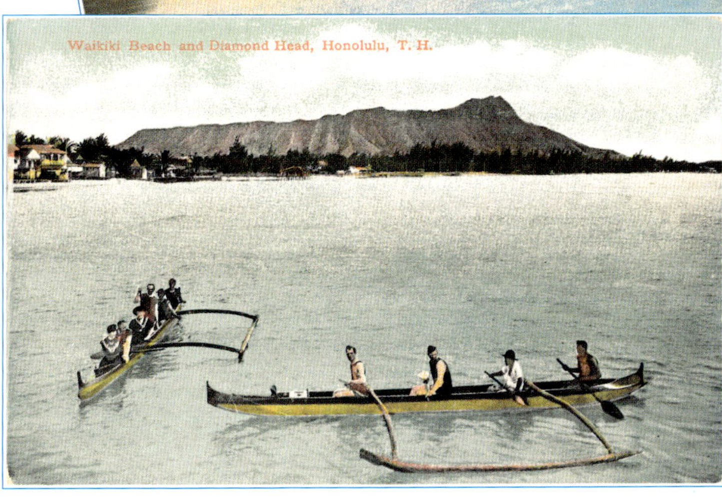

Tourists take a canoe ride off Diamond Head. [pre-1915, $10-12]

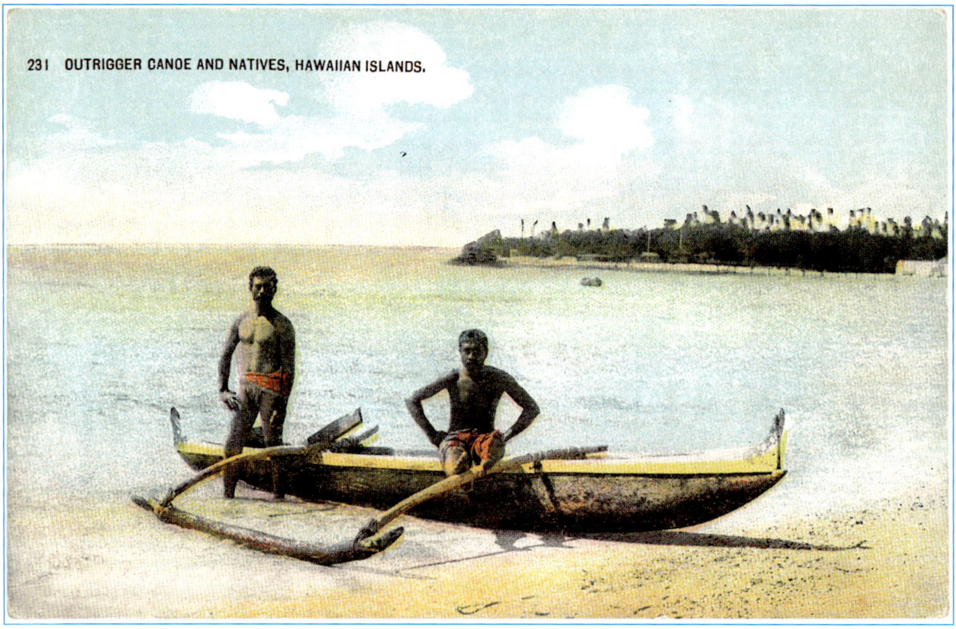

From the back: "The natives of Hawaii are expert fishermen and seldom cast their nets without landing a fine mess of fish. Their boats are long and narrow, kept in place on the water by two long outriggers, which prevent the canoe from upsetting and allow navigation in rougher seas than could otherwise be done. Frequently they are lashed together like a catamaran and are propelled by paddle or sail." [pre-1915, $15-18]

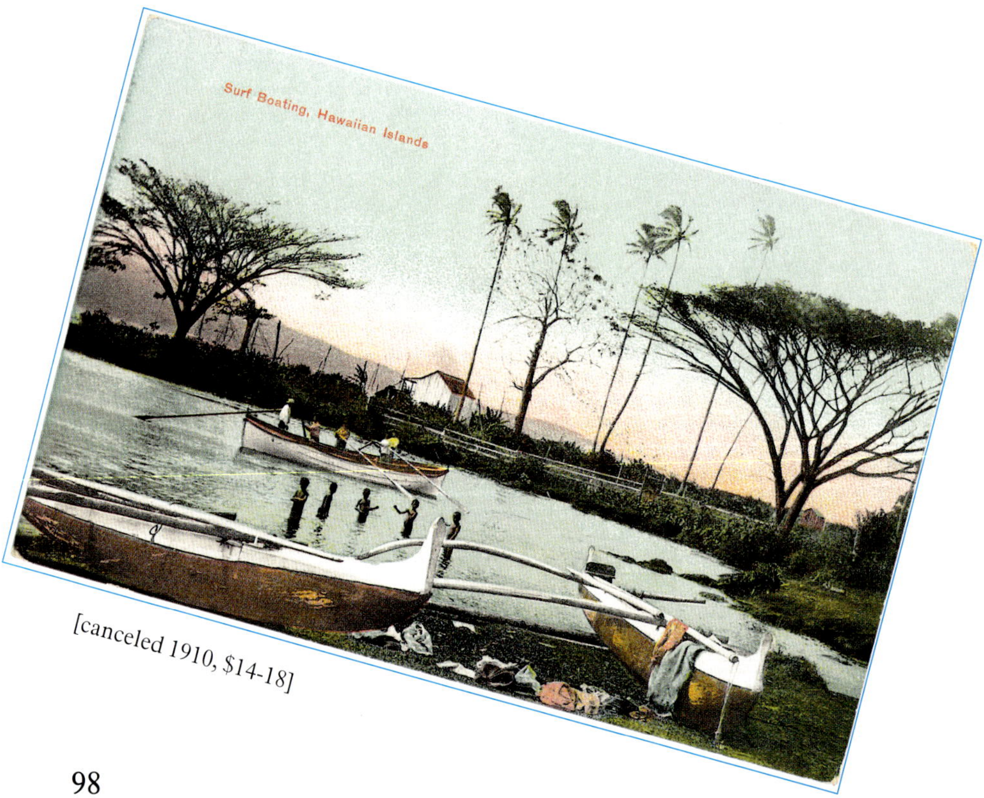

[canceled 1910, $14-18]

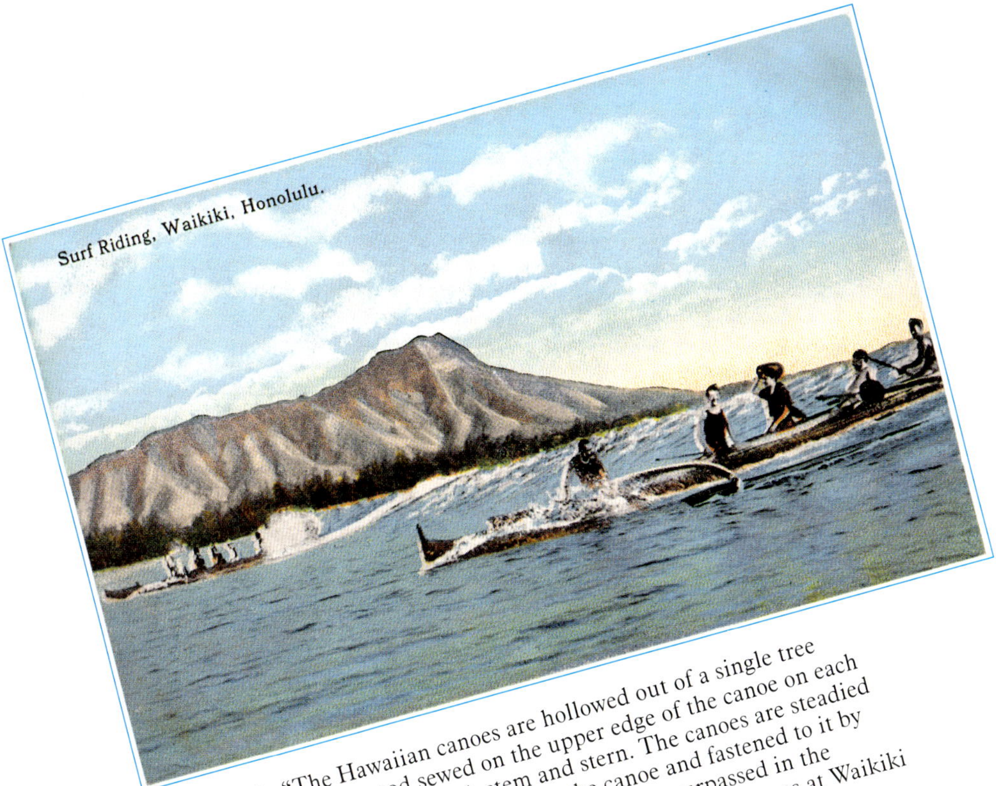

On the back: "The Hawaiian canoes are hollowed out of a single tree having strips of hardwood sewed on the upper edge of the canoe on each side, closing over the top at both stem and stern. The canoes are steadied by a slender log of light wood parallel to the canoe and fastened to it by curved cross pieces or lako. Canoe surf riding is unsurpassed in the Hawaiian Islands. Tourists are taken in these surf riding canoes at Waikiki near Honolulu." [pre-1915, $8-12]

[pre-1915, $8-12]

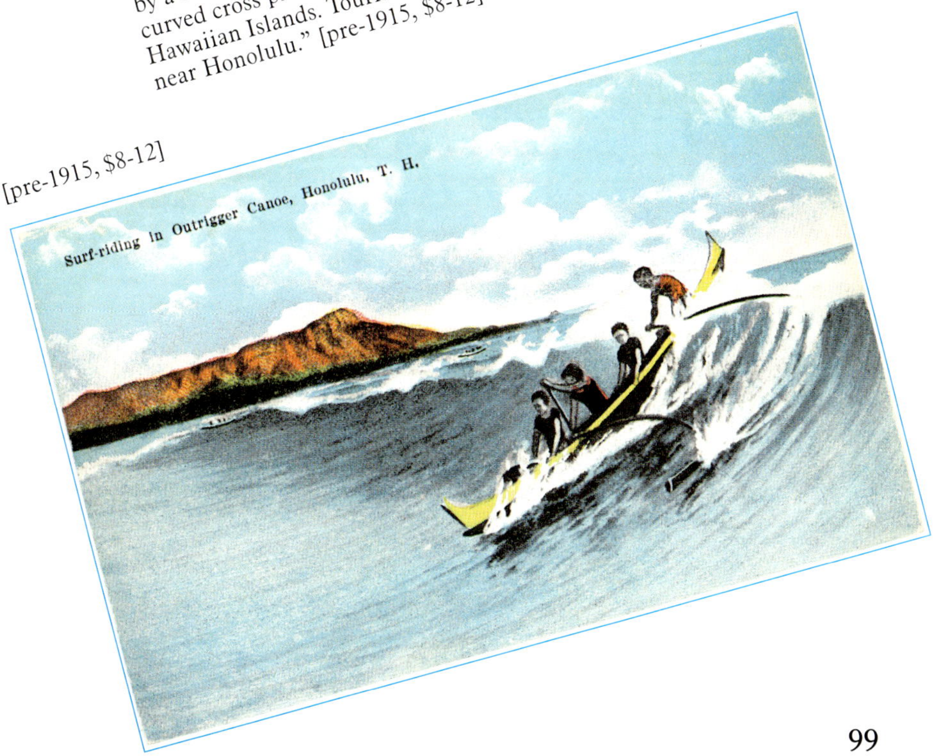

Surfs Up!

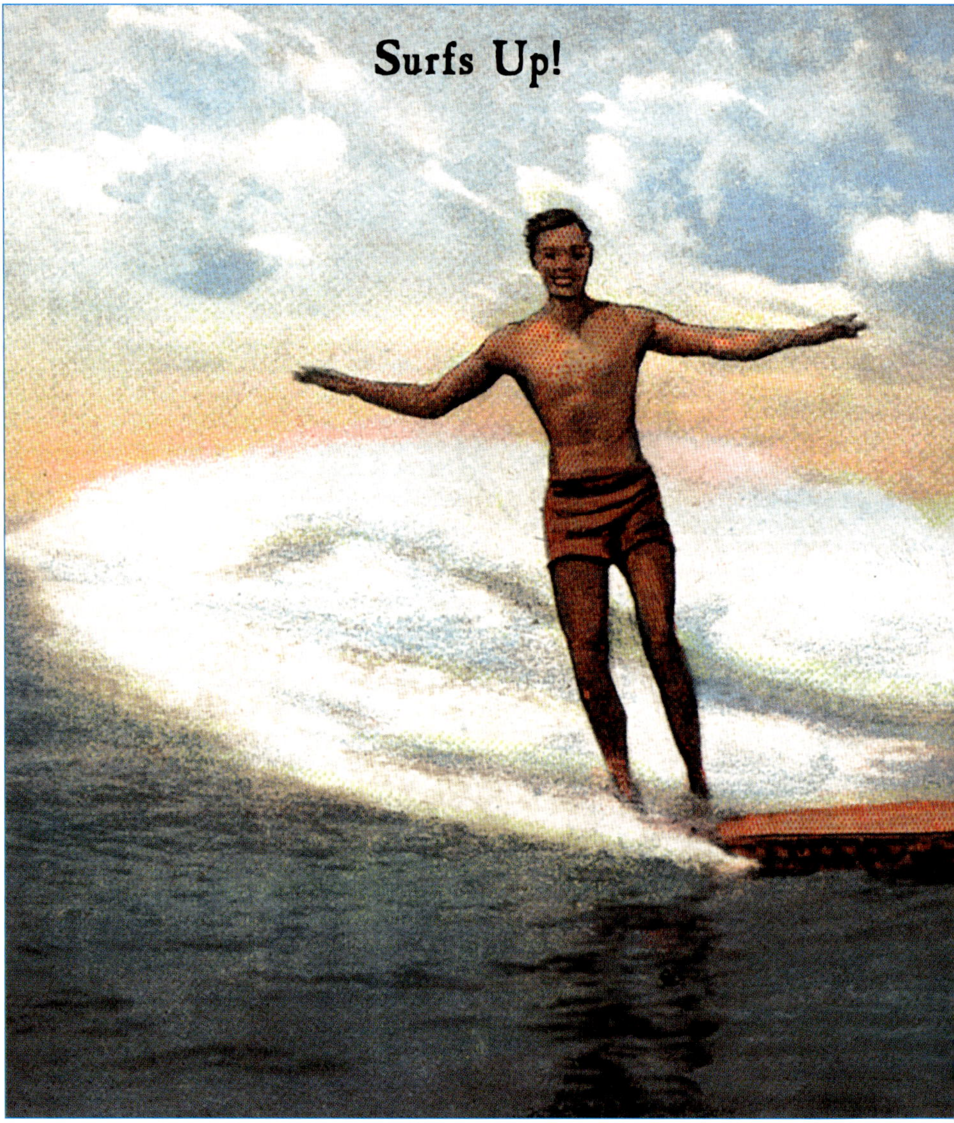

No one knows for sure when surfing on a long board became a sport as opposed a mode of aquatic transportation. What is known is that surfing has been enjoyed for centuries. In ancient Hawaii, is was the kings (and queens!) who were renowned as the highest skilled and most proficient of surfers. And no wonder. They had their own wave chanters, the most highly skilled board makers, and their own private beaches with the best waves. Woe to anyone who dared drop in on their wave. This was considered a crime for which the punishment was quite harsh. Because the sport was so highly thought of by the chiefly class, it quickly gained respectability among all classes. The best surfers were celebrated in song and dance and often enjoyed special privileges in royal circles.

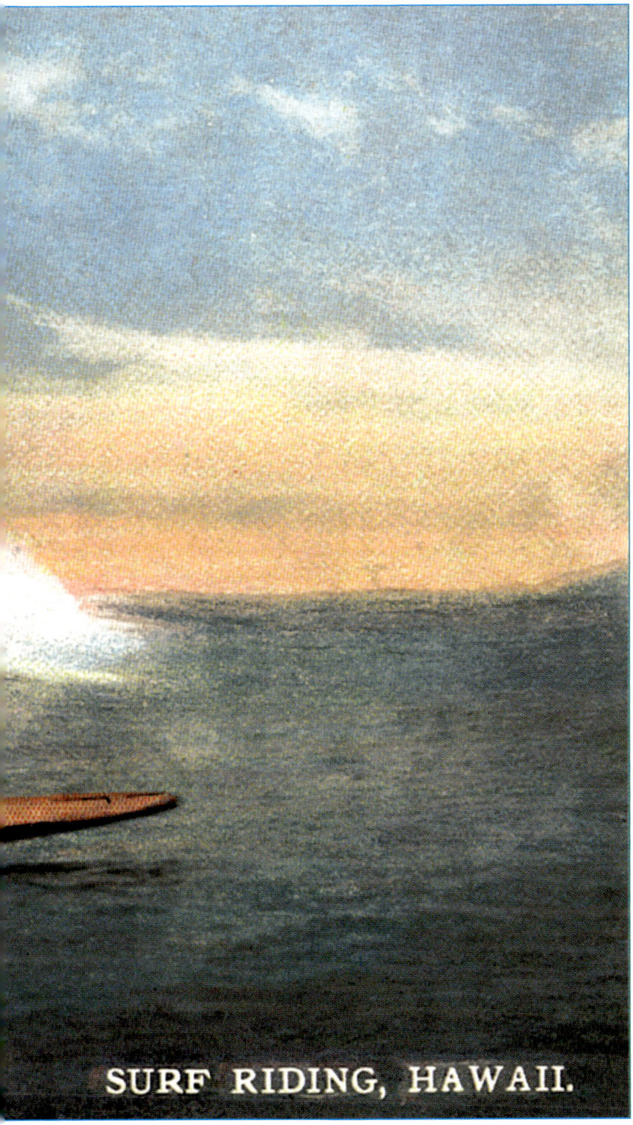

[pre-1915, $15-20]

By the turn of the 20th Century, tourists from the United States and Europe were discovering Waikiki, and surfing, for the first time. In 1901 the first major resort, the Moana Hotel, opened in Waikiki. A luxurious hotel, it was built in a Beaux-arts style of architecture which fronted the beach with a long pier extending to the waters edge. In order to promote itself as a popular attraction, the hotel advertised surfing and canoeing as exciting sports for tourists. Surfing continues to be one of Hawaii's most popular pastimes, attracting millions of surfers each year.

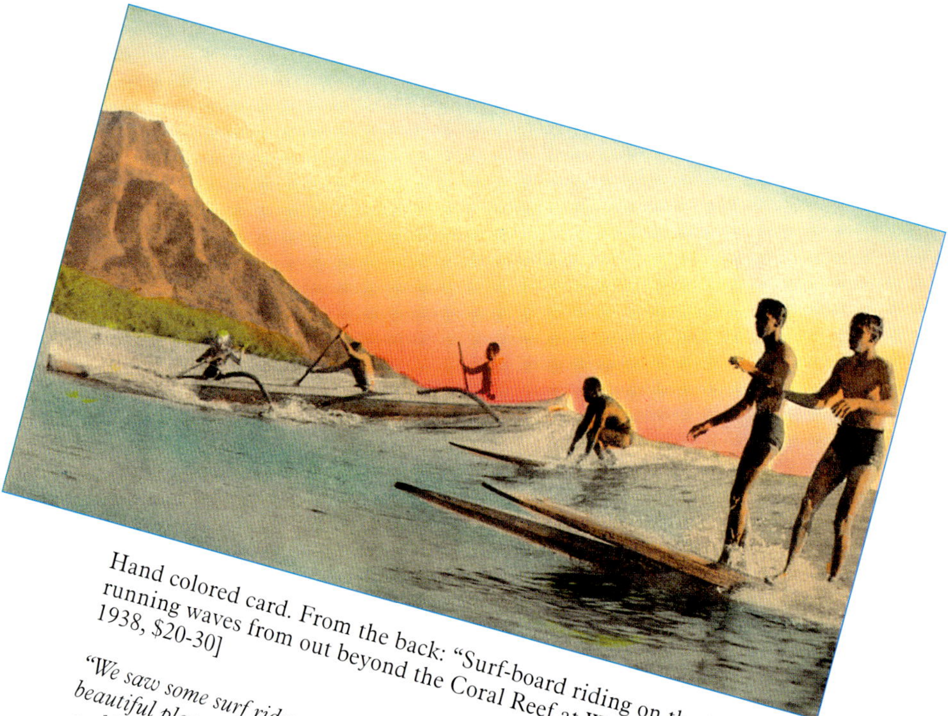

Hand colored card. From the back: "Surf-board riding on the long-running waves from out beyond the Coral Reef at Waikiki." [Cancelled 1938, $20-30]

"We saw some surf riders this morning, it looked like a lot of fun. This is a beautiful place and we have had a lovely day here." —1938

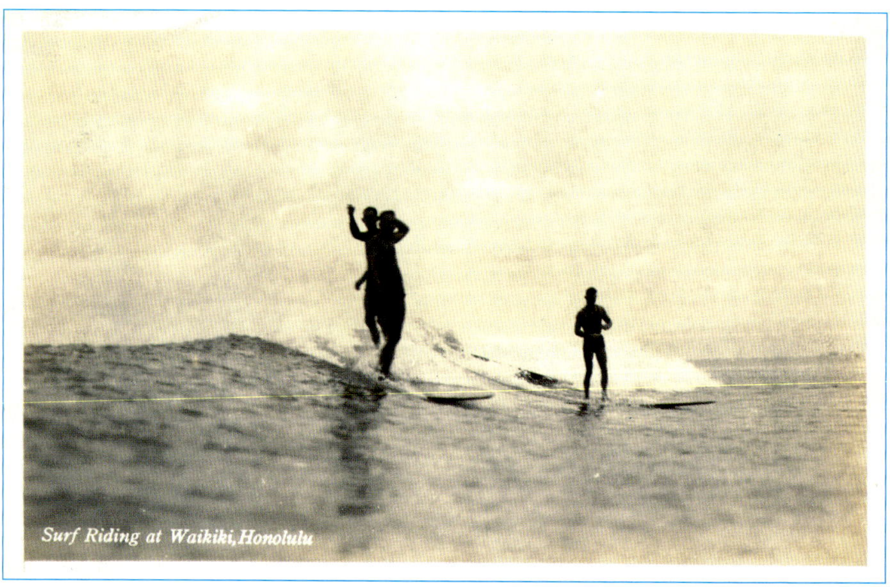

Early photo postcard. Surf Riding at Waikiki, Honolulu. [pre-1930, $25-45]

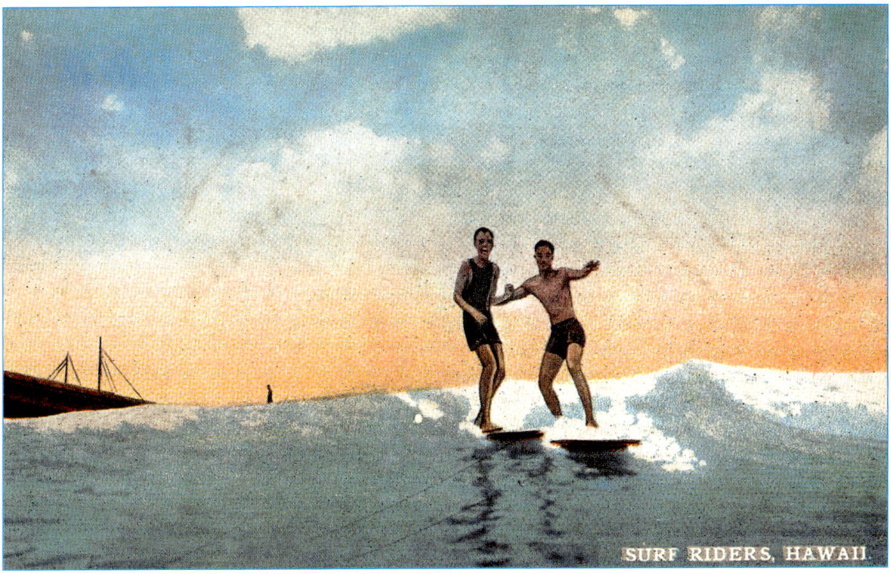

Surf riders, Hawaii. [pre-1915, $30-45]

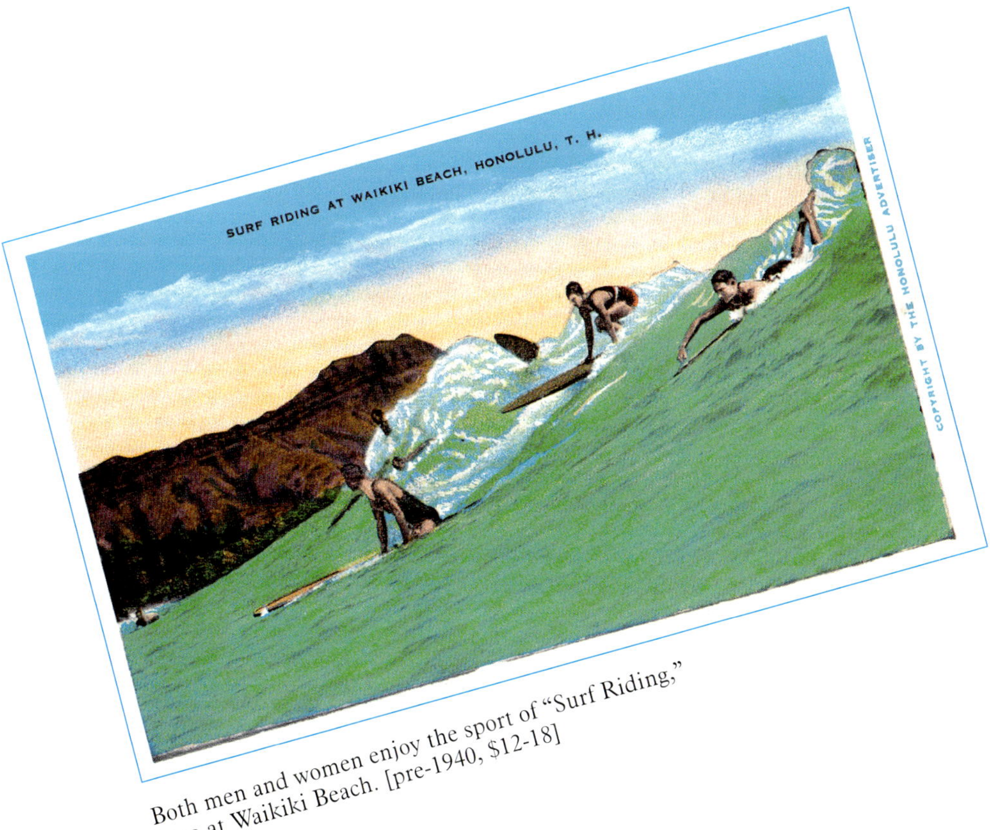

Both men and women enjoy the sport of "Surf Riding," here at Waikiki Beach. [pre-1940, $12-18]

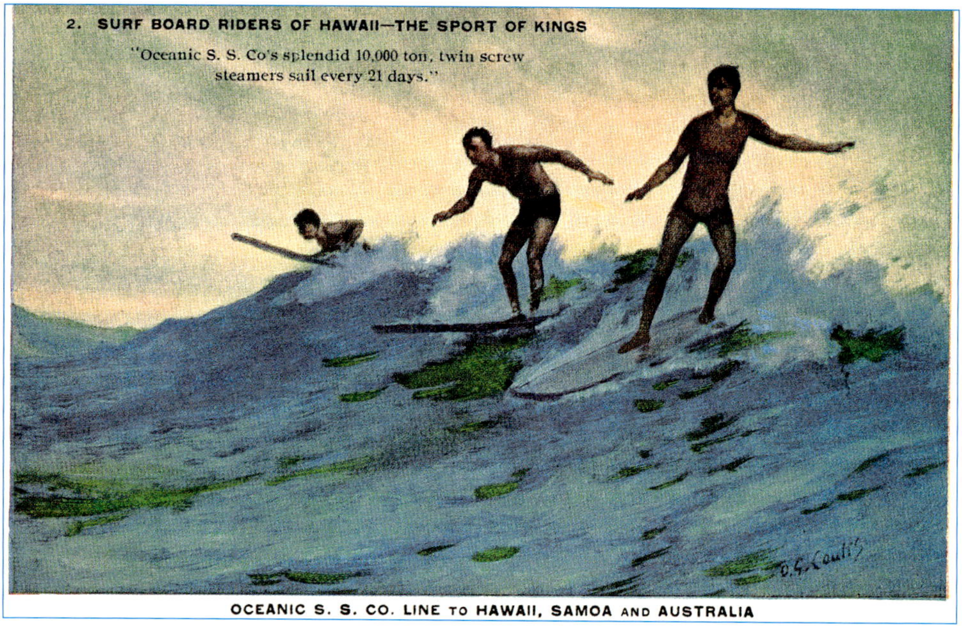

In addition to being used by tourists to send a greeting home, this card was used as advertising by Oceanic S.S. Co. Line to Hawaii, Samoa and Australia. From the front: "Oceanic S.S. Co's splendid 10,000 ton, twin screw steamers sail every 21 day's." [pre-1915, $35-65]

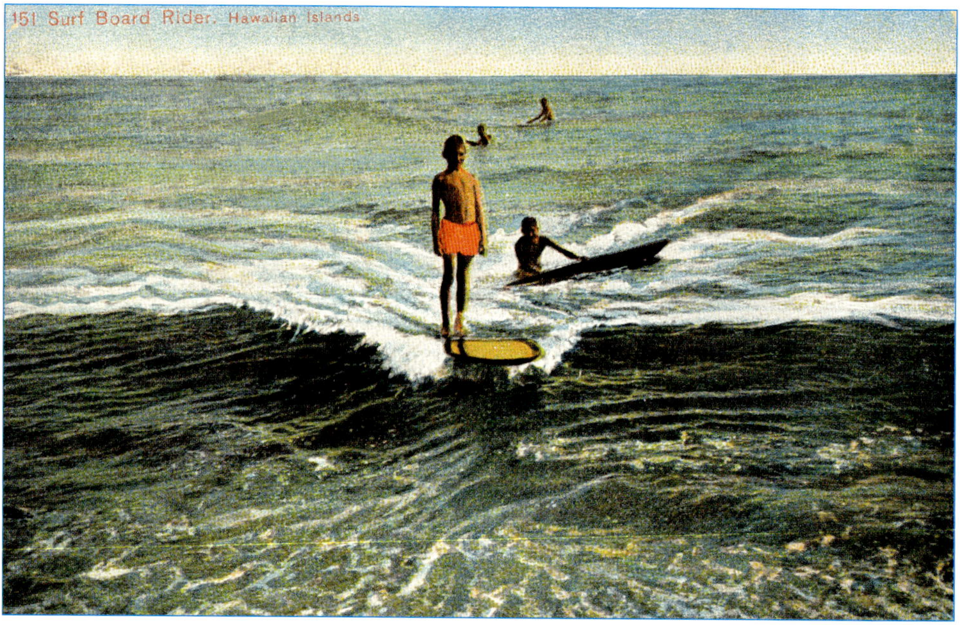

Making it look easy – Surf Board Rider, Hawaii. [pre-1940, $25-40]

"Xmas greetings from Honolulu, HI."
—1936

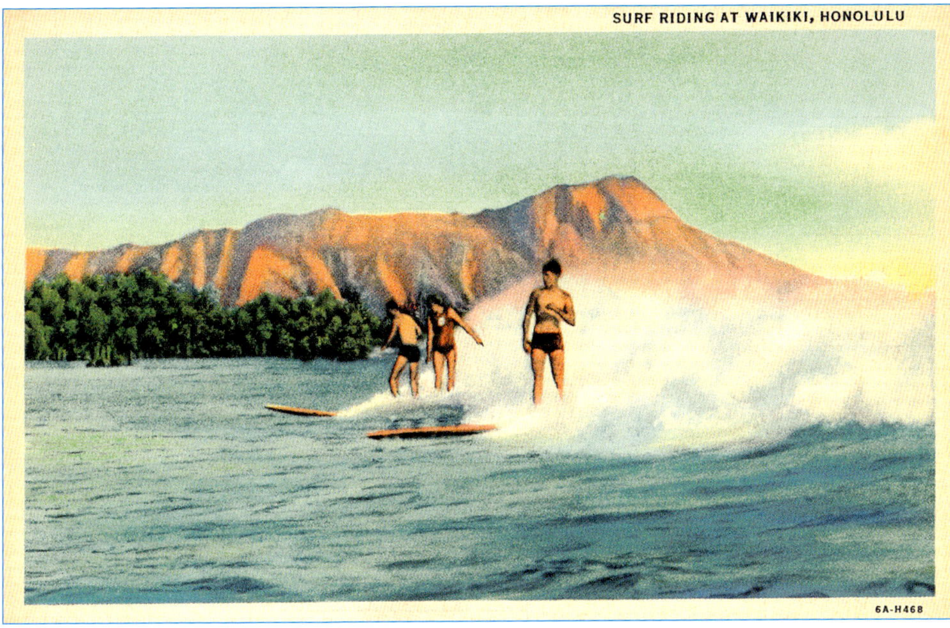

Surf Riding at Waikiki. [pre-1940, $5-9]

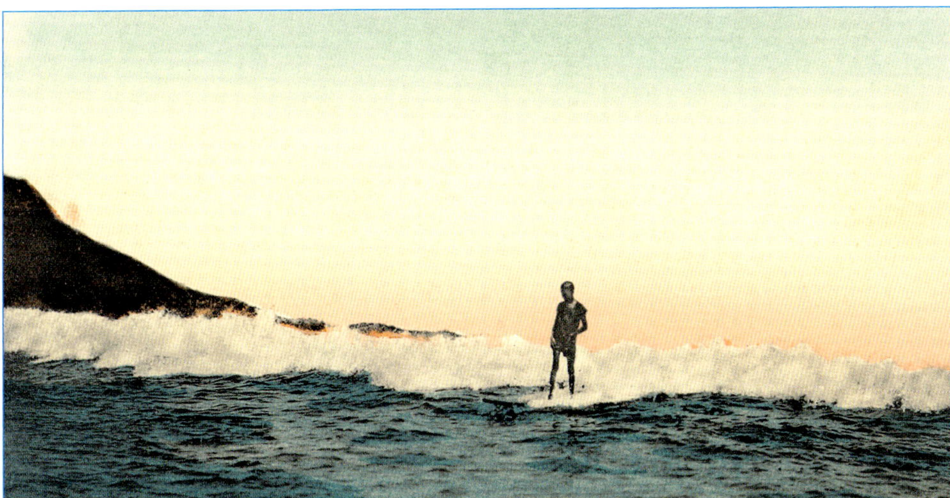

Surf-Board-Riding Waikiki, Honolulu.

Surf-Board-Riding Waikiki, Honolulu. [pre-1915, $25-45]

"We were pleased to here from Thomas this a.m and to learn that all were well [sic]. We feel quite as if we were home this place is so very American. 2-21-1913."
—1913

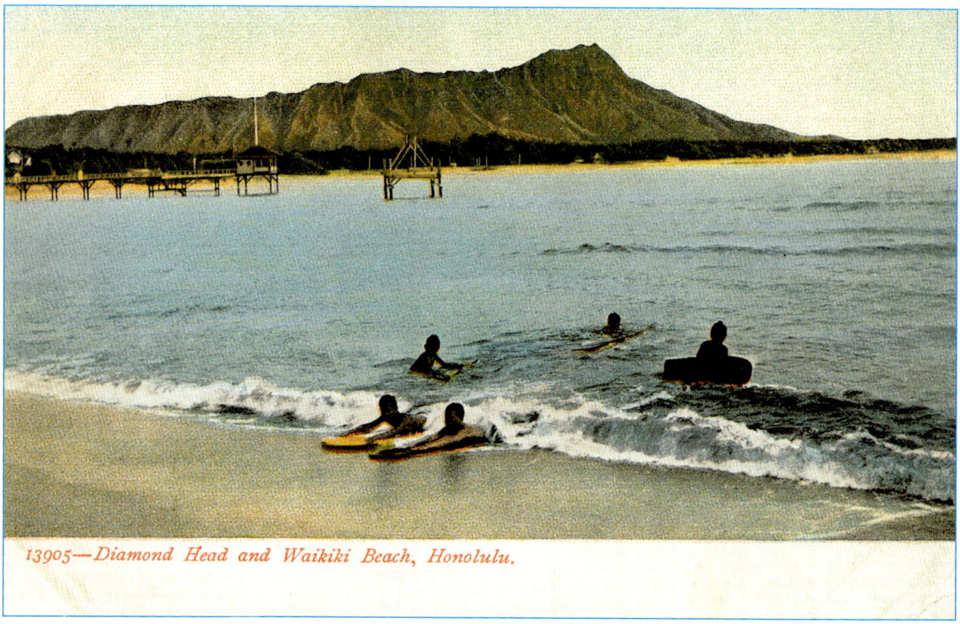

Surf Riding at Waikiki Beach, Honolulu. Diamond Head is silhouetted in the background. [pre-1915, $20-30]

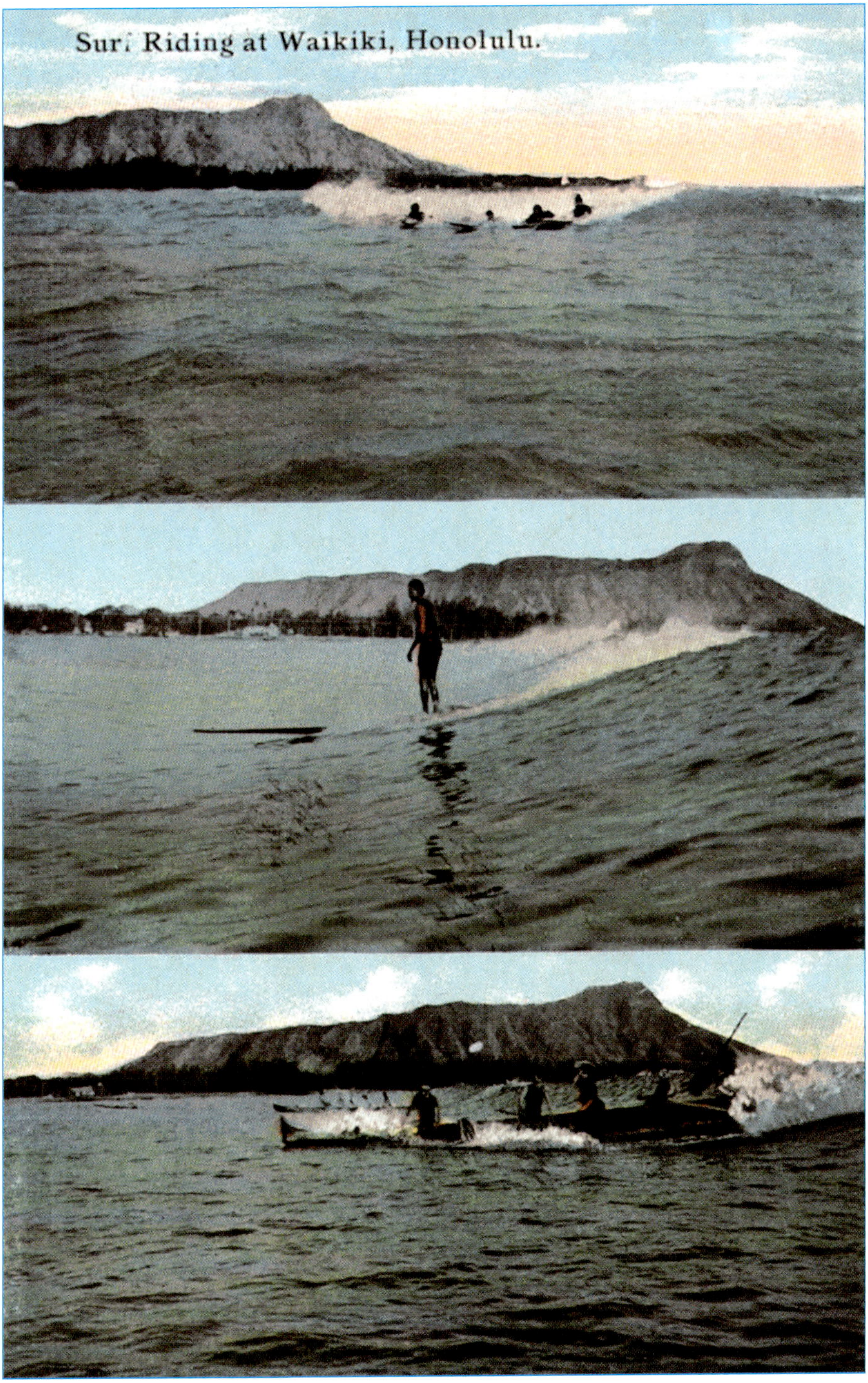

The near-perfect waves on Waikiki were a magnet for surf riding, whether on boards or Outrigger canoes. [pre-1915 $12-20]

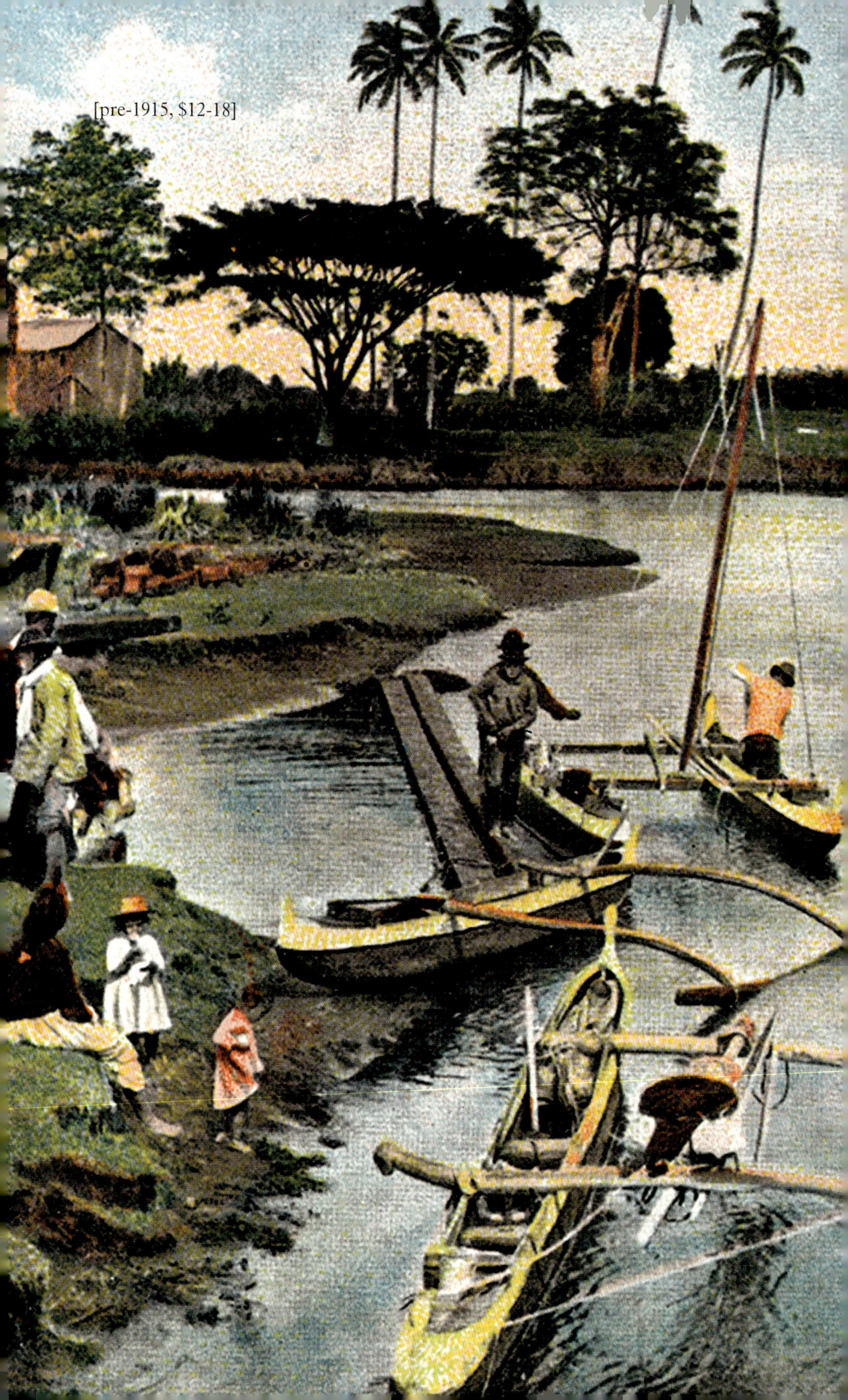

[pre-1915, $12-18]

Aquaculture

The colorful fish that surround Hawaii were also staples in the Hawaiian diet. As expected in an island culture, the ocean provided a bounty for the land inhabitants, and the Hawaiians were experts in the reaping of it.

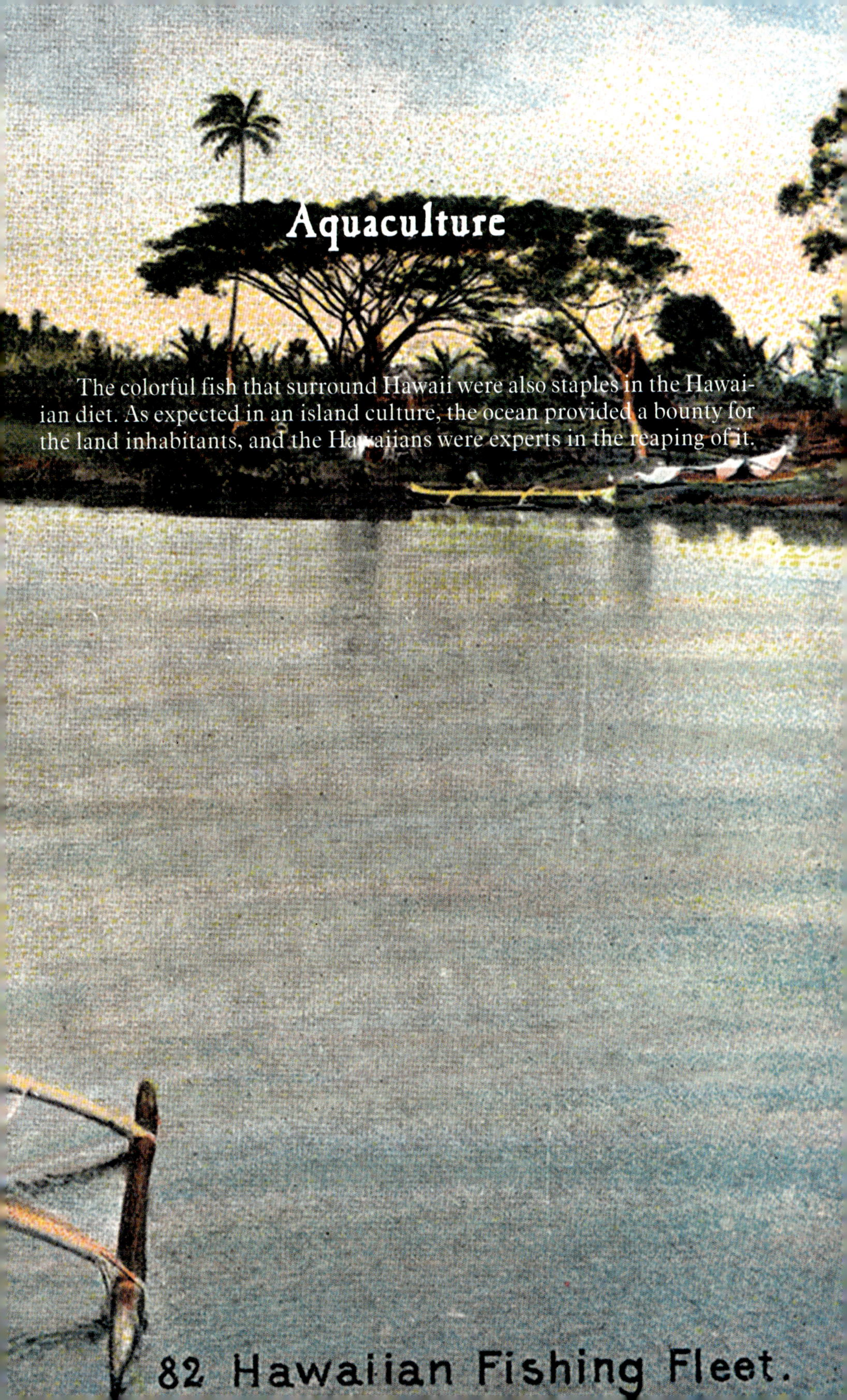

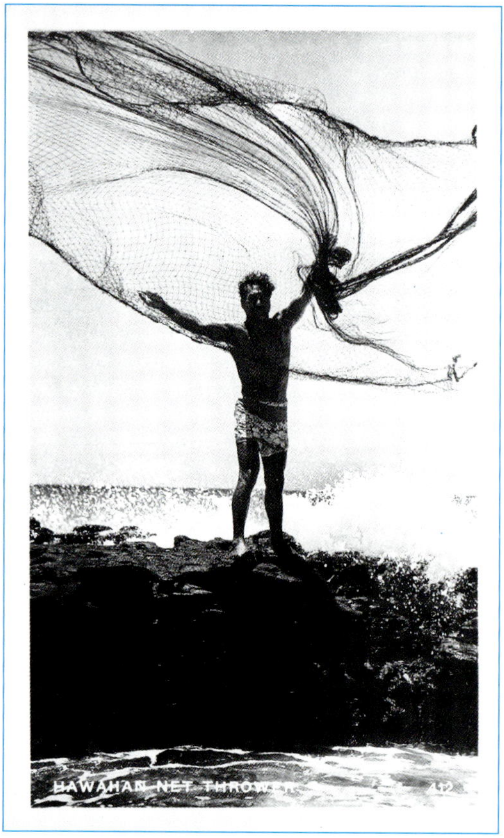

[pre-1940, $6-9]

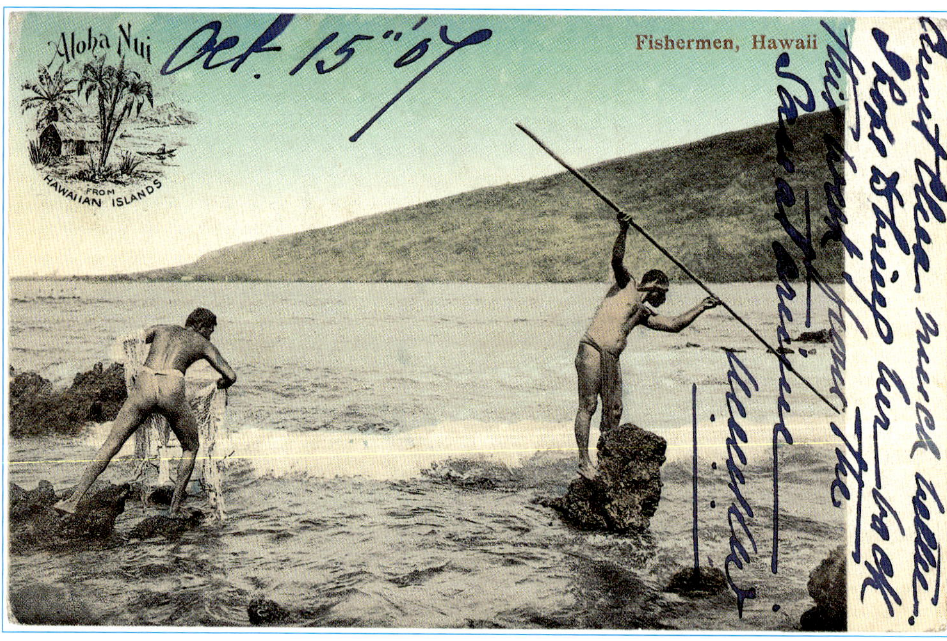

An early card depicts both a net caster and a spear fisherman. [canceled 1907, $20-30]

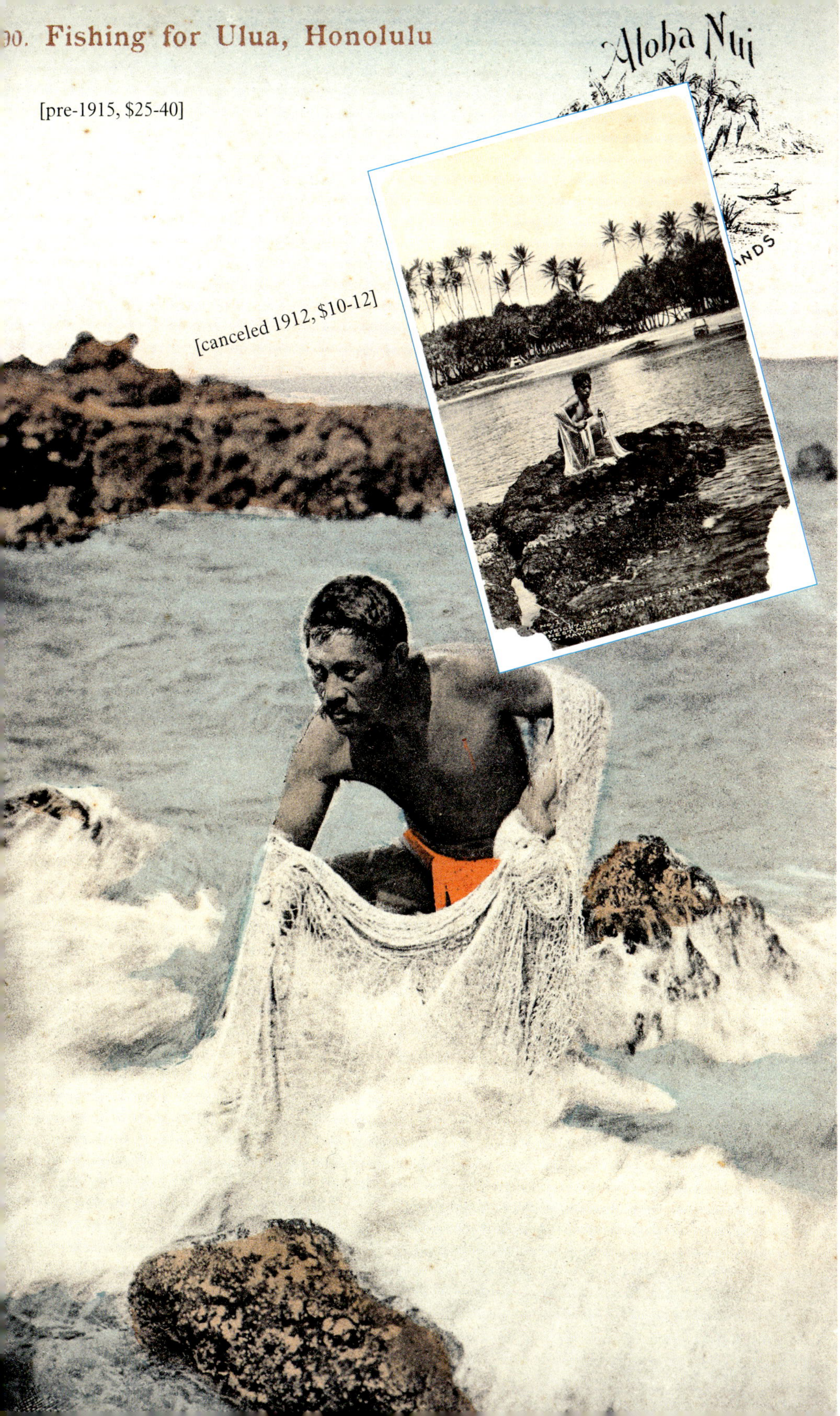

[pre-1915, $25-40]

[canceled 1912, $10-12]

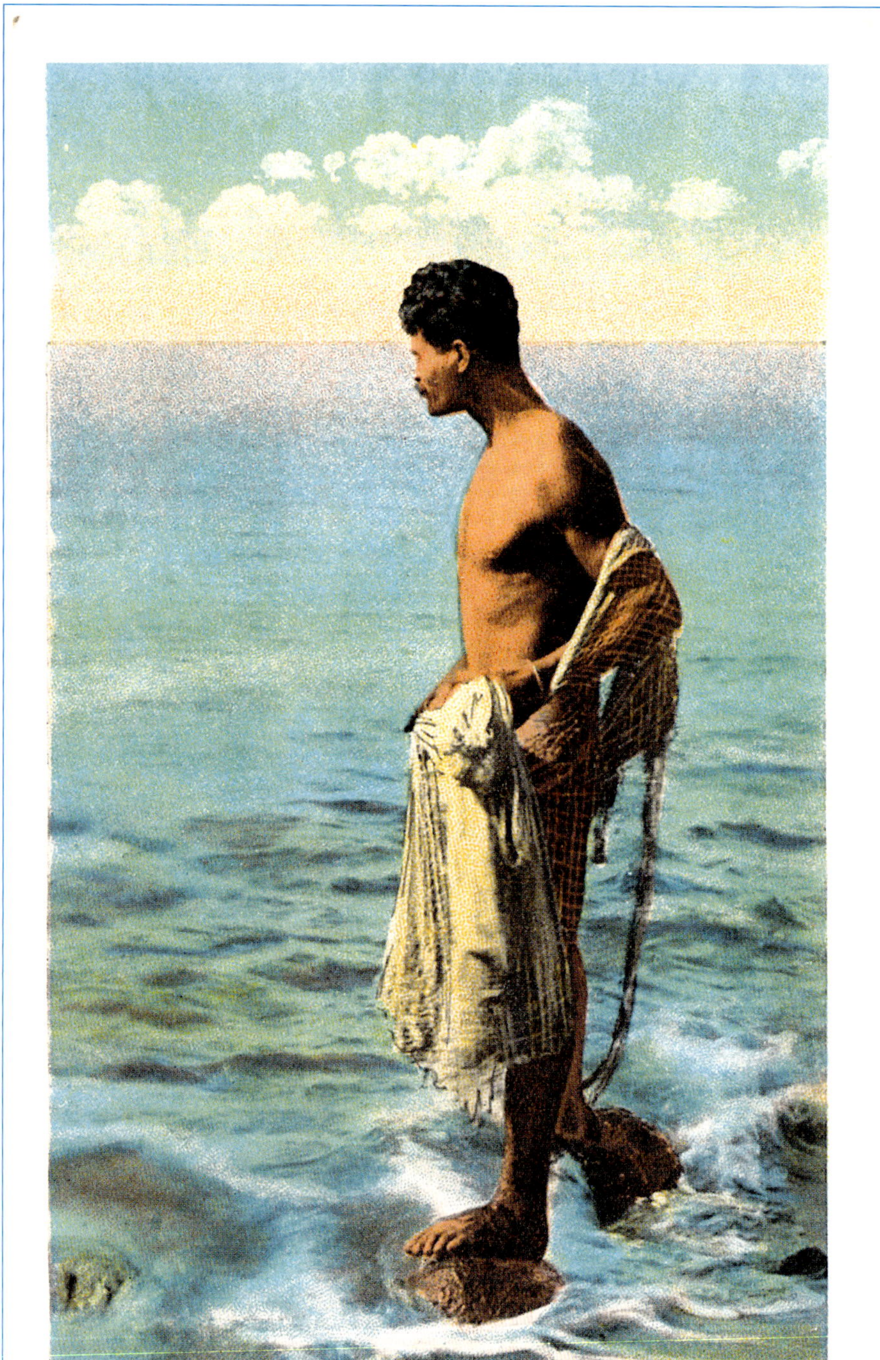

On the back: "The natives of the Hawaiian Islands, subsisting on fish to a great extent, have acquired a wonderful knowledge of their habits and have become the most expert and bravest fishermen of the world. The waters surrounding Hawaii teem with a great variety of eatable fish and native fishermen in their fishing boats can be seen almost any day of the Honolulu Harbor." [pre-1920, $9-13]

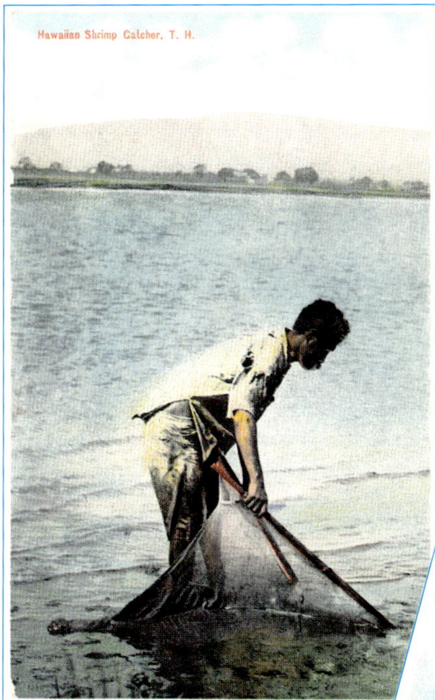

Hawaiian shrimp catcher.
[Postmarked 1911, $9-12]

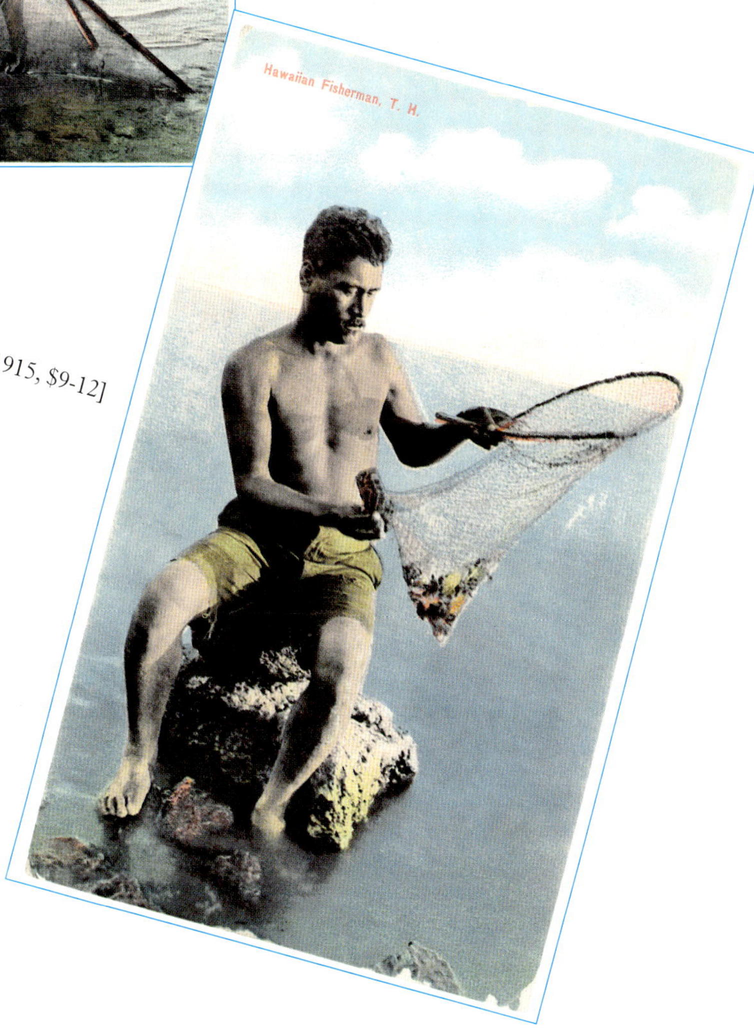

[pre-1915, $9-12]

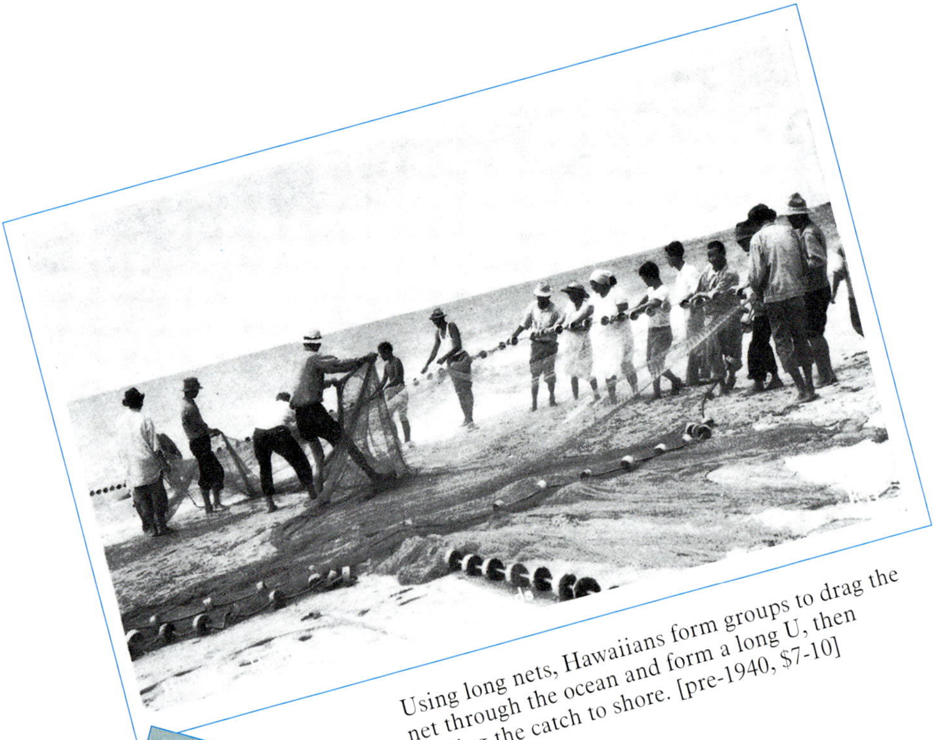

Using long nets, Hawaiians form groups to drag the net through the ocean and form a long U, then hauling the catch to shore. [pre-1940, $7-10]

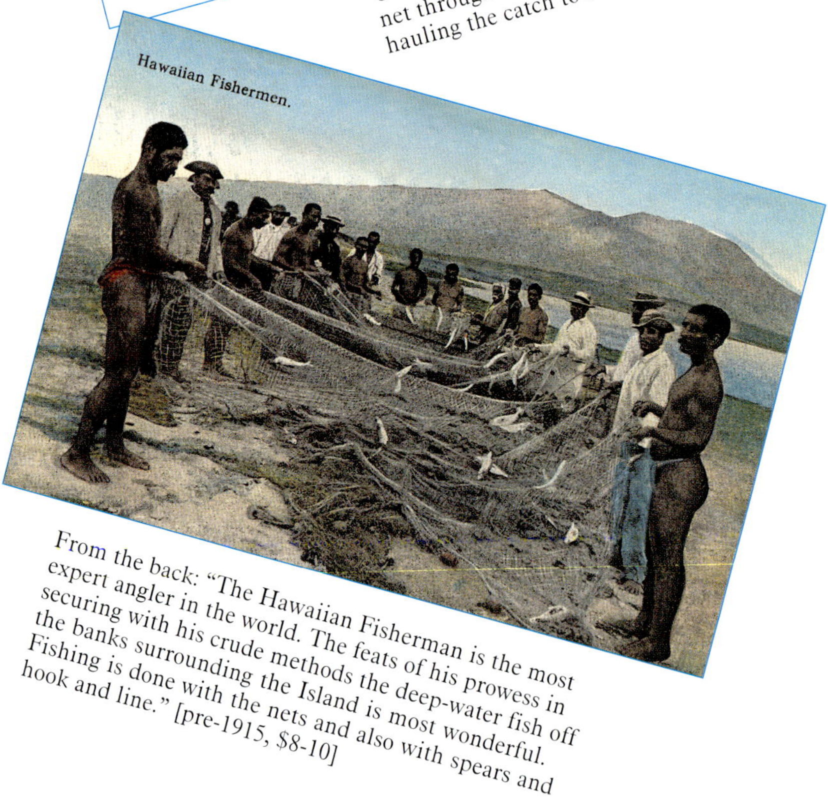

From the back: "The Hawaiian Fisherman is the most expert angler in the world. The feats of his prowess in securing with his crude methods the deep-water fish off the banks surrounding the Island is most wonderful. Fishing is done with the nets and also with spears and hook and line." [pre-1915, $8-10]

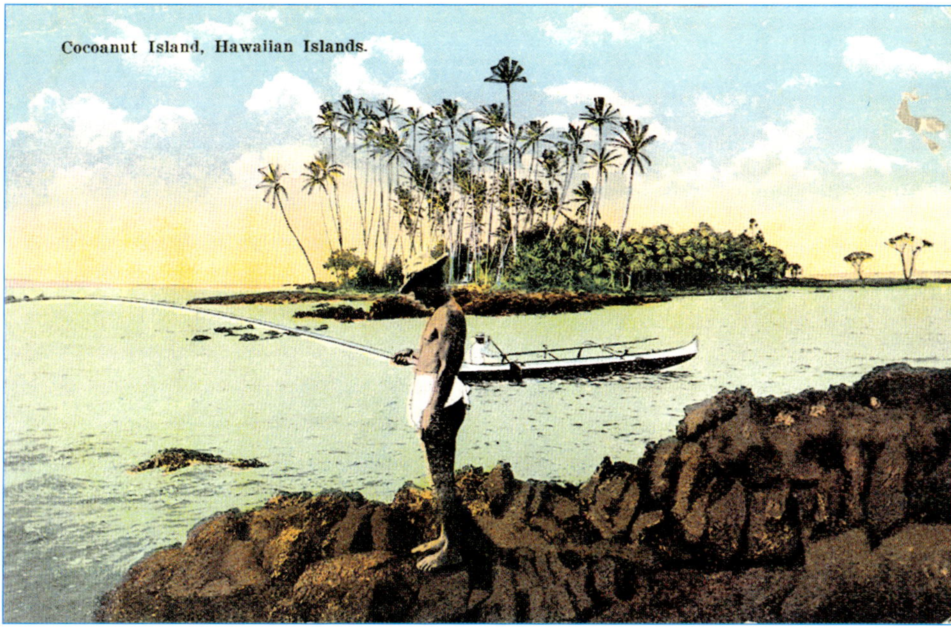

[pre-1915, $4-7]

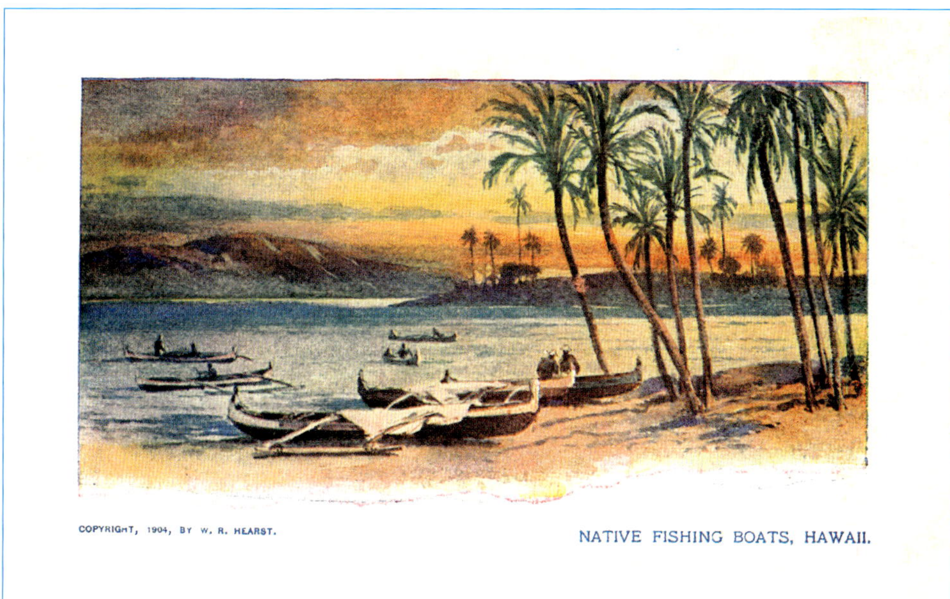

A painting turned postcard, copyright 1904 by W. R. Hearst, establishes the tropical ideal. [pre-1915, $4-6]

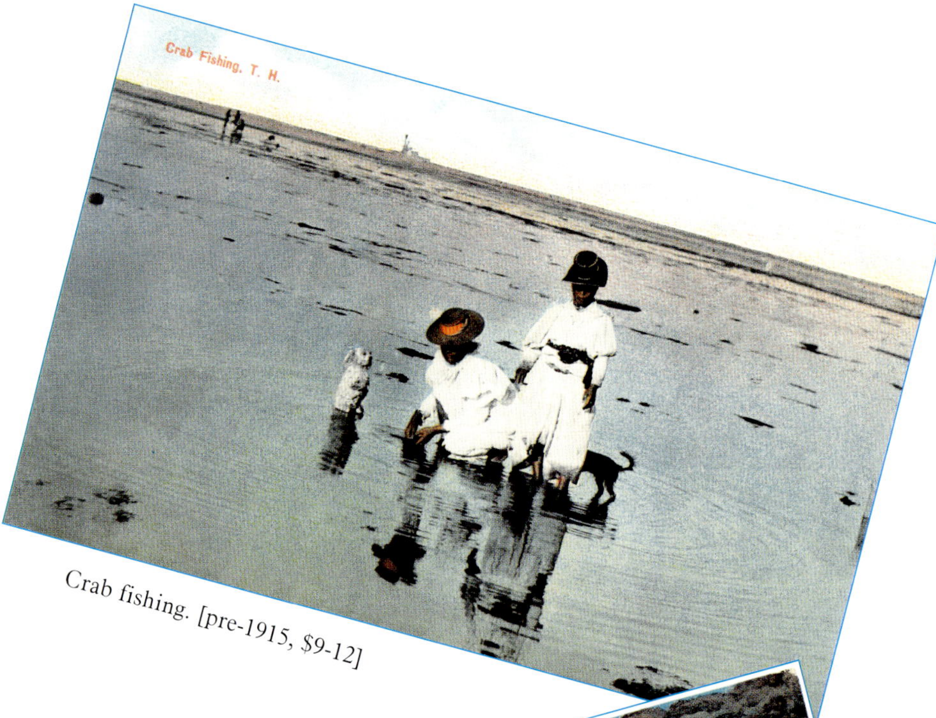

Crab fishing. [pre-1915, $9-12]

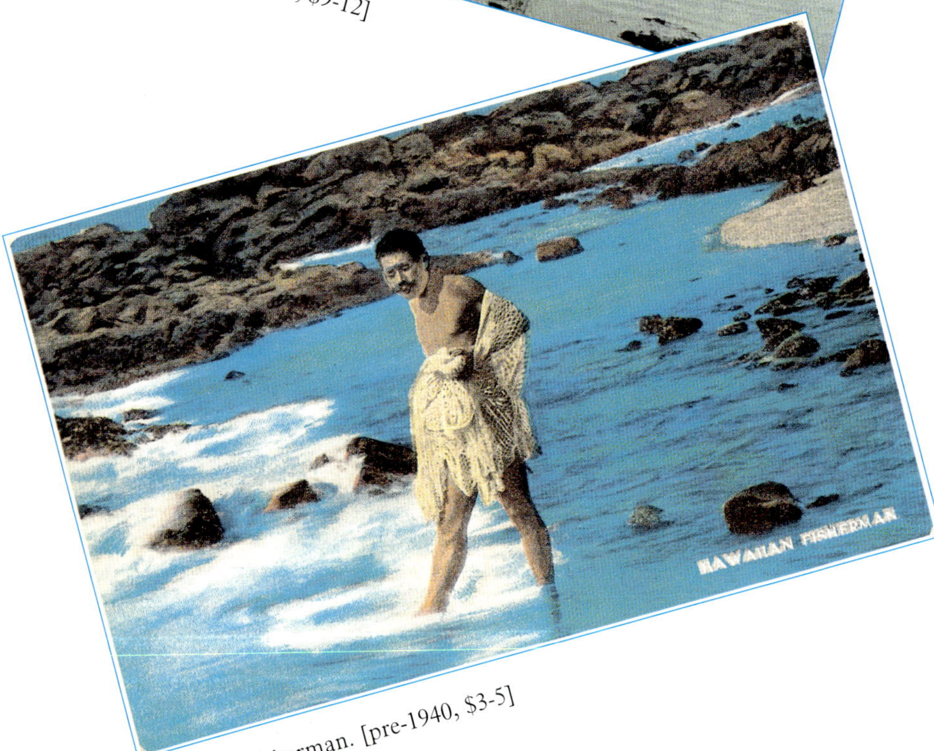

Hawaiian Fisherman. [pre-1940, $3-5]

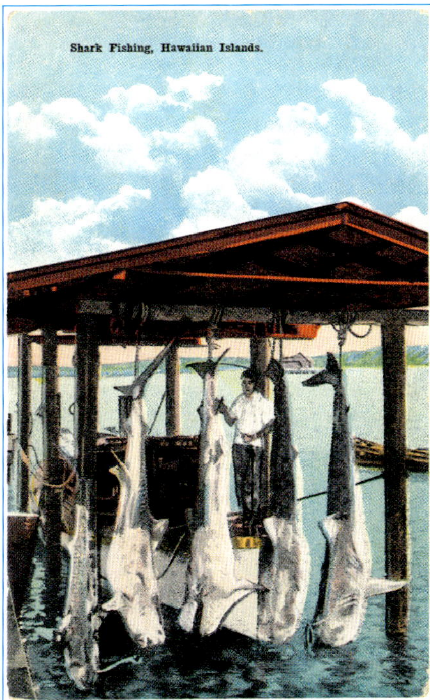

Shark Fishing. [pre-1915, $9-12]

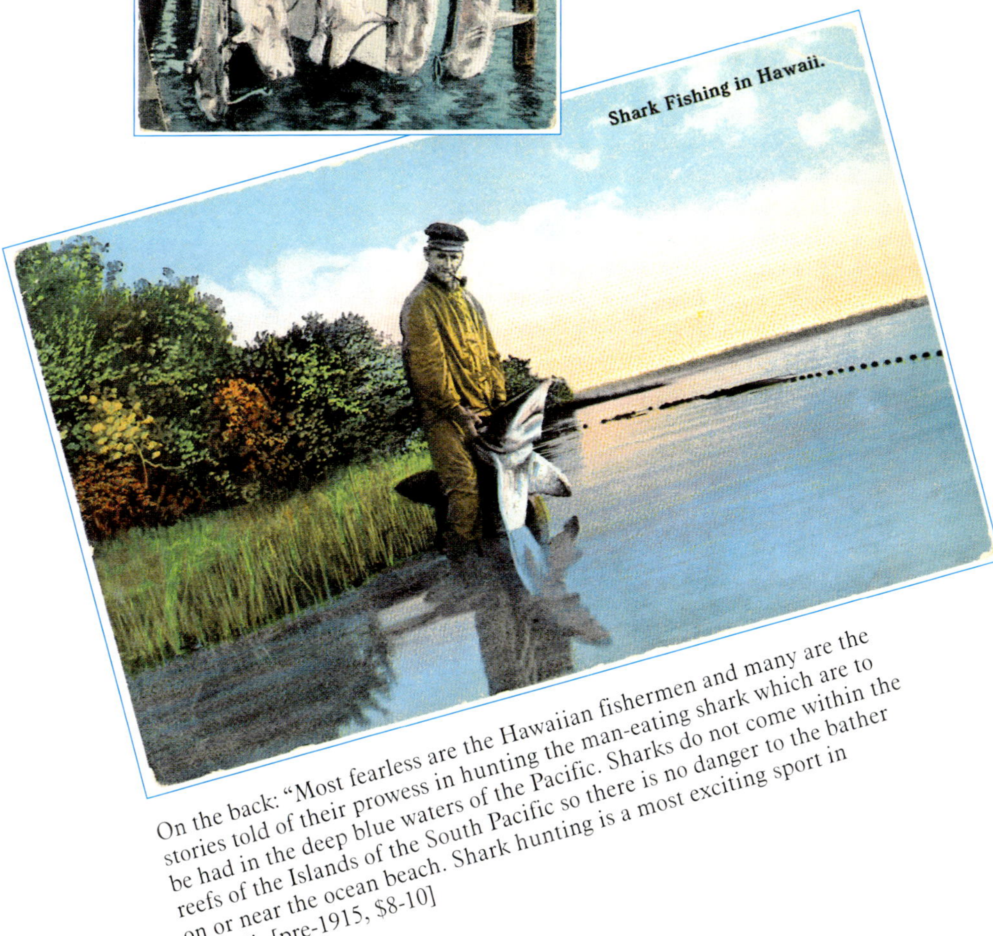

On the back: "Most fearless are the Hawaiian fishermen and many are the stories told of their prowess in hunting the man-eating shark which are to be had in the deep blue waters of the Pacific. Sharks do not come within the reefs of the Islands of the South Pacific so there is no danger to the bather on or near the ocean beach. Shark hunting is a most exciting sport in Hawaii. [pre-1915, $8-10]

[pre-1940, $2-4]

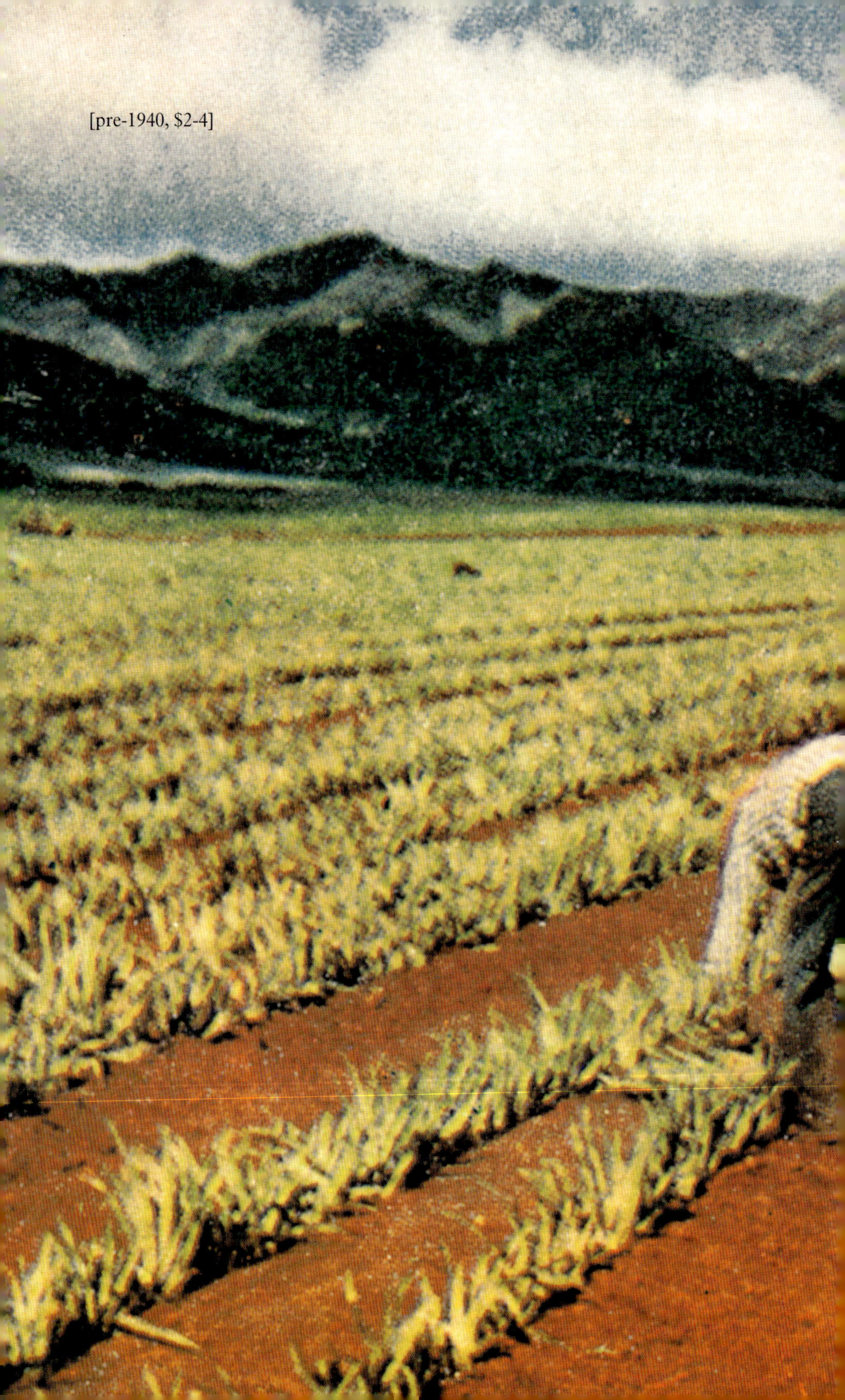

Agriculture

Taro and Poi

When the Ancient Polynesians first came to the islands of Hawaii, they brought several kinds of plants with them in their canoes. One of these was the taro plant, also known as kalo, or Haloa, which means "everlasting breath." The name reflects the importance of taro in the daily life of the Hawaiian people. Today there are eighty-seven different varieties of taro grown around the world in Africa, the West Indies, islands in the Pacific Ocean, South Asia, and of course, Hawaii.

According to legend, taro was a byproduct of the liaison between Wakea, the sky father, and his daughter Ho'ohokulani. The child that resulted from that union, Haloa-naka, was stillborn. After Haloa-naka was buried taro sprouted from his body. Wakea had another son who he also named Haloa. This Haloa eventually became the forefather of the Hawaiian people. Haloa was told to look after, care for, and respect his older brother and his older brother would sustain and provide for his descendants.

Taro is a perennial herb, which can be identified by clusters of arrowhead-shaped leaves on green, red, black, or variegated stems growing from a thick, brown tuber. It can be grown in a variety of soil types and reaches maturity in 6-10 months.

In Hawaii, taro was grown in two distinct ways. Dry land taro was grown in the low land forests where there was enough rainfall and the soil was rich enough to support the plant. Wetland taro was grown in manmade lo'i, or pond fields, along with several other varieties of plants including another important crop, sugar cane.

Taro had a variety of uses. It could be fed to the elderly to ease digestion and provide necessary vitamin supplements. A piece of taro stem can be applied to the skin to stop bleeding, or can be rubbed on insect bites. Taro leaves can be mashed and mixed with salt to make a poultice for infections. Poi was also used as a glue, to quiet an upset stomach, was put on sores that were infected, and when mixed with arrowroot starch served as a cure for diarrhea. Even the soil that taro was grown in was useful. The mud from taro patches was used as a dye to color cloth.

The leaves can also be cooked and eaten like spinach. Perhaps the most important use of the taro plant is in the making of poi, one of the staple dishes in the Hawaiian diet. Islanders were said to have eaten as much as fifteen pounds of poi a day. To make poi, the tuber of the taro plant is mashed and mixed with water until the mixture is smooth and sticky. Poi can be eaten fresh or fermented, which gives it a sour taste. The flavor of this dish is largely dependent on the type of taro used to make it.

The poi bowl is the center of the Hawaiian table and eating one at a time from it forms a basis of a ritual to bind the family together and to show appreciation for their ancestors.

However, before it can be eaten, taro must be cooked because it contains crystals made of calcium oxalate. These crystals, if ingested, can cause severe irritation to the lining of the throat and mouth. The tuber can be baked, boiled, or steamed.

Since taro and poi were so widely used in the daily life of the Hawaiians it was widely cultivated throughout the islands. Today, the Keanae Peninsula on Maui is the primary region where taro is still grown.

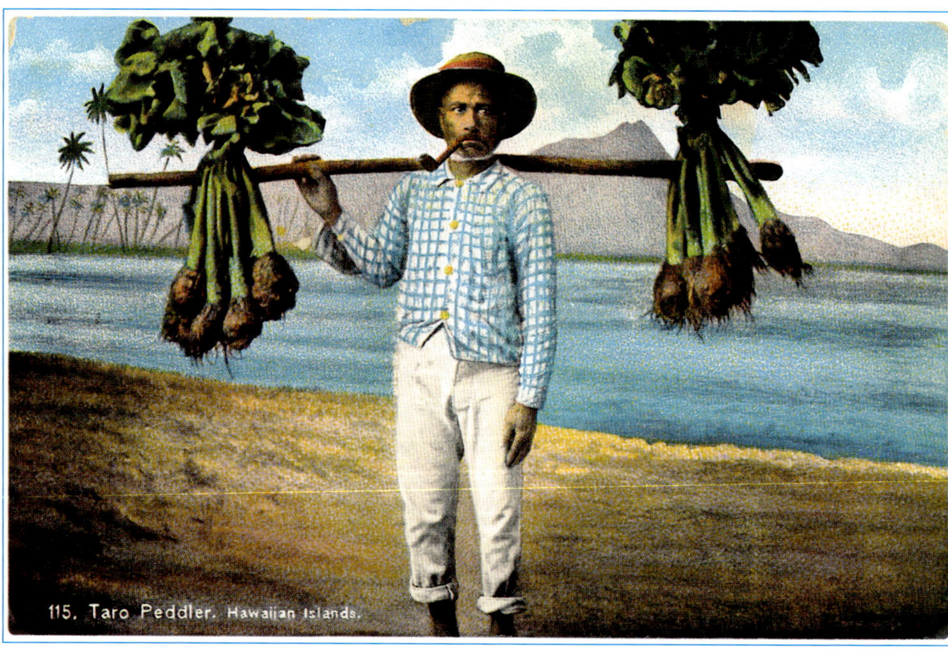

[pre-1915, $9-12]

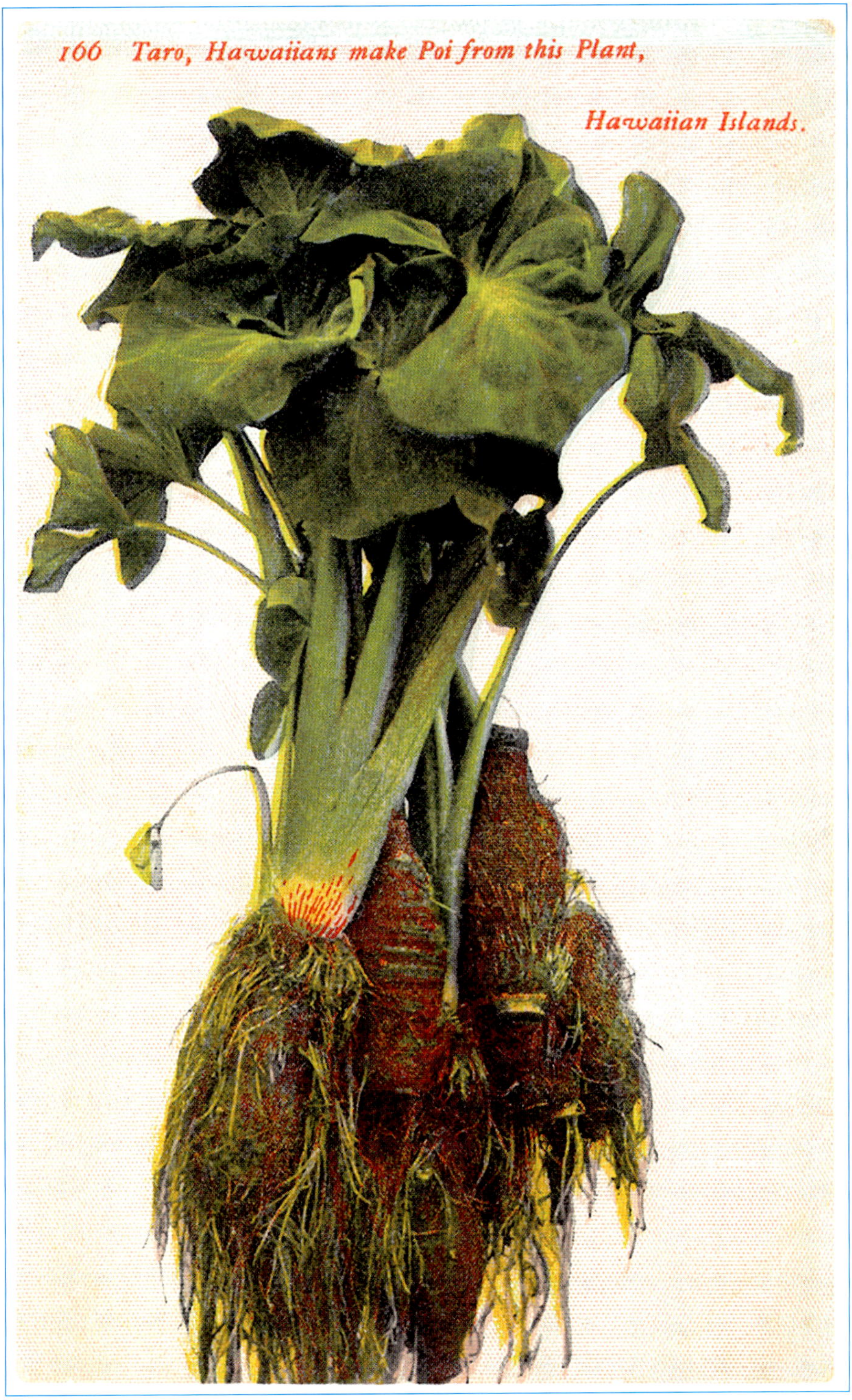

Like the Native Americans of the Plains of America did with the buffalo, the Ancient Hawaiians used every part of the taro plant. [pre-1915, $2-4]

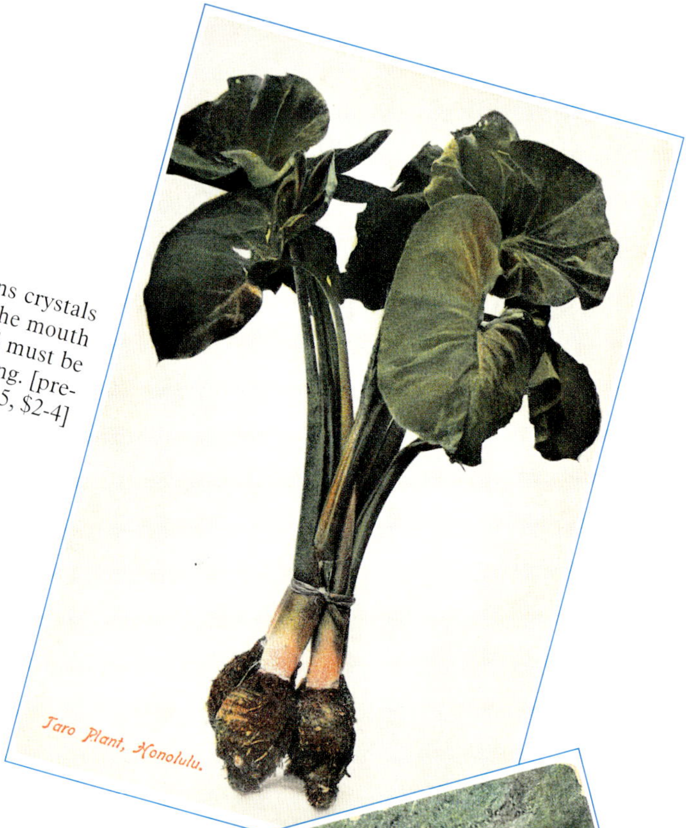

Taro contains crystals that irritate the mouth and throat, and must be cooked before eating. [pre-1915, $2-4]

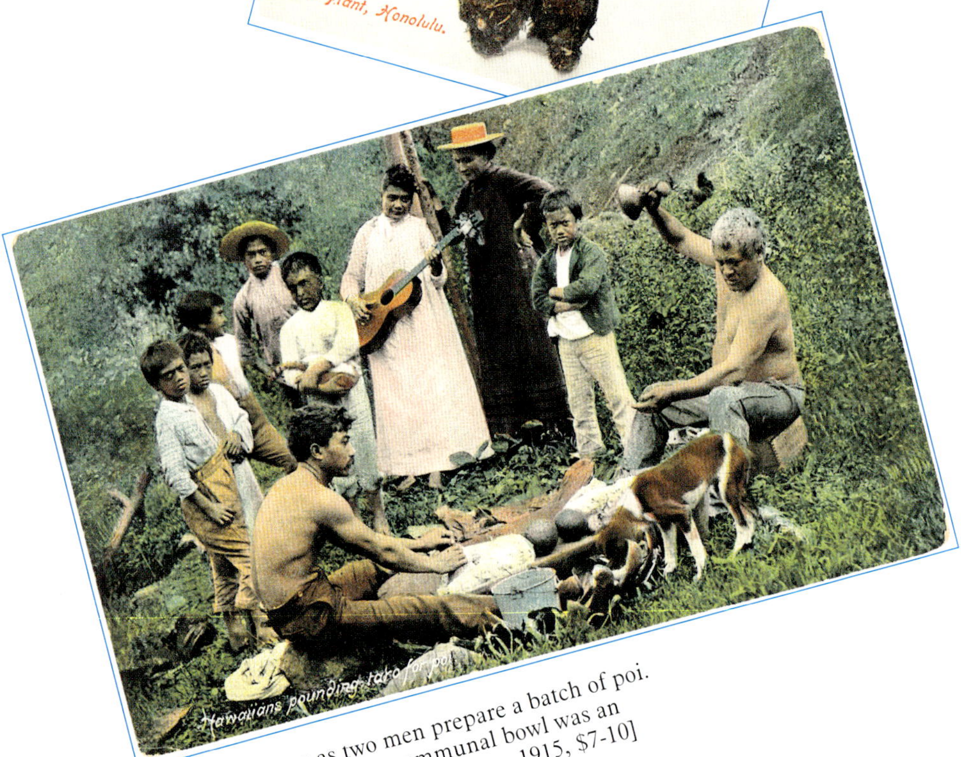

A family watches as two men prepare a batch of poi. The eating of poi from a communal bowl was an important part of family ritual. [pre-1915, $7-10]

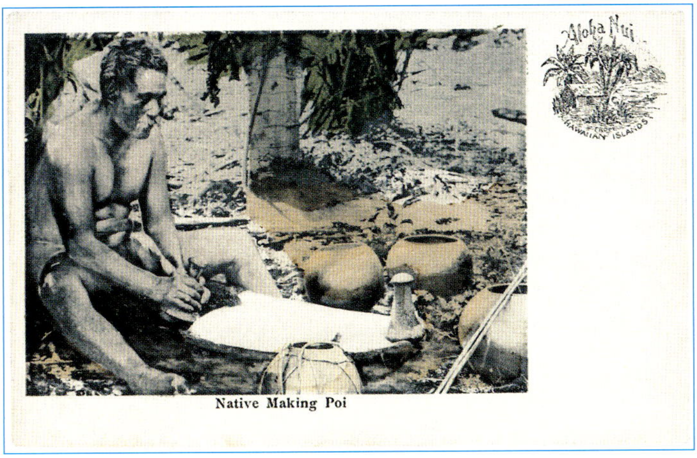

[pre-1915, $25-40]

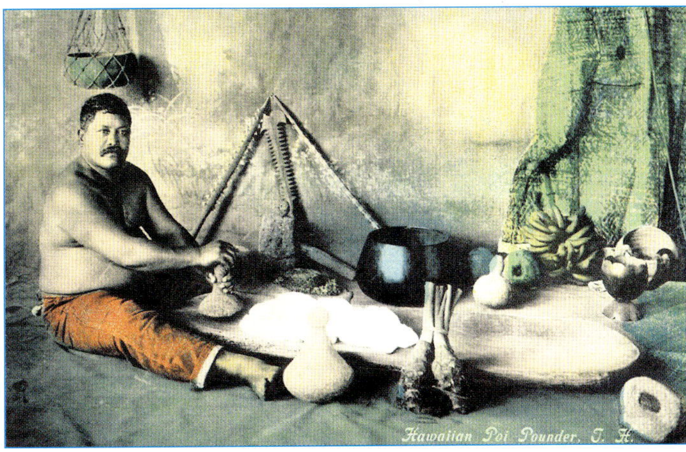

A special stone tool, called a "poi pounder," is used to mash the taro root. [pre-1915, $12-15]

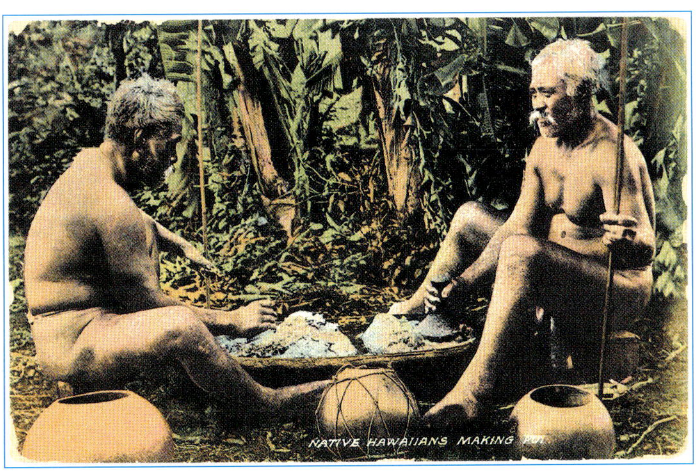

Two Hawaiian natives make poi by mashing the root and adding water to the mash. [canceled 1912, $12-15]

Sugar Cane

Ancient Polynesians brought sugar cane, or "ko," to the Hawaiian Islands and it soon became part of the Islands' ecology.

The Hawaiians grew forty varieties of sugar cane and used them for a variety of purposes. Not only was sugarcane an excellent way to sweeten foods, it also was used as medicine. The juice of a young shoot of sugar cane was an ingredient in a poultice that was applied to cuts and lacerations and also served as a sweetener for many other bitter-tasting medical concoctions. The plant's leaves grow up to two feet in length and were used as thatching for huts. The stalks, which grew anywhere from six to twenty feet high and one to two inches thick, were planted to serve as windbreaks.

Sugarcane was grown extensively as a subsistence crop for many years and it was not until the mid 1800s that it became a commercial crop. In 1825, John Wilkinson built the first sugar plantation in Koloa on the island of Kauai. His first harvest yielded two tons of raw sugar. Since sugar cane requires a great deal of moisture, growers had to dig wells and irrigation canals. The last sugarcane plantation on the Big Island, Hawaii, closed in 1995.

Today the sugarcane industry in Hawaii is concentrated primarily on the islands of Kauai and Maui and produces harvests of 340,00 tons of raw sugar, making sugarcane the biggest cash crop grown in Hawaii.

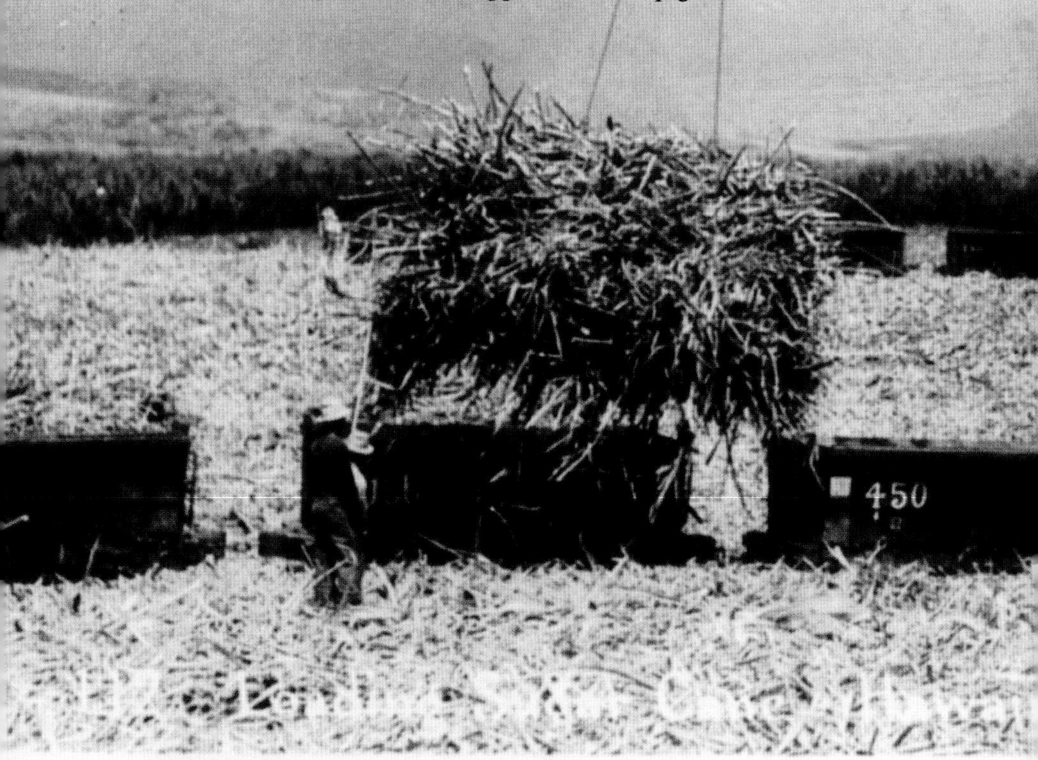

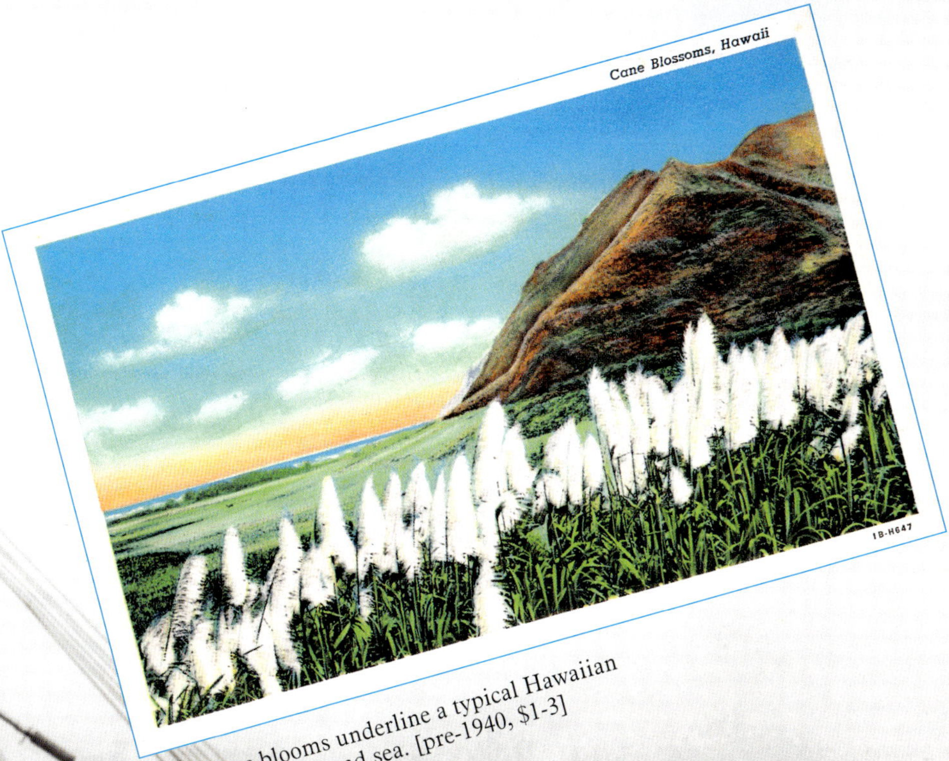

Sugar cane blooms underline a typical Hawaiian view of mountain and sea. [pre-1940, $1-3]

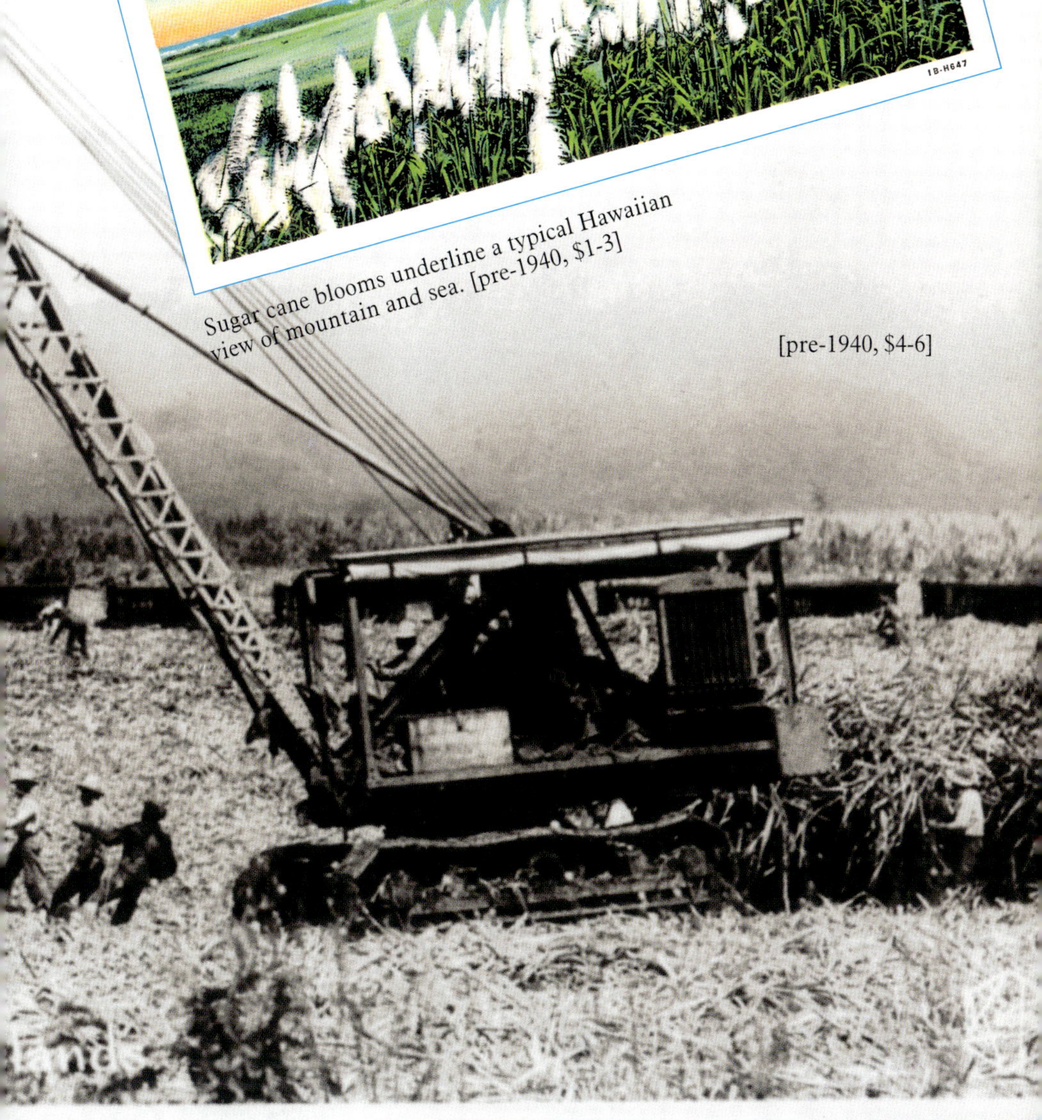

[pre-1940, $4-6]

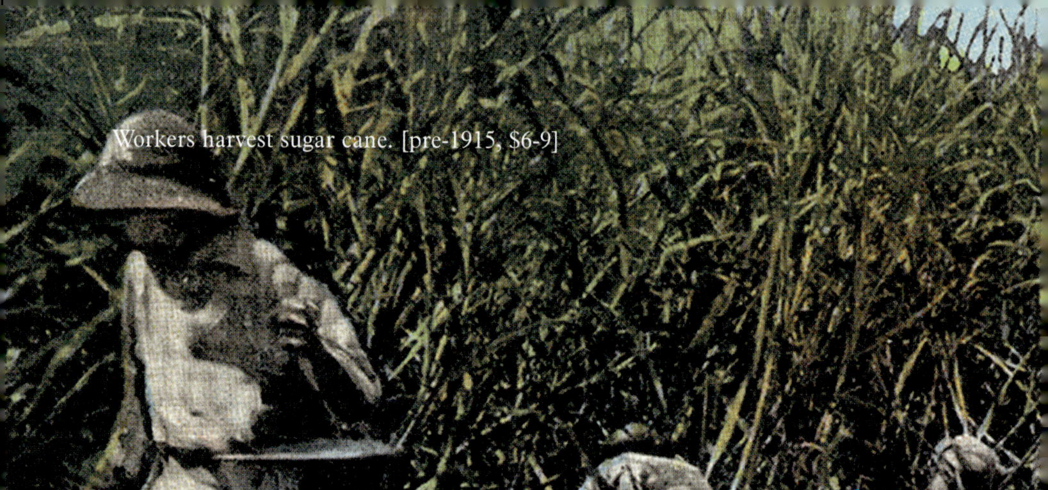

Workers harvest sugar cane. [pre-1915, $6-9]

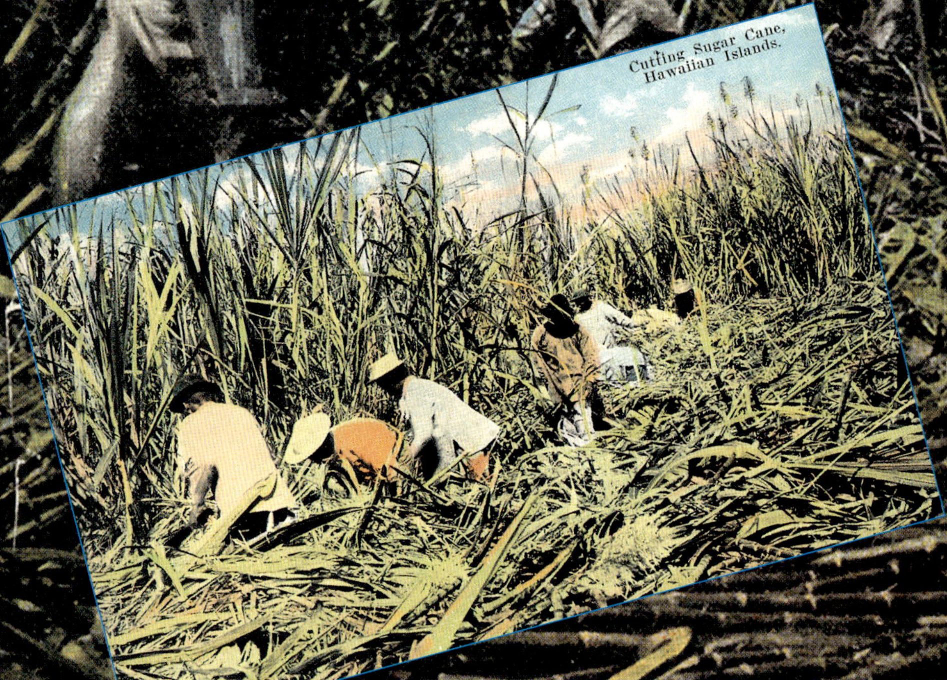

The sugar industry in Hawaii was so great that labor was brought in from other countries in order to supplement the local work force. [pre-1915, $6-9]

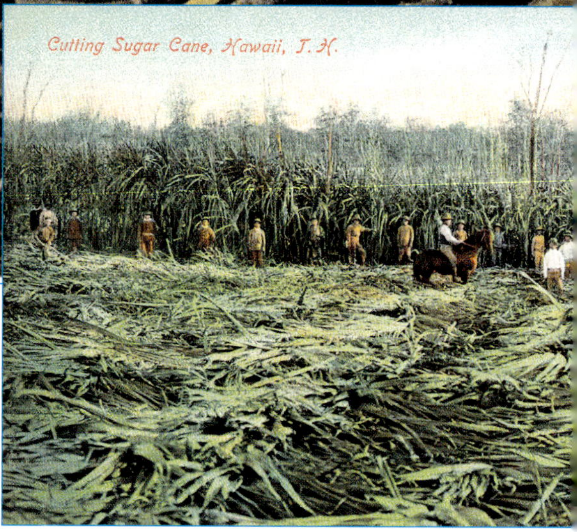

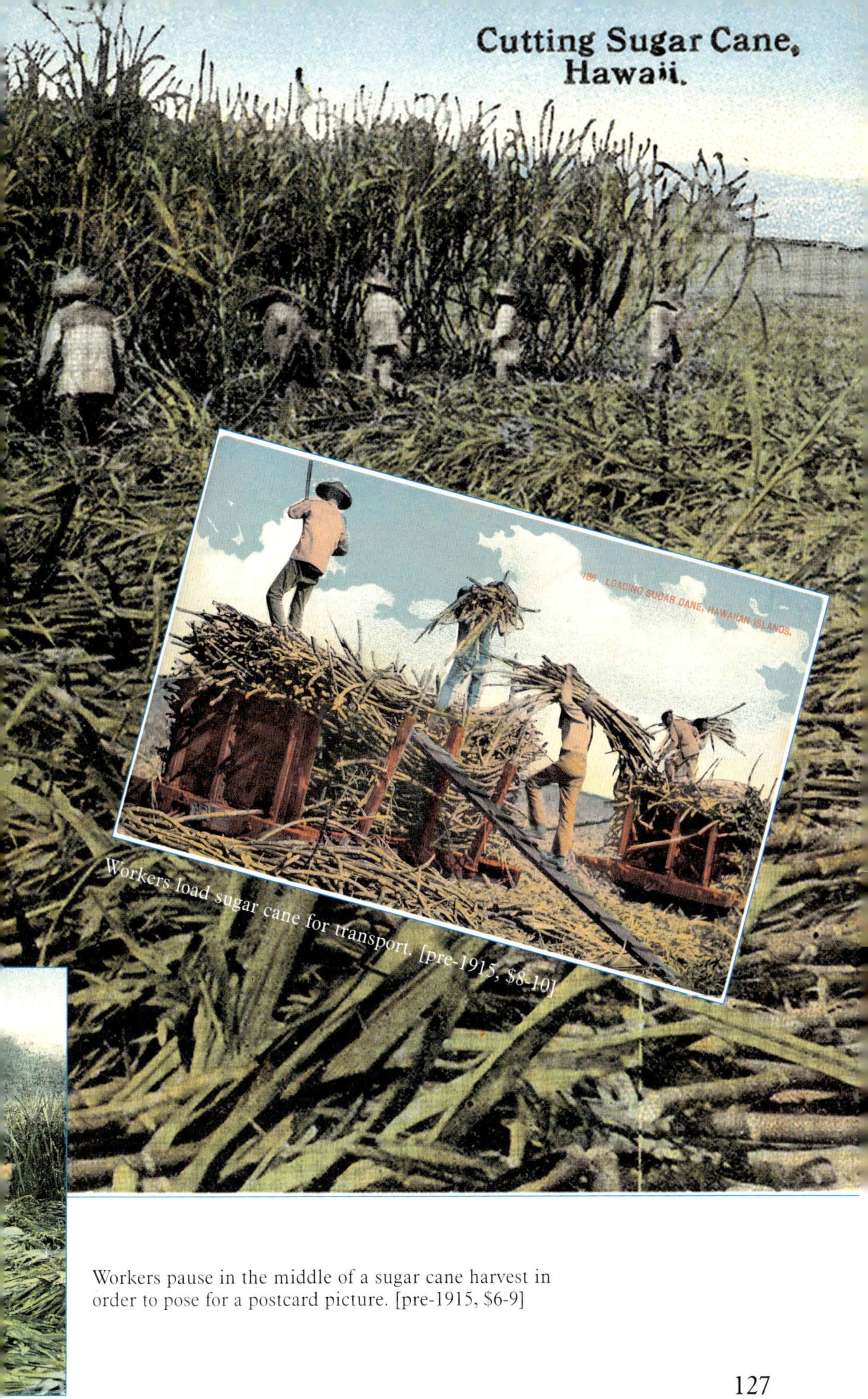

Workers load sugar cane for transport. [pre-1915, $8-10]

Workers pause in the middle of a sugar cane harvest in order to pose for a postcard picture. [pre-1915, $6-9]

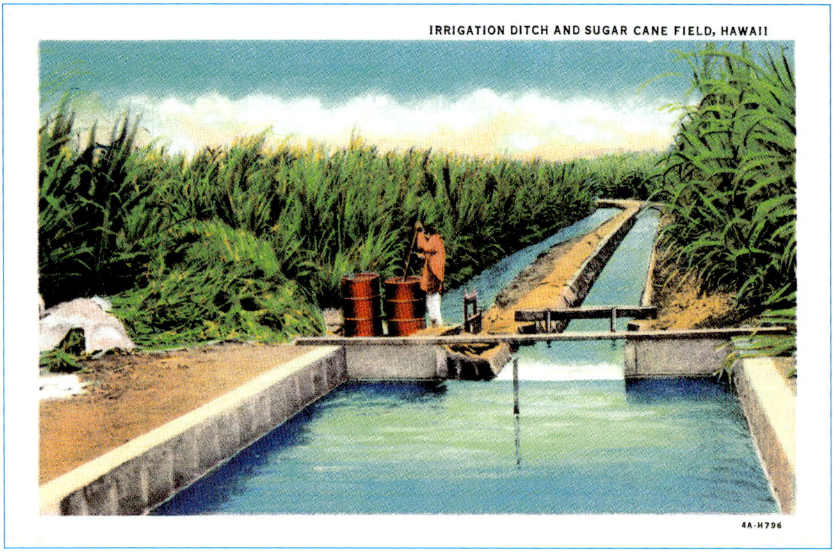

From the back: "Sugar fields are always thirsty. Careful planning, hard work, and millions of dollars spent on scientific research have made this Hawaii's greatest industry. Nearly a hundred million tons of sugar are shipped from Hawaii every year." [Cancelled 1935, $2-4]

"When I went on a picnic the 30th of May I passed fields of sugarcane as well as pineapple fields; but I did not see any ditches like this one. I suppose they were further in from the road. A narrow gauge railroad runs through the fields, on which the cane is hauled. The tracks cross the street in many places and signs have to be put up because one time there was a terrible accident when one of the trains collided with an auto."
—1935

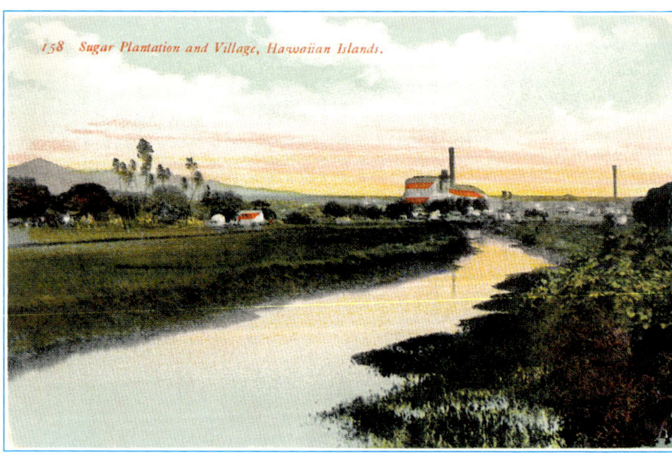

A canal provides the necessary irrigation for a sugar plantation. [pre-1915, $10-12]

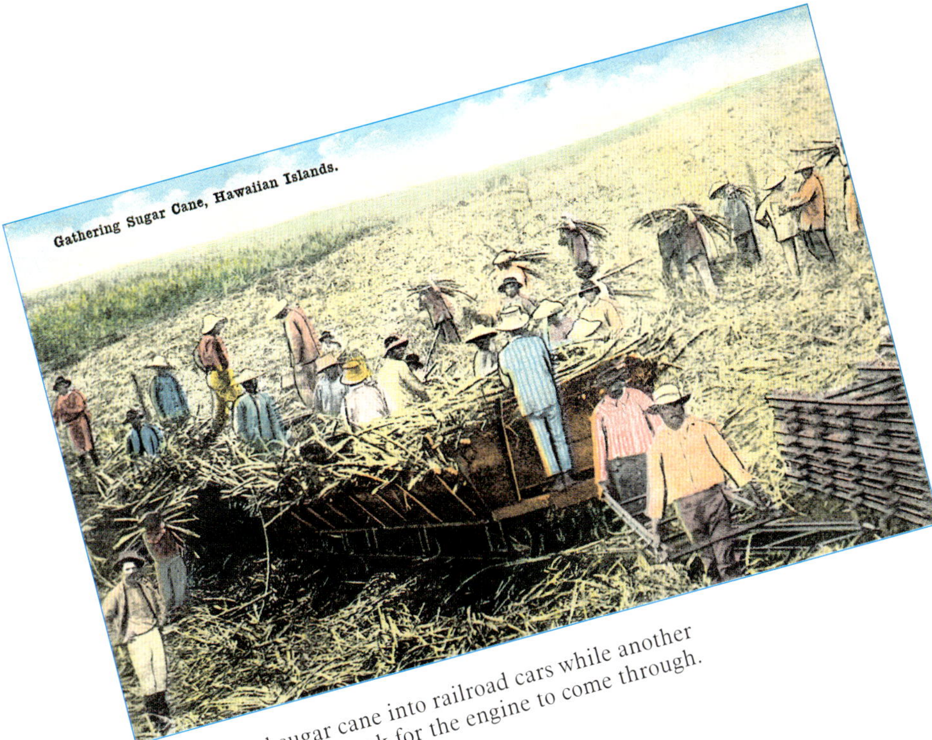

Workers load sugar cane into railroad cars while another pair of workers lay track for the engine to come through. [pre-1915, $10-12]

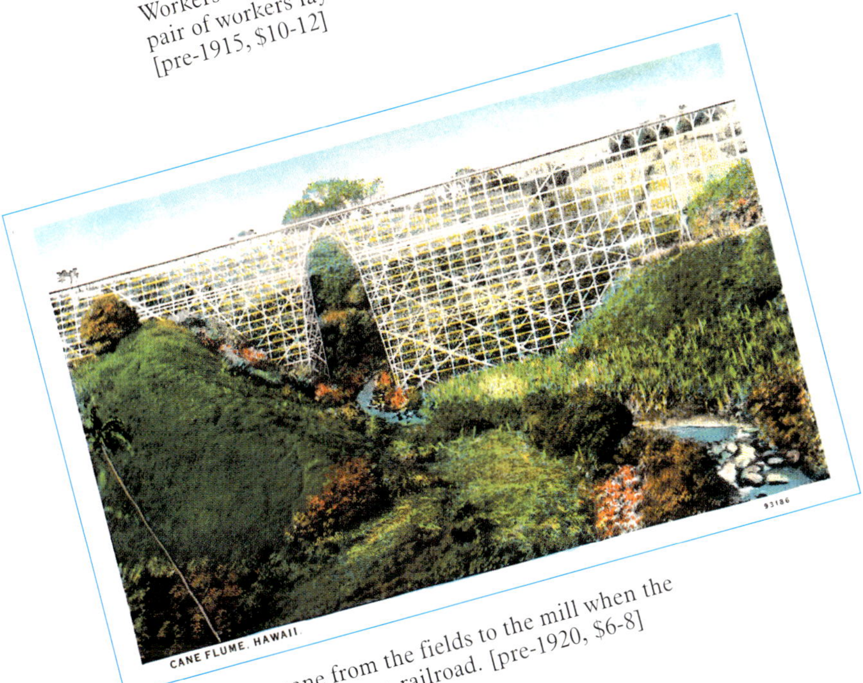

A flume moves cane from the fields to the mill when the terrain in unsuitable for a railroad. [pre-1920, $6-8]

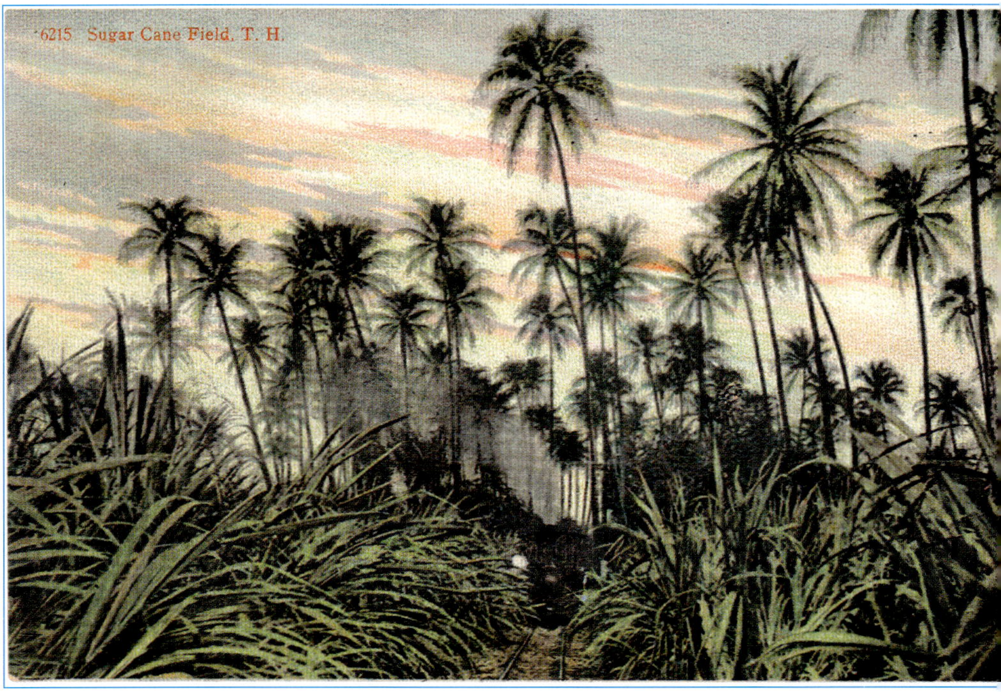

A railroad running through a field of sugarcane, is able to transport the harvested cane directly to the mill. [pre-1915, $7-9]

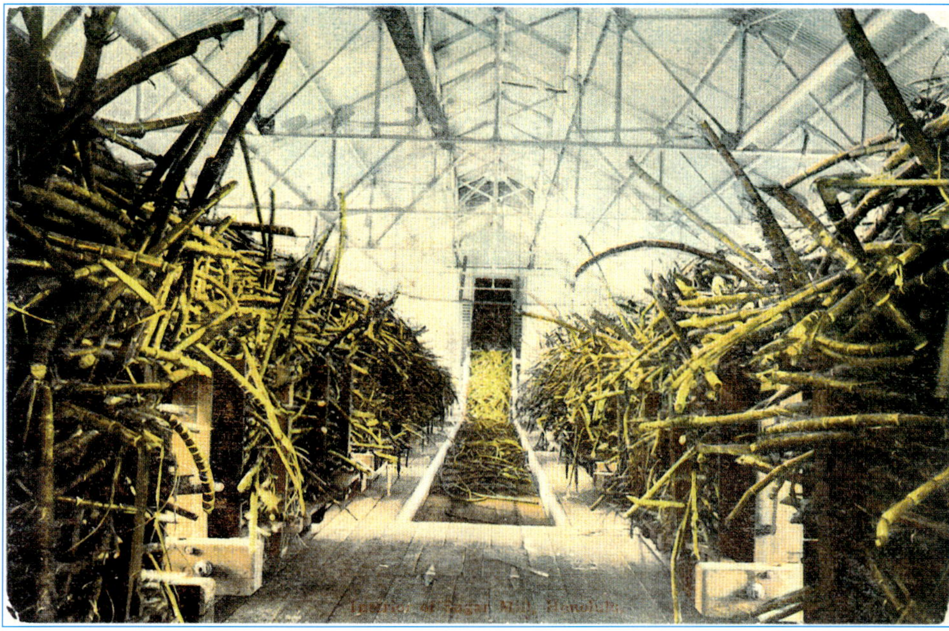

After being harvested and stripped of its leaves, sugarcane is taken to a mill for processing. [pre-1915, $8-10]

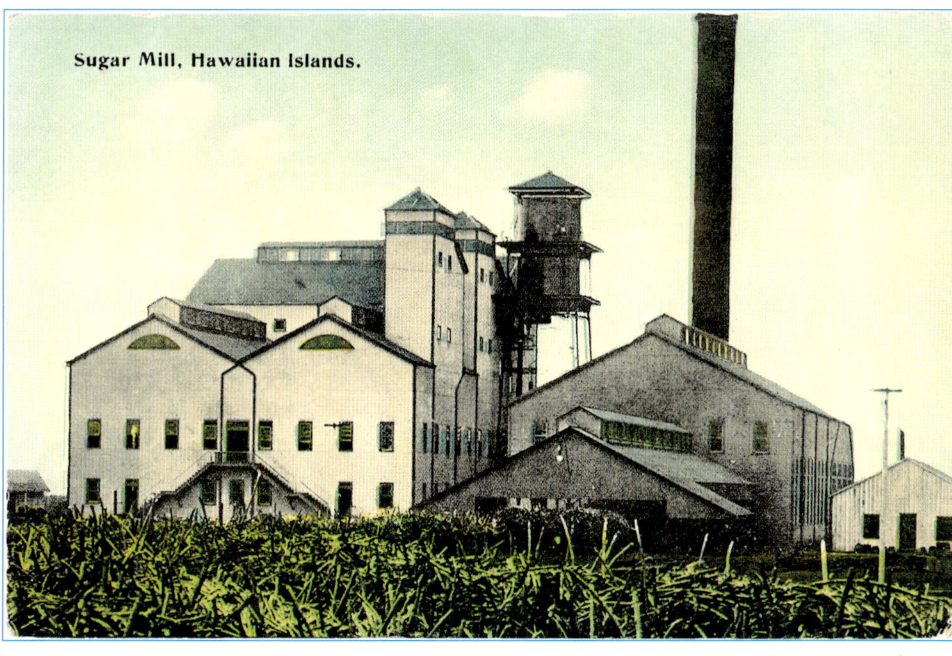

Sugar mills were a common sight. [pre-1915, $9-12]

Rice

Rice was first introduced to the Hawaiian Islands in 1858 and became an important staple of the Islands' agricultural economy during the 1900s.

Rice requires plenty of moisture, so much that it is classified as a semi-aquatic plant, and it can grow in a variety of environments and soil types. However, rice does not share the exotic nature of pineapple or the necessity of sugar, and as a result does not share the spotlight with Hawaii's other agricultural exports.

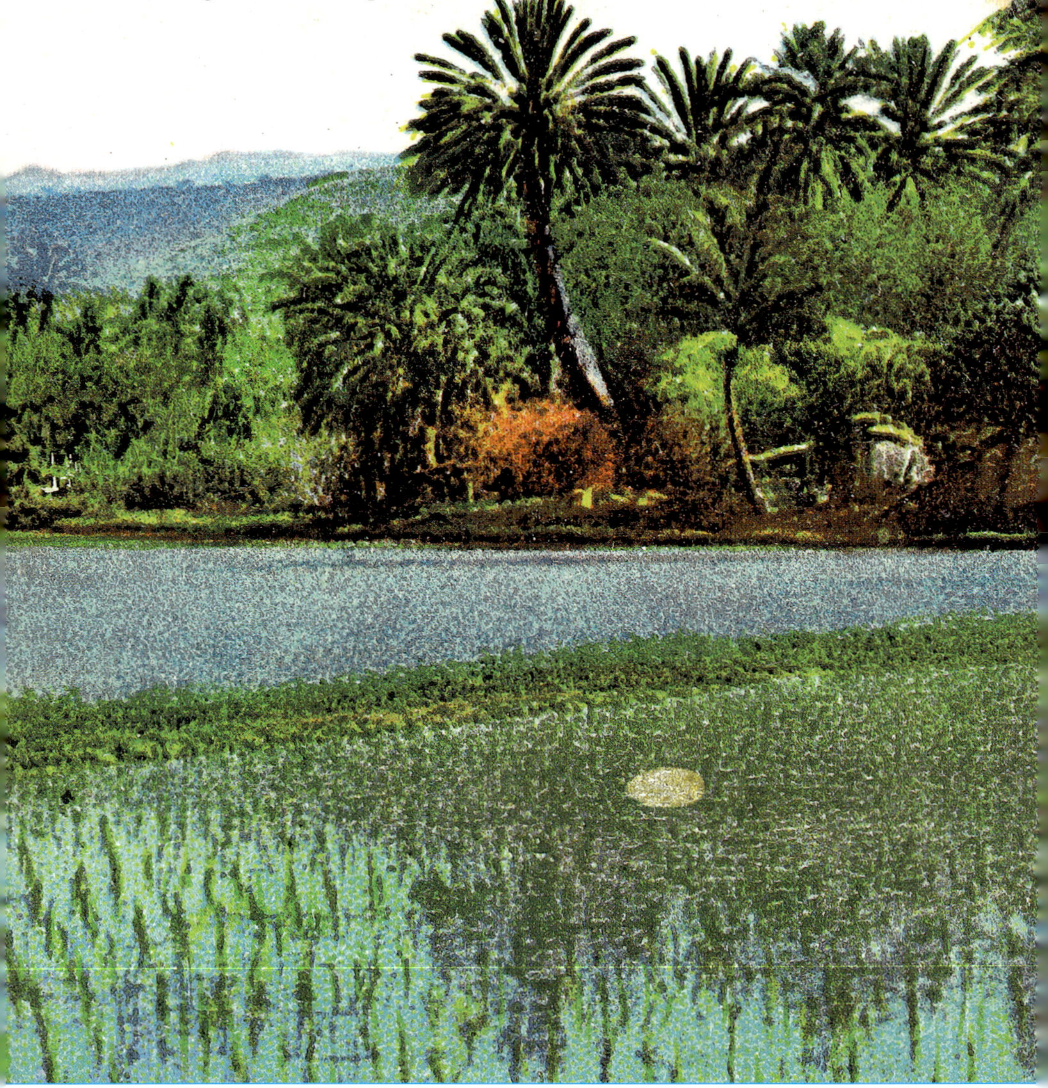

A hut on the edge of a rice paddy gives a farmer easy access to his crops. [pre-1915, $4-6]

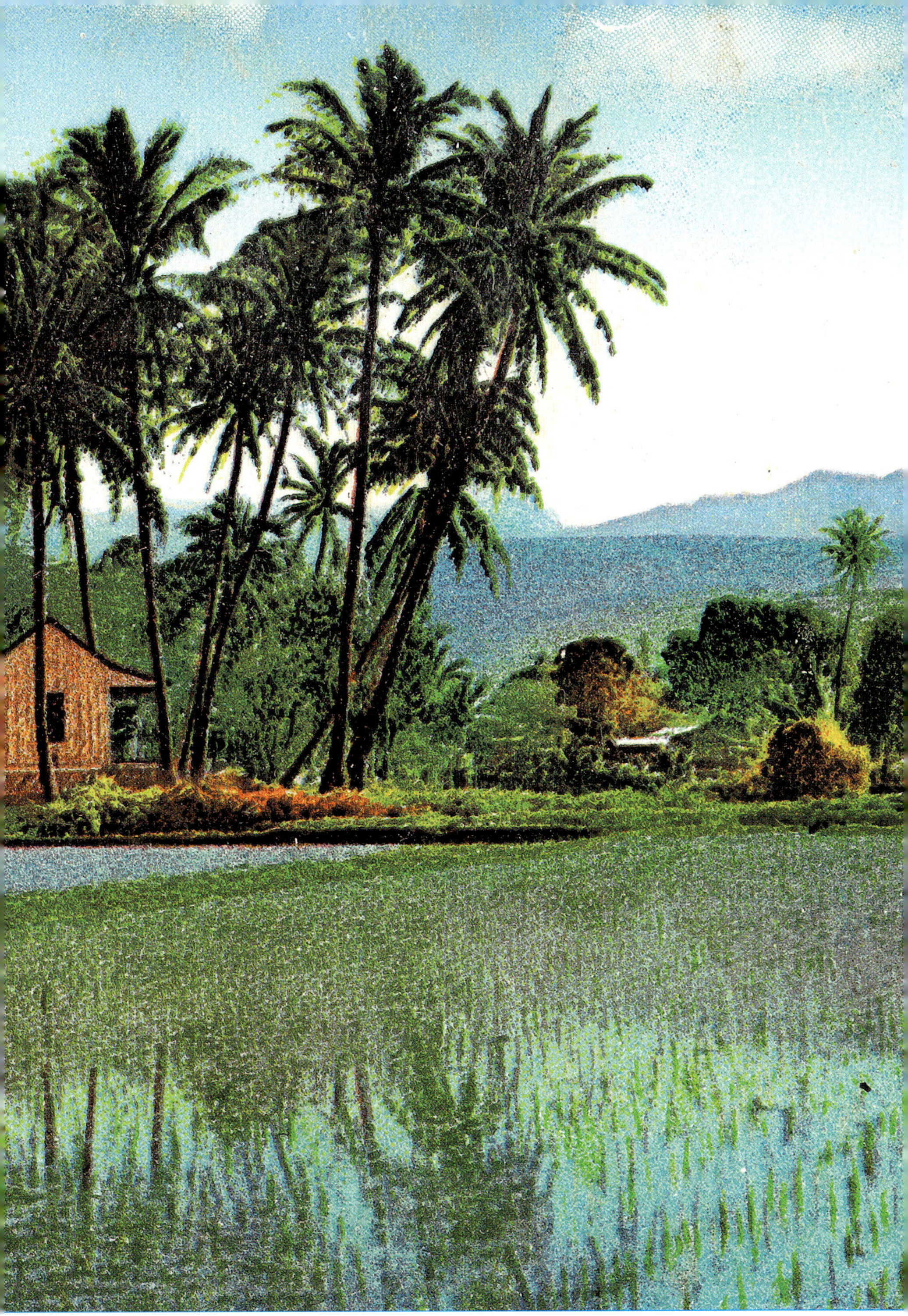

"Too early to see rice fields. Lots of sugarcane, mountains, ocean, rivers, waterfalls, and farms. Lovely estates back up the mountainside, their lights at night like fire flys [sic]."
—1912

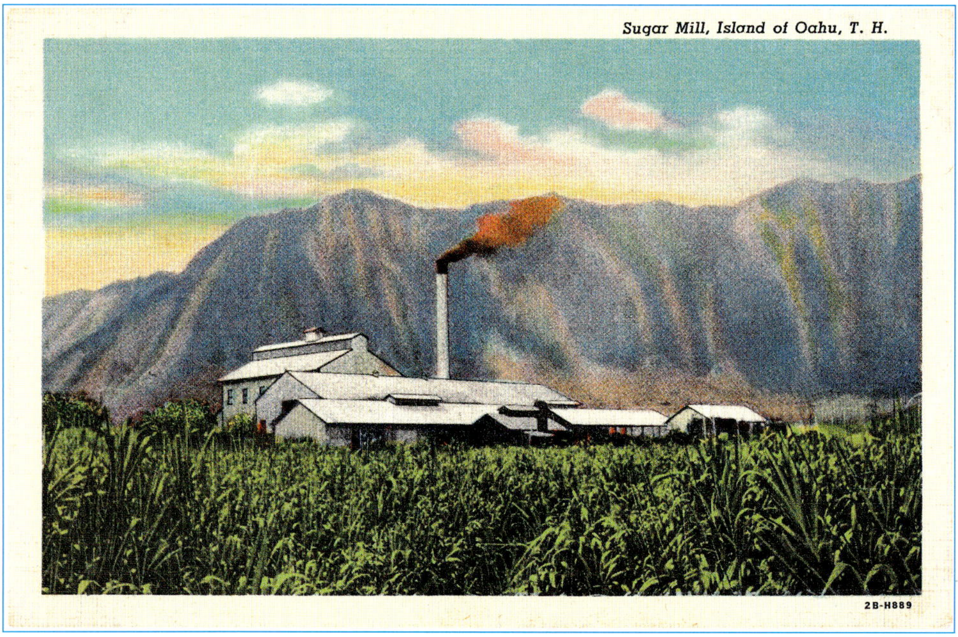

Many sugar mills were built on the islands to help deal with the demands of the industry. [pre-1940, $2-5]

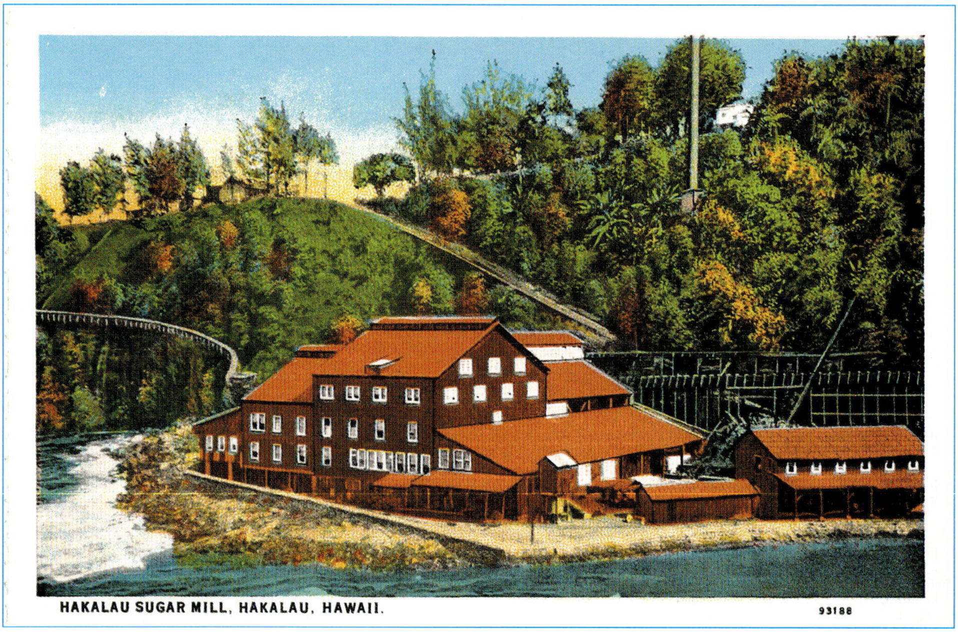

Flumes transport harvested cane to this mill, located on the coast. [pre-1920, $5-7]

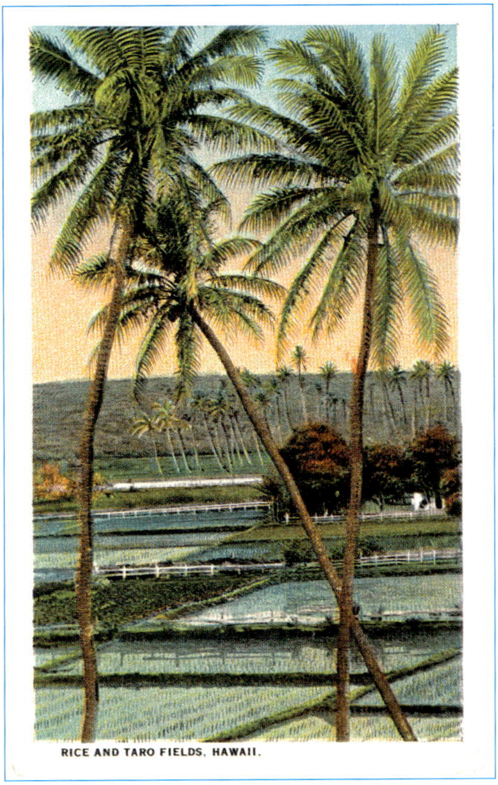

Palm trees take advantage of the extra moisture that a rice paddy provides. [pre-1920, $3-5]

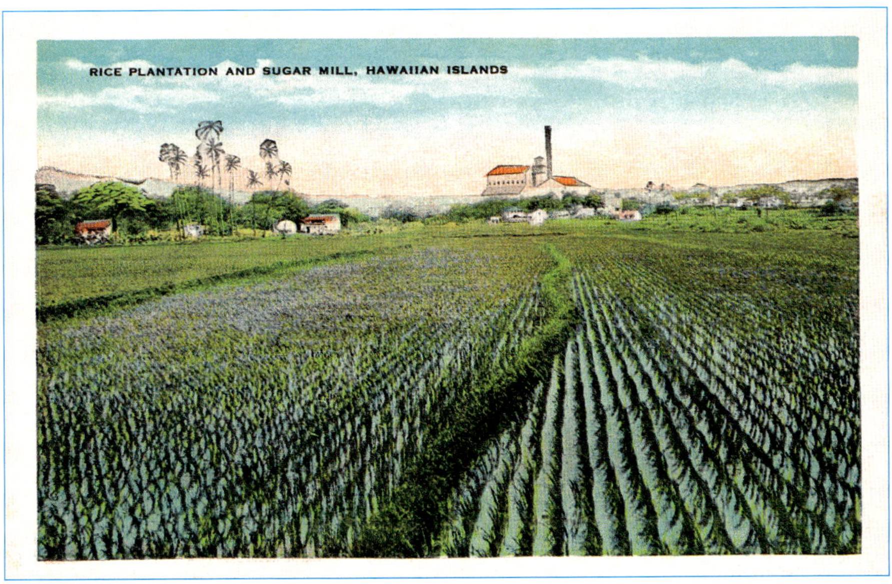

A sugar mill overlooks rice paddies. Both rice and sugar cane require a great deal of moisture to survive. [pre-1920, $4-8]

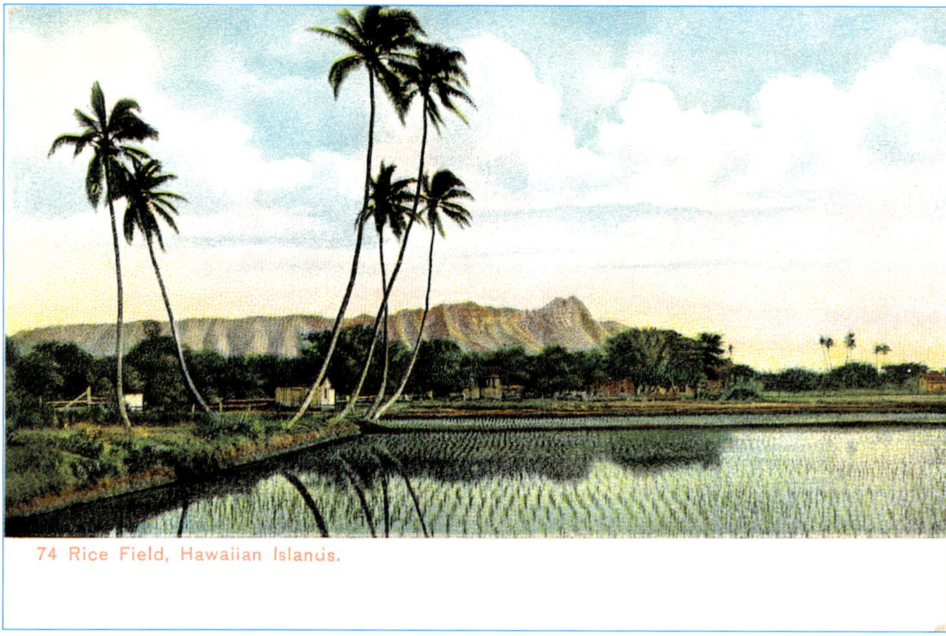

Palm trees and rice paddies are often seen side-by-side because each requires much moisture. [pre-1915 $4-7]

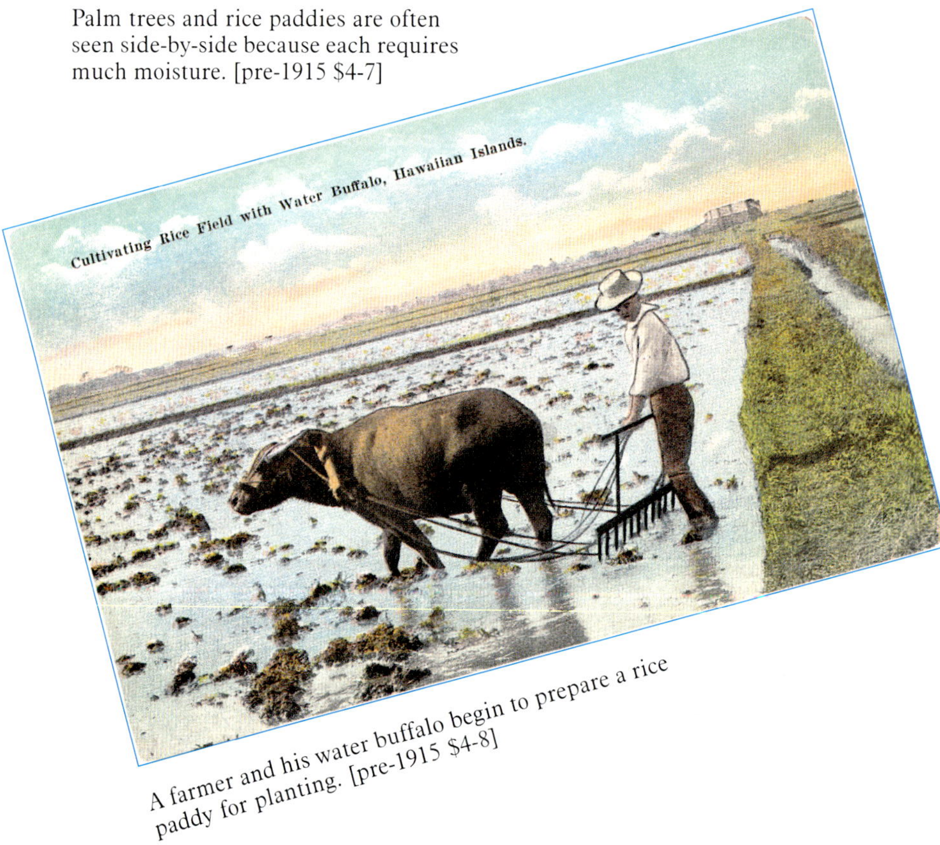

A farmer and his water buffalo begin to prepare a rice paddy for planting. [pre-1915 $4-8]

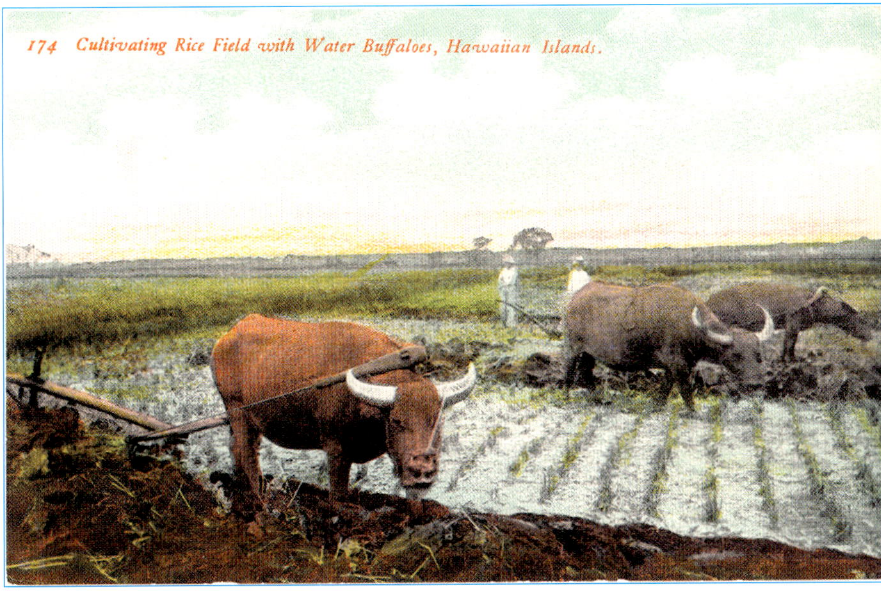

Water buffalos were used extensively in the rice farming industry to cultivate rice paddies. [pre-1915, $8-12]

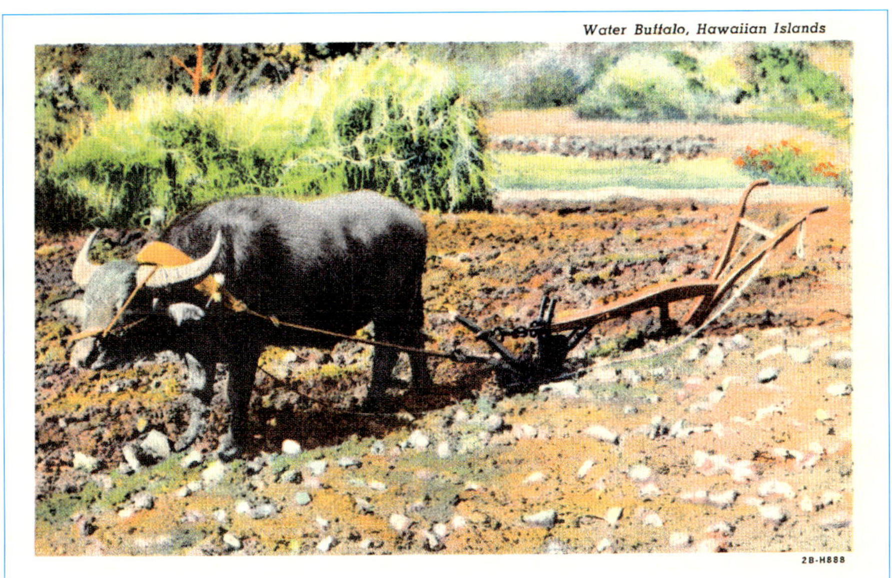

[Passed by US Army Examiner." Canceled 1943, $1-3]

"I was surprised to find this animal being used in these islands. It's used in Asia very much."
—1943

Pineapples

Pineapples, along with surfboards, volcanoes, hula dancers, and leis, are a popular and widely recognized symbol of the Hawaiian Islands. The pineapple is not a native Hawaiian plant, but was imported as a cash crop by Europeans and Americans.

A pineapple plant grows close to the ground, will reach heights of five feet, and will grow outwards anywhere from three to four feet. They reach maturity in a year and a half. Pineapples require a loose, dry sandy loam, which makes them ideally suited for the rich volcanic ash-ridden soil of the Hawaiian islands. They also require a lot of heat and therefore thrive well in Hawaii's tropical climate.

Captain John Kidwell is credited with being the pioneer of the pineapple industry, bringing several different varieties of pineapple plants to Oahu and experimenting with growing them in 1958. However there are records of pineapples being brought to Hawaii by Don Francisco de Paula y Marin, an advisor of King Kamehameha I.

In 1900, James Drummond Dole purchased sixty acres in Wahiawa and a year later founded the Hawaiian Pineapple Company, which became responsible for growing and processing the majority of the pineapples in Hawaii.

Because the means of transporting the fruit was so slow, most of the pineapples were shipped preserved in cans, rather than whole and fresh. During the 1960s, Hawaii was responsible for producing eighty percent of the world's canned pineapple. While production has slowed from the frantic boom of the 1960s, pineapples still remain one of Hawaii's major agricultural exports.

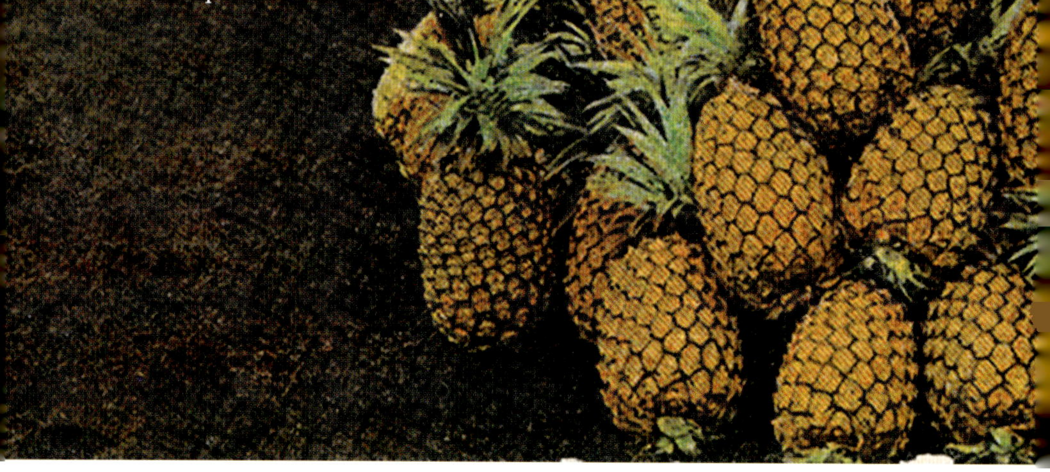

[pre-1915, $1-3]

Right:
Pineapple fields stretch as far as the eye can see near Honolulu. [pre-1940, $1-3]

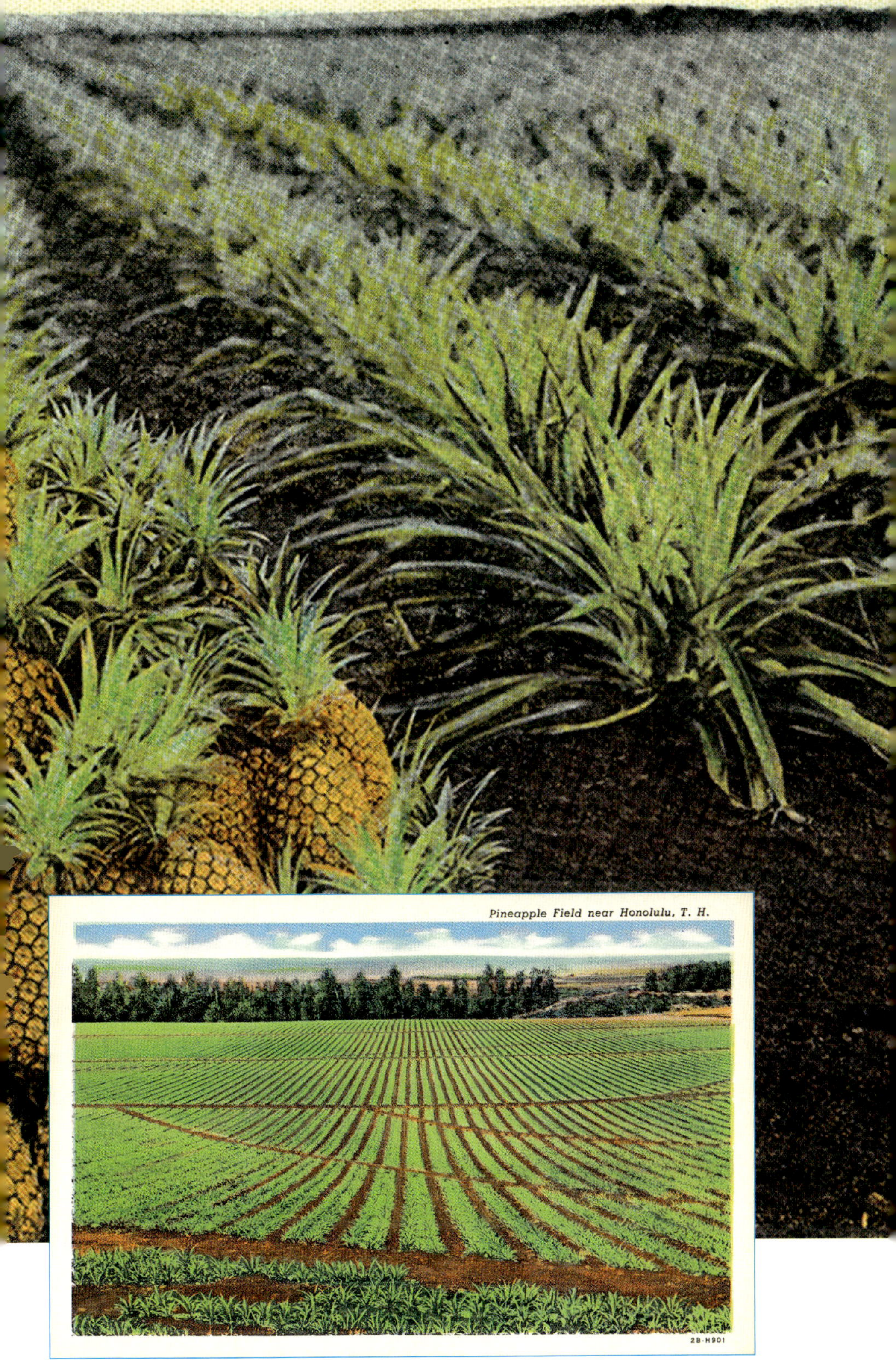
Pineapple Field near Honolulu, T. H.
2B-H901

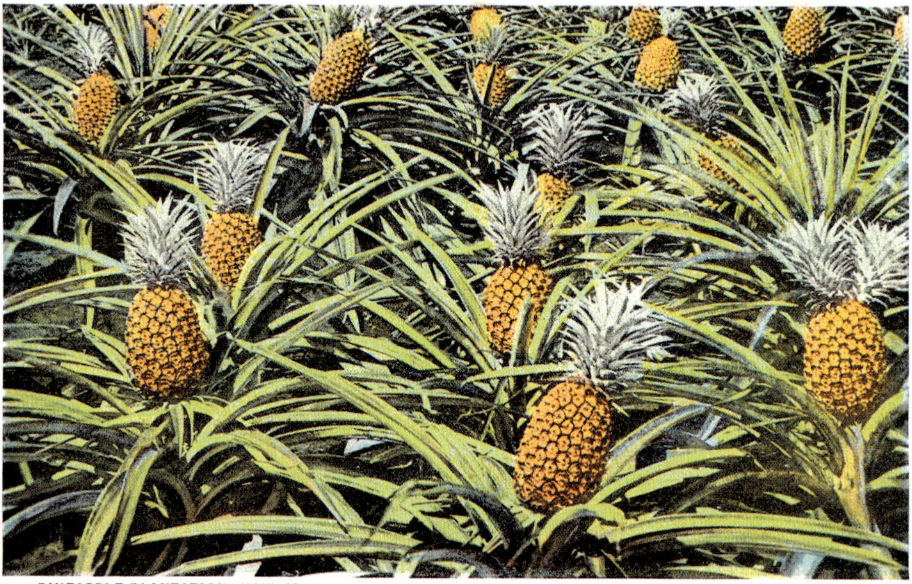

PINEAPPLE PLANTATION, HAWAII.

From the back: "The chief market for this product is the United States. A large quantity of the fruit is consumed in Hawaii and the juice is used for making a most refreshing and cooling drink." [pre-1920, $2-5]

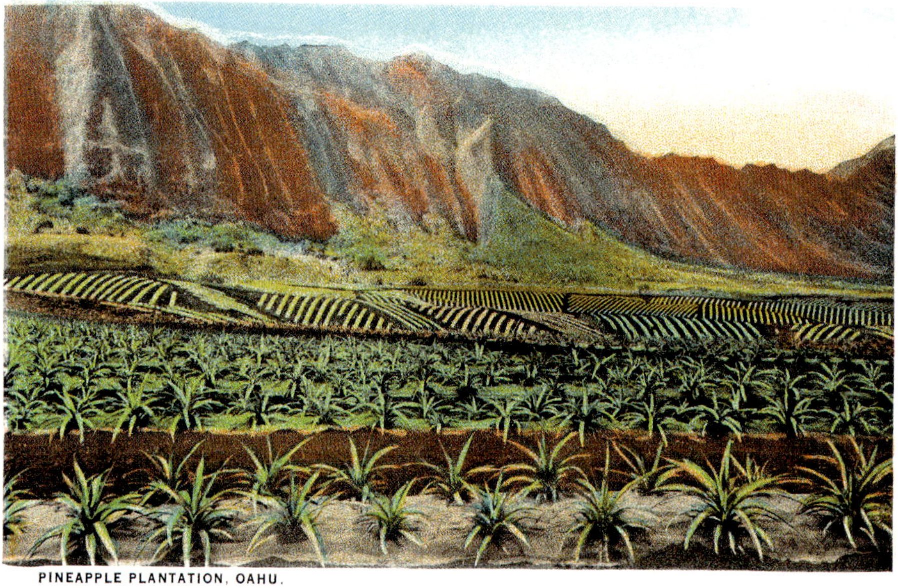

PINEAPPLE PLANTATION, OAHU.

From the back: "Pineapple plantation 'on the other side' (Koolau District) of Oahu Island. Note also the steep precipices of the Koolau mountain range and the Pali needle to the left. The pale silvery green of double rows of pineapple plants extends in all directions as far as your eye can see." [pre-1920, $2-5]

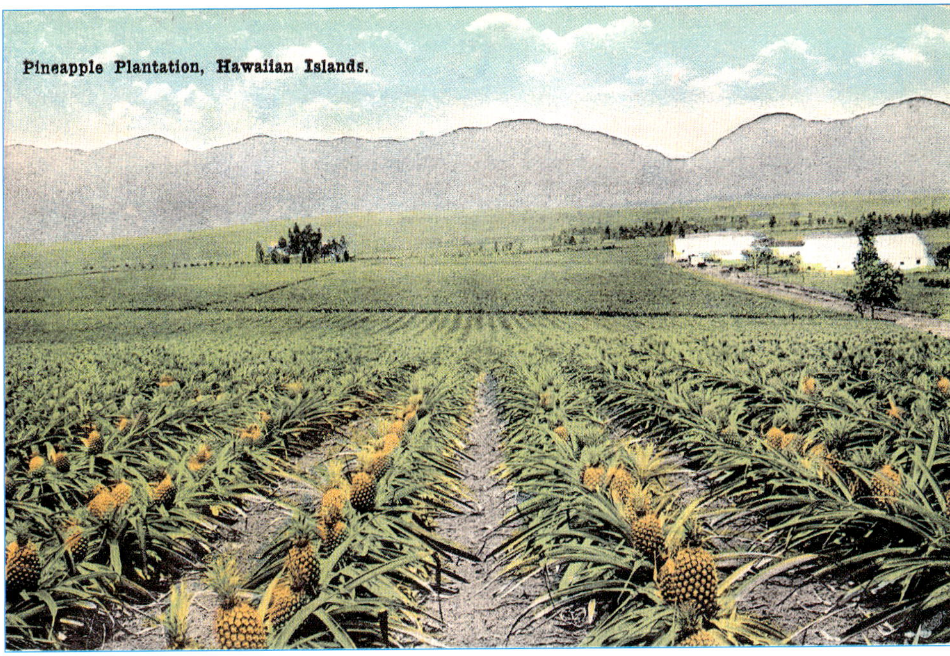

Pineapple plants can attain heights of up to five feet. [pre-1915, $4-7]

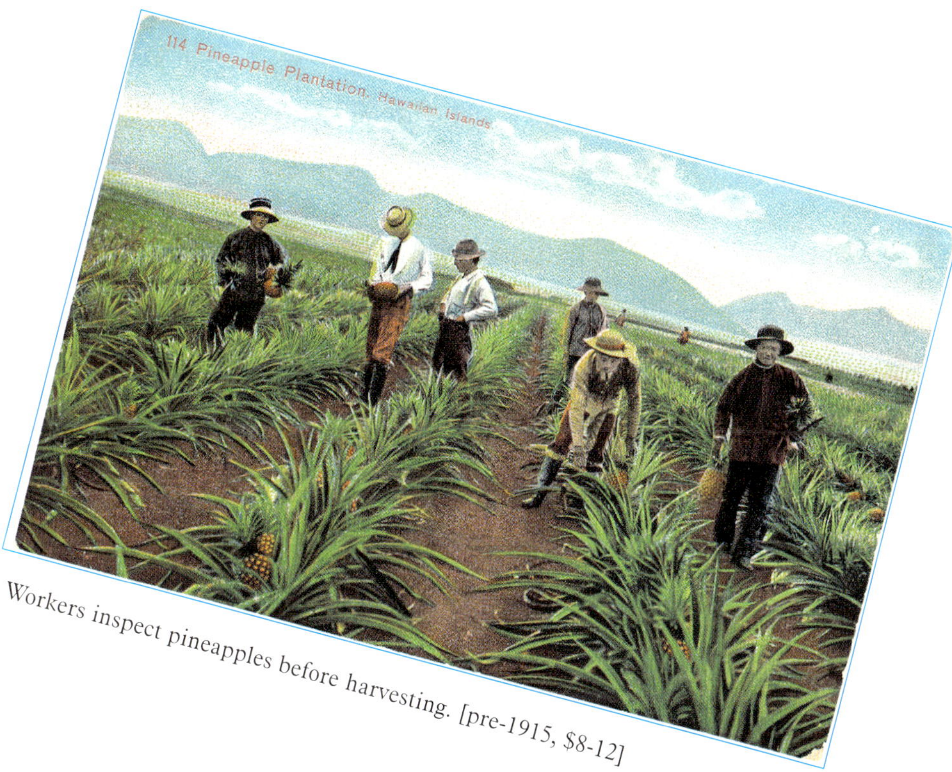

Workers inspect pineapples before harvesting. [pre-1915, $8-12]

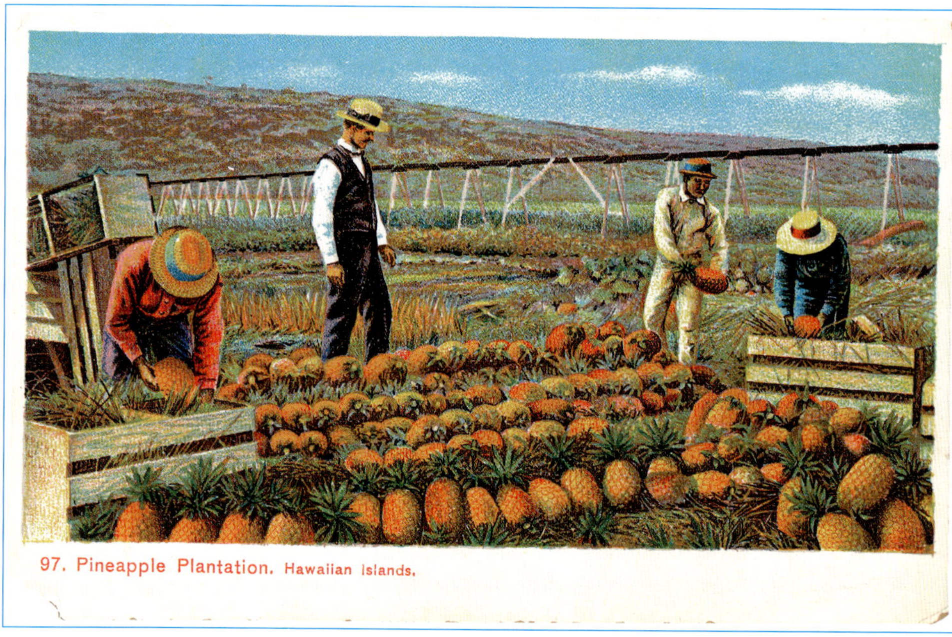

Workers prepare pineapples to be transported to processing plants, shearing off the tops so that more can be packed into the crates. [pre-1915, $13-17]

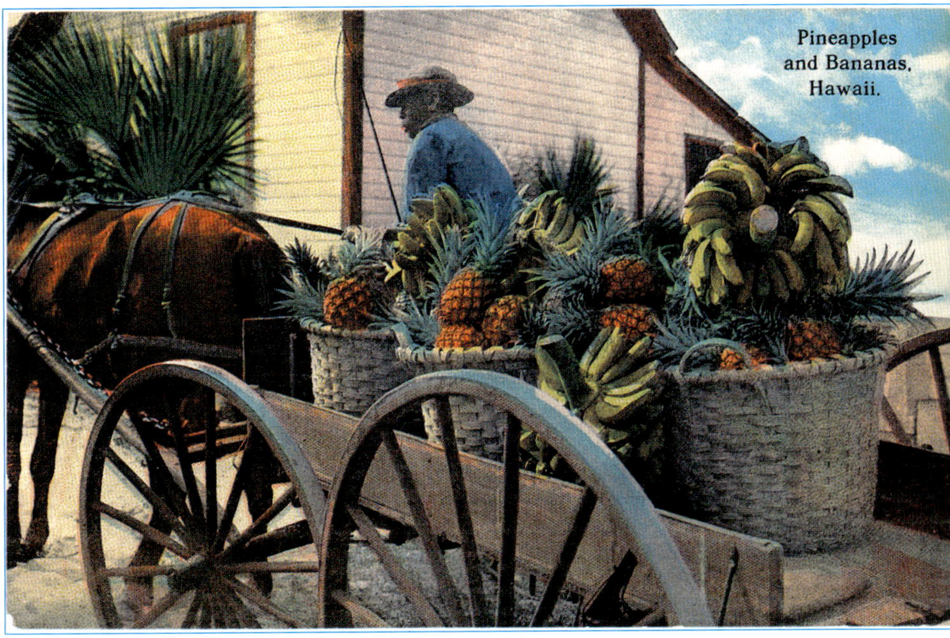

A local merchant sells pineapples and bananas off the back of his cart. [pre-1915, $6-9]

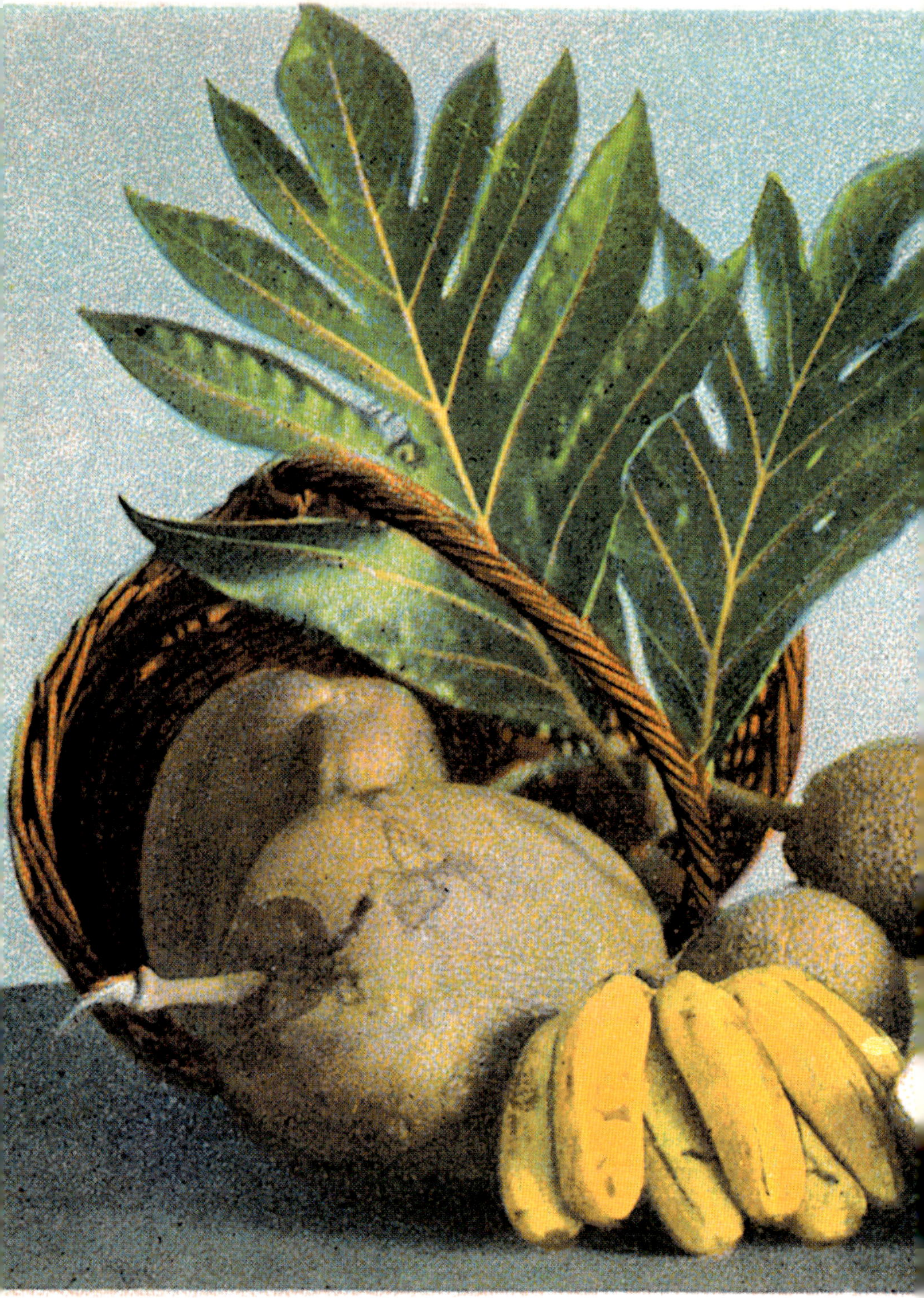

HAWAIIAN FRUITS.

[pre-1915, $3-5]

Fruits in Abundance

Hawaii presented visitors with a virtual cornucopia of fresh fruits to be savored. The flavors of pineapple, banana, mango, papaya, and coconut embody the tropical experience, so it's little wonder that their images were often used as mementoes of paradise.

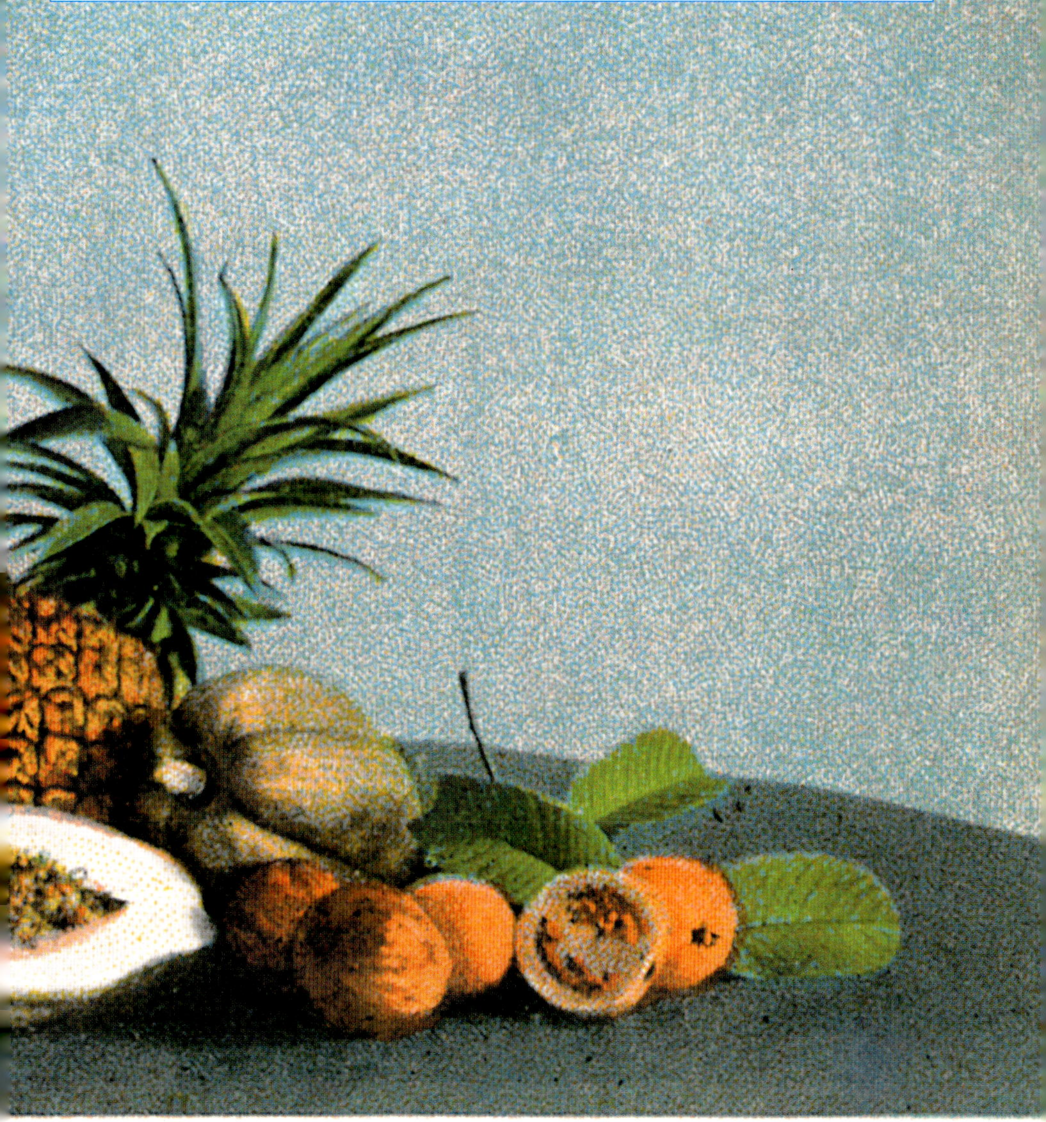

93194

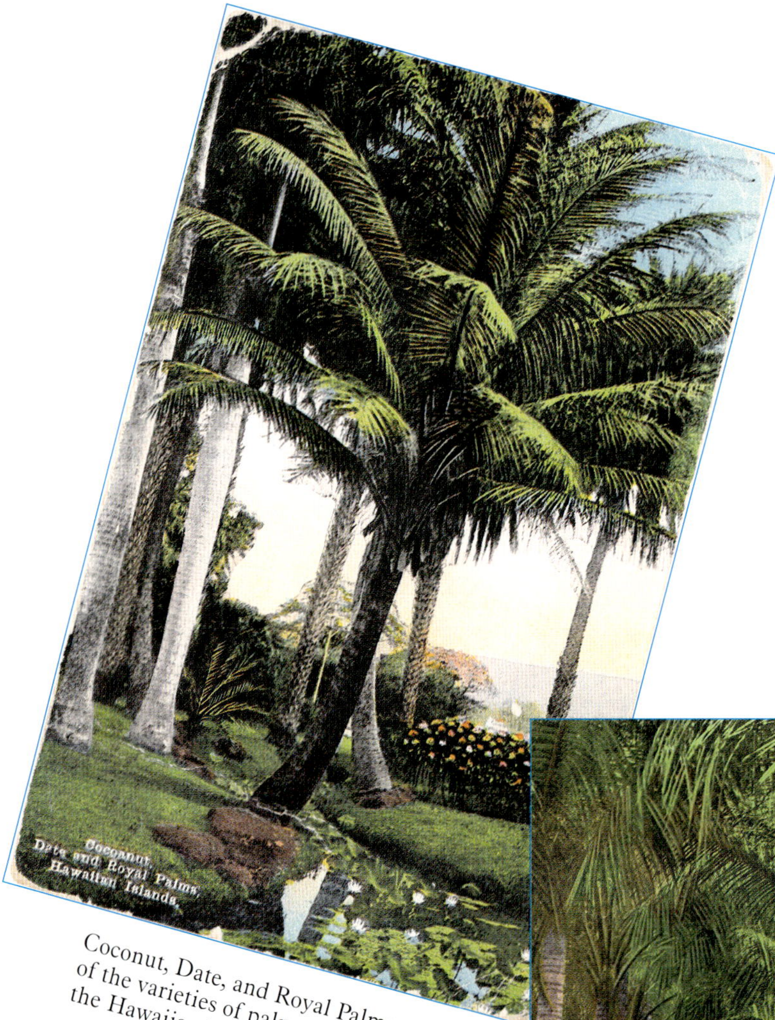

Coconut, Date, and Royal Palms are three of the varieties of palm that are grown on the Hawaiian Islands. [pre-1915, $2-4]

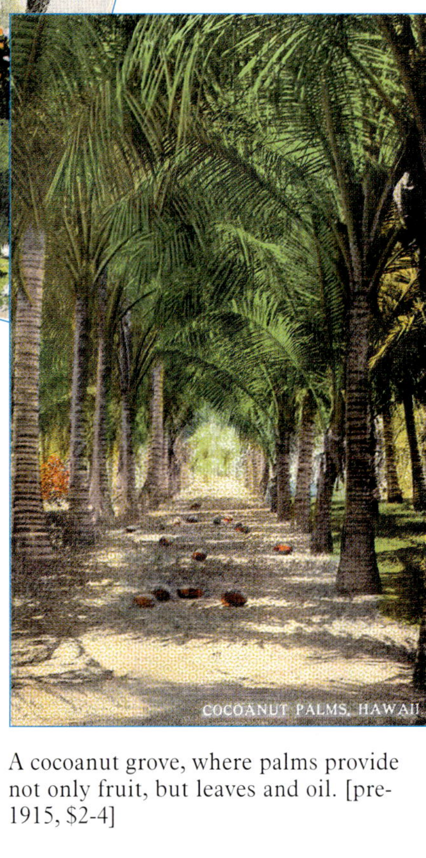

A cocoanut grove, where palms provide not only fruit, but leaves and oil. [pre-1915, $2-4]

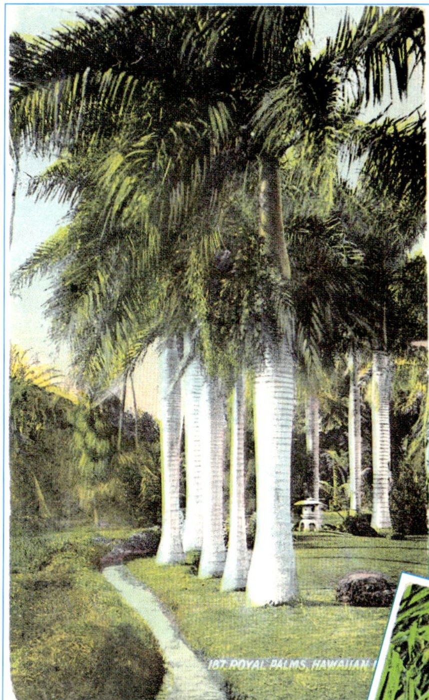

The Royal Palm can sometimes grow to heights of fifty feet or taller. [pre-1915, $2-4]

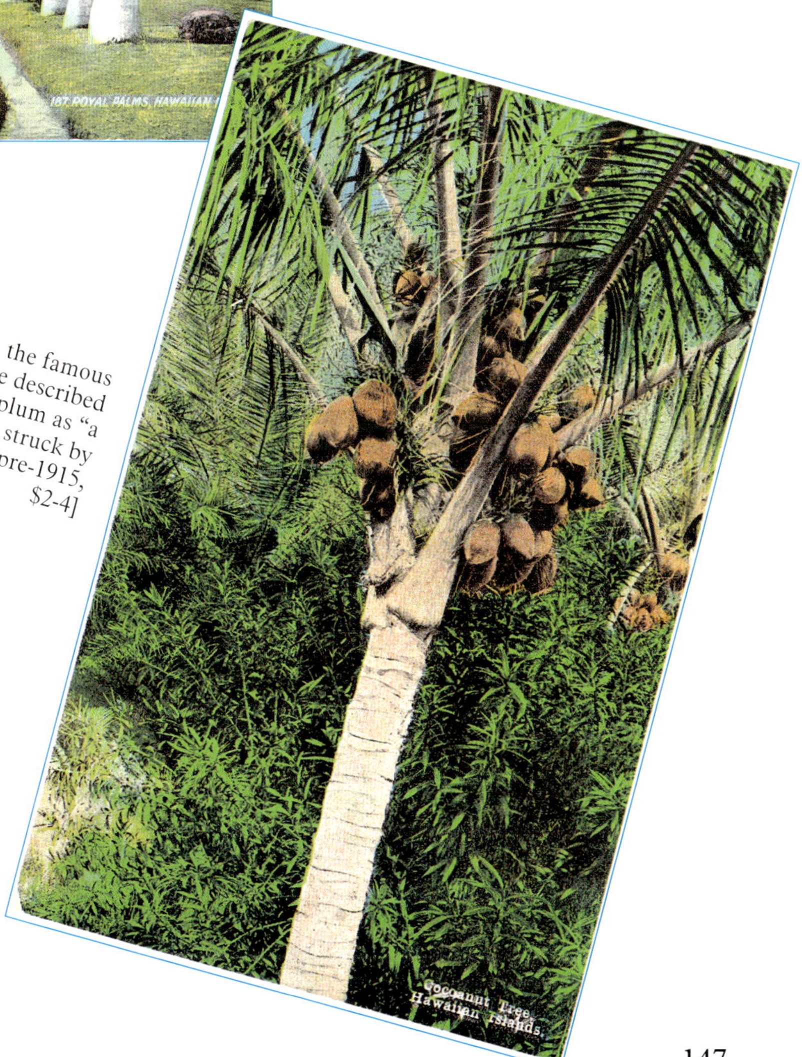

Mark Twain, the famous author, once described the coconut plum as "a feather duster struck by lightning." [pre-1915, $2-4]

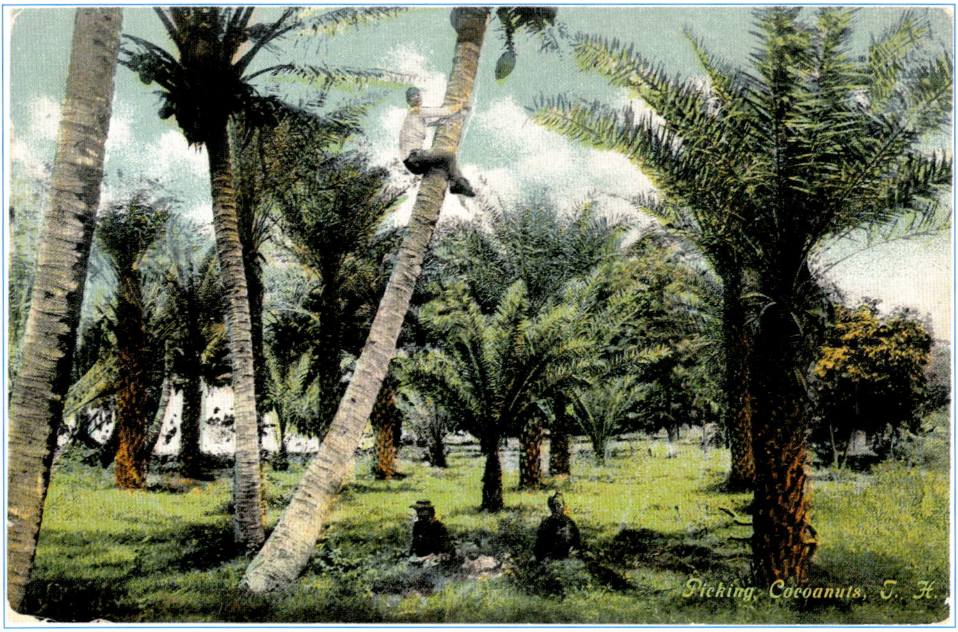

A memorable sight for tourists was watching natives defy gravity to climb palm trees and gather coconuts. The coconut palm's rough bark and sloping trunk aids in the endeavor. [pre-1915, $3-5]

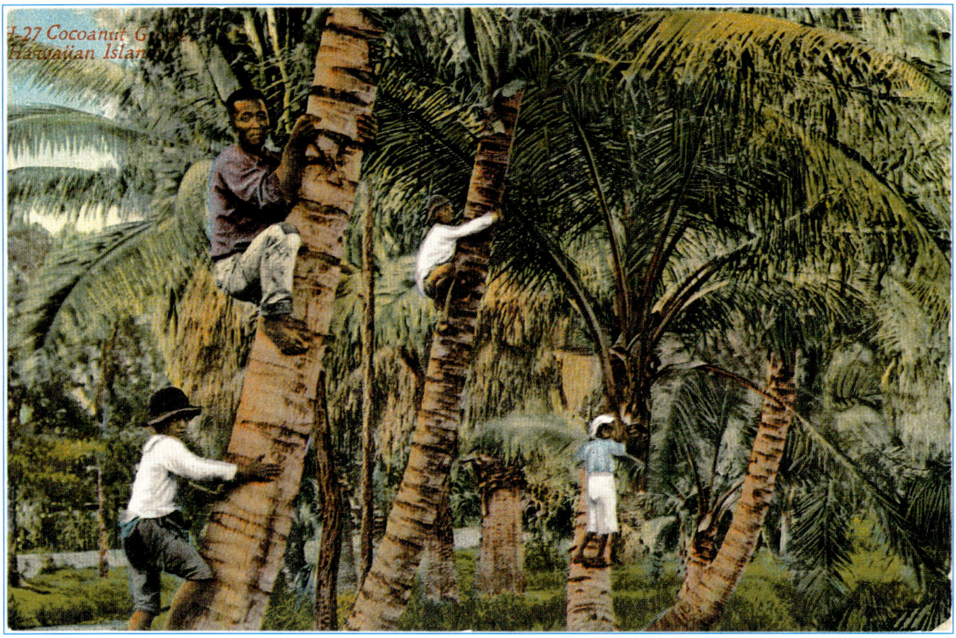

[pre-1915, $3-7]

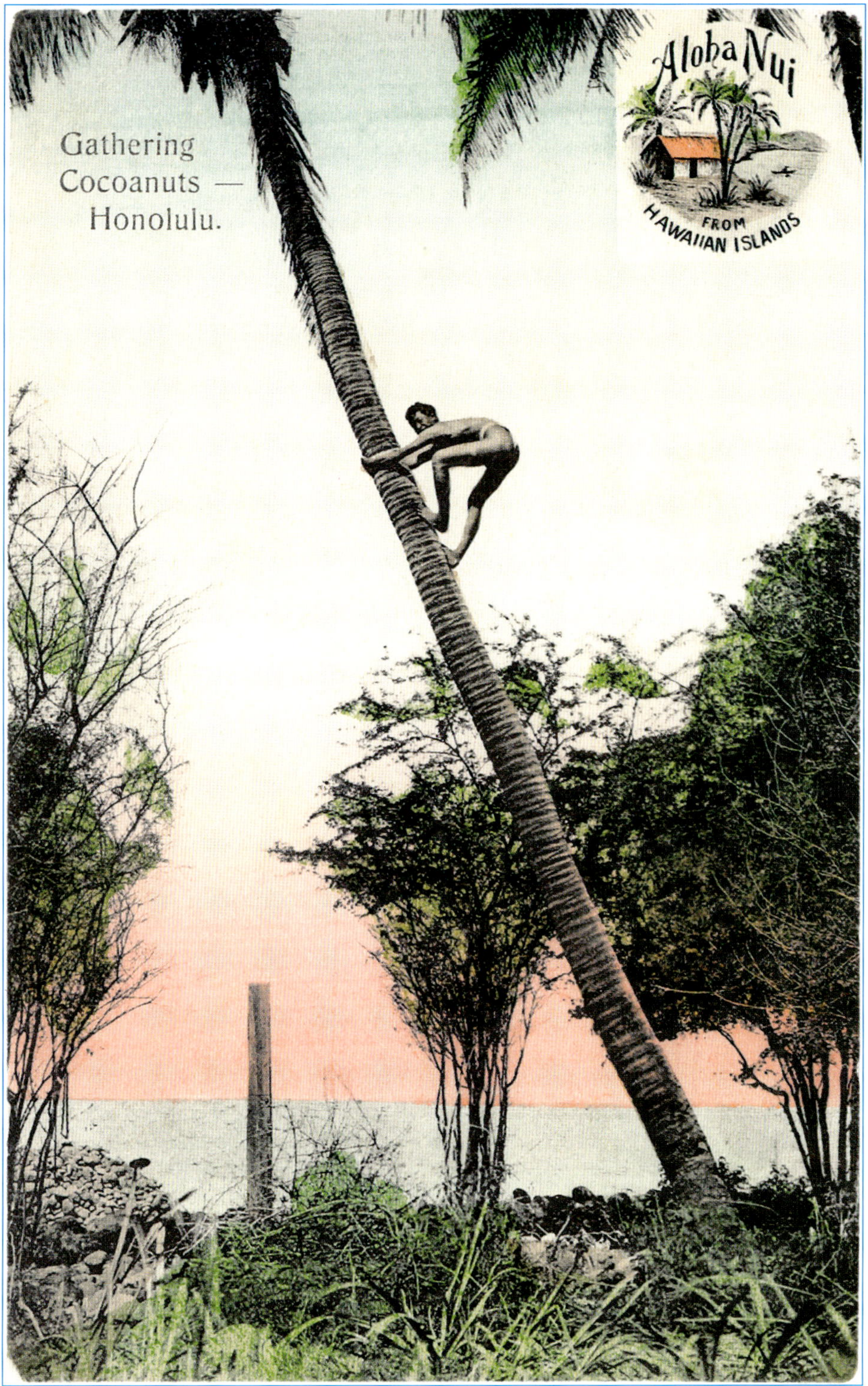

[pre-1915, $20-30]

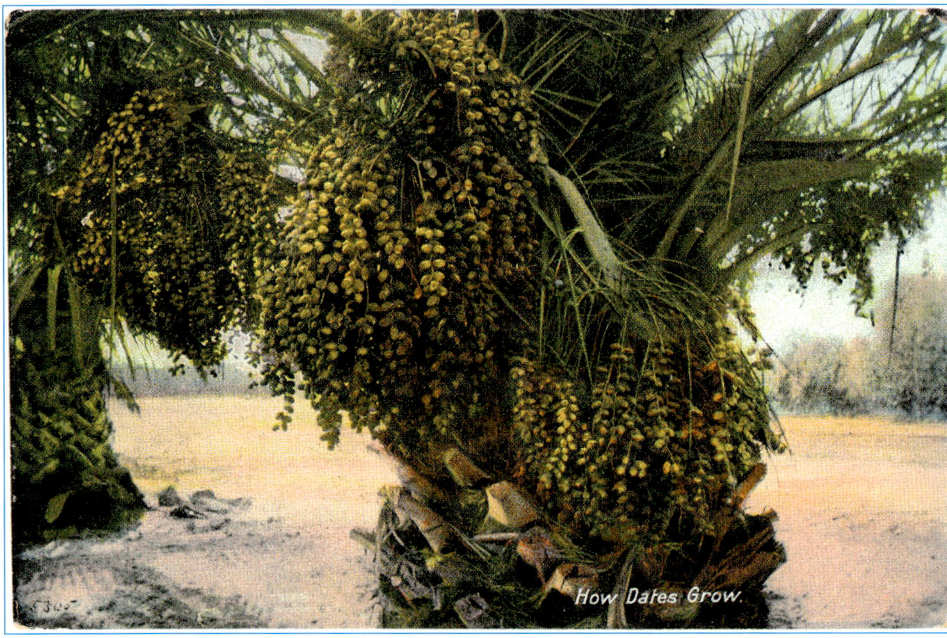

Date Palms only produce fruit when they reach five feet or taller in height. [canceled 1908, $2-4]

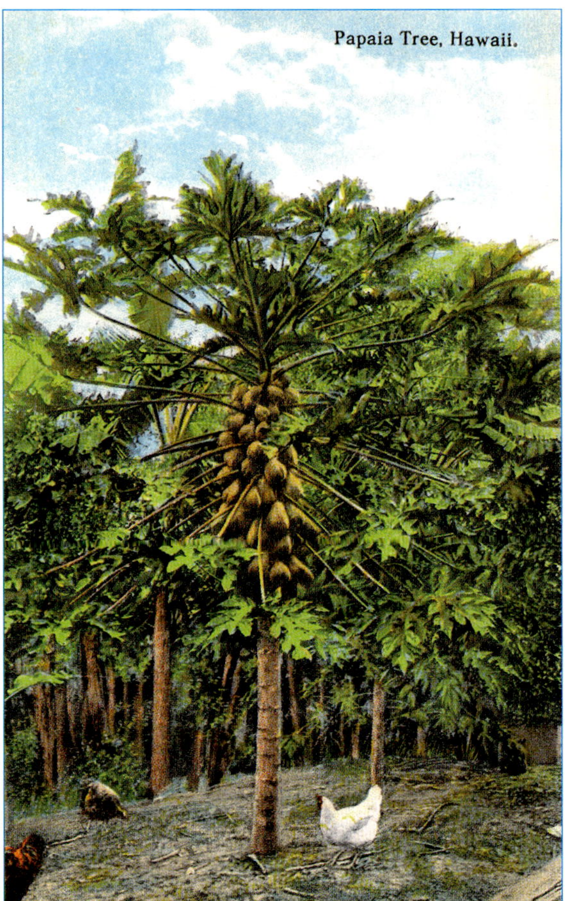

The fruit of the papaya tree is technically a berry, even though it looks like a melon. [pre-1915, $2-4]

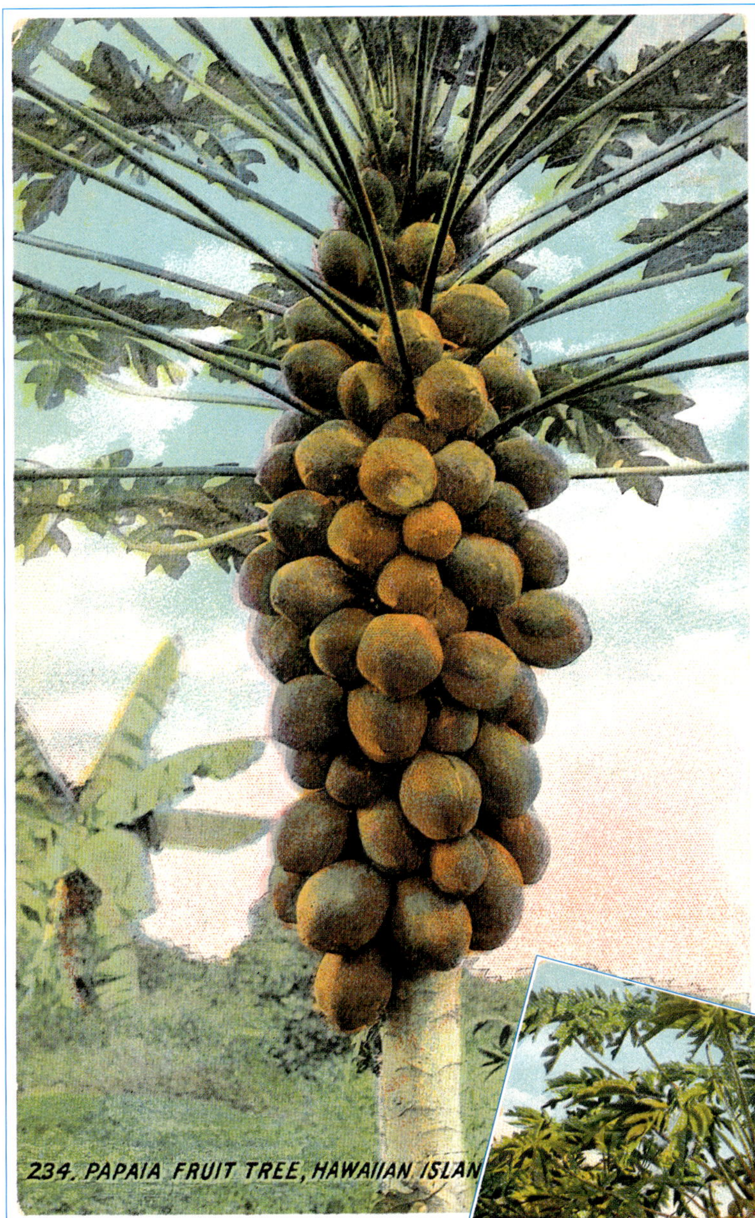

[pre-1915, $1-3]

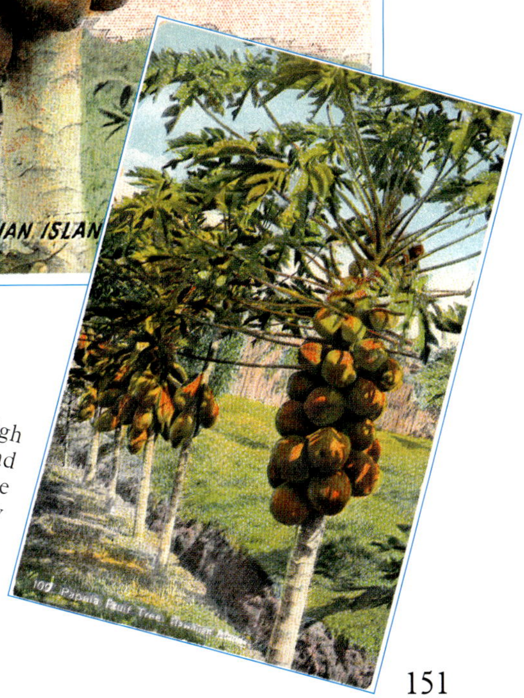

Papayas contain a high amount of pepsin and are considered by some to be an excellent remedy for poor digestion. [pre-1915, $1-3]

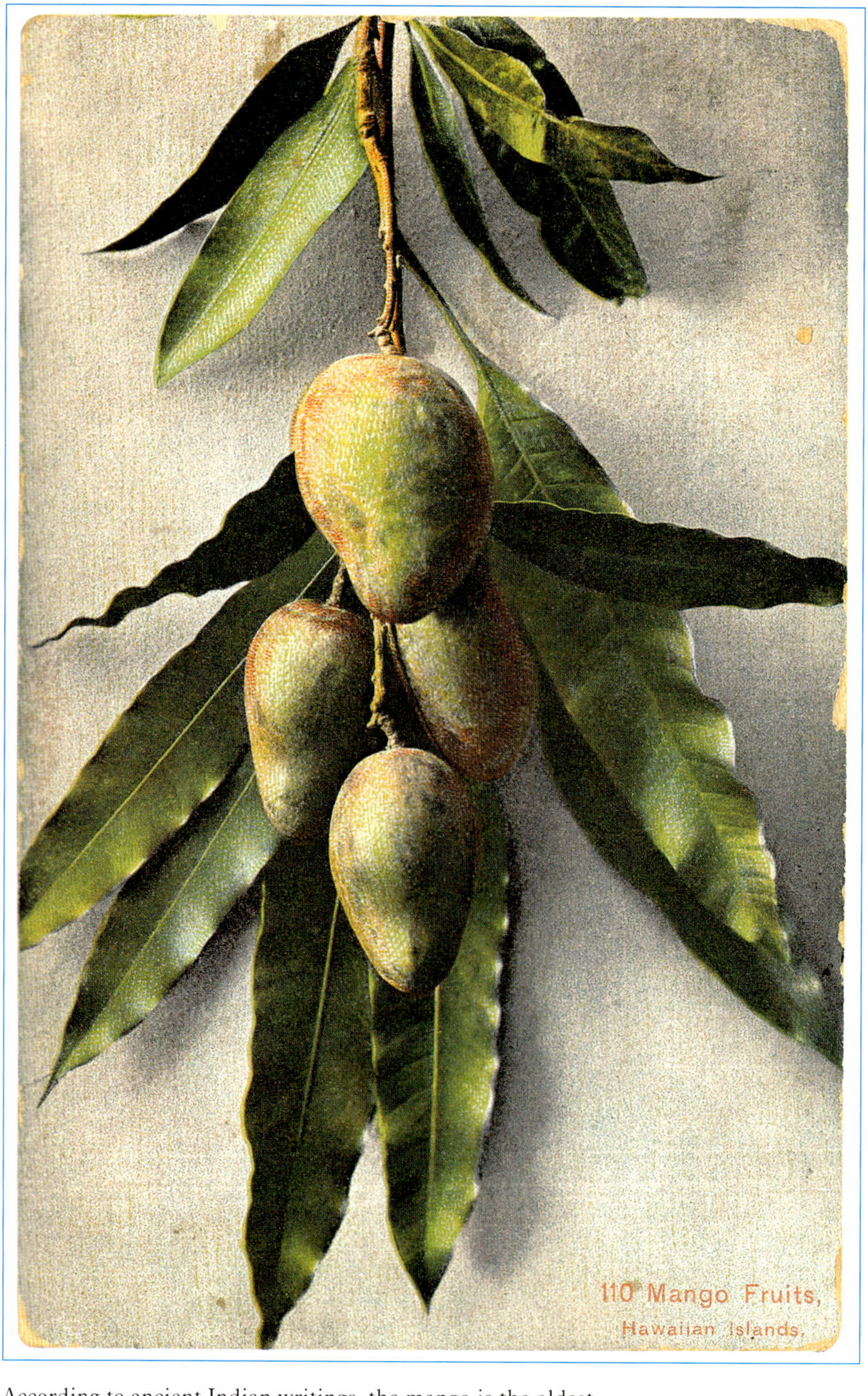

According to ancient Indian writings, the mango is the oldest cultivated plant in the world. [canceled 1913, $1-3]

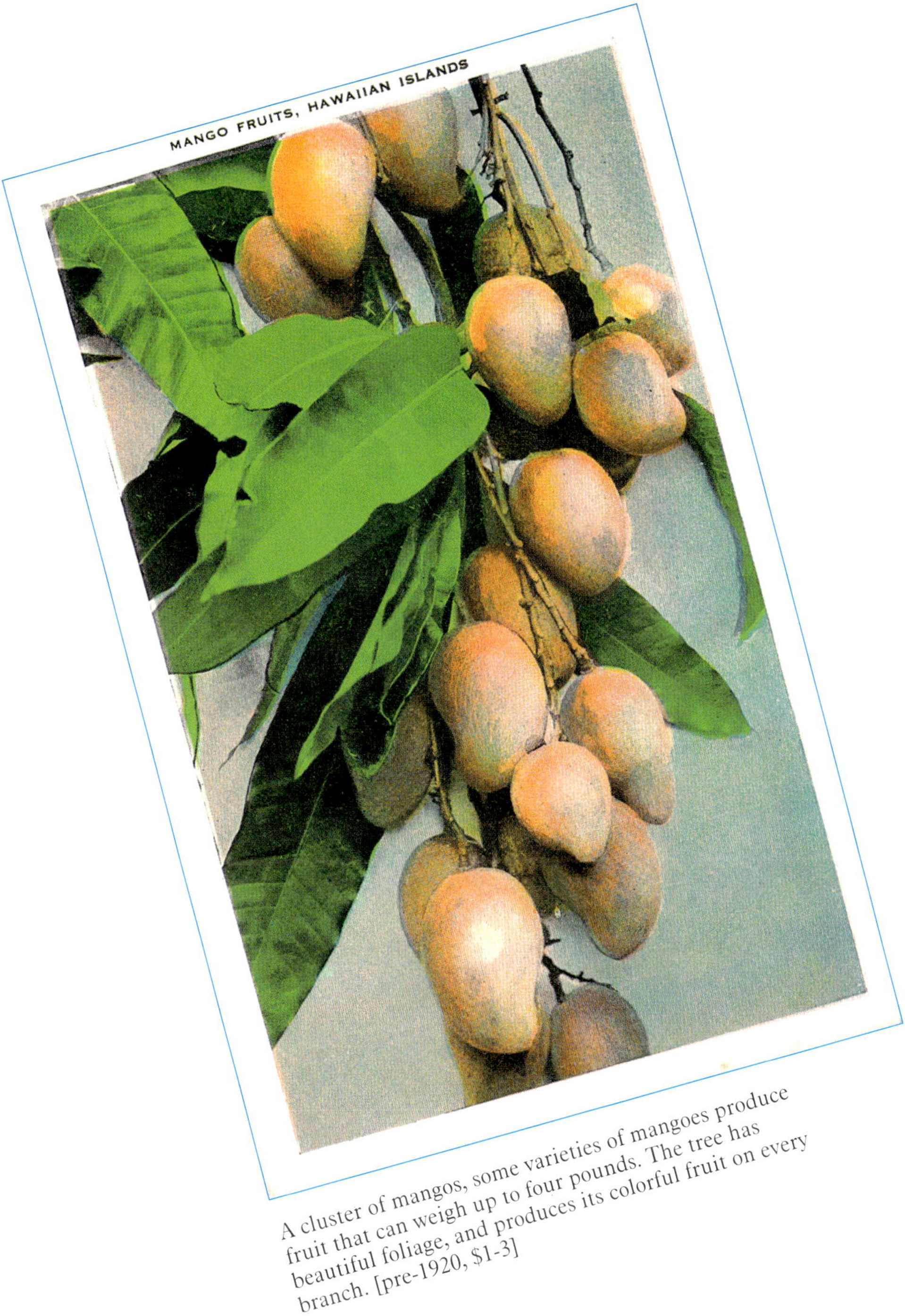

A cluster of mangos, some varieties of mangoes produce fruit that can weigh up to four pounds. The tree has beautiful foliage, and produces its colorful fruit on every branch. [pre-1920, $1-3]

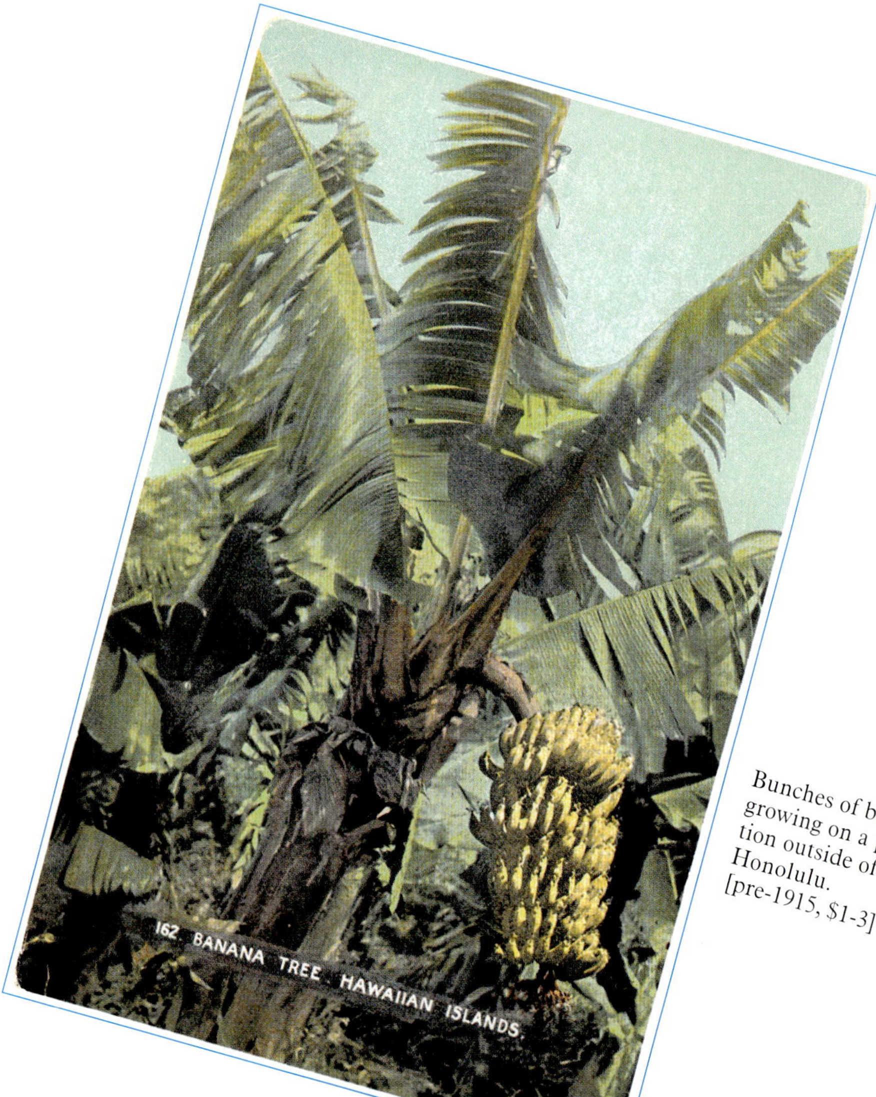

Bunches of bananas growing on a plantation outside of Honolulu. [pre-1915, $1-3]

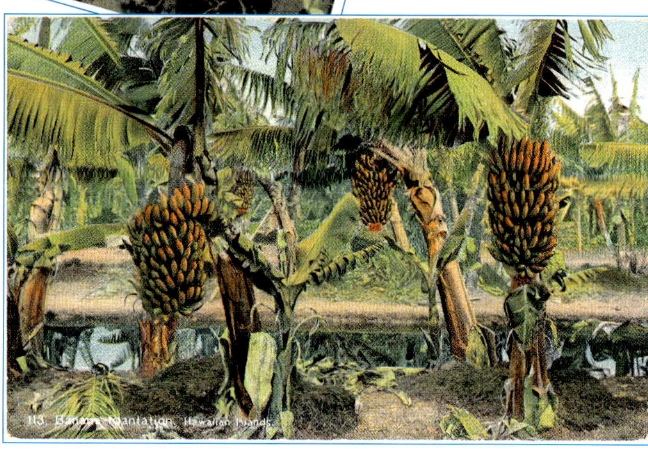

Ancient superstition said it was bad luck to dream about bananas or to take them on a fishing trip. [canceled 1909, $1-3]

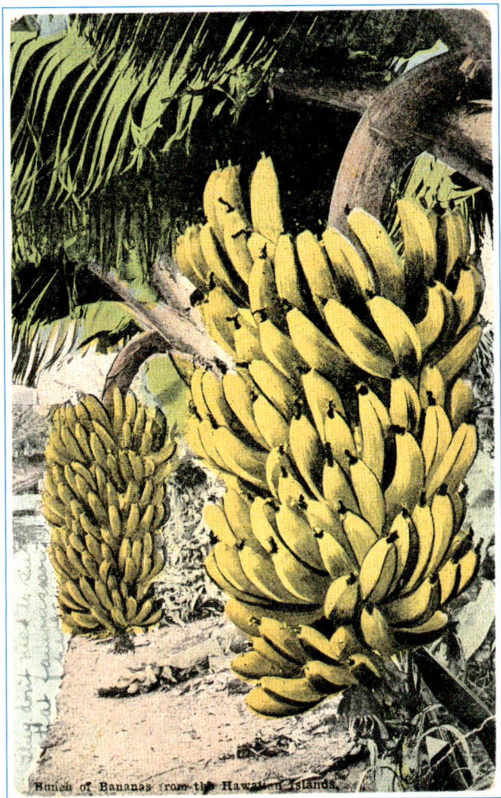

Banana trees need plenty of rich moist soil to grow. [canceled 1925, $2-4]

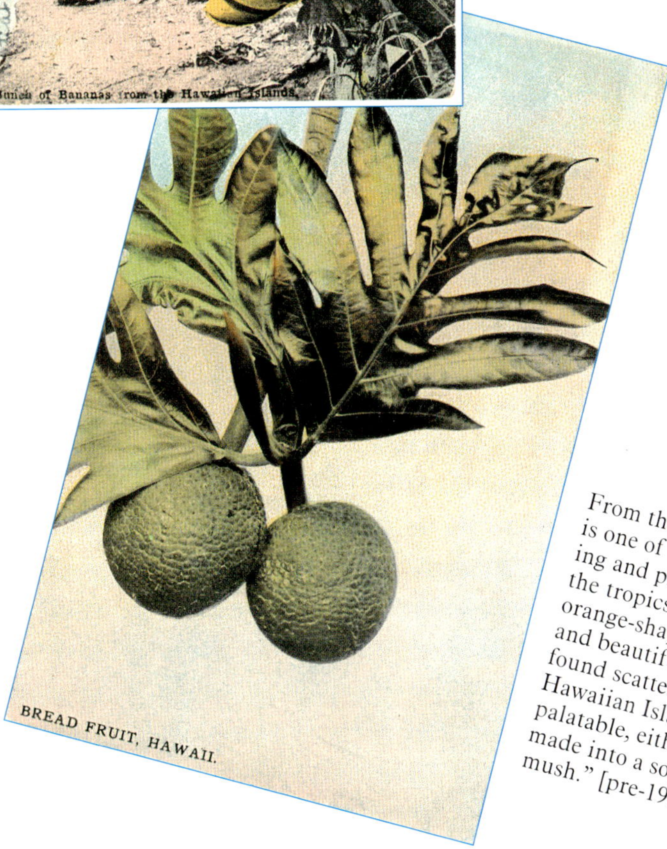

From the back: "Breadfruit is one of the most nourishing and plentiful foods of the tropics. It hangs, orange-shaped, from a large and beautiful tree, which is found scattered all over the Hawaiian Islands. It is very palatable, either baked or made into a sort of poi or mush." [pre-1915, $1-3]

East Meets West

Westerners invaded Hawaii all out, from the tourists and plantation owners, to the government advisors who eventually oversaw the union with the United States. The following pictures help chronicle the evolution toward Western development of the islands.

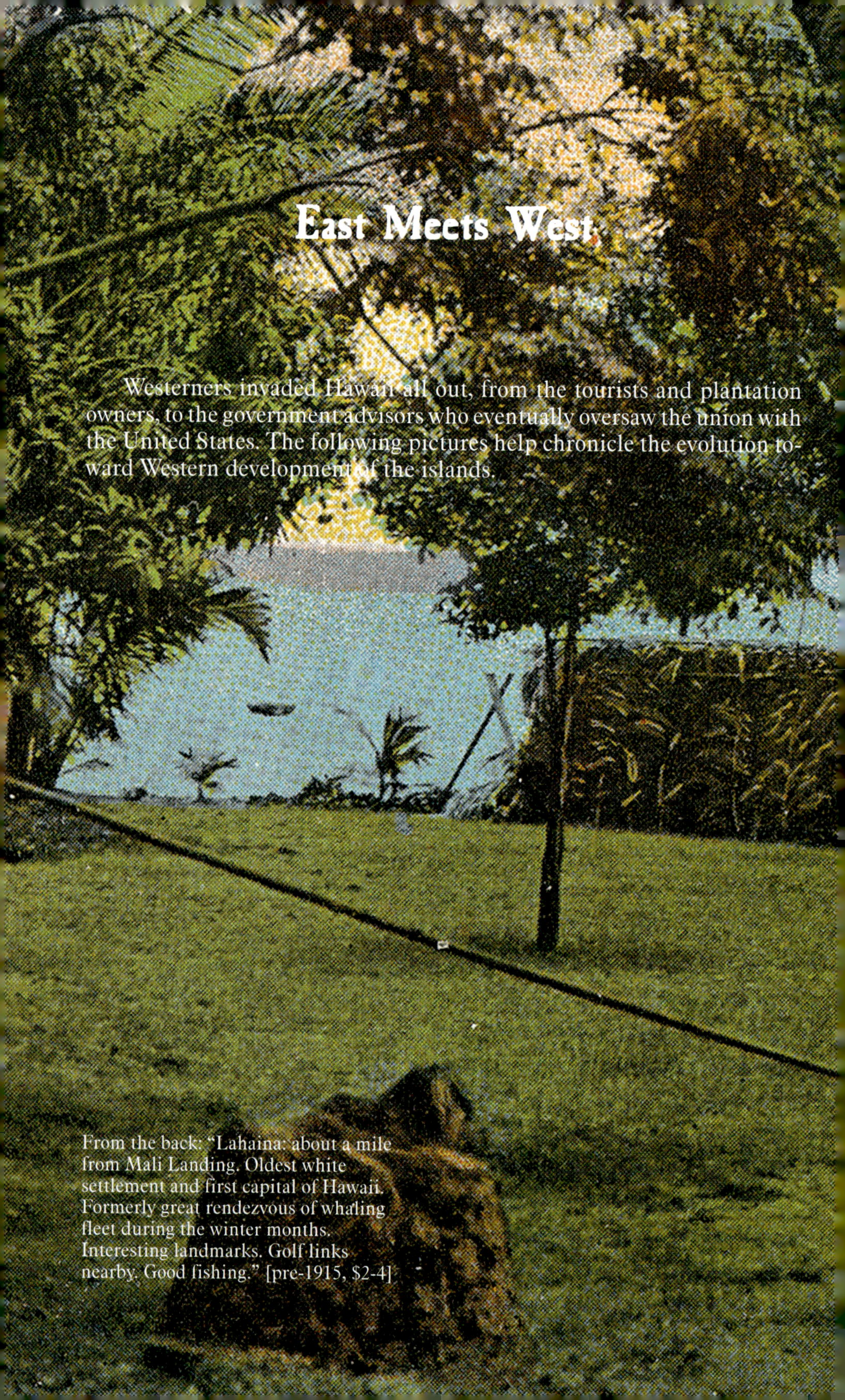

From the back: "Lahaina: about a mile from Mali Landing. Oldest white settlement and first capital of Hawaii. Formerly great rendezvous of whaling fleet during the winter months. Interesting landmarks. Golf links nearby. Good fishing." [pre-1915, $2-4]

Early Settlements

From the back: "Lahaina: about a mile from Mali Landing. Oldest white settlement and first capital of Hawaii. Formerly great rendezvous of whaling fleet during the winter months. Interesting landmarks. Golf links nearby. Good fishing."

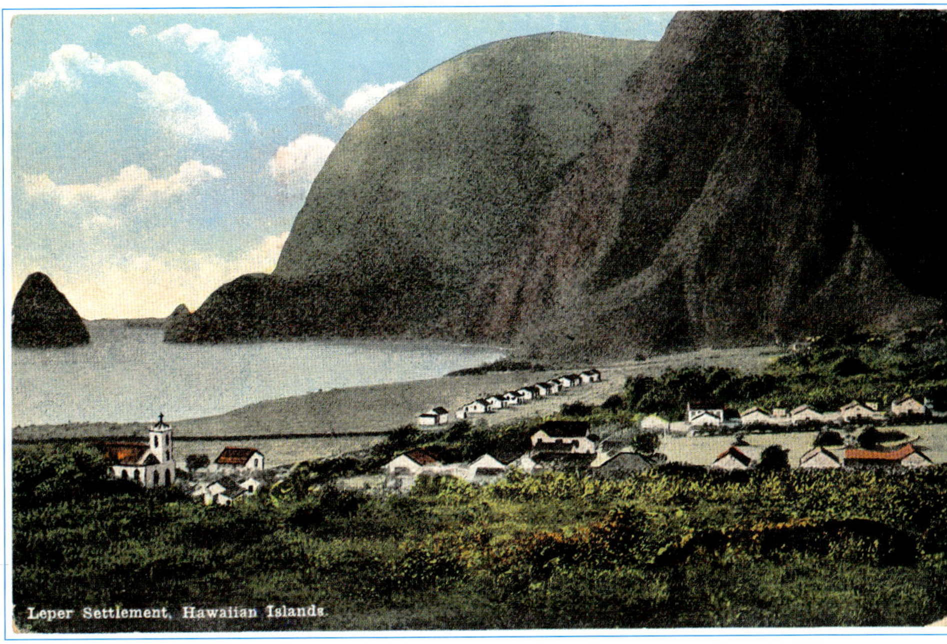

Leper settlement, Hawaiian Islands. [canceled 1928, $7-12]

Laupahoehoe Hawaii, one of the many landing places on the coast of Hawaii. [pre-1915, $7-12]

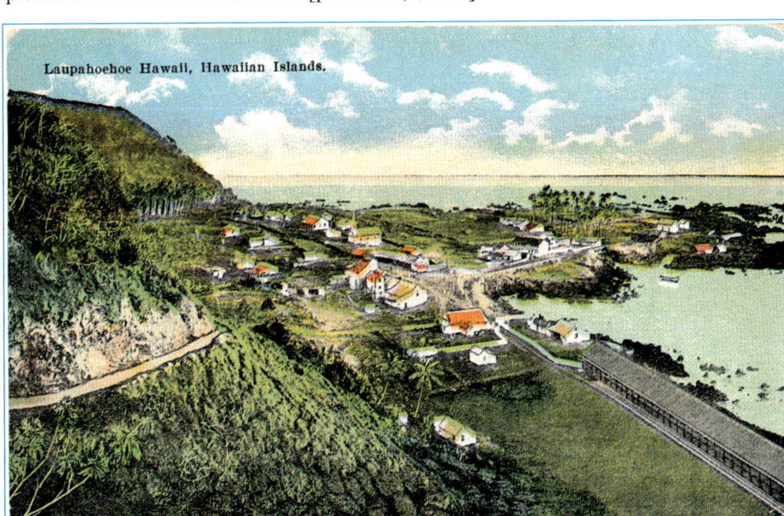

Honolulu

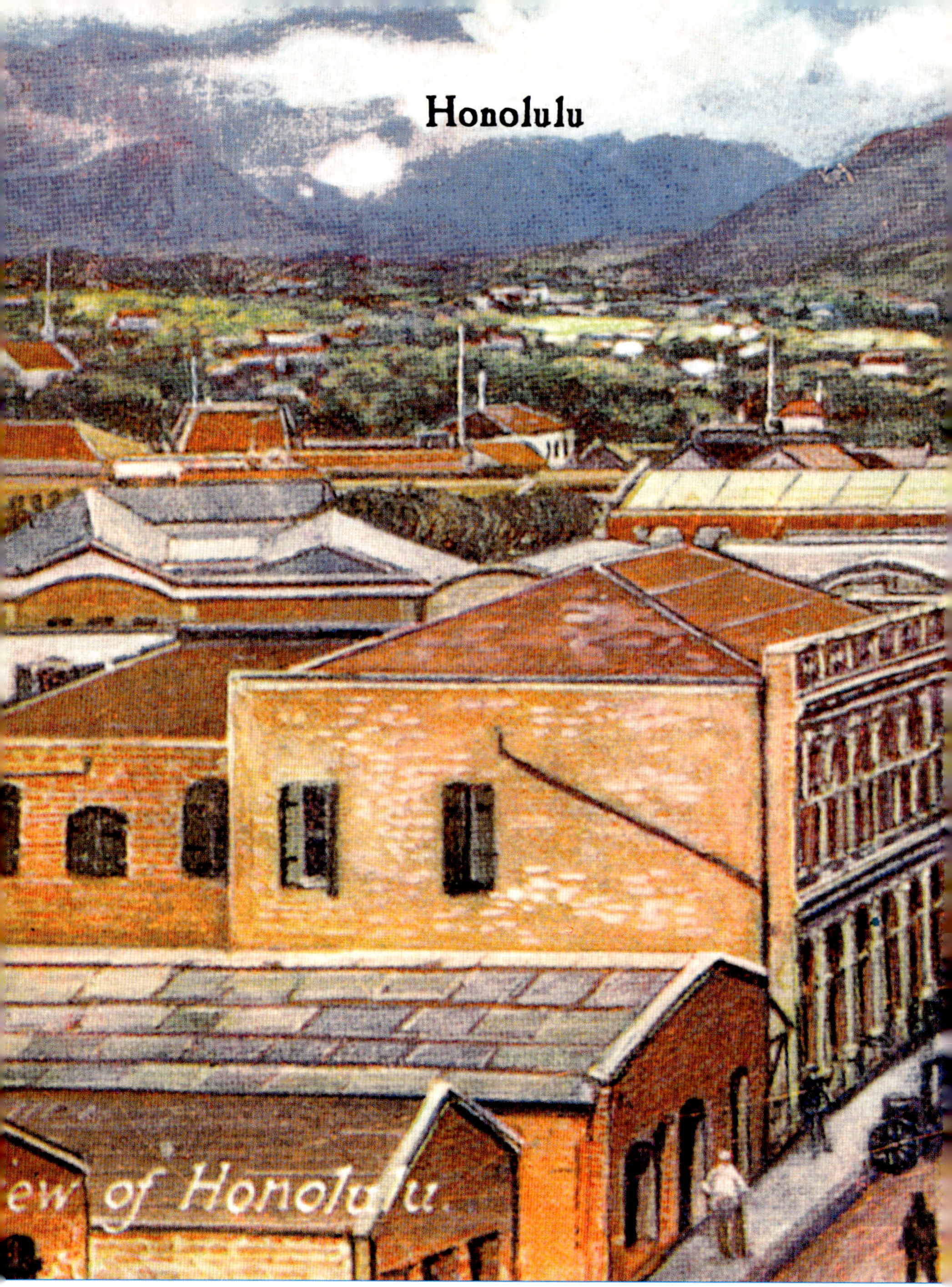

Located on the southeast coast of the island of Oahu, Honolulu was overlooked by Captain James Cook when he explored the islands in 1778. It was not until 1794 that William Brown, an English captain entered the harbor, whose name means "sheltered harbor." Honolulu's history from 1820, when missionaries arrived on the islands, is much

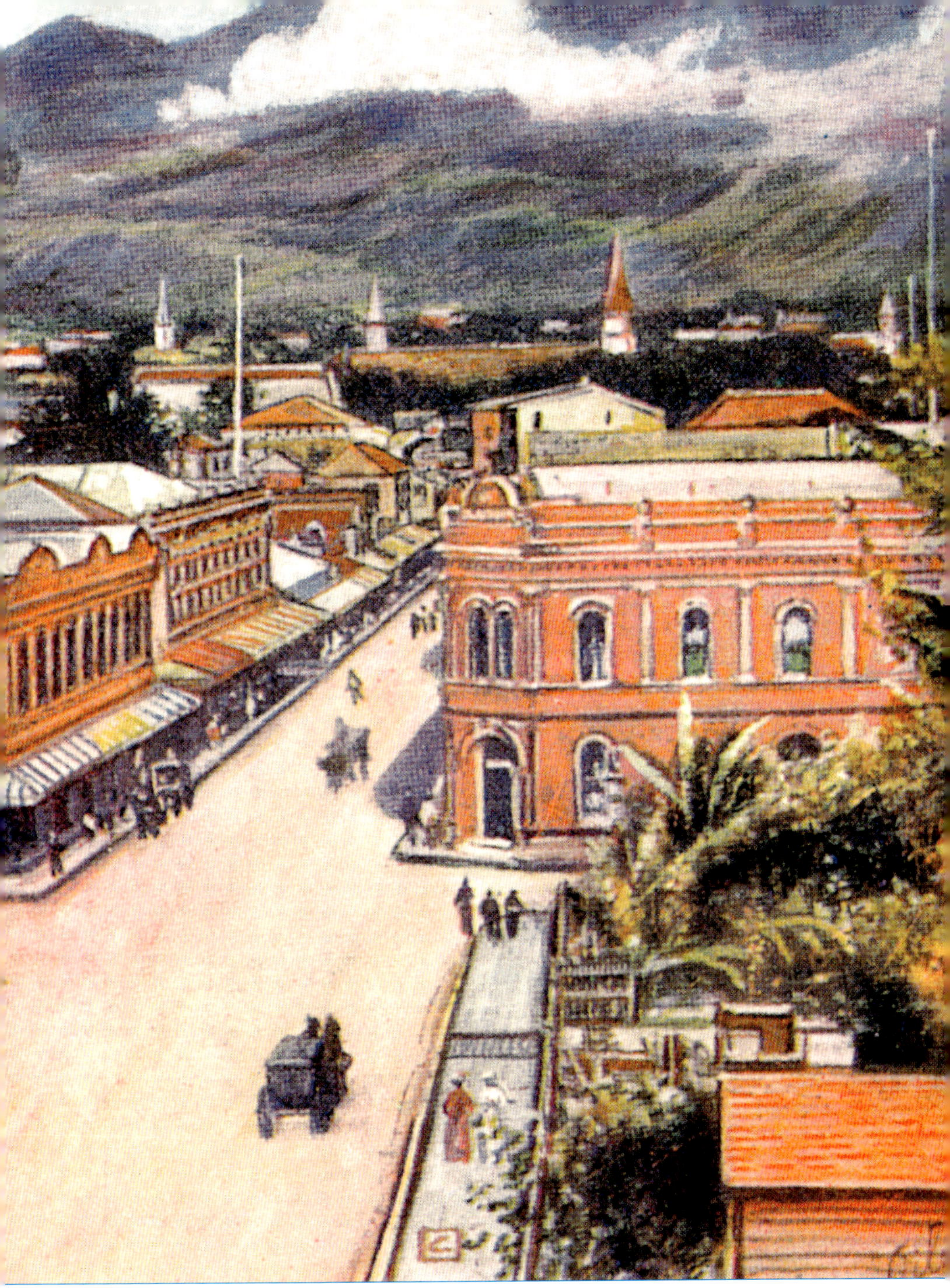

From the back: "Honolulu is a charming picturesque city, alluring in its wealth of tropical vegetation. It is built upon low ground, with towering hills at the back and a delightful sea in front. The streets are wide and irregular, but remarkably well paved and kept; and the buildings, in the main, are substantial and of modern construction. Honolulu contains fine stores, hotels and residences, such as are found in any large American city." [pre-1915, $8-10]

the same as that of Hawaii. Growing from a settlement of mud huts into the main residence of Hawaiian royalty and later of foreign consuls, Honolulu became the permanent capital of the kingdom of Hawaii in 1845. In the 19th century, it bacame an important port for European as well as American merchants, sandalwood traders, and whalers.

Today, Honolulu is the principal port of the Hawaiian Islands and is known as the crossroads of the Pacific. The city is famous for its beauty and the variety of its ethnic groups.

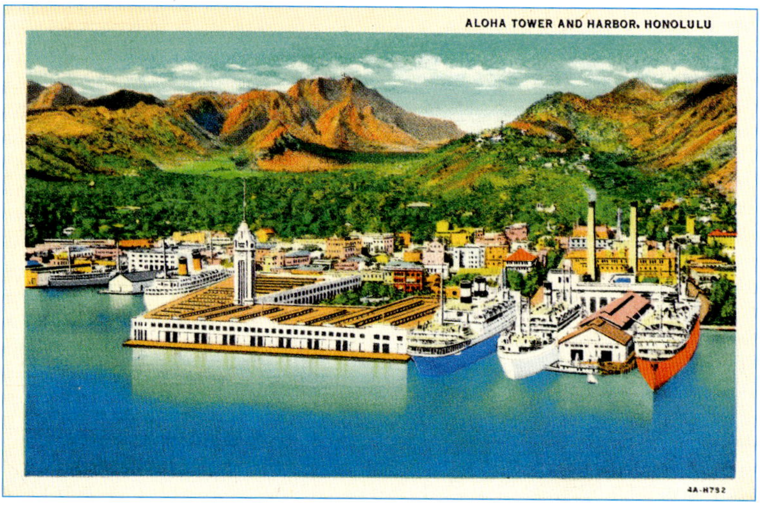

Honolulu Harbor, the "Crossroads of the Pacific, where steamer lines converge from North America, Australia, New Zealand, the Orient, and around the world." [canceled 1941, $5-6]

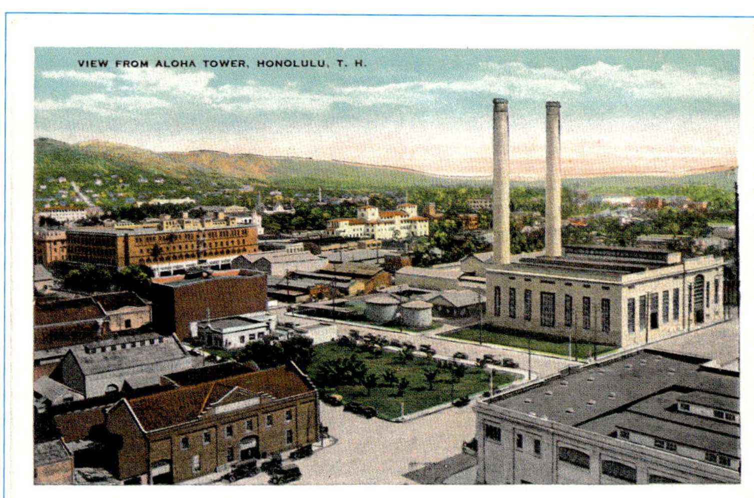

A view of downtown Honolulu as seen from the top of the Aloha Tower. [pre-1915, $15-17]

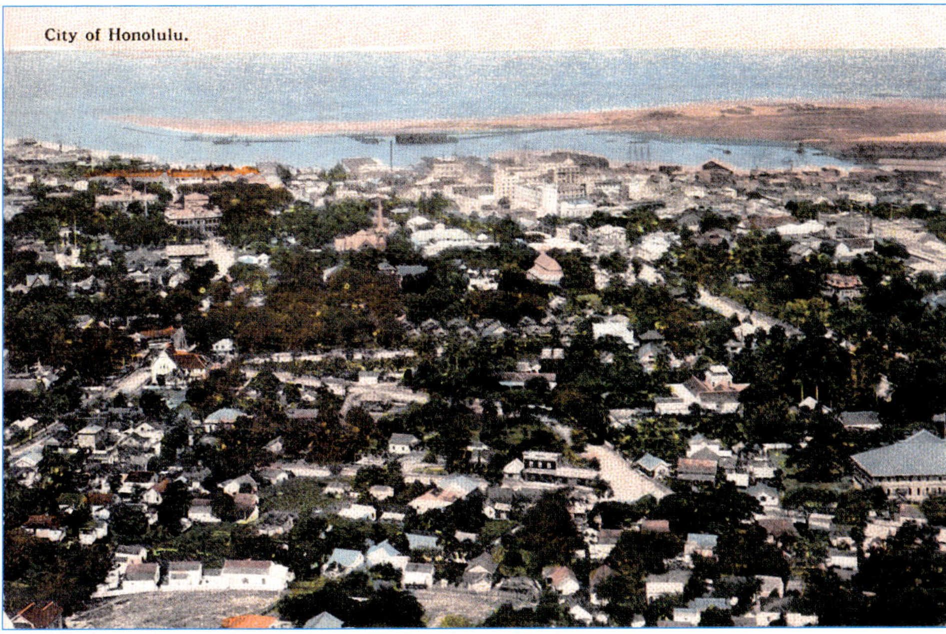

Honolulu, the Capital of Hawaii, and "the most beautiful city in the world." [pre-1915, $12-15]

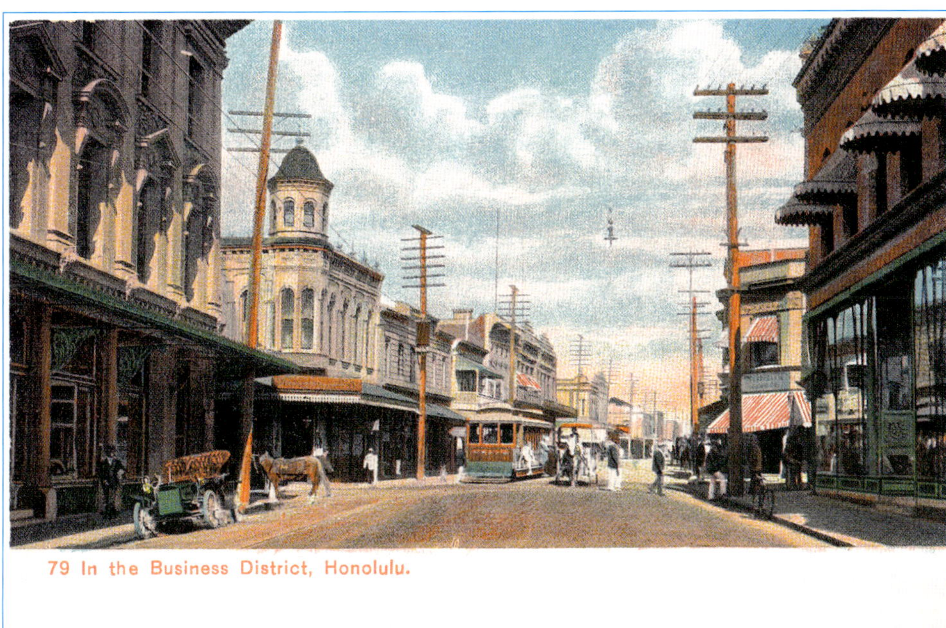

The Business District of Honolulu at King and Fort Streets. [pre-1915, $15-22]

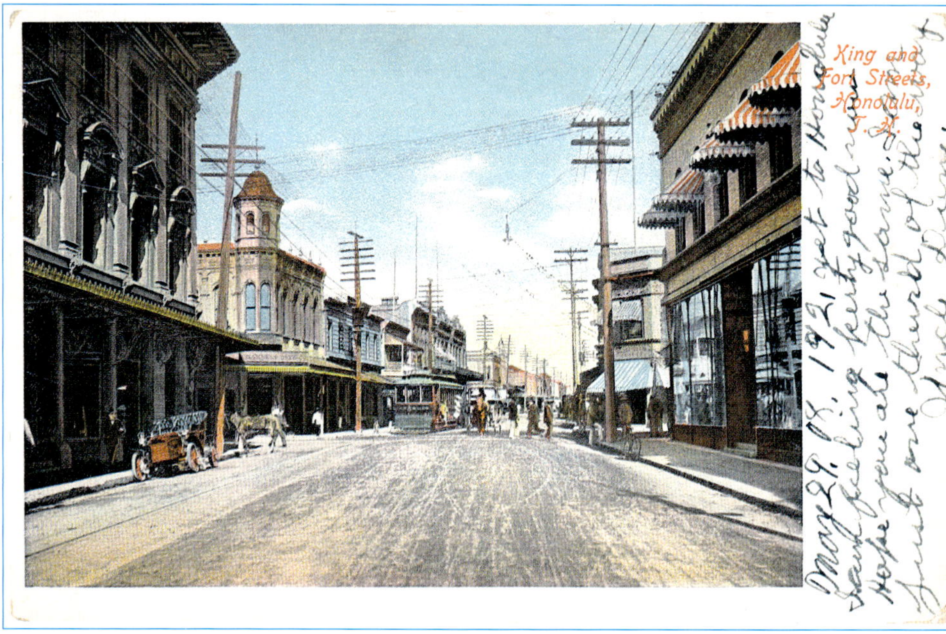

A greater perspective of the business district. [canceled 1908, $15-20]

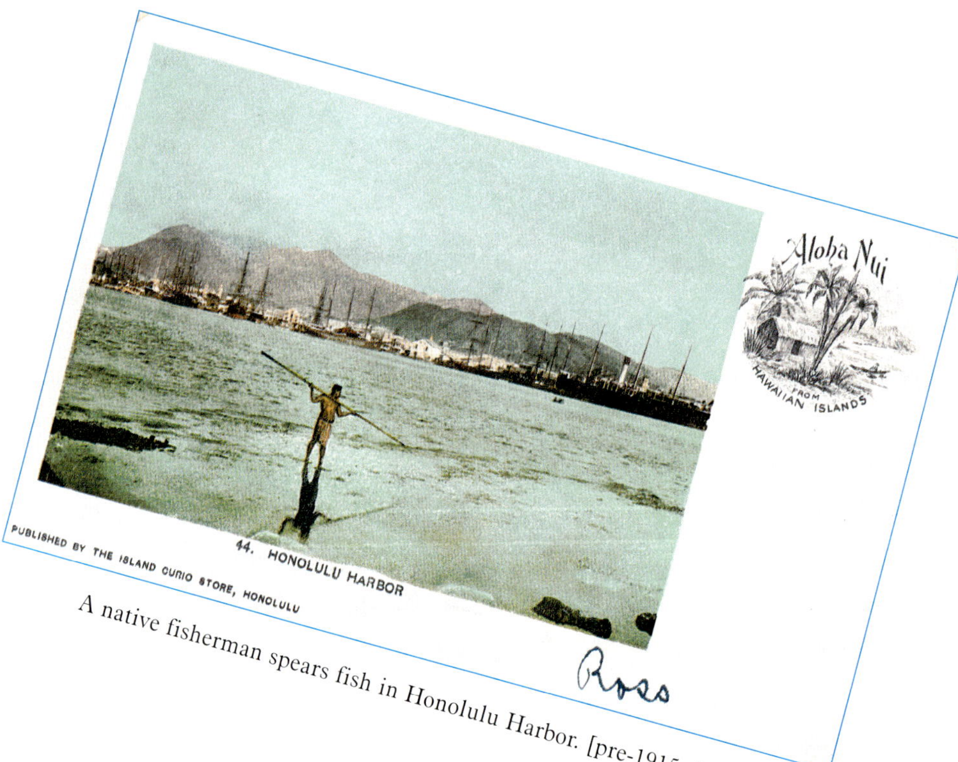

A native fisherman spears fish in Honolulu Harbor. [pre-1915, $20-35]

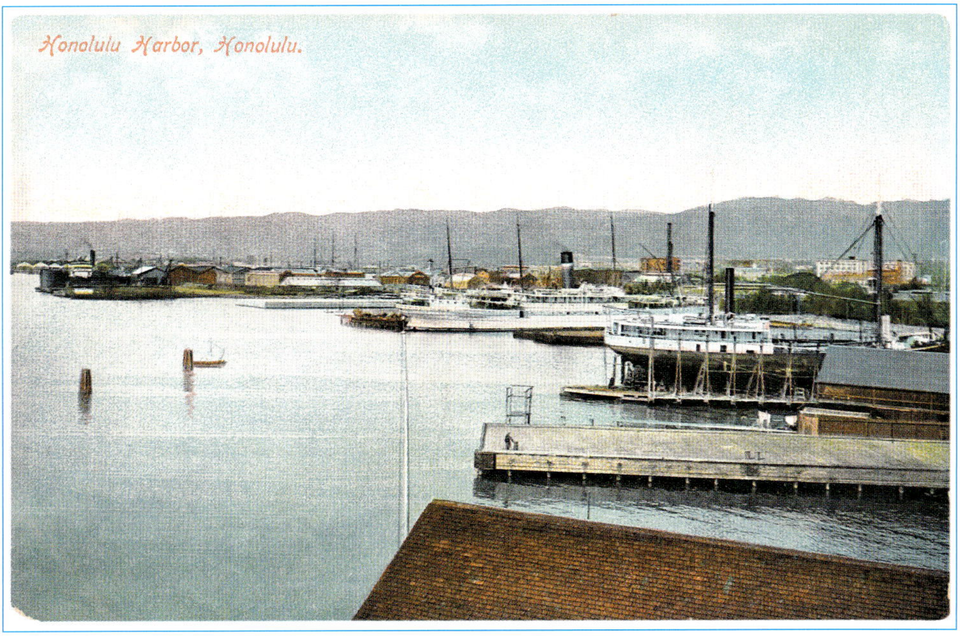

Honolulu Harbor is the destination for cruise ships from around the world. [pre-1915, $12-15]

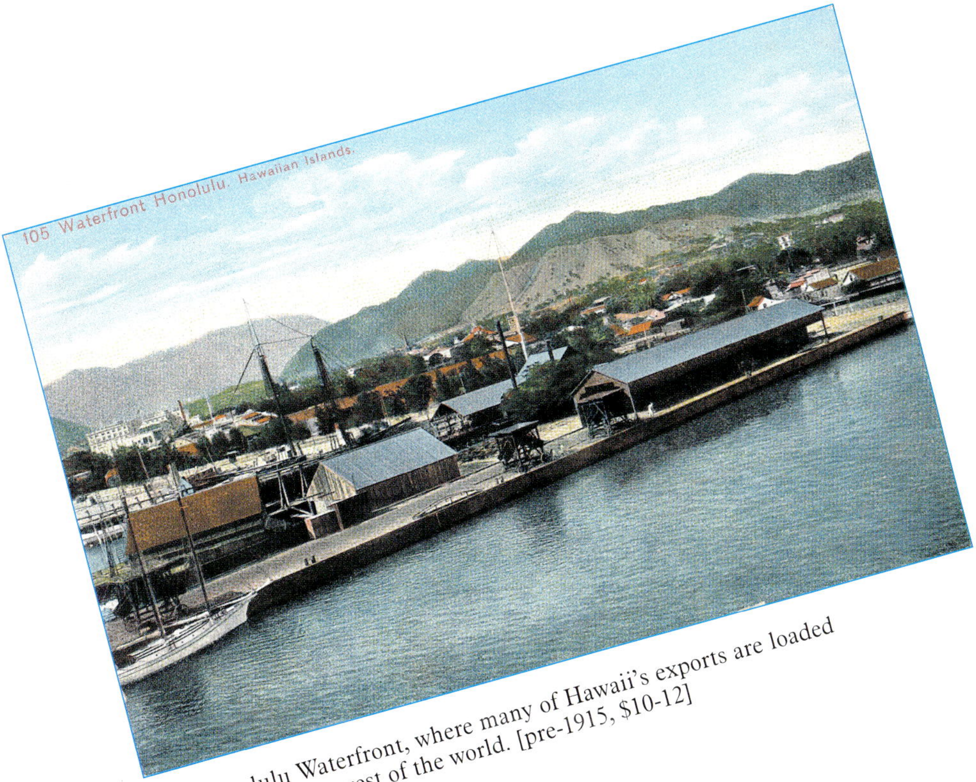

The Honolulu Waterfront, where many of Hawaii's exports are loaded and shipped to the rest of the world. [pre-1915, $10-12]

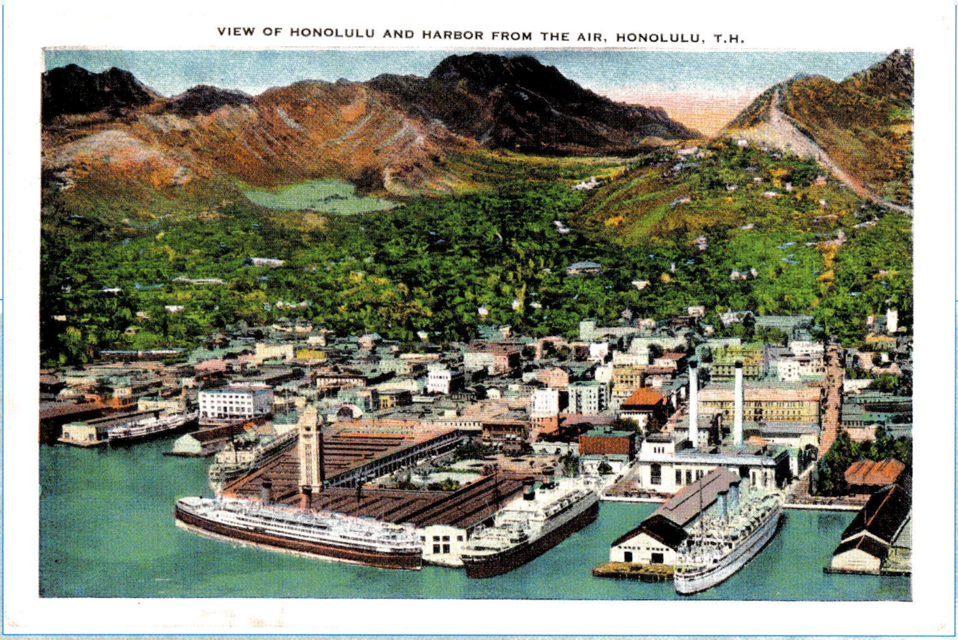

An aerial view of Honolulu Harbor. Mt. Tantalus is in the immediate background. [canceled 1911, $10-12]

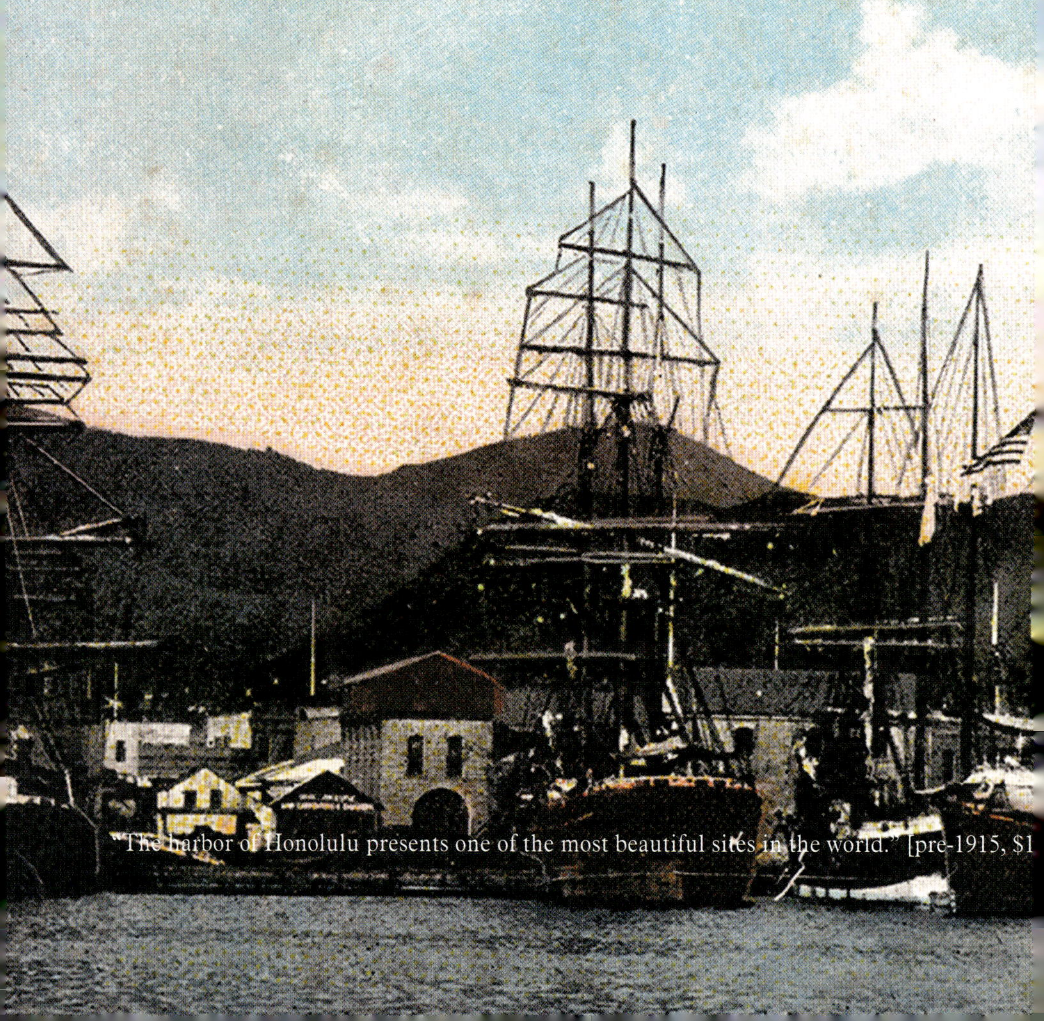

"The harbor of Honolulu presents one of the most beautiful sites in the world." [pre-1915, $1

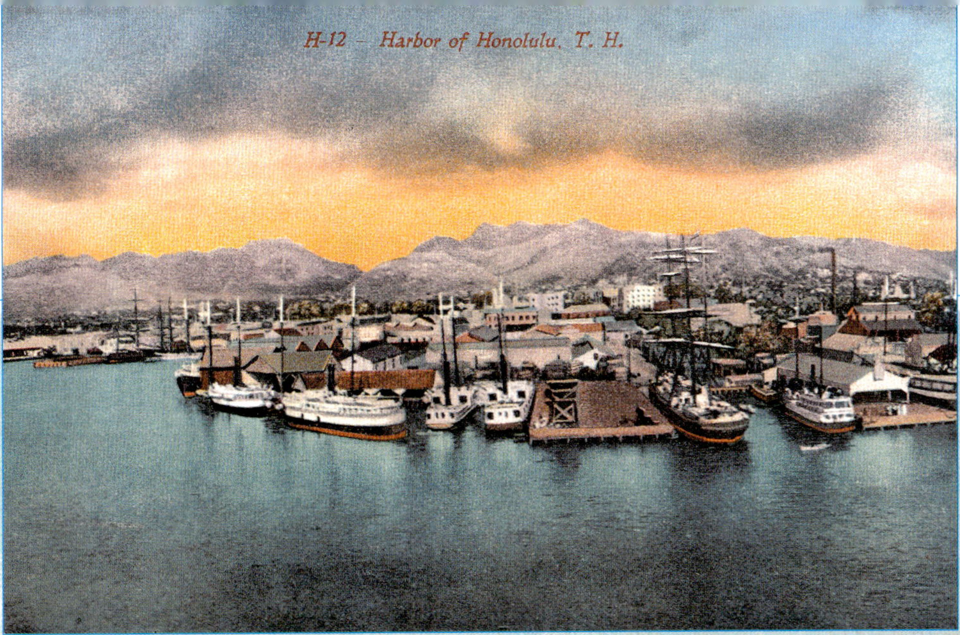

Ships lie in dock at Honolulu Harbor. "The largest steamers in the world can enter Honolulu Harbor." [pre-1915, $12-15]

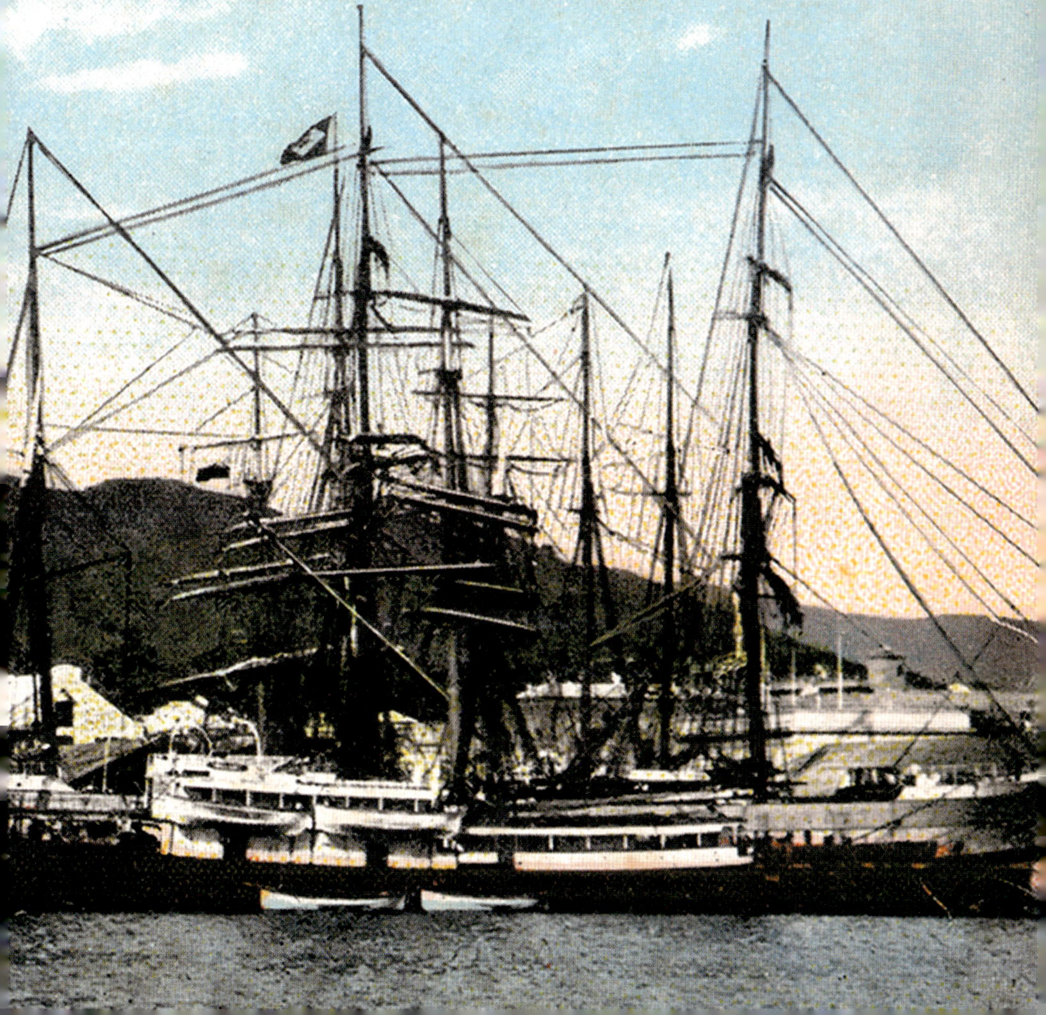

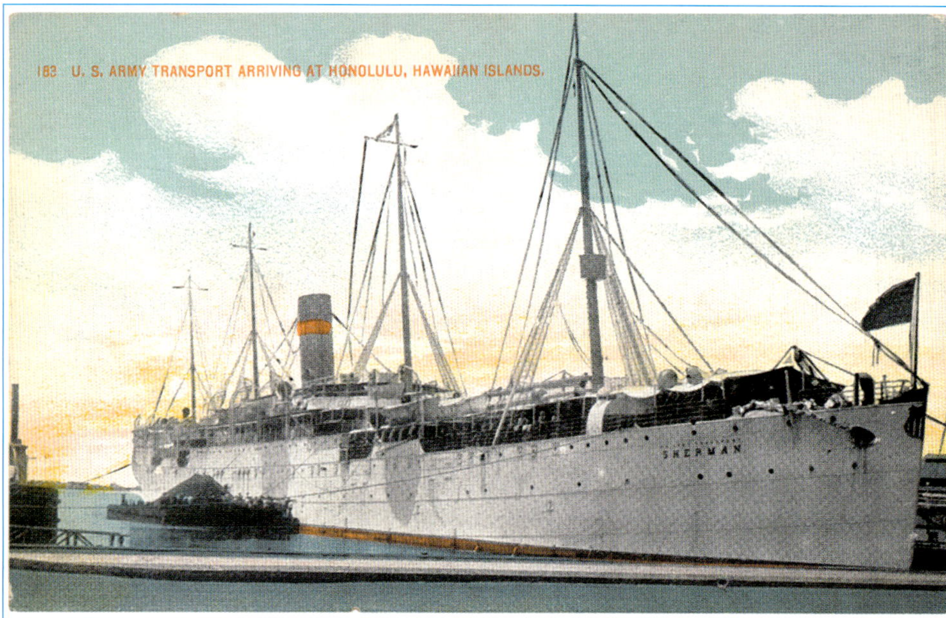

The U.S. Army transport *Sherman* arriving in Honolulu. The Hawaiian Islands are home to several military bases. [pre-1915, $12-15]

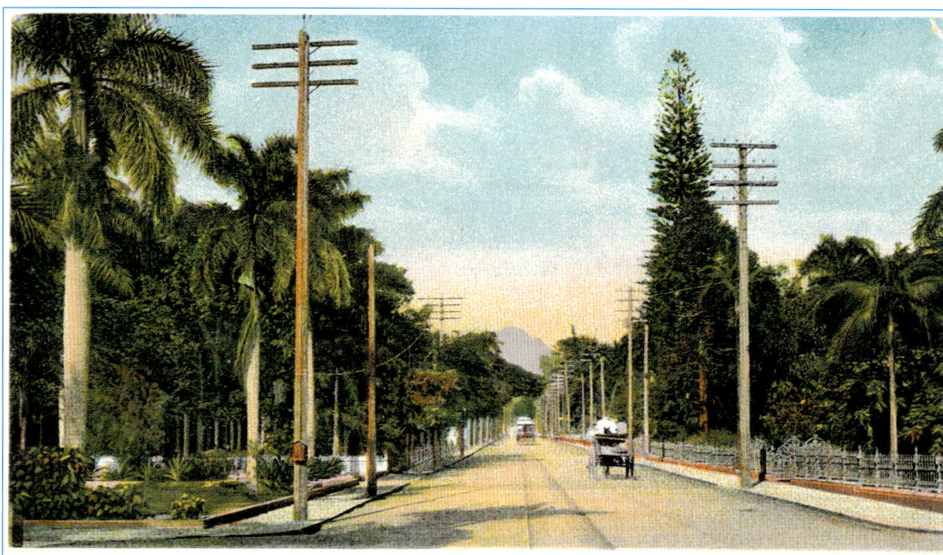

78 Nuuanu Avenue, Honolulu.

Looking down Nuuanu Avenue. [pre-1915, $4-6]

Right: An avenue lined with royal palms leads up to the Queen's Hospital. [pre-1915, $11-13]

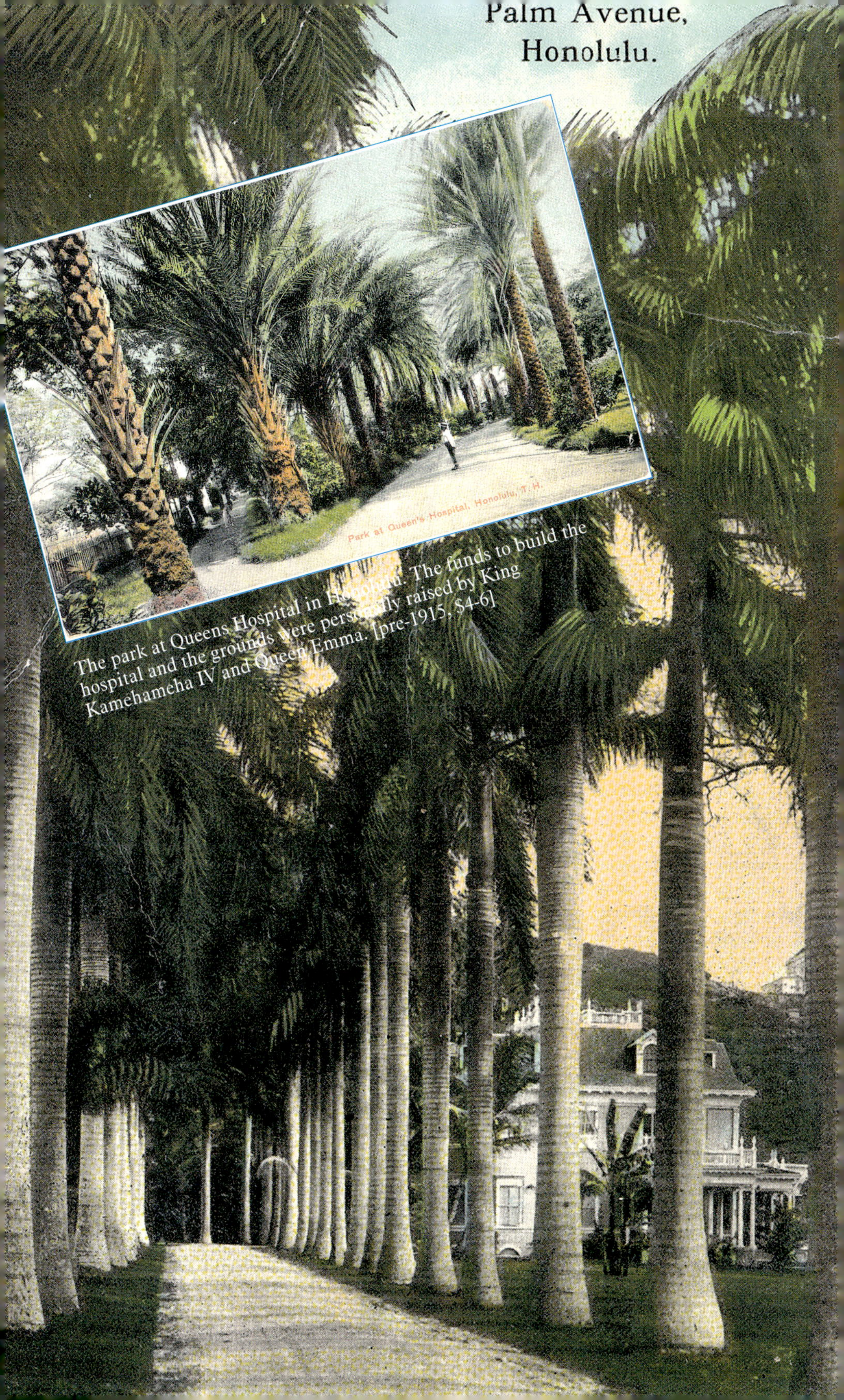

The park at Queens Hospital in Honolulu. The funds to build the hospital and the grounds were personally raised by King Kamehameha IV and Queen Emma. [pre-1915, $4-6]

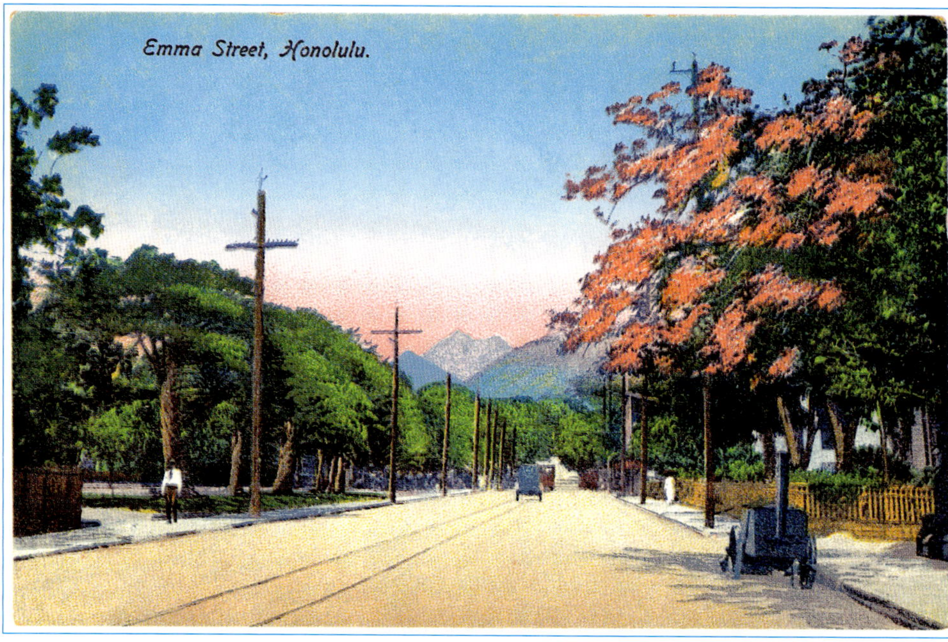

Royal Poinciana trees draw the admiration of both residents and visitors on Emma Street. [pre-1940, $7-10]

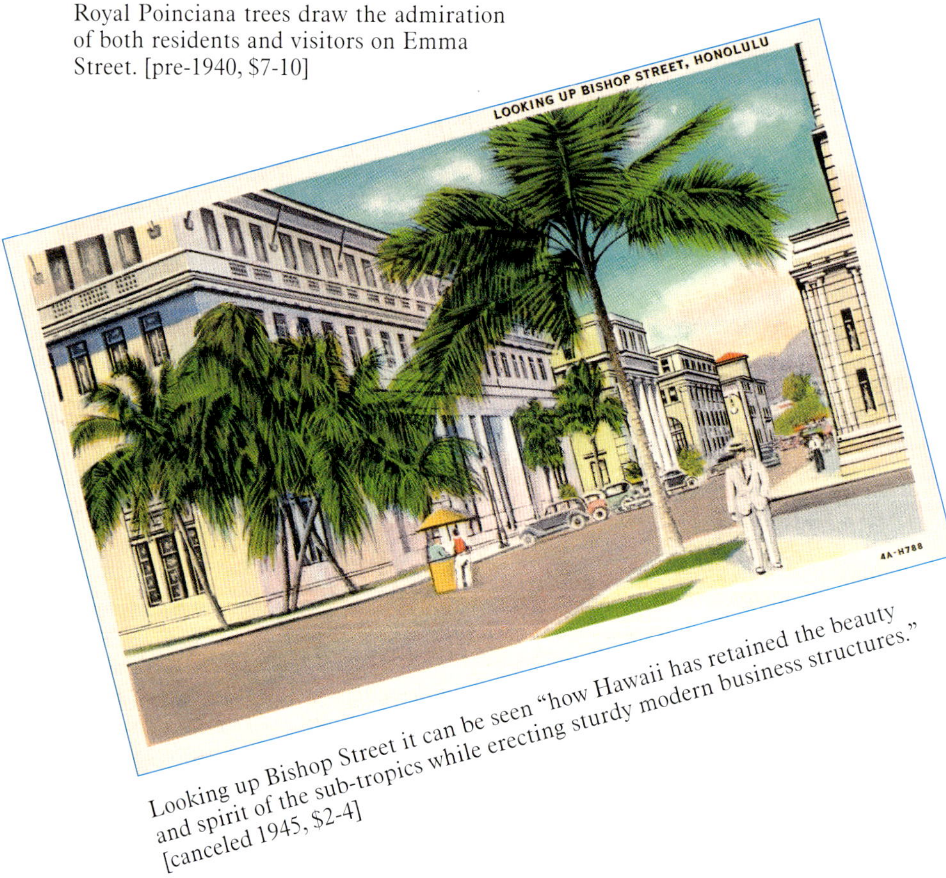

Looking up Bishop Street it can be seen "how Hawaii has retained the beauty and spirit of the sub-tropics while erecting sturdy modern business structures." [canceled 1945, $2-4]

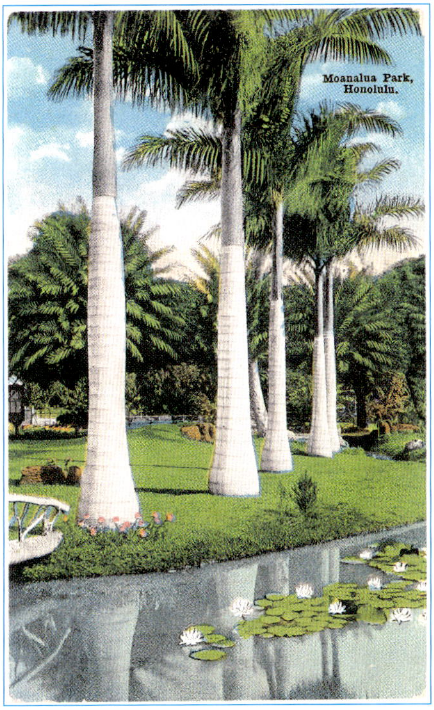

Stately Royal Palms in Moanalua Park. [pre-1915, $2-5]

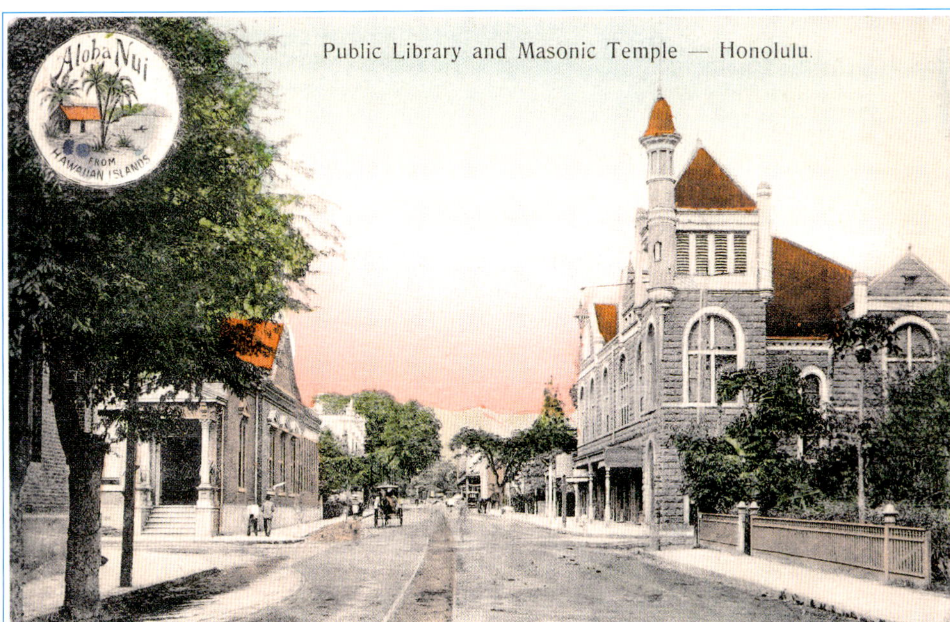

The Honolulu Public Library, across the street from the Masonic Temple. [canceled 1909, $25-45]

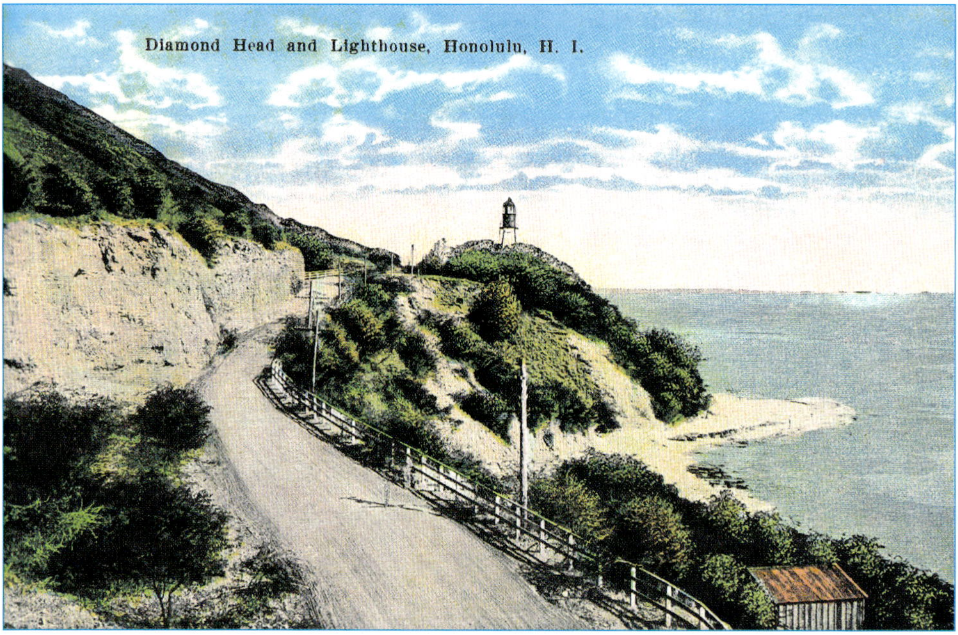

The lighthouse on Diamond Head was built in 1899 after a steamer ran aground nearby. [pre-1915, $5-8]

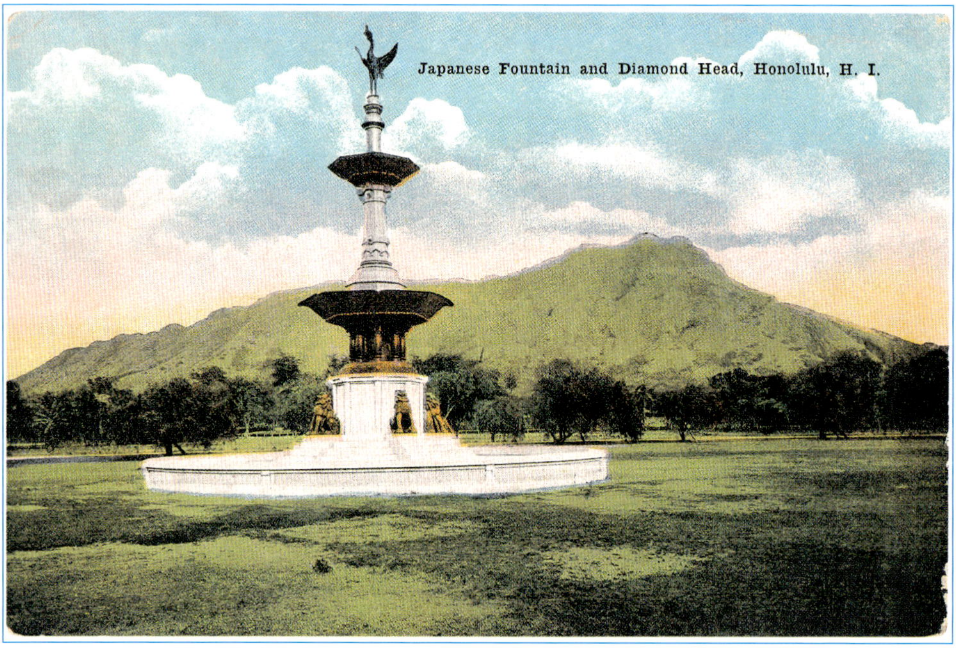

The Japanese Fountain with Diamond Head in the background. The Japanese played an important role in the general development of the Hawaiian Islands. [canceled 1920, $5-7]

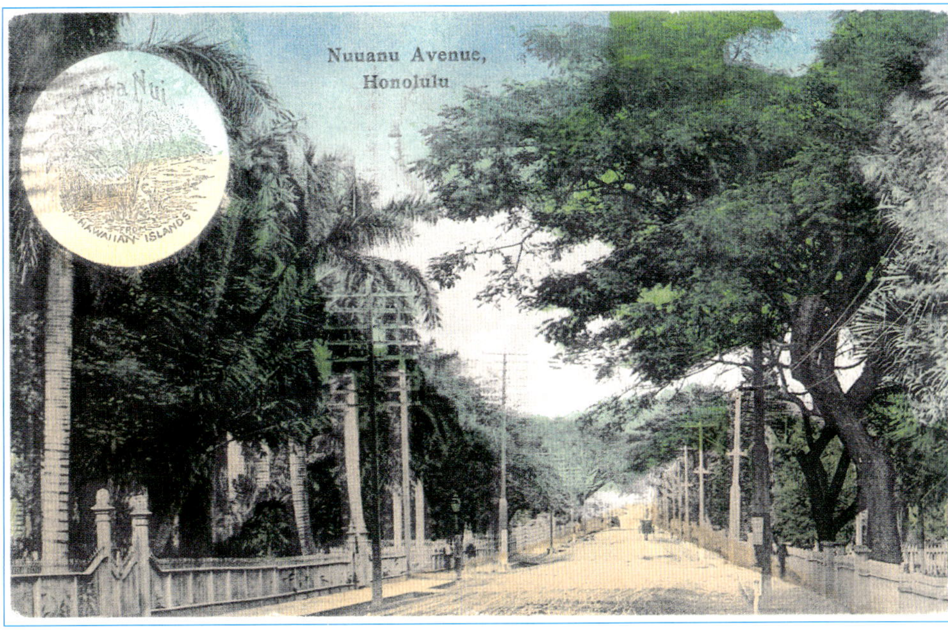

Nuuanu Avenue, Honolulu. [canceled 1912, $20-30]

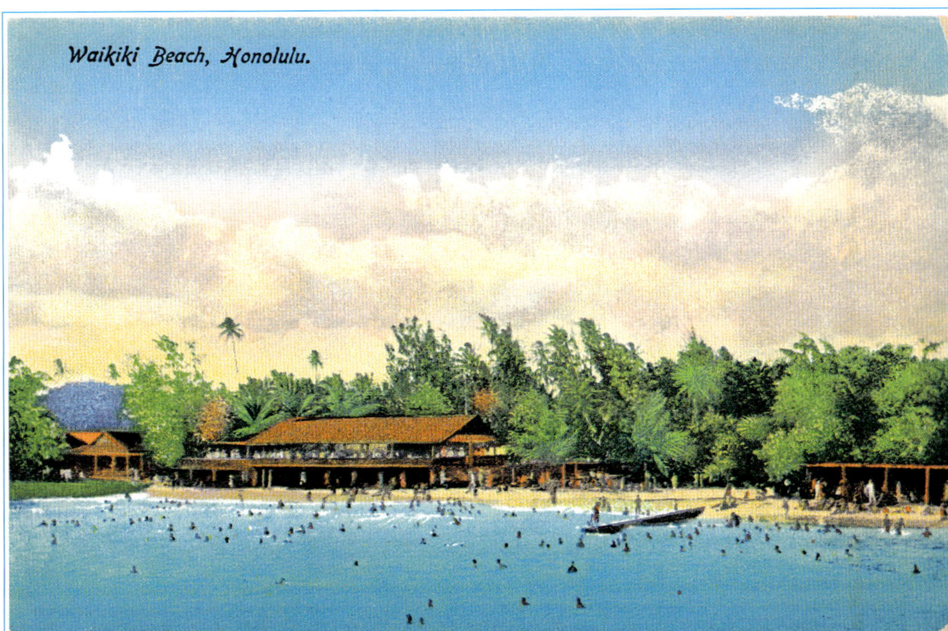

Waikiki Beach, "famed in song and story, lies some four miles from the city." [pre-1915, $8-12]

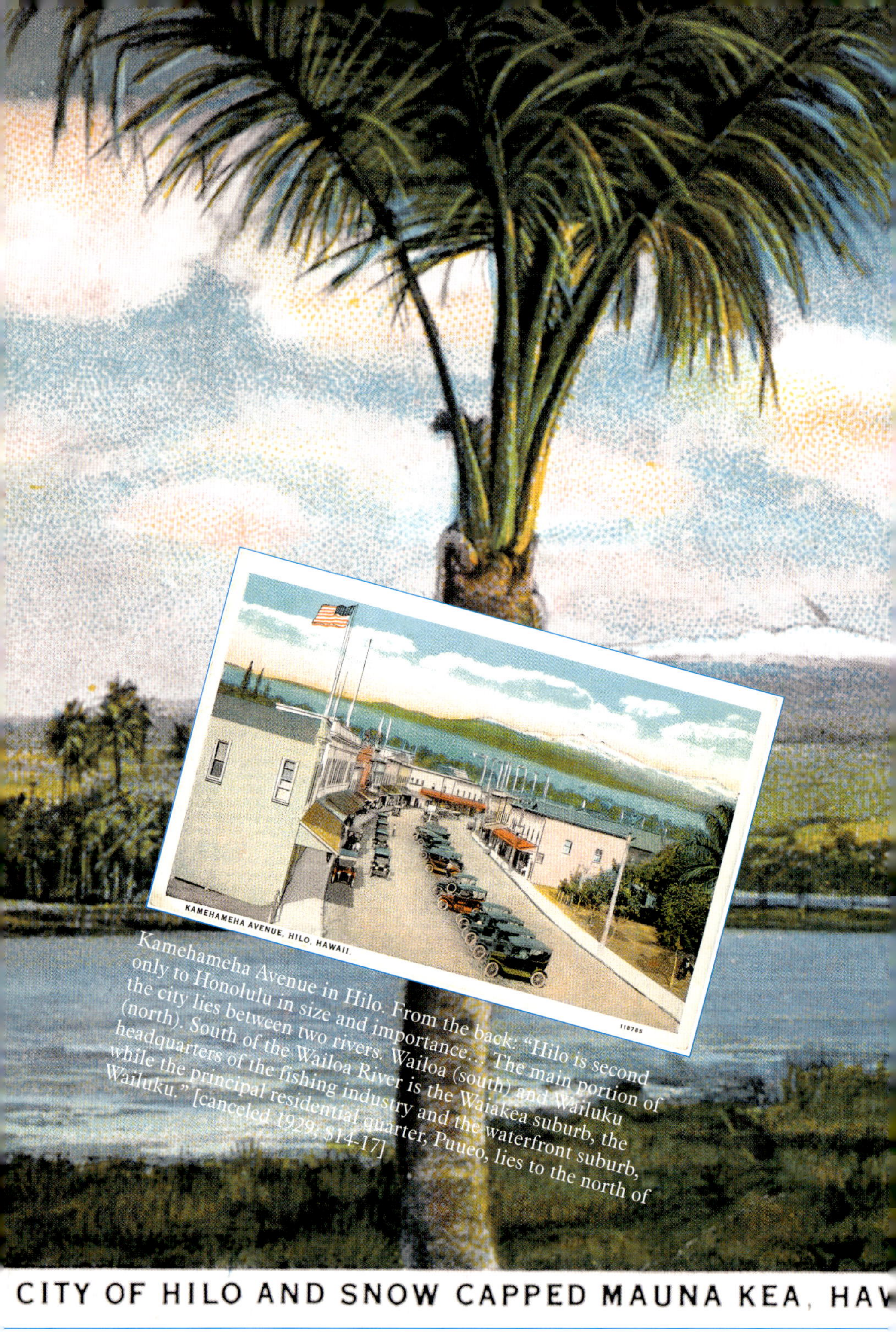

Kamehameha Avenue in Hilo. From the back: “Hilo is second only to Honolulu in size and importance… The main portion of the city lies between two rivers. Wailoa (south) and Wailuku (north). South of the Wailoa River is the Waiakea suburb, the headquarters of the fishing industry and the waterfront suburb, while the principal residential quarter, Puueo, lies to the north of Wailuku.” [canceled 1929; $14-17]

Hilo

Hilo was founded on the slope rising from a crescent shaped bay. The city enjoys a theater-like atmosphere with the sea as stage. The fine sand beach and palm-fringed Cocoanut Island near the wharf are part of the show. In the background, the snow-capped summits of Mauna Kea and Mauna Loa stand sentinel. The city has long served tourists flocking to visit the active volcano nearby.

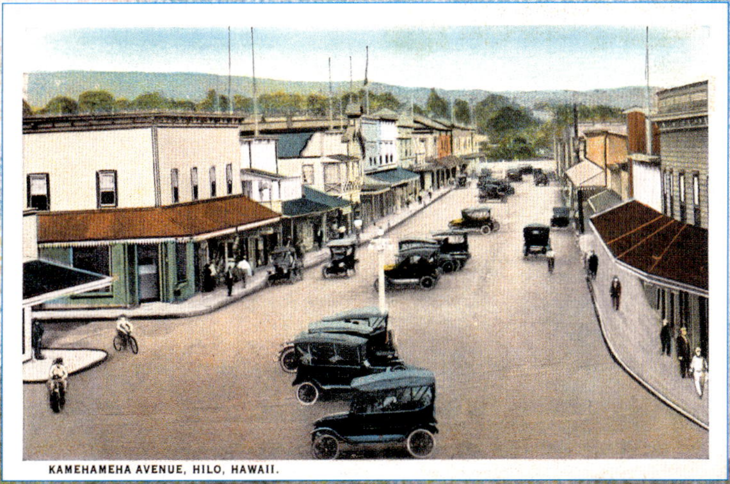

Another view of Kamehameha Avenue. This street was once one of the main streets in the city. [pre-1920, $14-17]

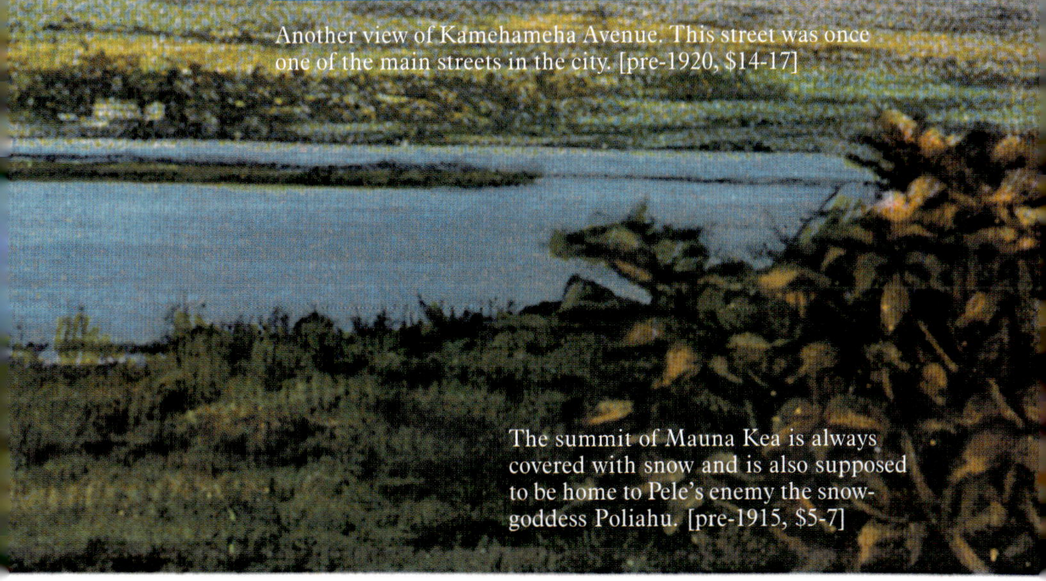

The summit of Mauna Kea is always covered with snow and is also supposed to be home to Pele's enemy the snow-goddess Poliahu. [pre-1915, $5-7]

118775

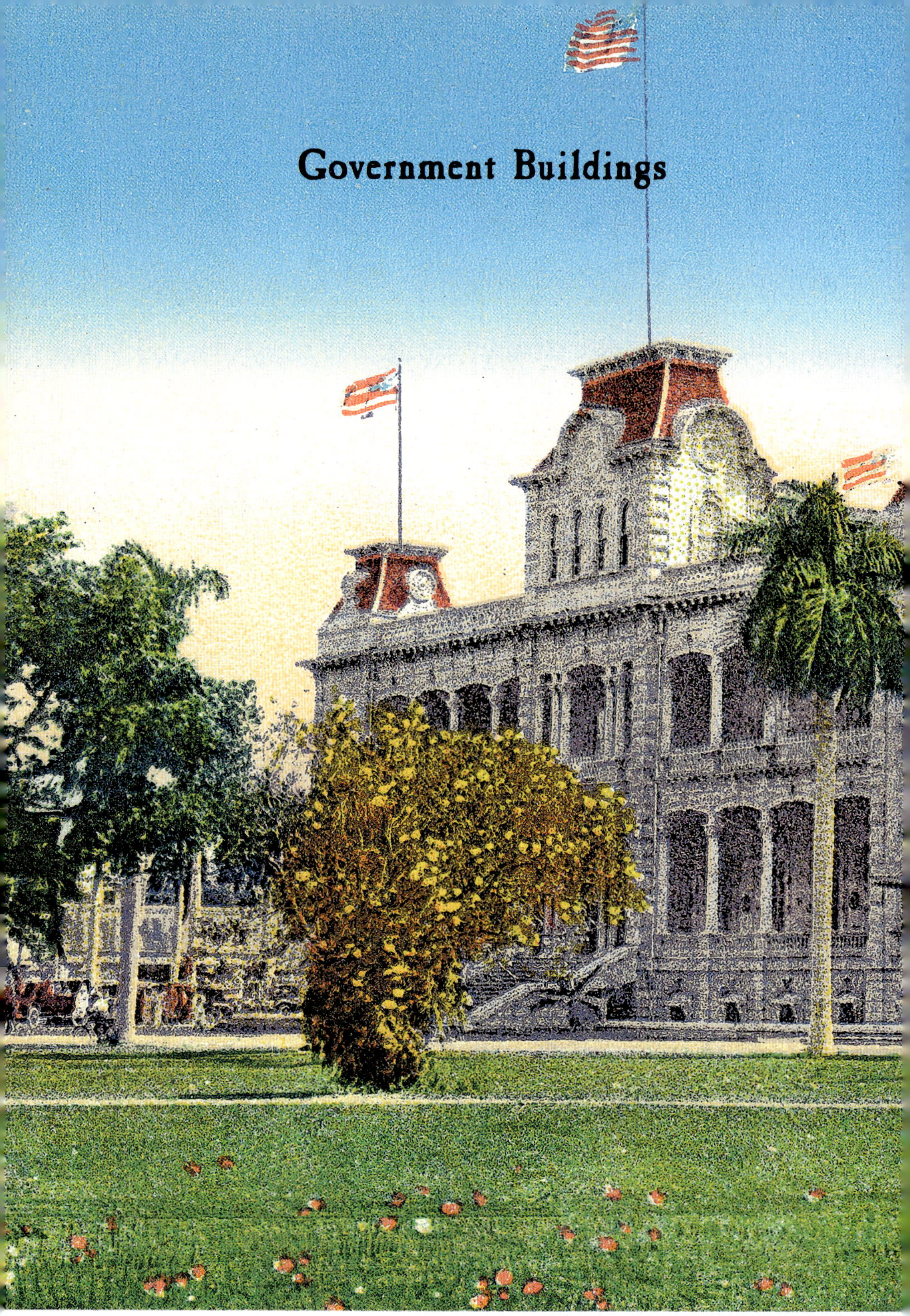

After the overthrow of the Hawaiian Monarchy in 1893, the Palace was converted into the capitol building for the Republic of Hawaii. [pre-1915, $6-9]

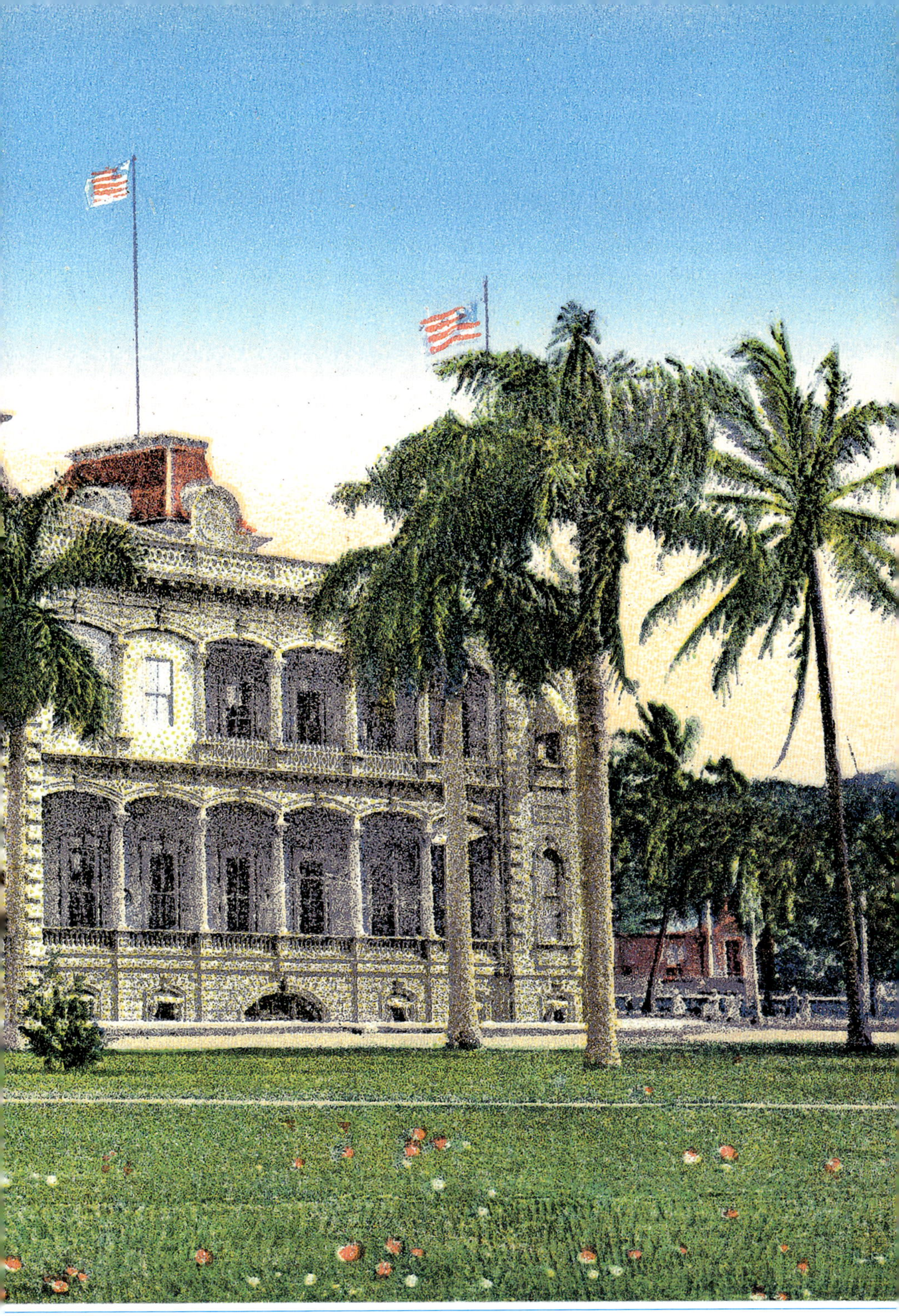

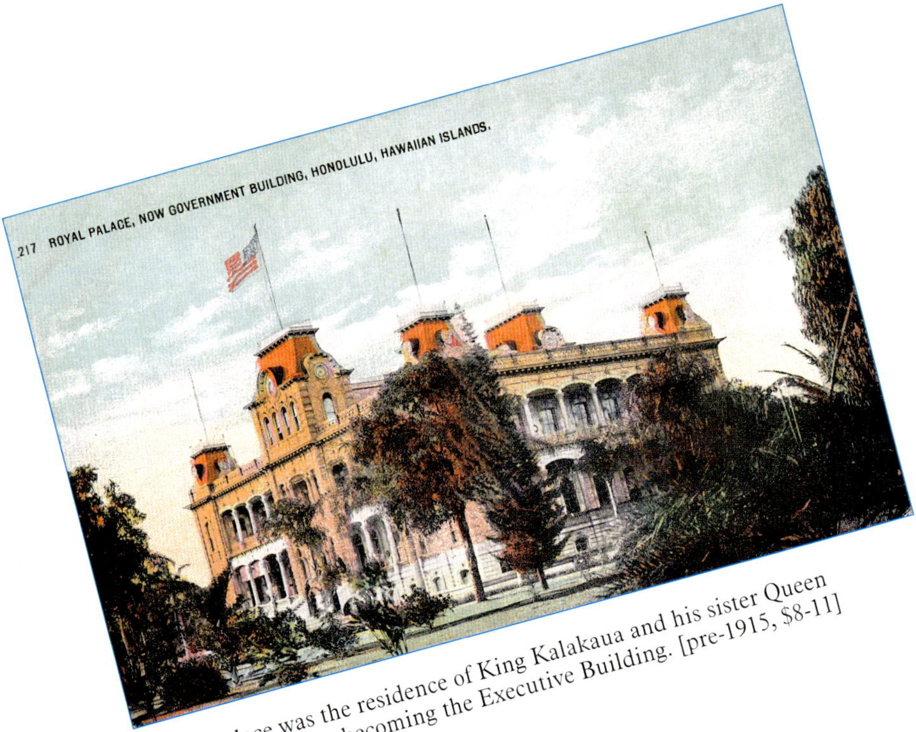

'Iolani Palace was the residence of King Kalakaua and his sister Queen Liliuokalani before becoming the Executive Building. [pre-1915, $8-11]

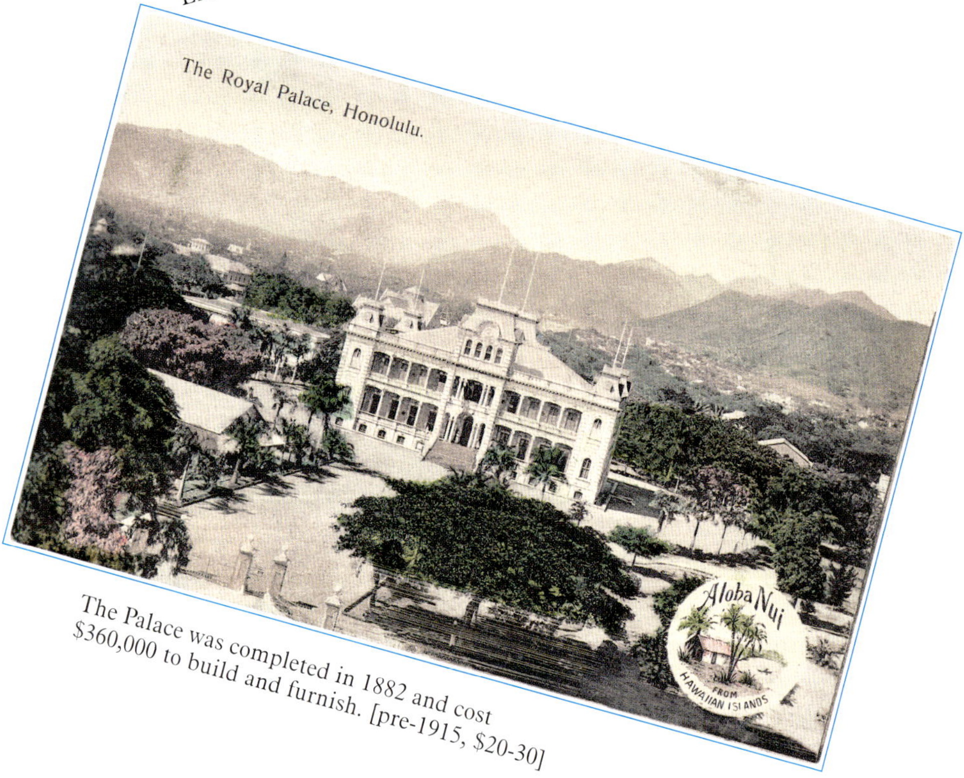

The Palace was completed in 1882 and cost $360,000 to build and furnish. [pre-1915, $20-30]

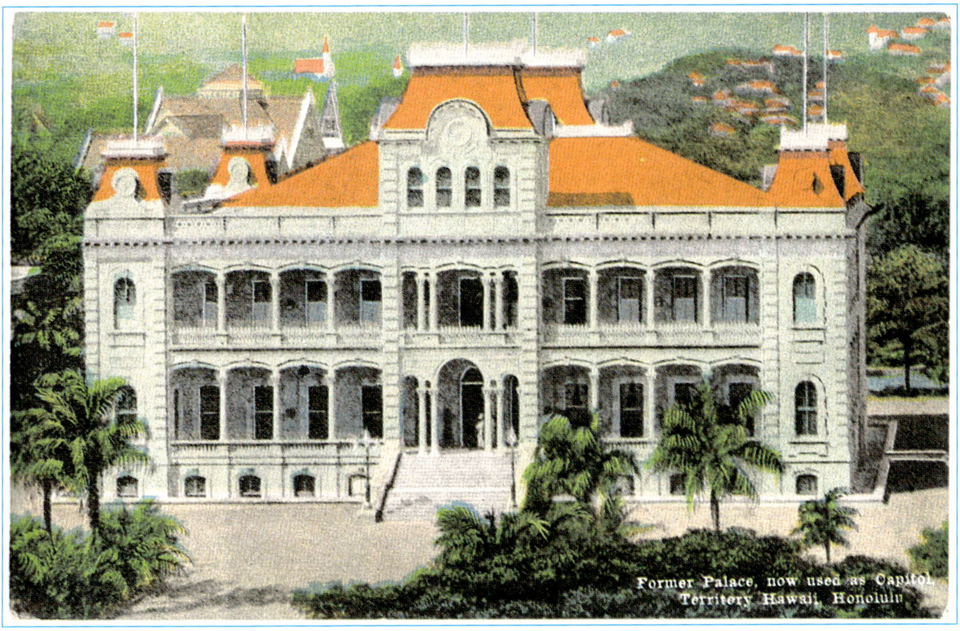

The Palace was built close to the location of the previous Royal Palace, which had to be torn down due to extensive termite damage. [pre-1915, $7-9]

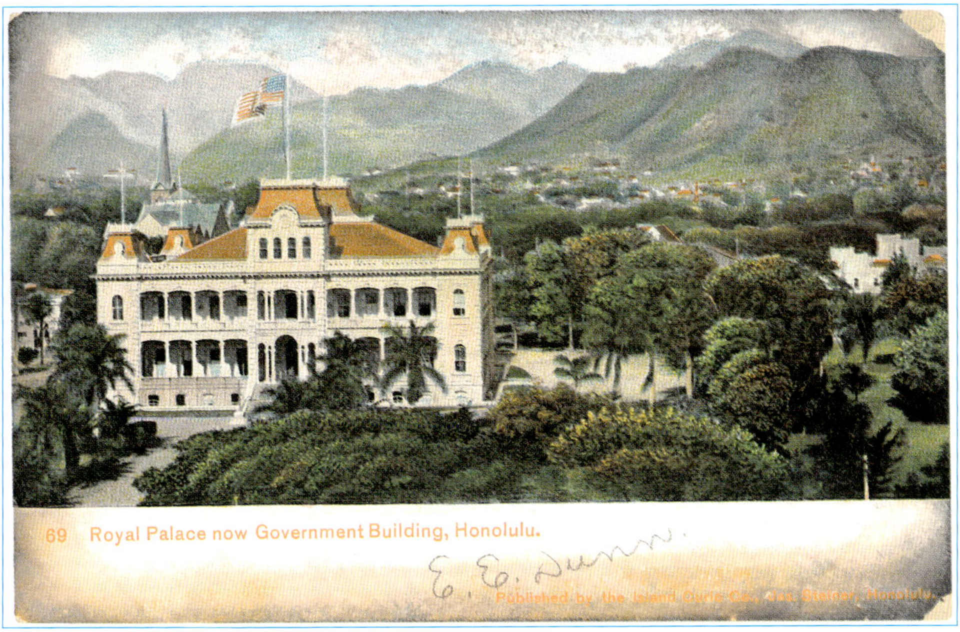

After the overthrow of the Hawaiian Monarchy in 1893, the Palace was converted into the capitol building for the Republic of Hawaii. It then served as the capitol building for the Territory and the State of Hawaii until 1968. [pre-1915, $7-12]

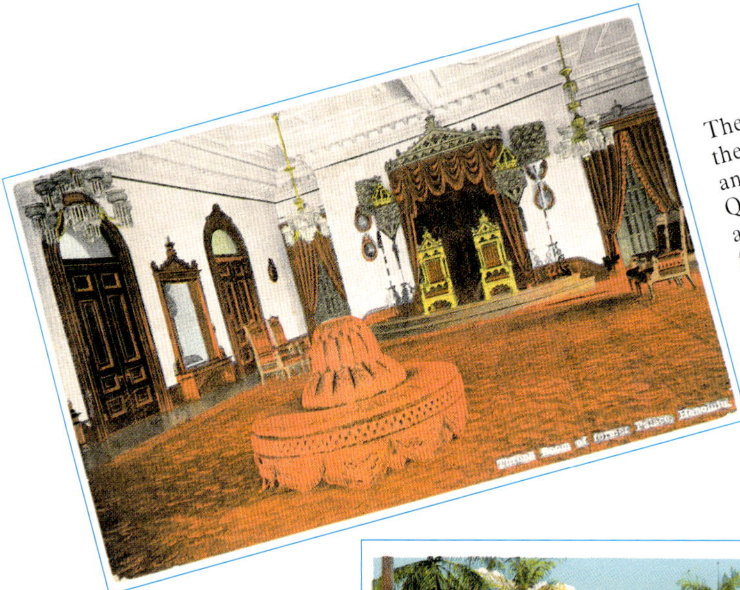

The Throne Room was the site of many royal and state functions. Queen Liliuokalani was also tried in this room for concealing knowledge from Republic officials concerning a royalist rebellion in 1895. [pre-1920, $7-9]

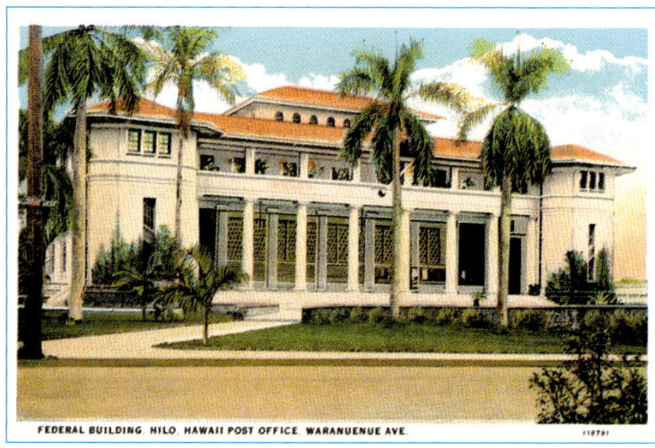

The Federal Building in Hilo, also the location of the city's post office. [pre-1920, $6-8]

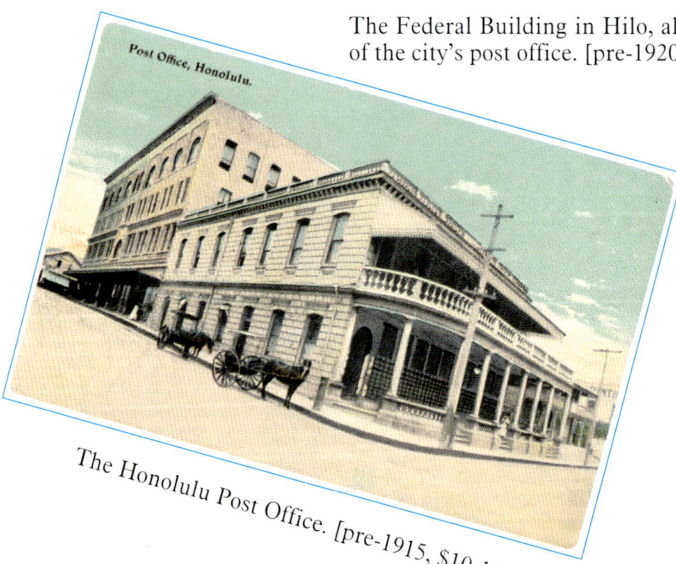

The Honolulu Post Office. [pre-1915, $10-12]

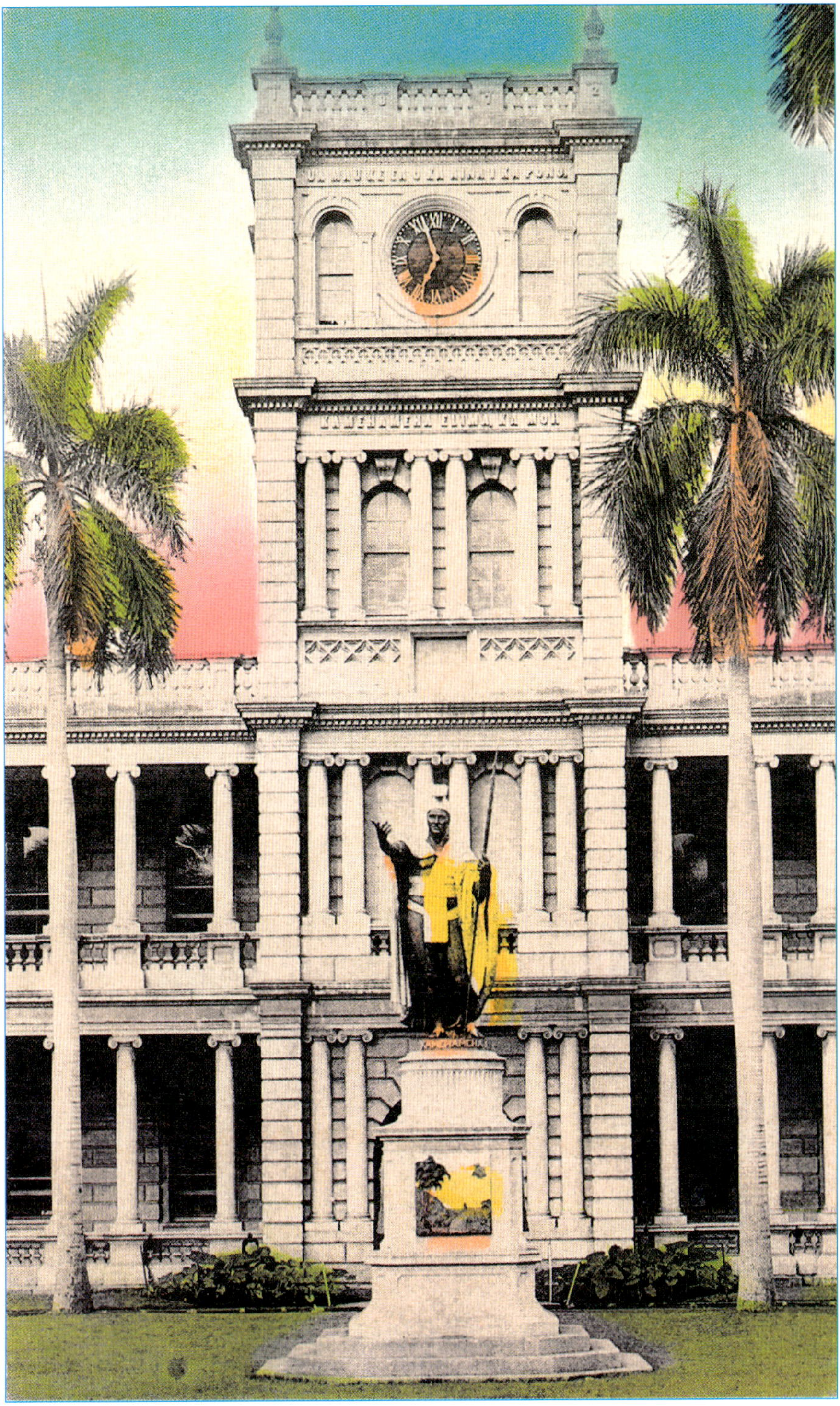

The statue of King Kamehameha I is one of three statues cast in Paris, France. This statue was dedicated in 1883. [canceled 1938, $6-9]

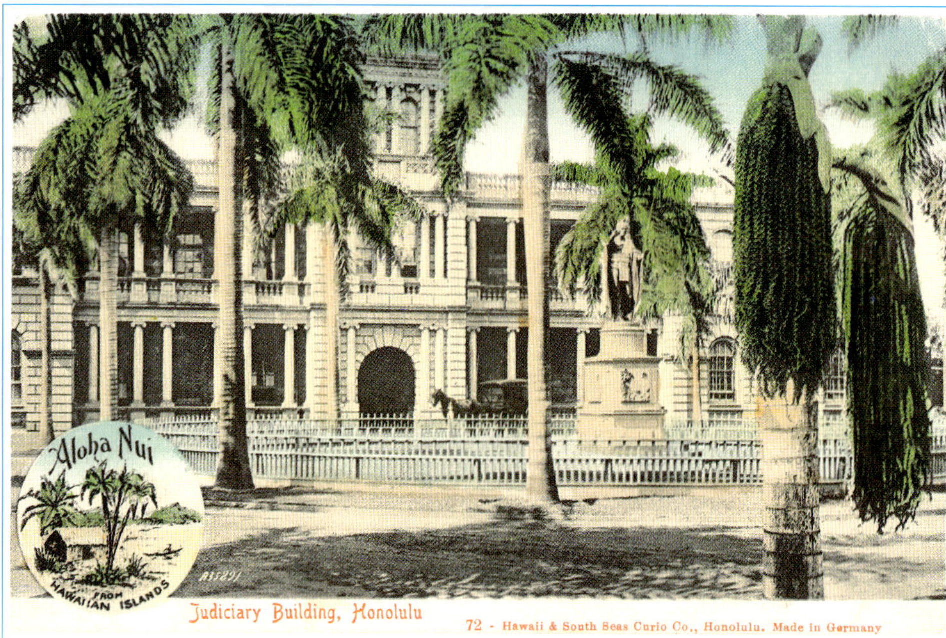

The Judiciary Building was constructed in 1874 by King Kamehameha V, who planned to use the building as his official residence. [pre-1915, $20-30]

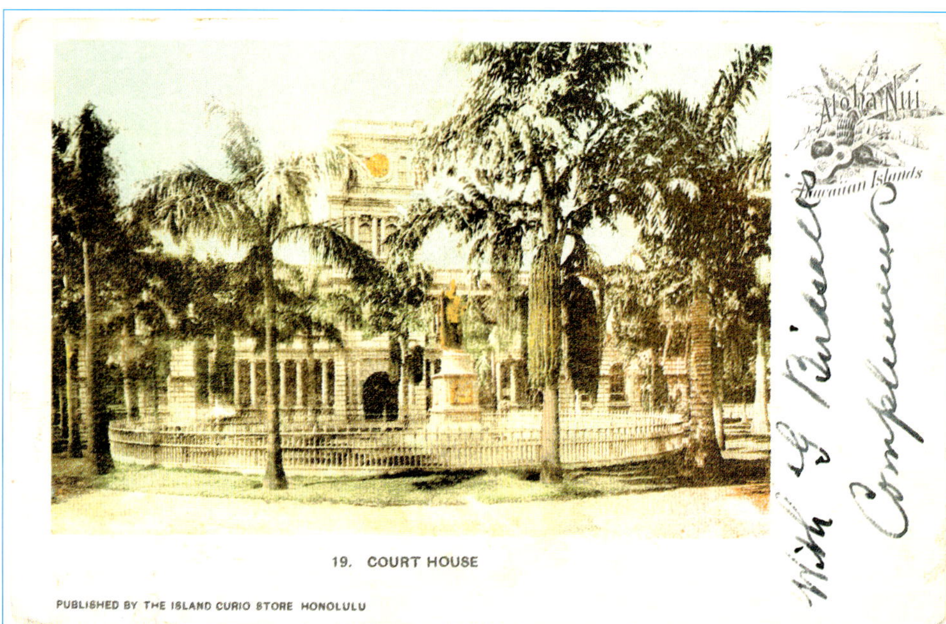

The Judiciary Building is the oldest government building in Hawaii. [canceled 1904, $20-30]

Home of Queen Liliuokalani, Washington Place, from 1895 until her death in 1917. [pre-1915, $7-9]

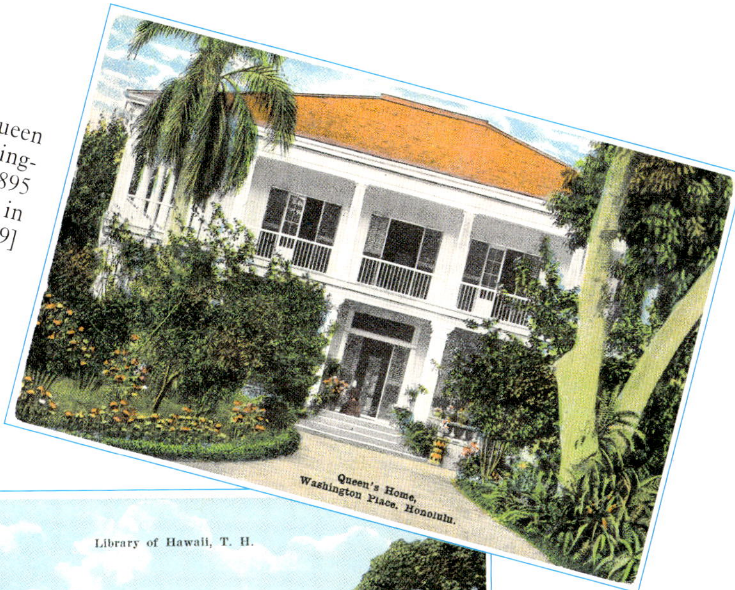

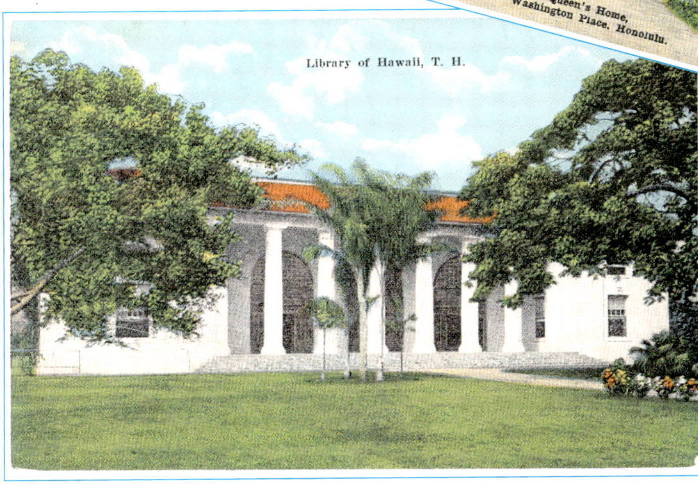

The Library of Hawaii was completed in 1913 and partially funded by Andrew Carnegie. [pre-1915, $7-9]

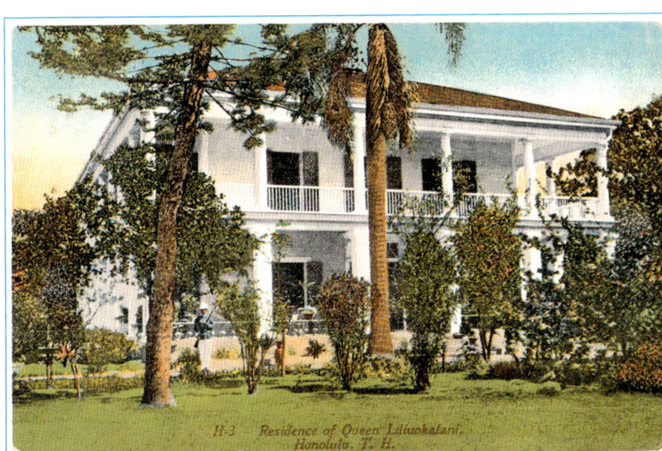

Washington Place was built by John Dominis in 1846. His son, John Owen Dominis, would eventually marry Queen Liliuokalani. [canceled 1914, $7-9]

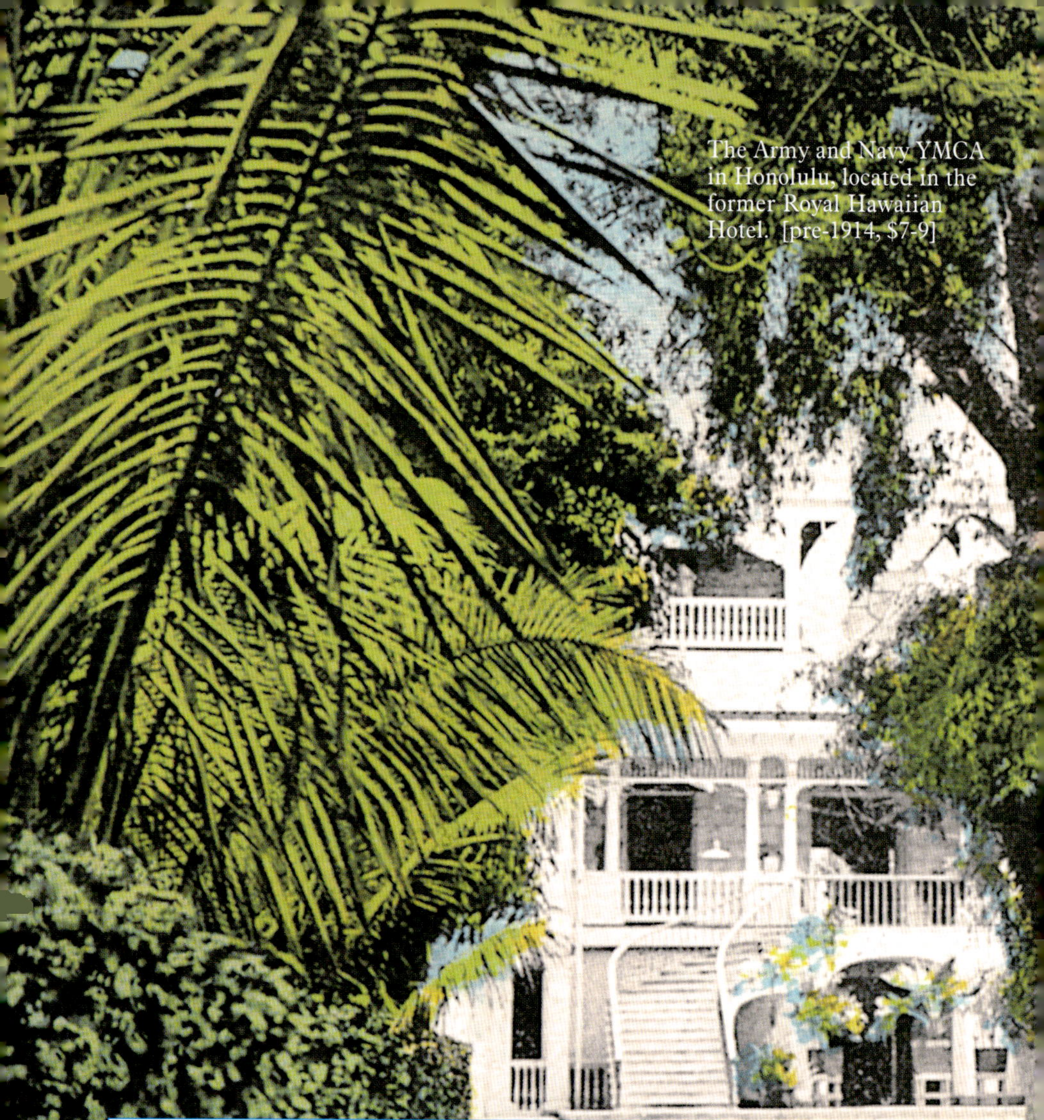

The Army and Navy YMCA in Honolulu, located in the former Royal Hawaiian Hotel. [pre-1914, $7-9]

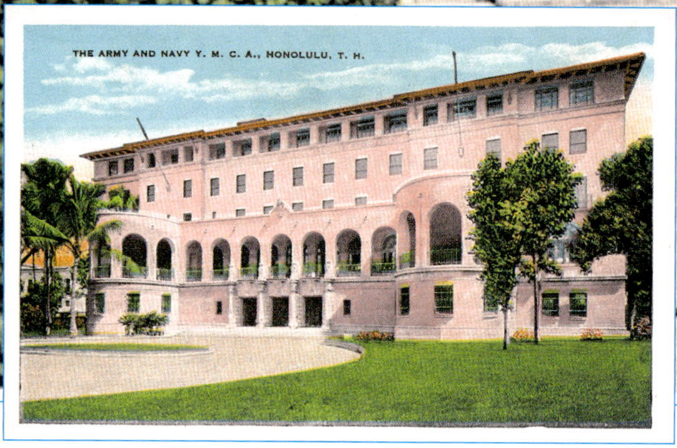

The Army and Navy YMCA was established in Honolulu in 1917. [pre-1915, $7-9]

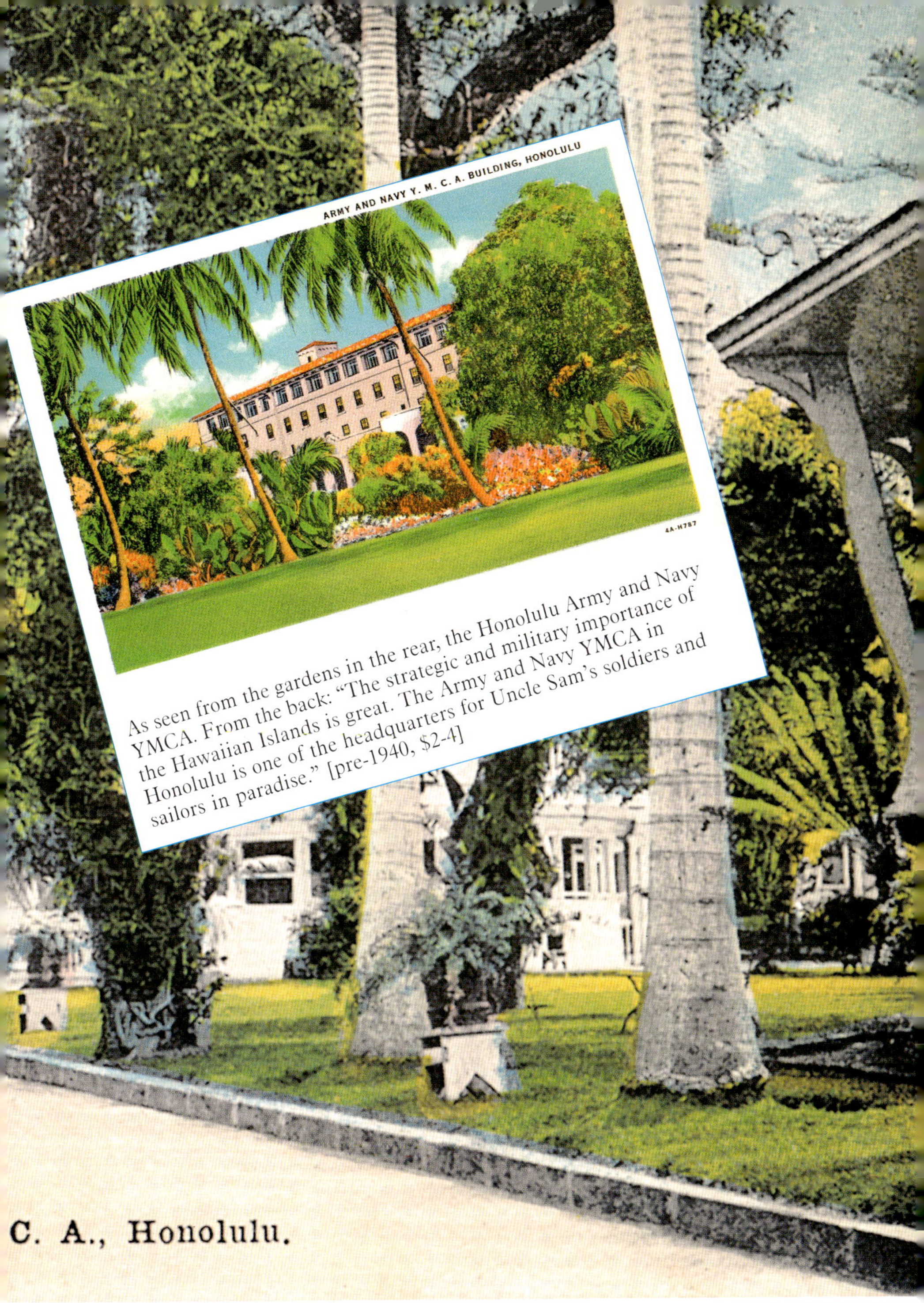

As seen from the gardens in the rear, the Honolulu Army and Navy YMCA. From the back: "The strategic and military importance of the Hawaiian Islands is great. The Army and Navy YMCA in Honolulu is one of the headquarters for Uncle Sam's soldiers and sailors in paradise." [pre-1940, $2-4]

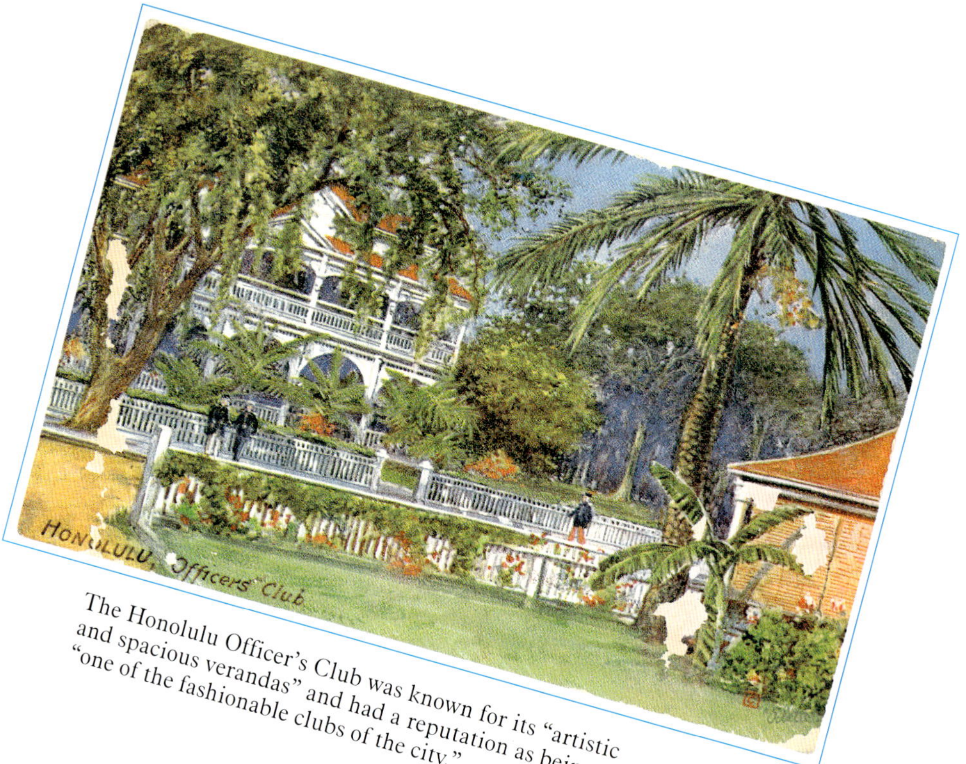

The Honolulu Officer's Club was known for its "artistic and spacious verandas" and had a reputation as being "one of the fashionable clubs of the city."

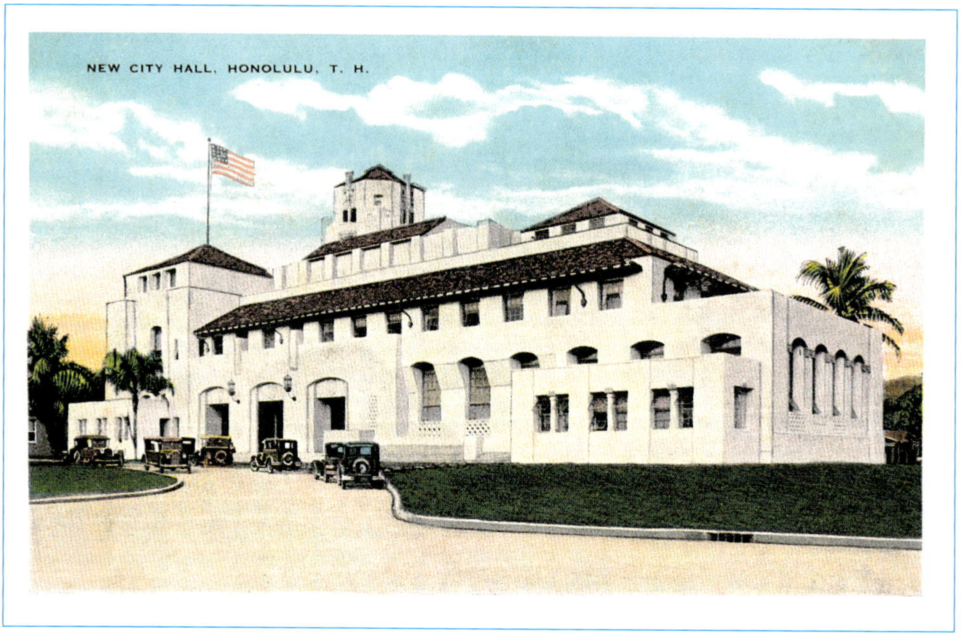

The Honolulu New City Hall was built in 1928. Much of the interior was modeled after a 13th Century Florentine palace.

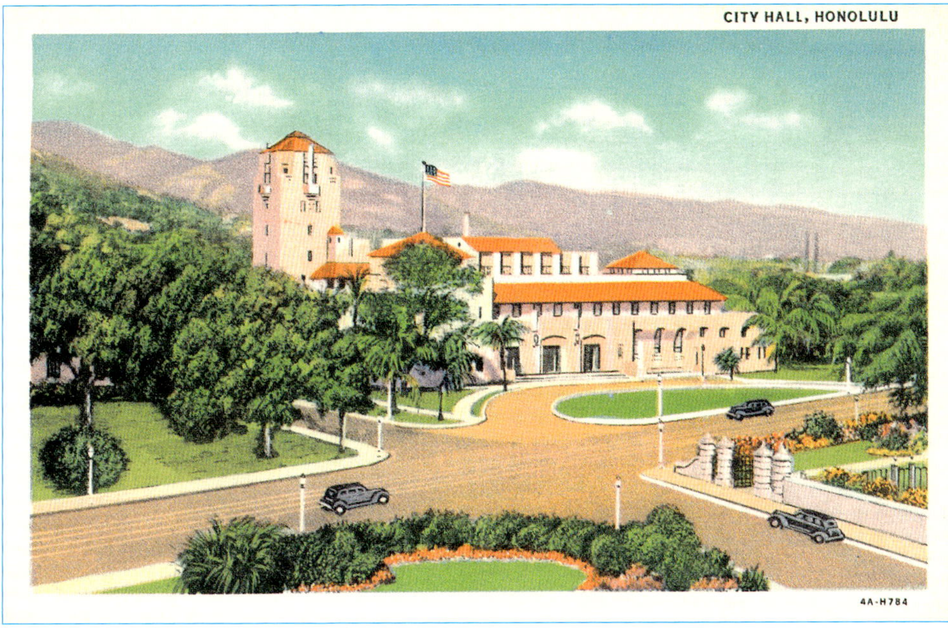

Honolulu City Hall is also called Honolulu Hale, which means "Honolulu House." [pre-1940, $2-4]

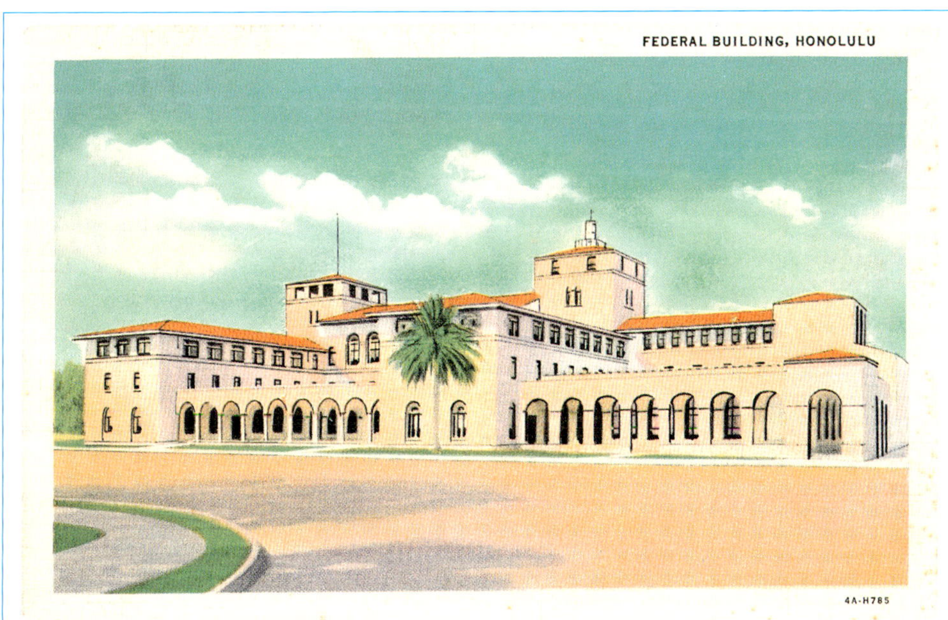

Construction for the Federal Building in Honolulu began in 1917, but was halted due to World War I and did not resume until 1922. [pre-1940, $2-4]

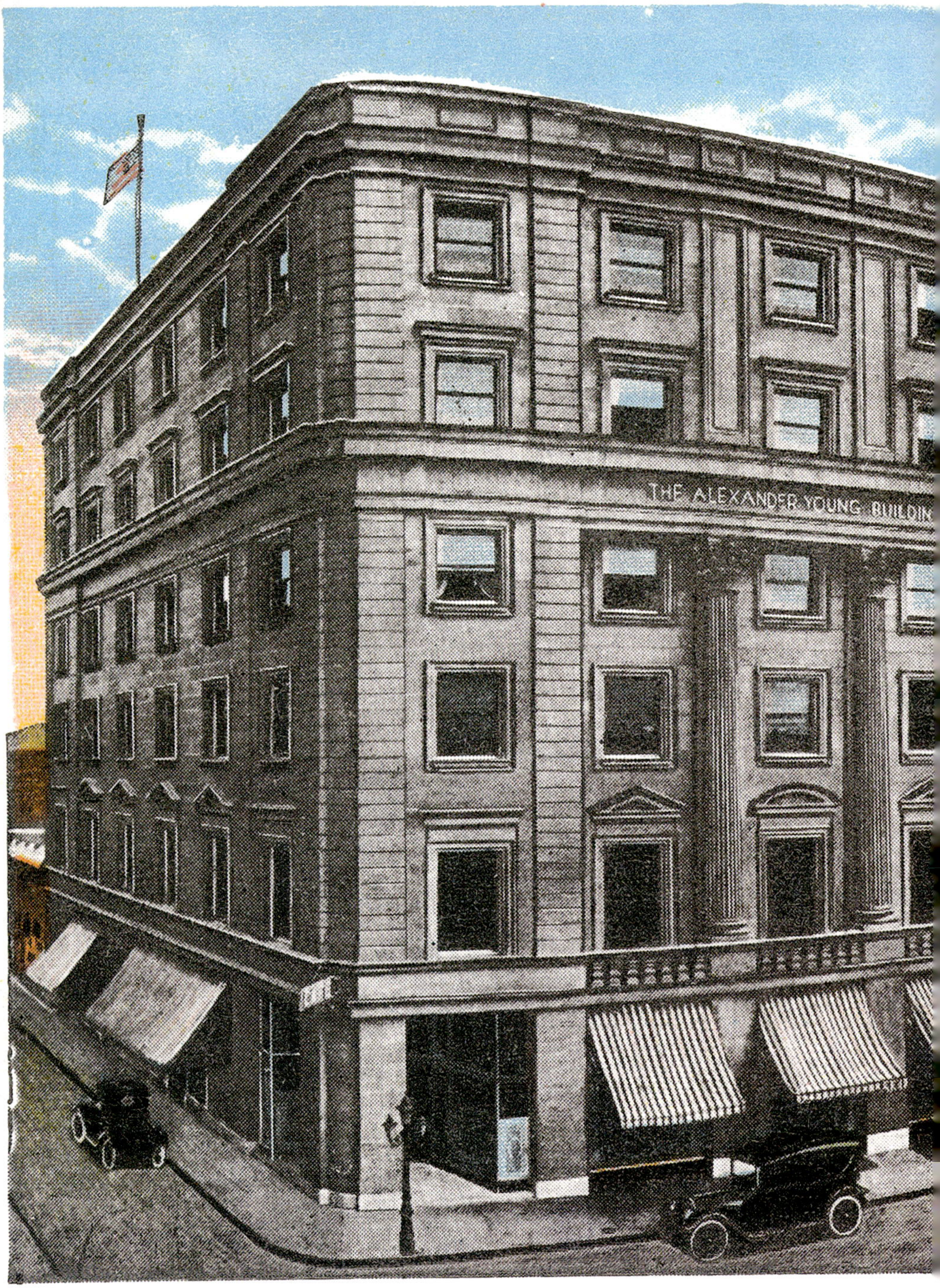

The Alexander Young Hotel was built in 1900 by Alexander Young Esq. a "pioneer planter." [pre-1920, $8-10]

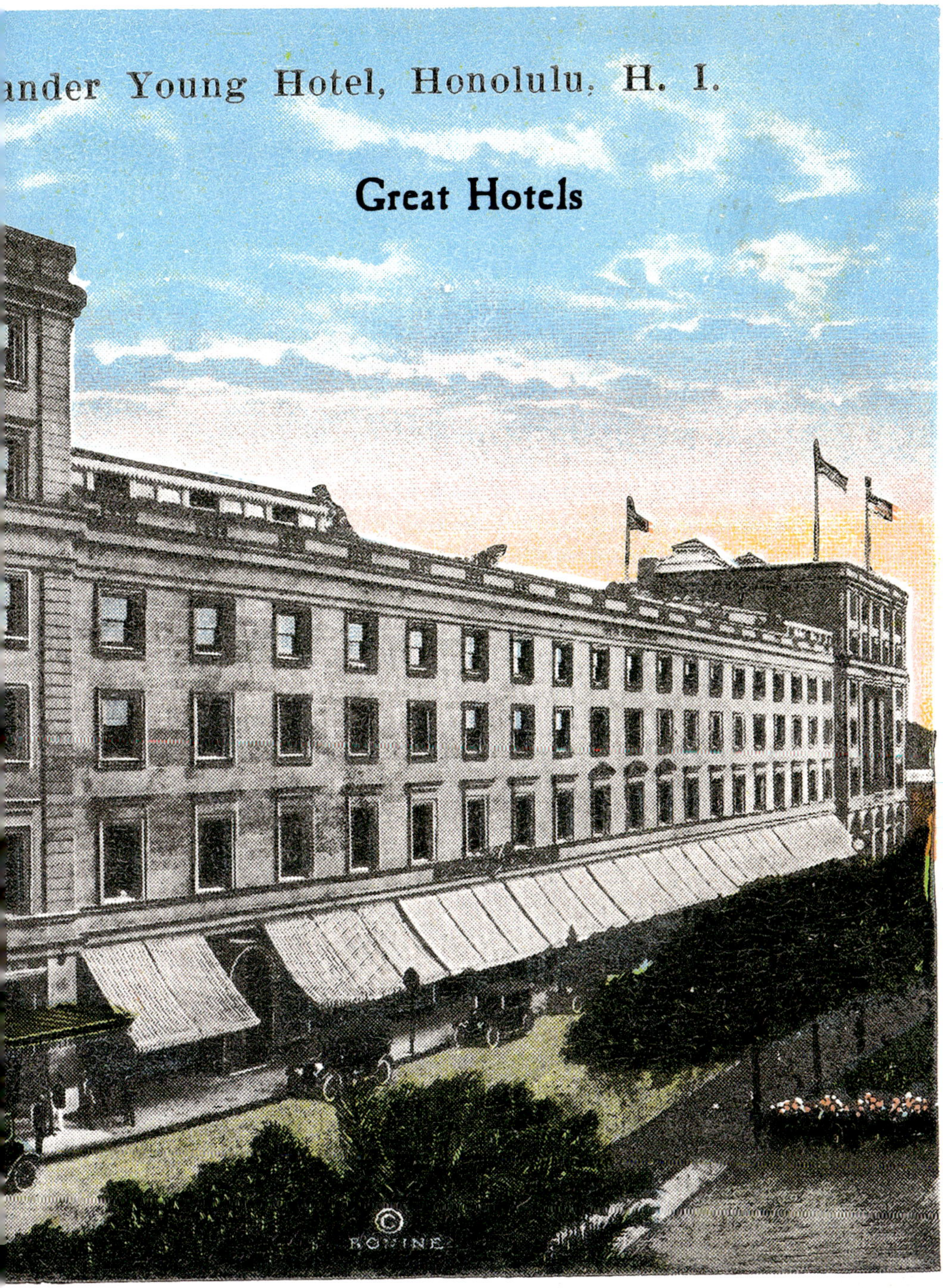
ander Young Hotel, Honolulu, H. I.
© BONINE

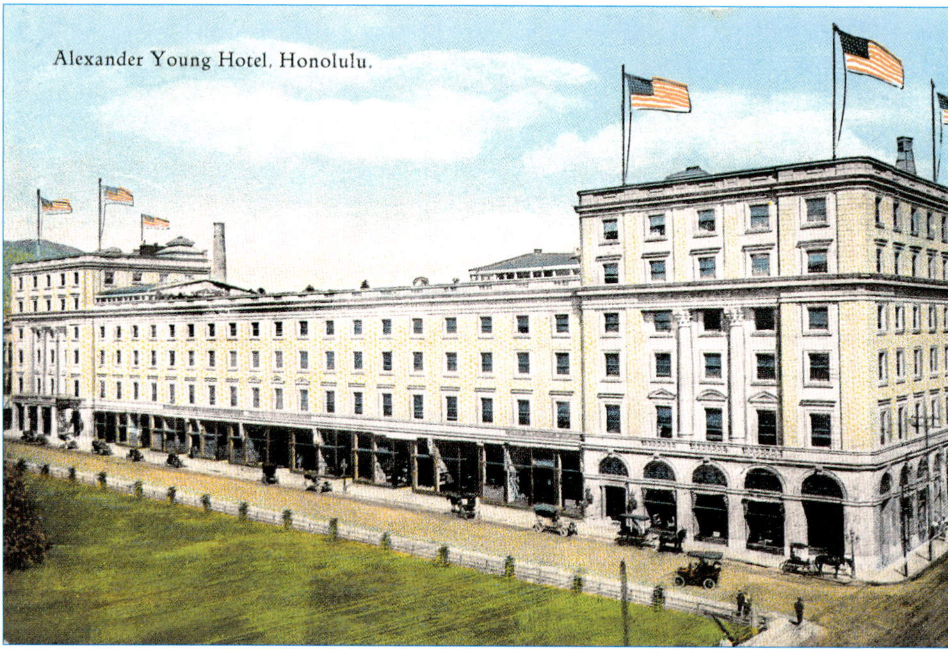

The hotel itself cost Alexander Young over $2,000,000 to build. [pre-1915, $8-12]

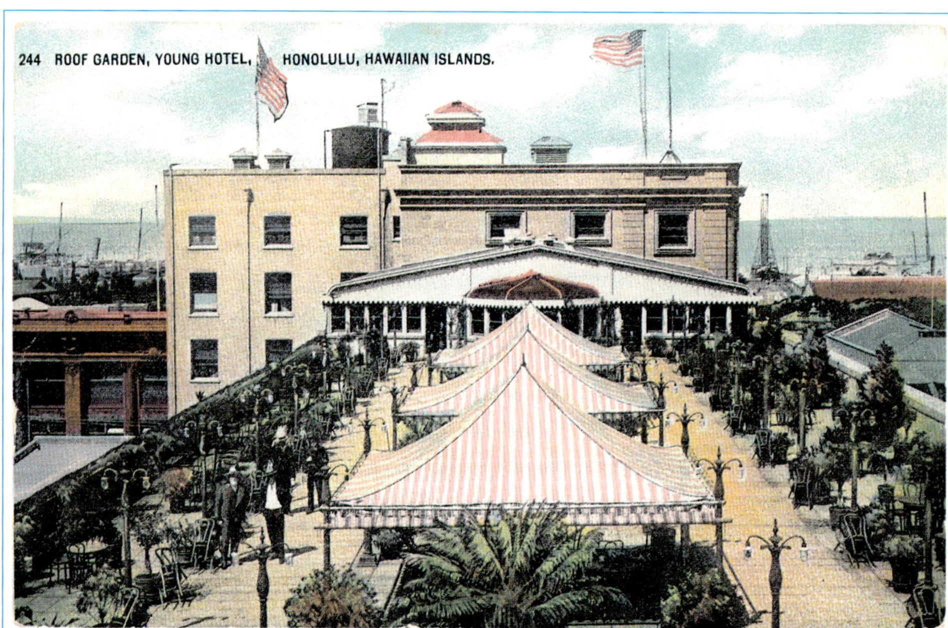

Perhaps the most magnificent feature of the Young Hotel, the roof gardens. [canceled 1917, $8-12]

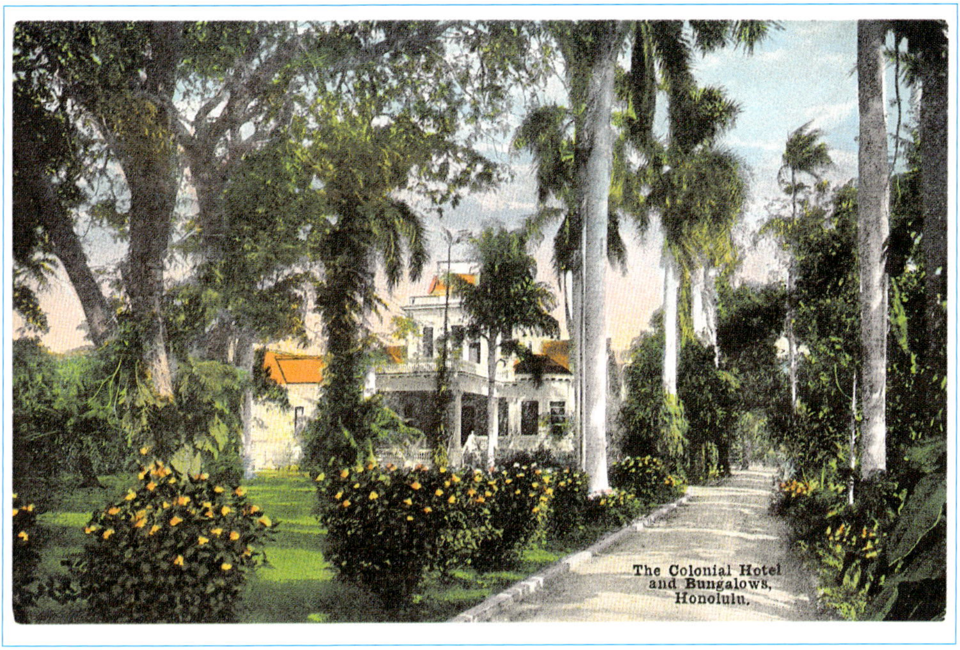

The Colonial Hotel and Bungalows in Honolulu. [pre-1915, $8-10]

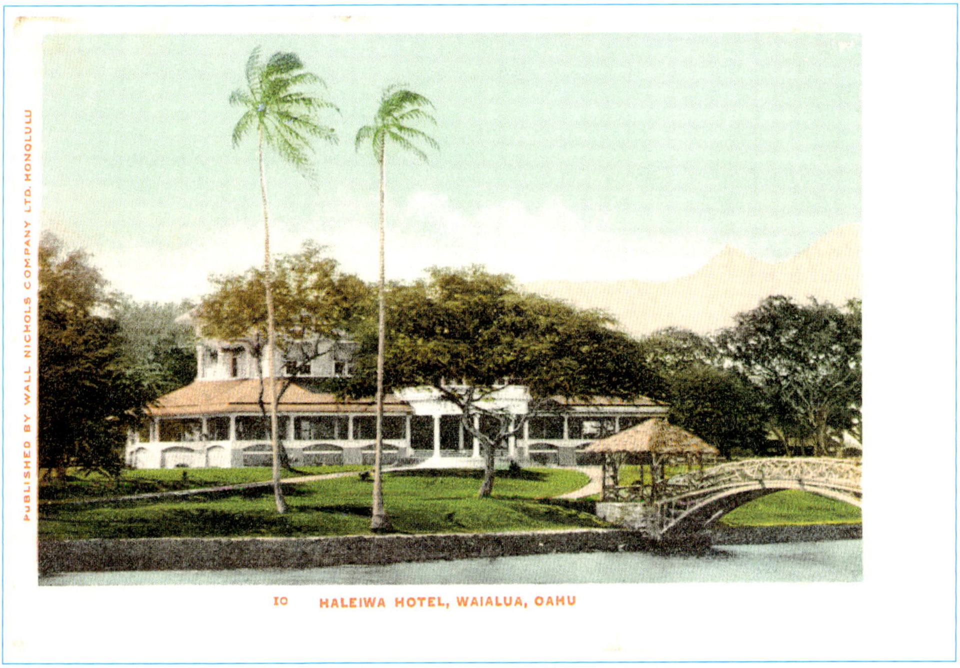

The Haleiwa Hotel was built by Benjamin Franklin Dillingham in 1899. [pre-1915, $8-10]

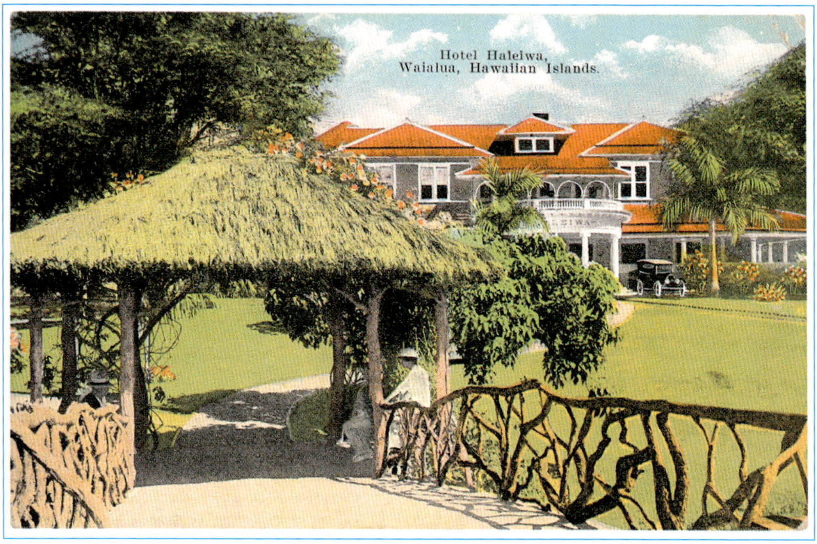

Tourists enjoy the shade provided by a grass-thatched gazebo outside the Hotel Haleiwa. [canceled 1921, $8-10]

Guests cross a primitive looking bridge to the "modern" luxuries of the Haleiwa Hotel. [pre-1915, $8-10]

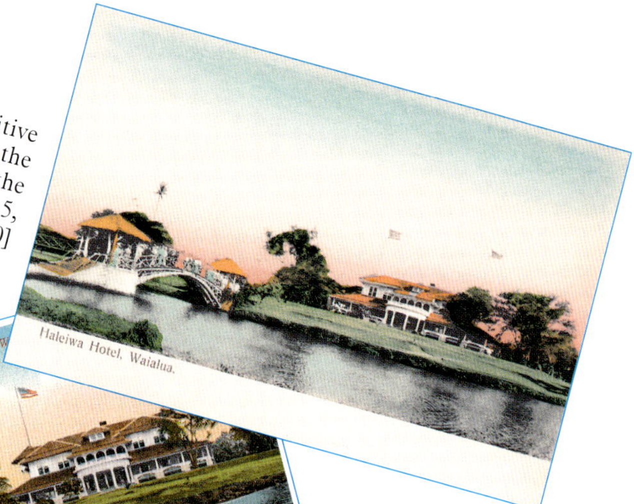

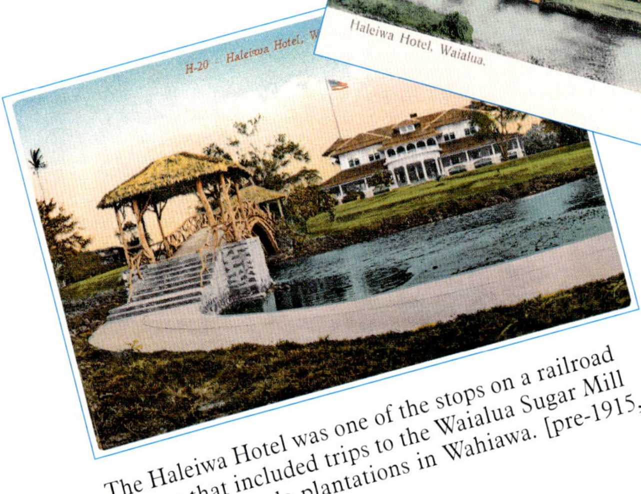

The Haleiwa Hotel was one of the stops on a railroad journey that included trips to the Waialua Sugar Mill and the pineapple plantations in Wahiawa. [pre-1915, $7-9]

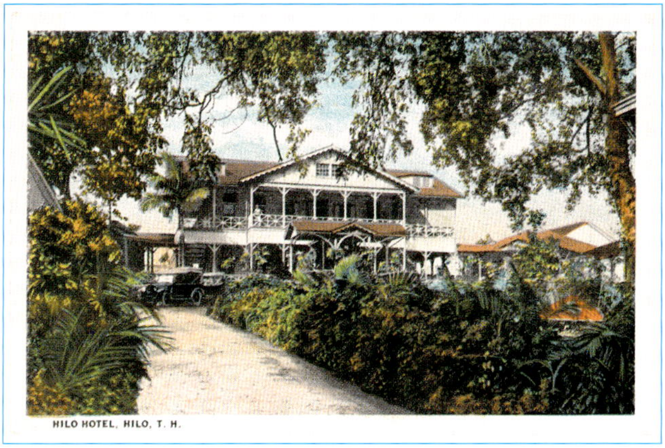

Hilo Hotel, "the leading hotel in the City of Hilo." [pre-1920, $6-9]

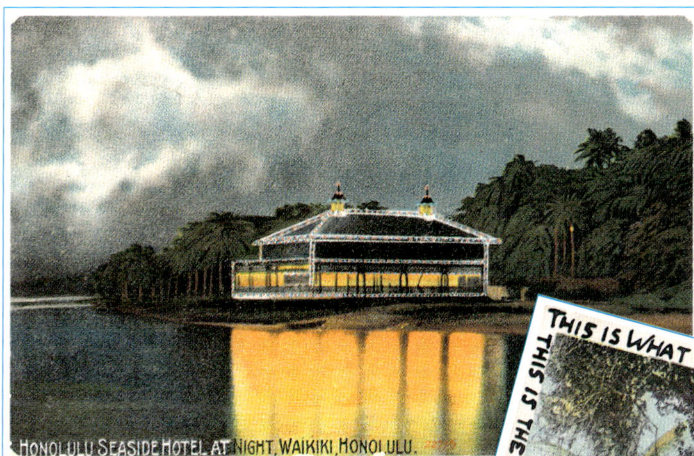

The Honolulu Seaside Hotel all-aglow at night. [canceled 1910, $7-10]

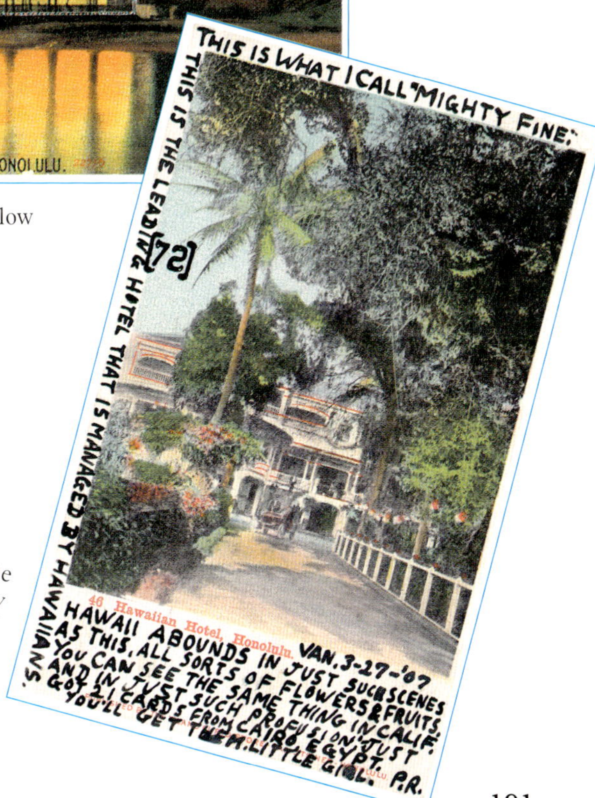

The Hawaiian Hotel, "the leading hotel managed by Hawaiians." [canceled 1901, $6-9]

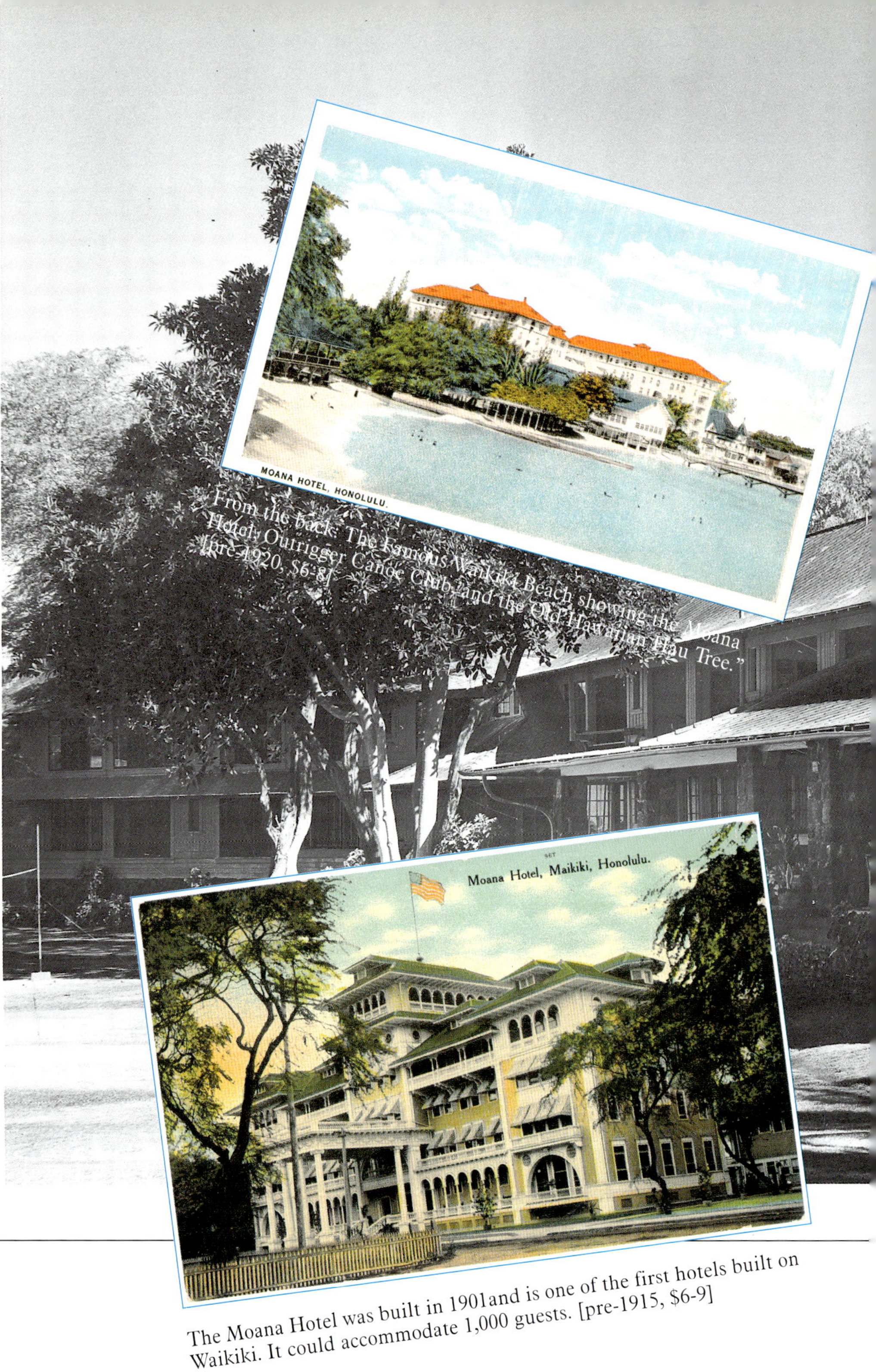

From the back: "The Famous Waikiki Beach showing the Moana Hotel, Outrigger Canoe Club, and the Old Hawaiian Hau Tree." [pre-1920, $6-8]

The Moana Hotel was built in 1901and is one of the first hotels built on Waikiki. It could accommodate 1,000 guests. [pre-1915, $6-9]

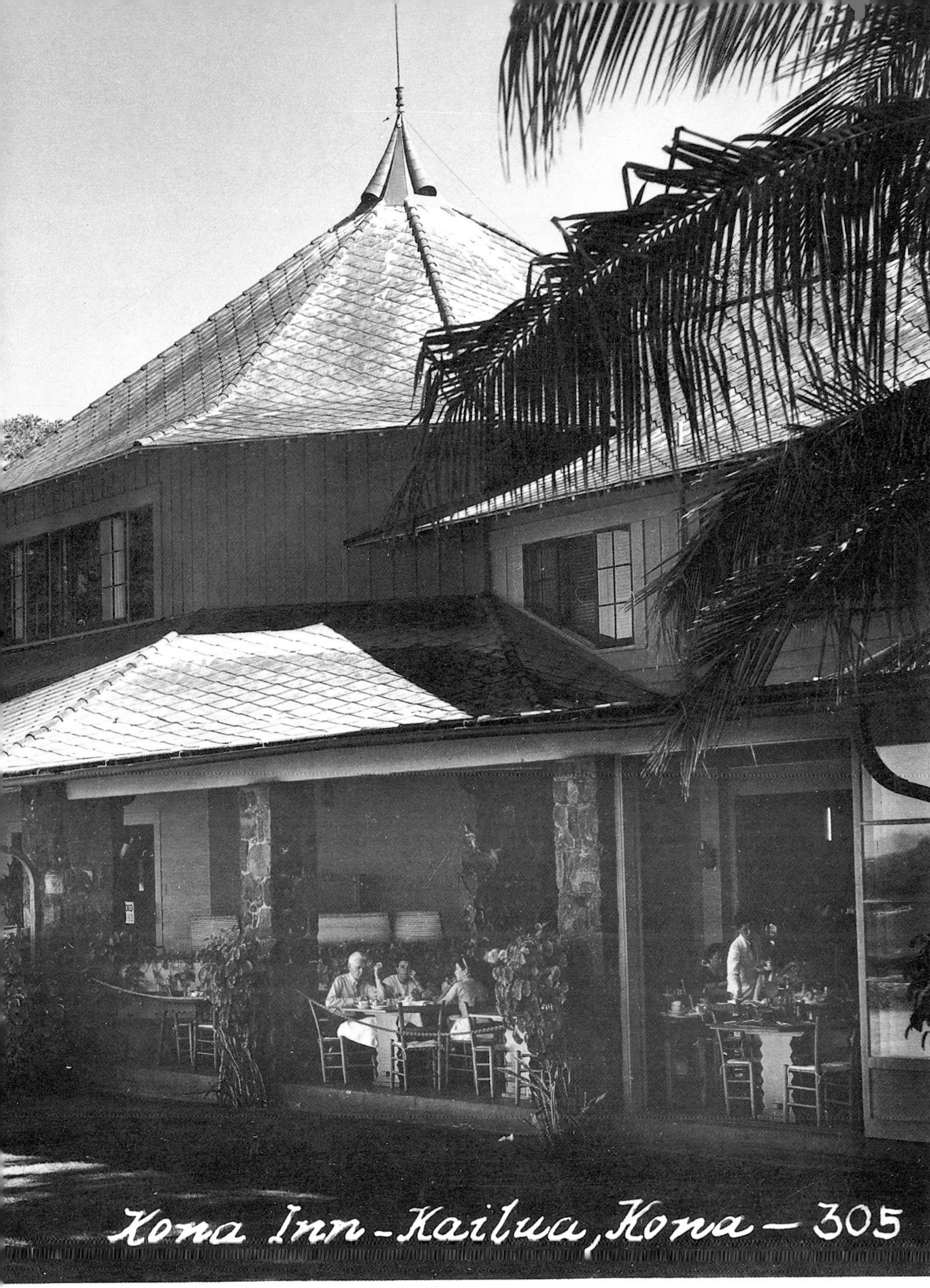

The Kona Inn in Kailua. [pre-1940, $8-10]

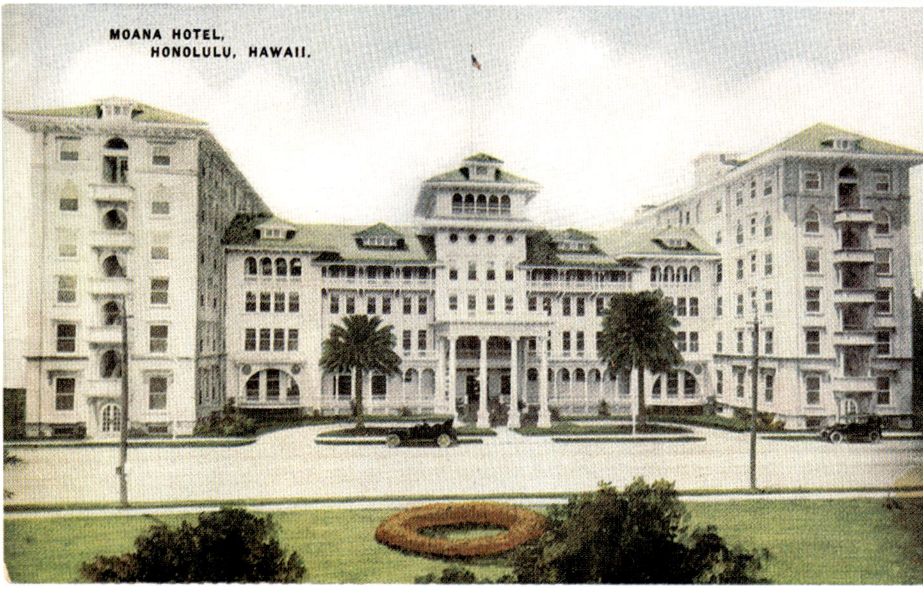

From the back: "The Moana Hotel is of concrete and wood construction and practically fire proof… Moonlight bathing parties, dances and concerts are nightly features of life at the Moana." [pre-1915, $8-10]

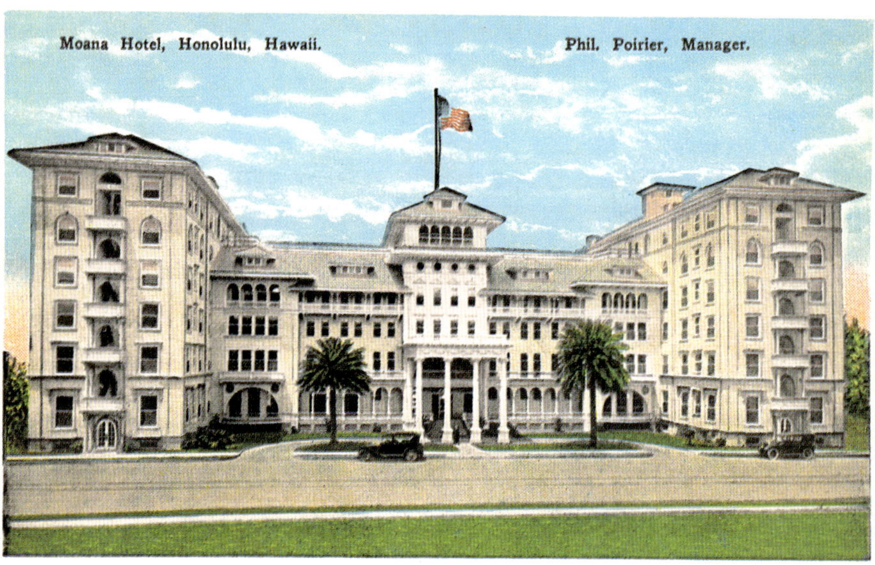

From the back: "A beautiful pier extends far into the ocean from the hotel and from its deck can be witnessed the wonderful aquatic sports which occur at all hours on Waikiki Beach." [pre-1920, $6-8]

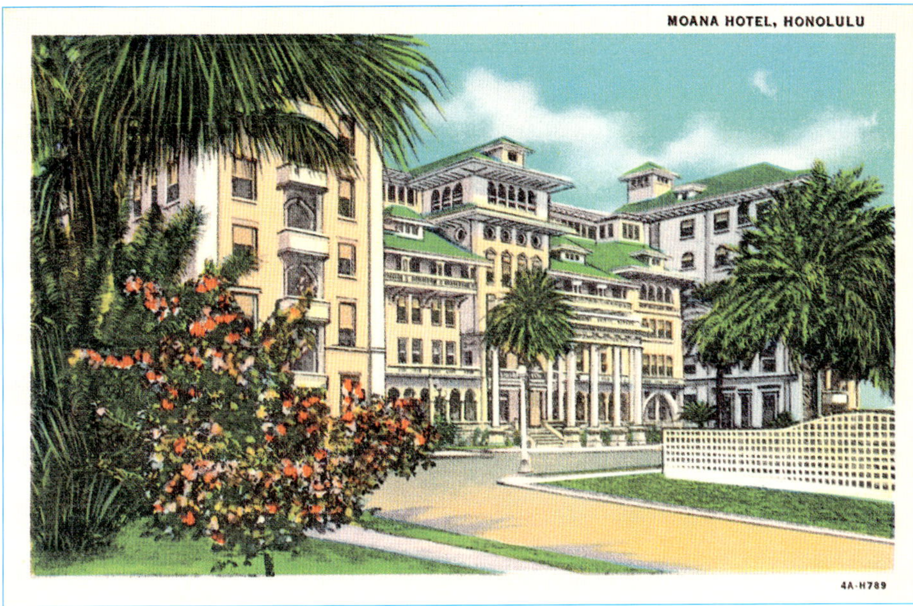

From the back: "Entertaining vacationists [sic] in the 'Paradise of the Pacific' has become the third most important industry of the islands." [pre-1940, $2-4]

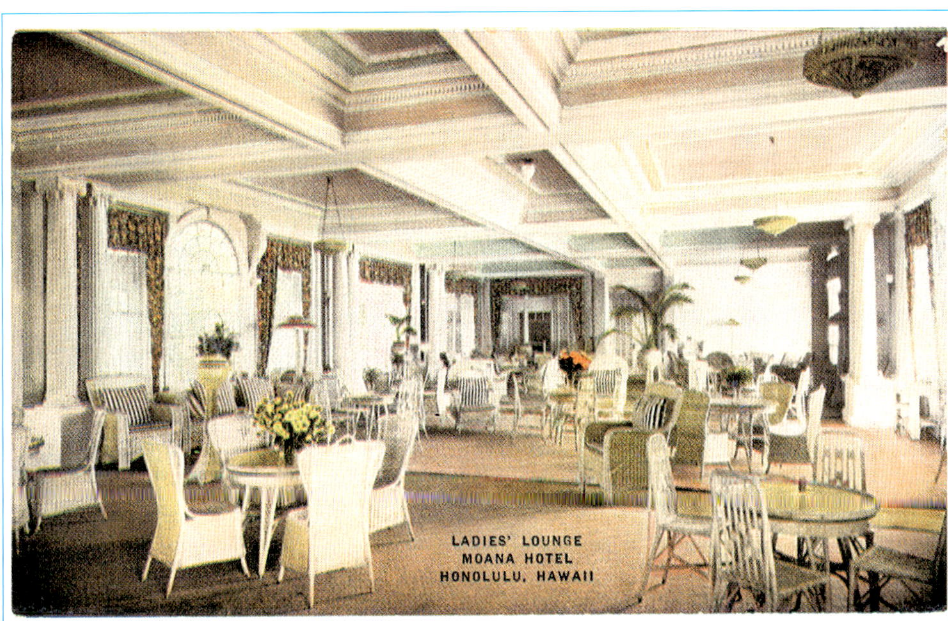

The Ladies Lounge in the Moana Hotel, where fashionable ladies would gather to sit, chat, and perhaps take a cup of tea. [pre-1930, $6-9]

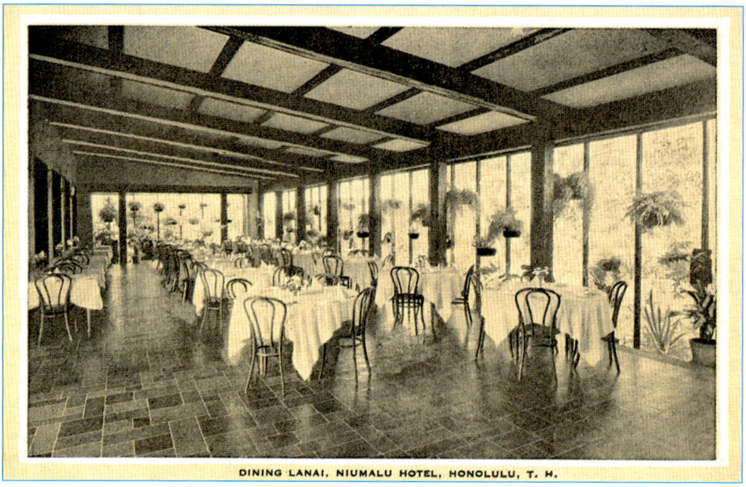

The dining *lanai* (patio) of the Niumalu Hotel. [pre-1940, $6-8]

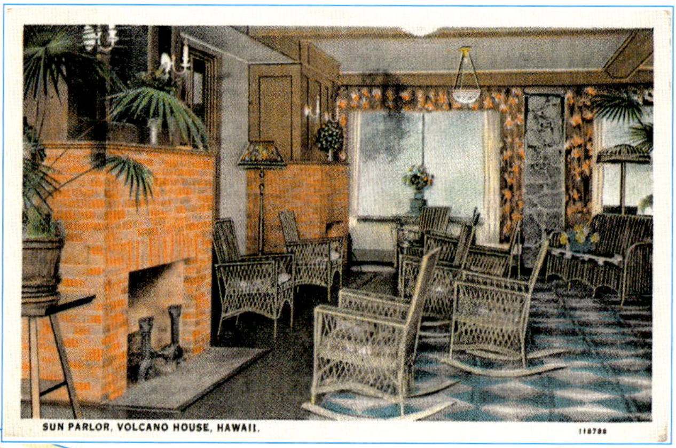

The sun parlor in Volcano House. From the back: "It has a spacious lobby and entrance hall, a ladies' drawing room, lounge and sun-parlor, together with smoking, writing, billiard rooms, etc." [canceled 1929, $8-10]

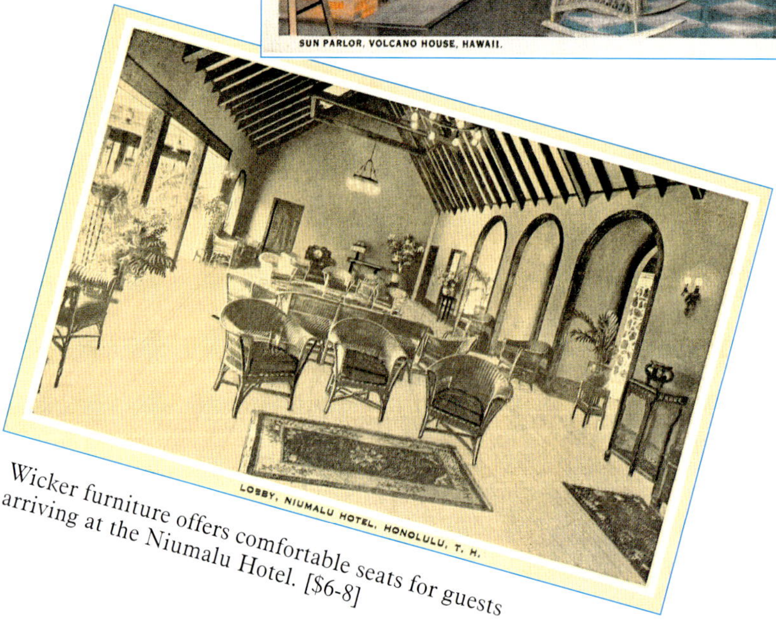

Wicker furniture offers comfortable seats for guests arriving at the Niumalu Hotel. [$6-8]

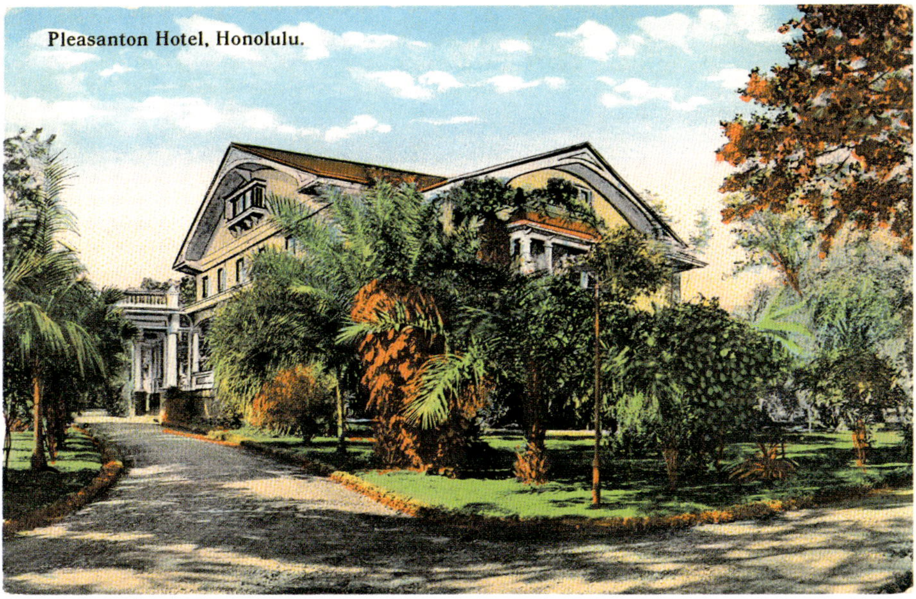

The Pleasanton Hotel, "in the most beautiful residential portion of Honolulu Punahou." [pre-1915, $6-8]

"When I go to my little bungalow the walk passes under giant ferns. I don't have to even bend my head to go under them. On the sides are flowering pomegranits [sic], hibiscus, pointcettas [sic] and the white surf and blue sea show through the blossoms and fern fronds."
—1930

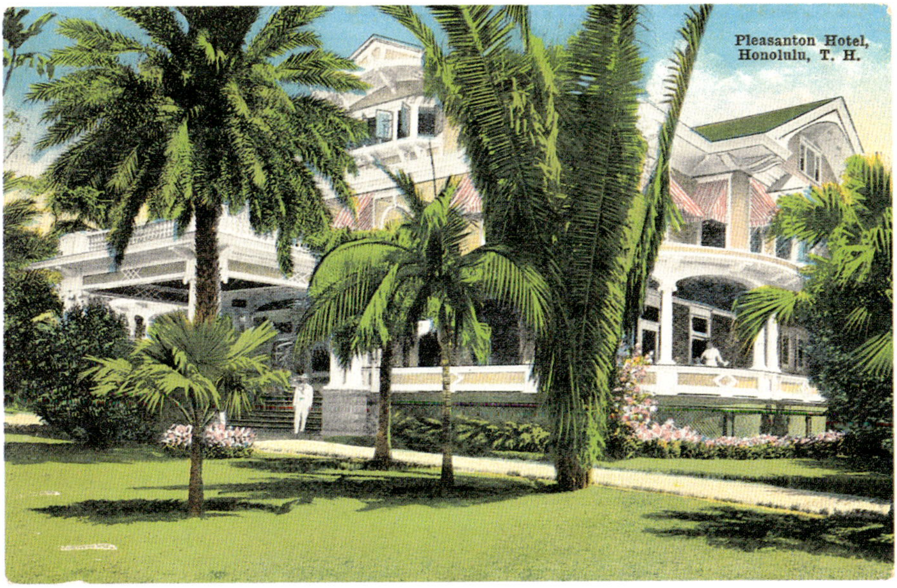

At the Pleasanton, "Lovely grounds occupying five acres of tropical garden surround the palatial building." [pre-1915, $6-8]

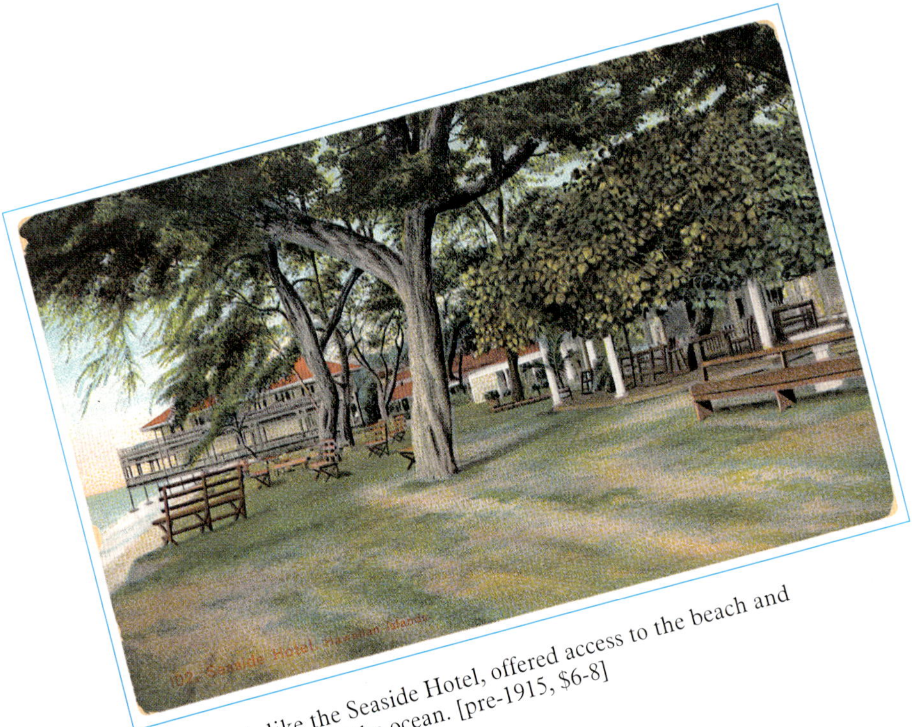

Many hotels like the Seaside Hotel, offered access to the beach and magnificent views of the ocean. [pre-1915, $6-8]

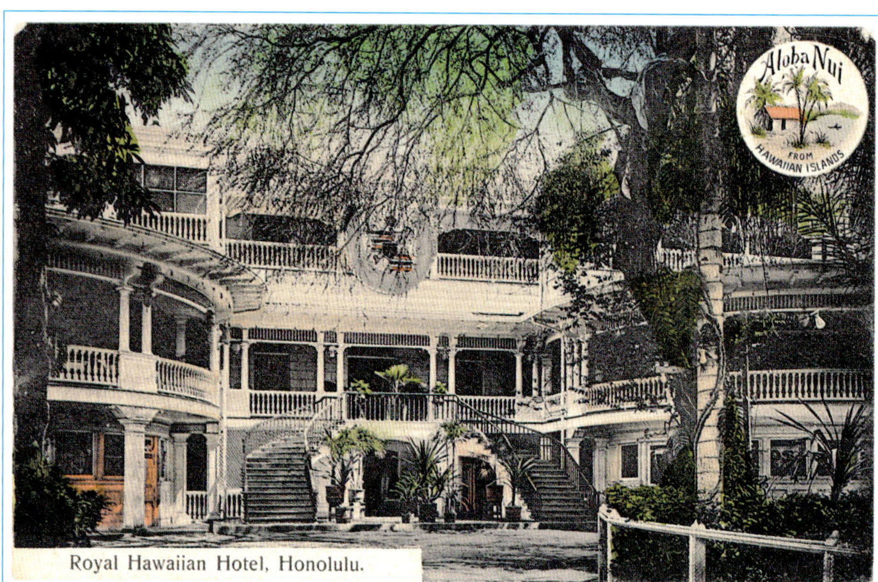

The style is vaguely reminiscent of a Southern plantation or mansion and resembles many of the hotels built during the late part of the 19th Century. [pre-1915, $30-40]

Right:
The famous Royal Hawaiian Hotel as seen from Waikiki Beach. [pre-1940, $10-15]

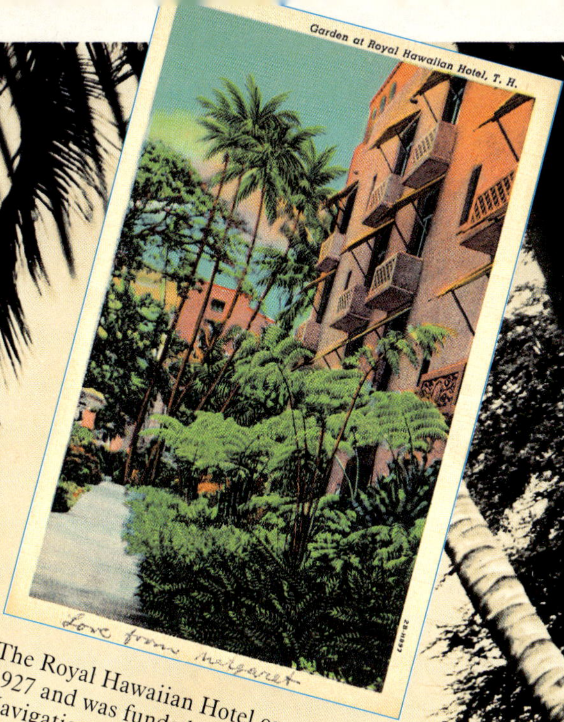

The Royal Hawaiian Hotel opened in 1927 and was funded by the Matson Navigation Company. [canceled 1949, $2-4]

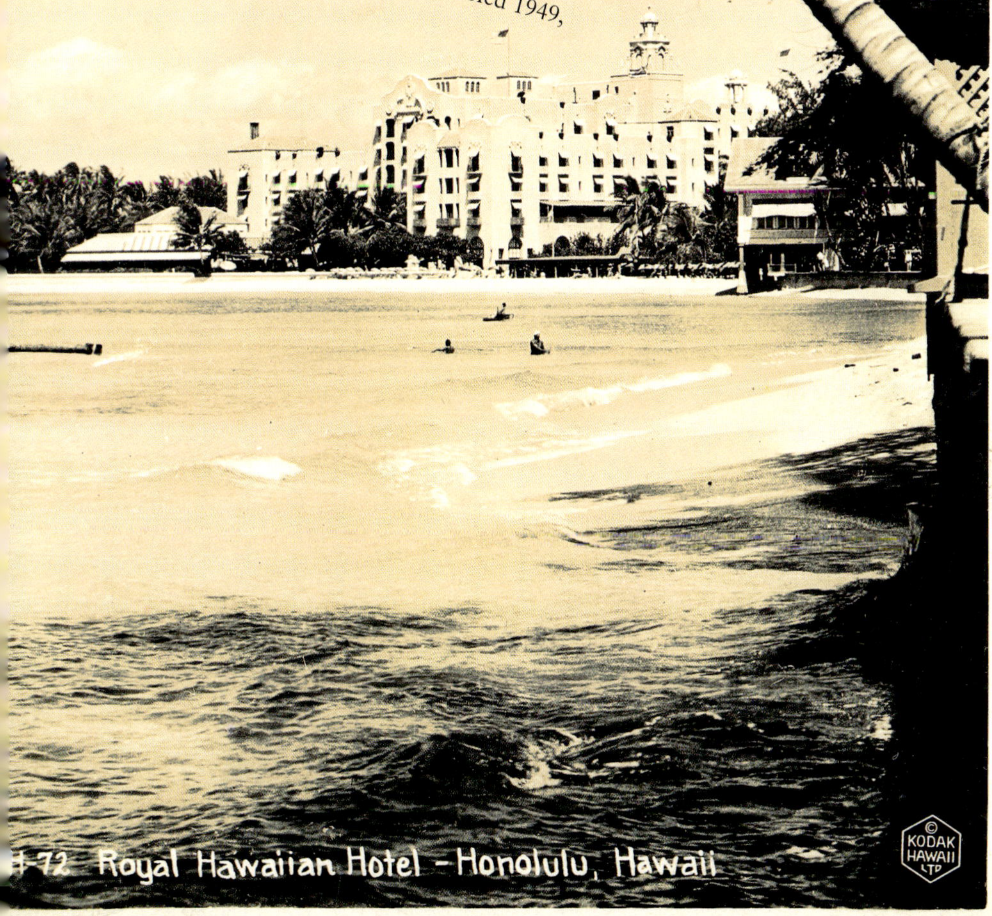

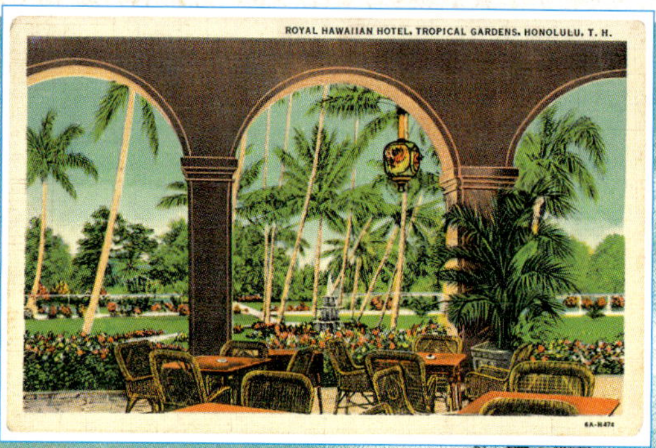

Visitors could sit on the veranda of the Royal Hawaiian and enjoy the view of the Tropical Gardens. [pre-1940, $2-4]

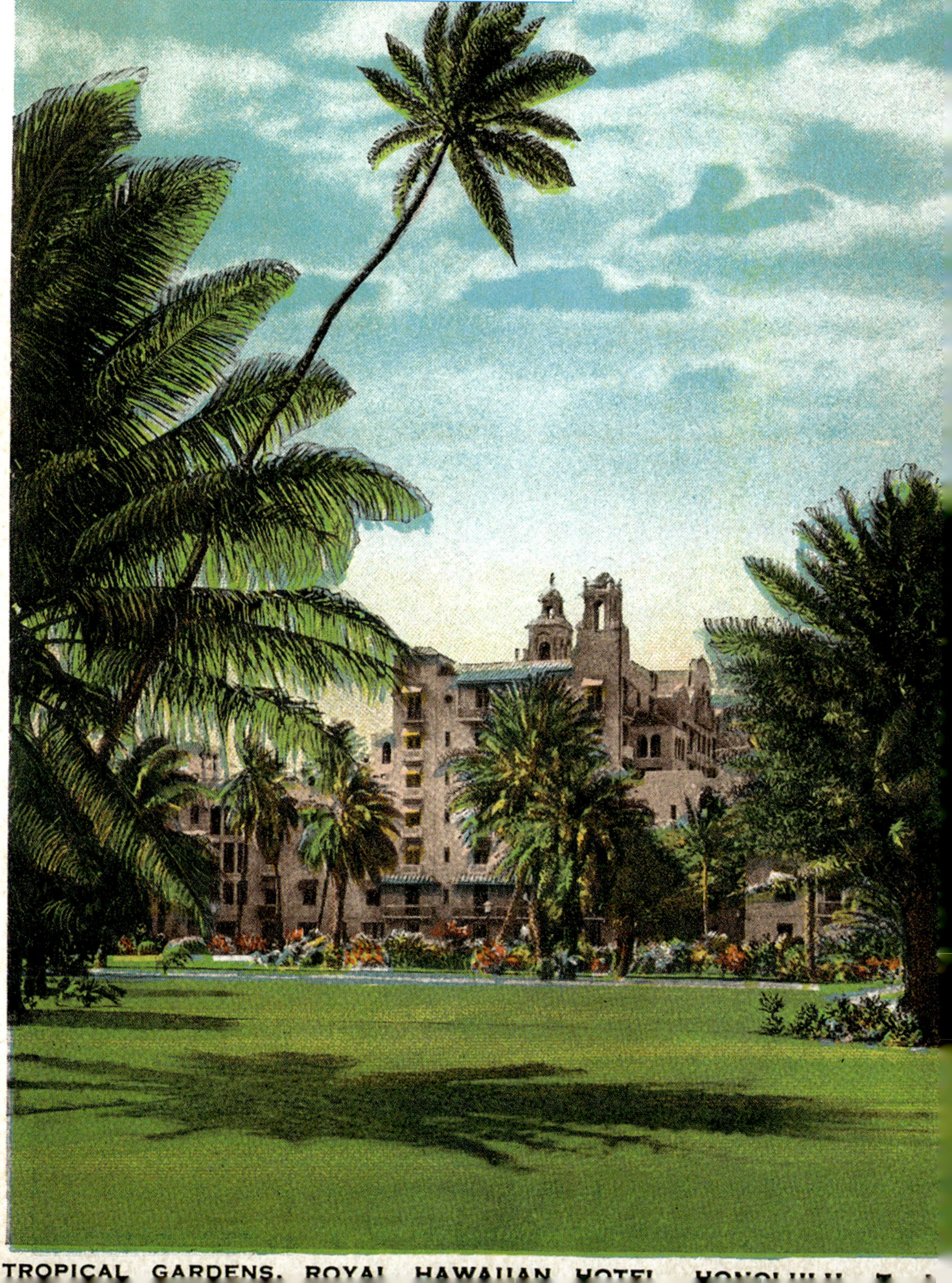

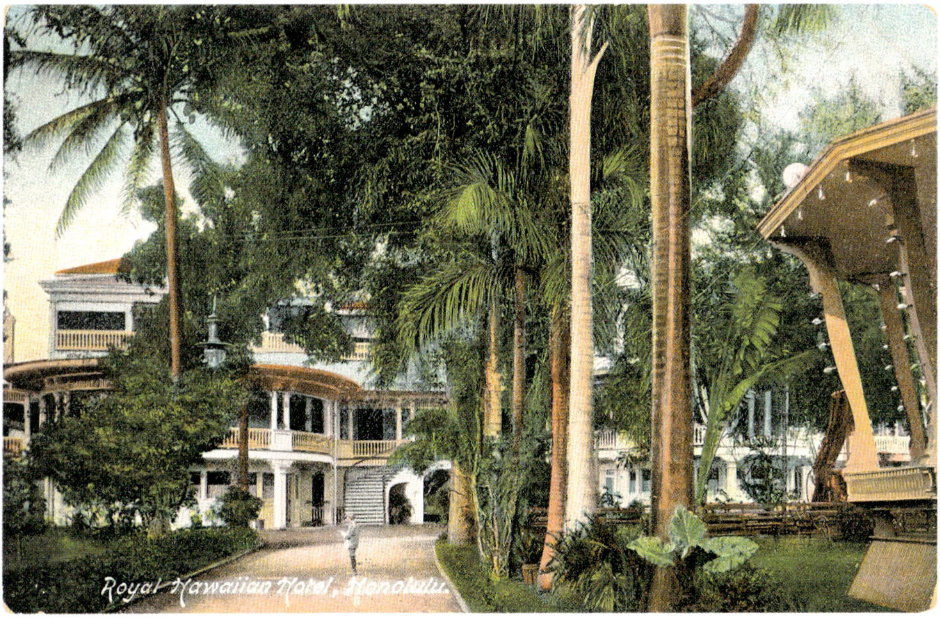

Stately palms line the entranceway to the Royal Hawaiian Hotel. [pre-1915, $7-9]

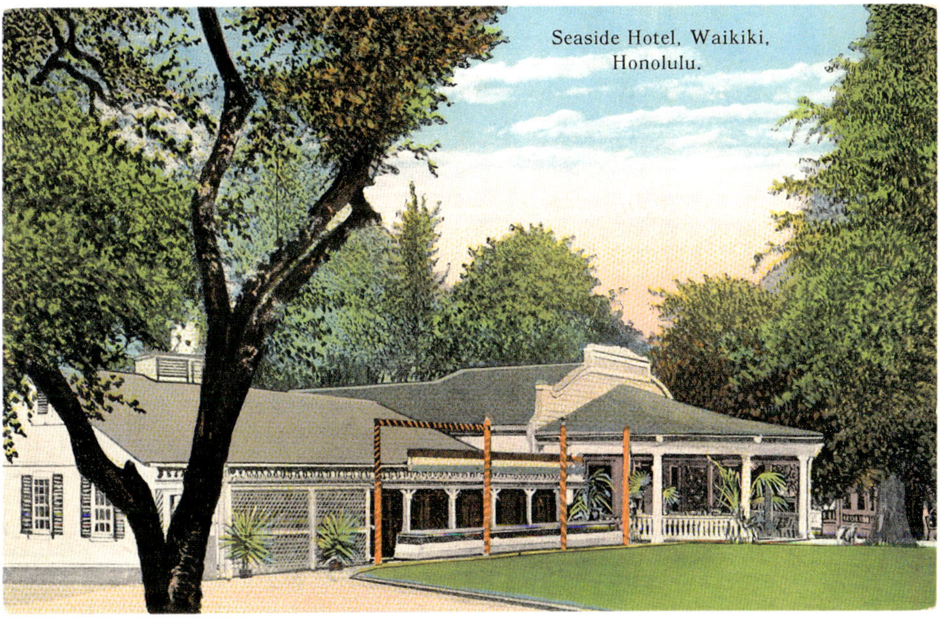

Waikiki's Seaside Hotel, "situated in the grove of coconut trees." [pre-1915, $7-9]

Left:
The "Pink Palace" of the Royal Hawaiian, as seen from the Tropical Gardens located on the Hotel Grounds. [pre-1920, $6-8]

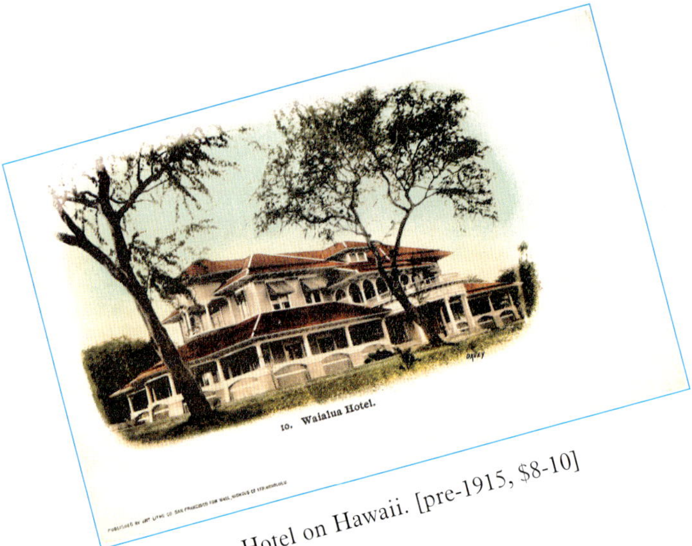

The Waialua Hotel on Hawaii. [pre-1915, $8-10]

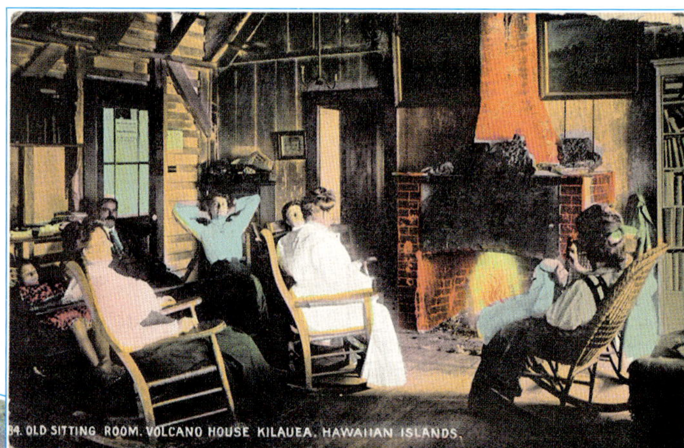

Visitors at the old sitting room in the first, wooden Volcano House constructed in 1877. [pre-1915, $8-10]

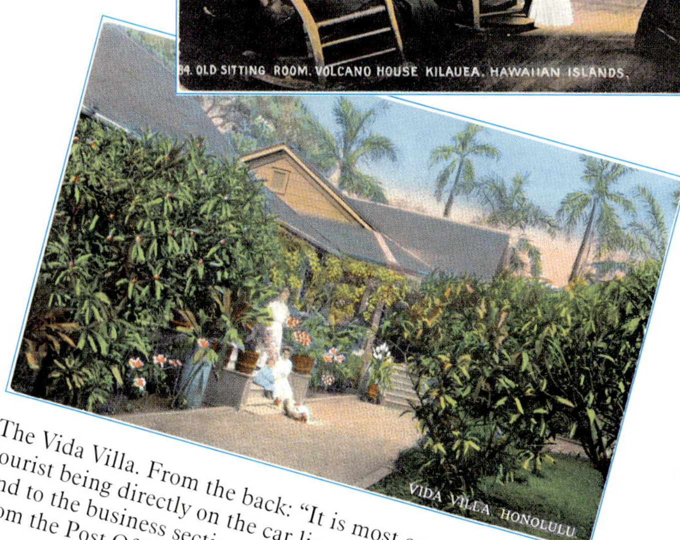

The Vida Villa. From the back: "It is most convenient to the tourist being directly on the car lines running to Waikiki and to the business section of the city, about ten minutes from the Post Office." [pre-1915, $7-9]

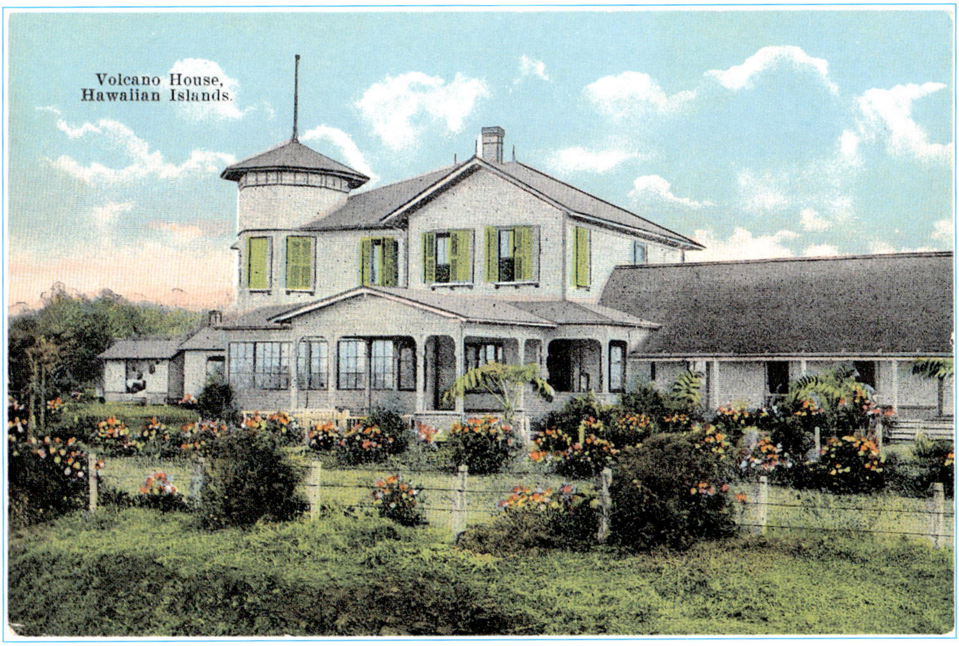

Volcano House is Hawaii's oldest continually operating hotel. [pre-1915, $7-9]

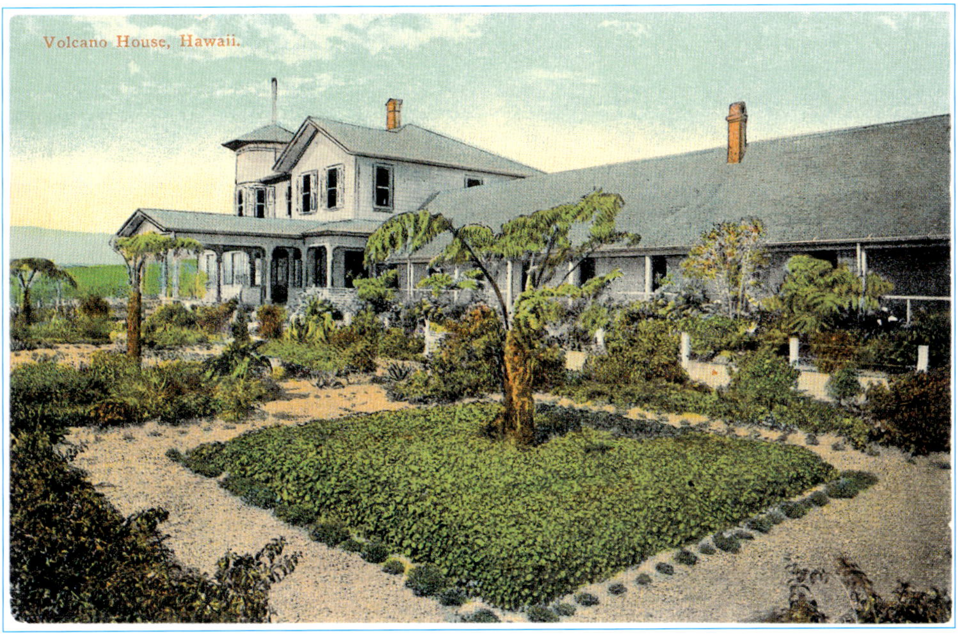

Volcano House is only about a mile and a half from the crater of Kilauea. In fact, the crater could be seen quite clearly from the hotel. [pre-1915, $7-9]

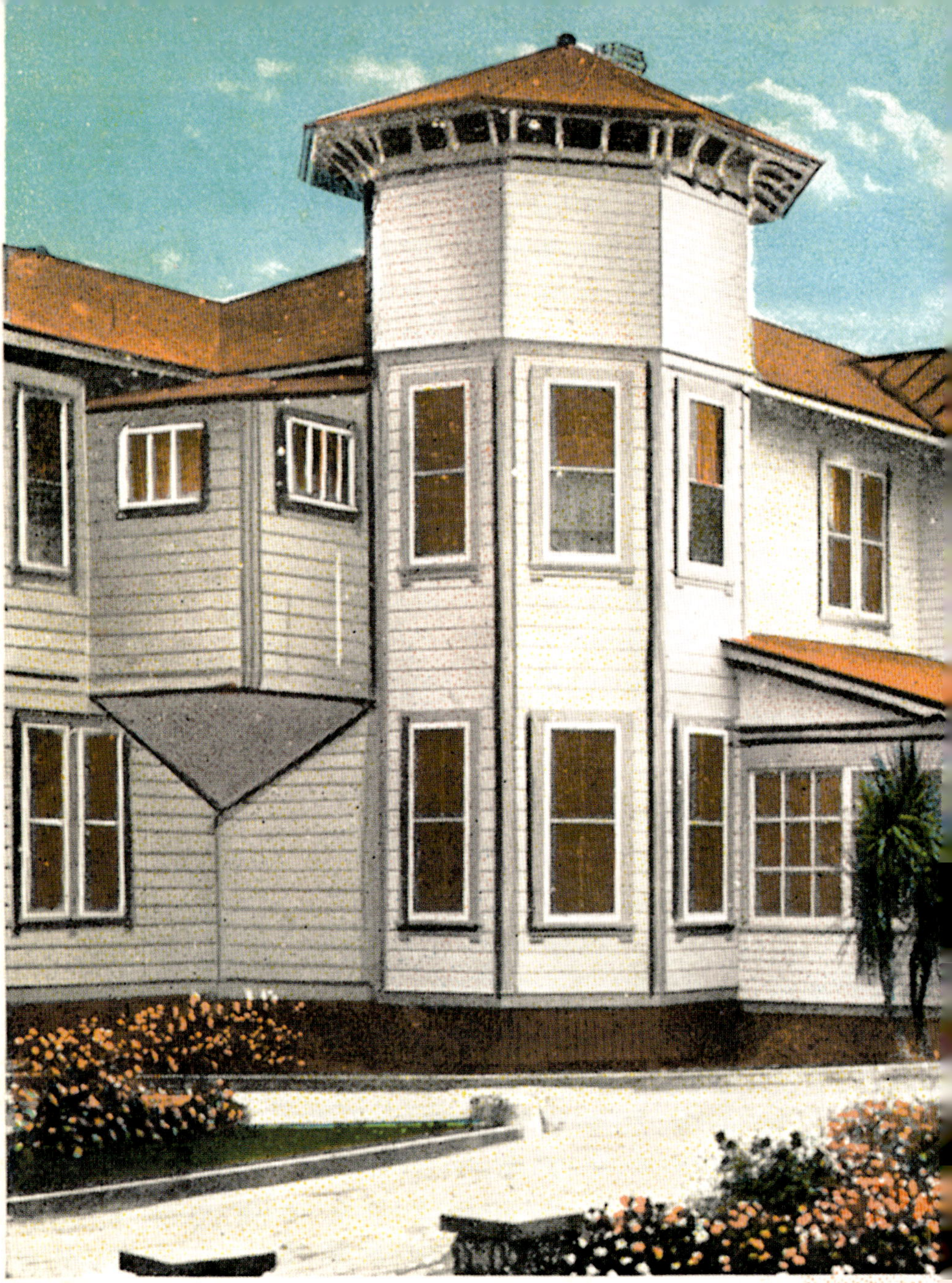

PORTION OF HOTEL FRONTAGE, VOLCANO HOUSE

From the back: "The cuisine is in charge of a first-class chef and is beyond reproach. The Volcano House maintains its own private poultry farm and dairy herds, and possesses extensive grounds with fruit, flower and vegetable gardens, tennis courts, etc., etc... The location of the Volcano House is unique. It stands in an absolutely safe position on the very brink of the vast active crater of Kilauea Volcano ... [and] also overlooks the largest individual mountain on the surface of the globe." [pre-1915, $7-9]

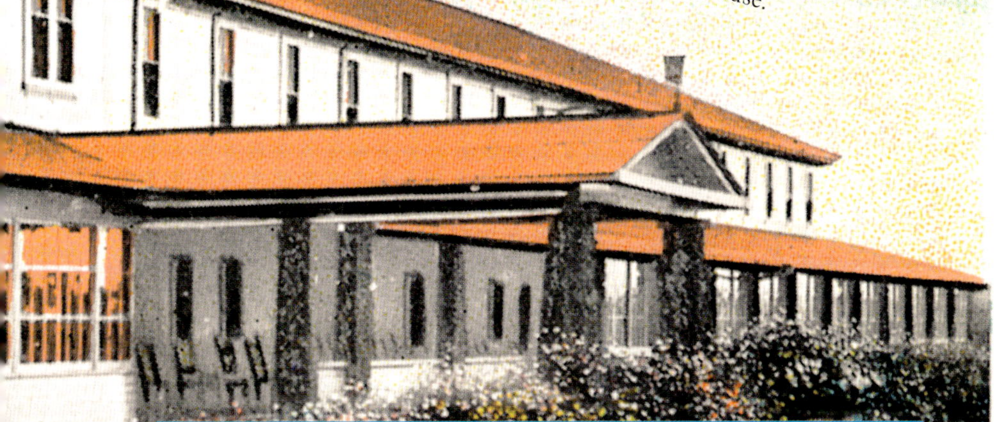

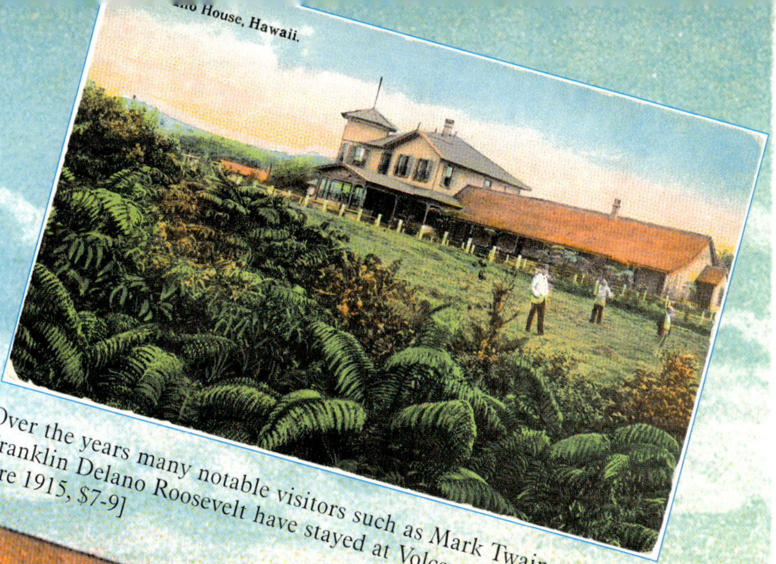

Over the years many notable visitors such as Mark Twain and Franklin Delano Roosevelt have stayed at Volcano House. [pre 1915, $7-9]

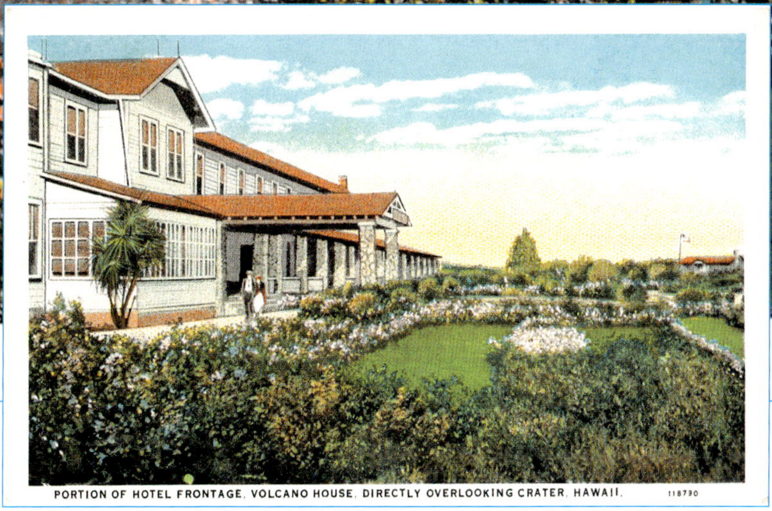

The Volcano House had one hundred-fifty bedrooms, "many of which have private bathrooms attached." [pre-1920, $6-8]

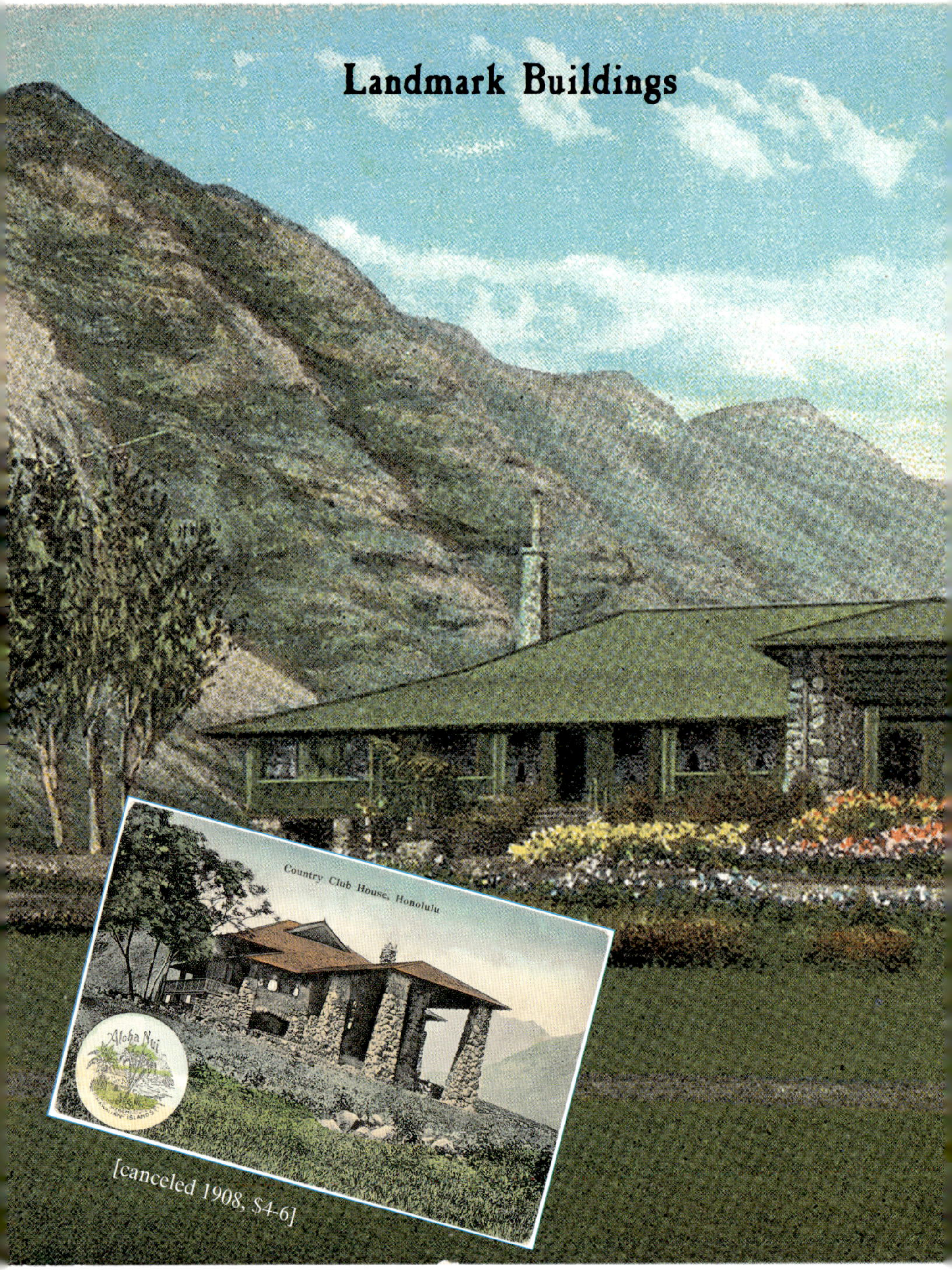

[canceled 1908, $4-6]

From the back: "In the charming valley of Nuuanu and probably the most picturesque site in the world, the Country Club of Honolulu purchased a large expanse of beautiful grounds about 1906. The golf links are perfect and crowded with devotees of the sport every afternoon. It is easily reached by the street cars or by a short and pleasant walk from the city." [pre-1920, $25-40]

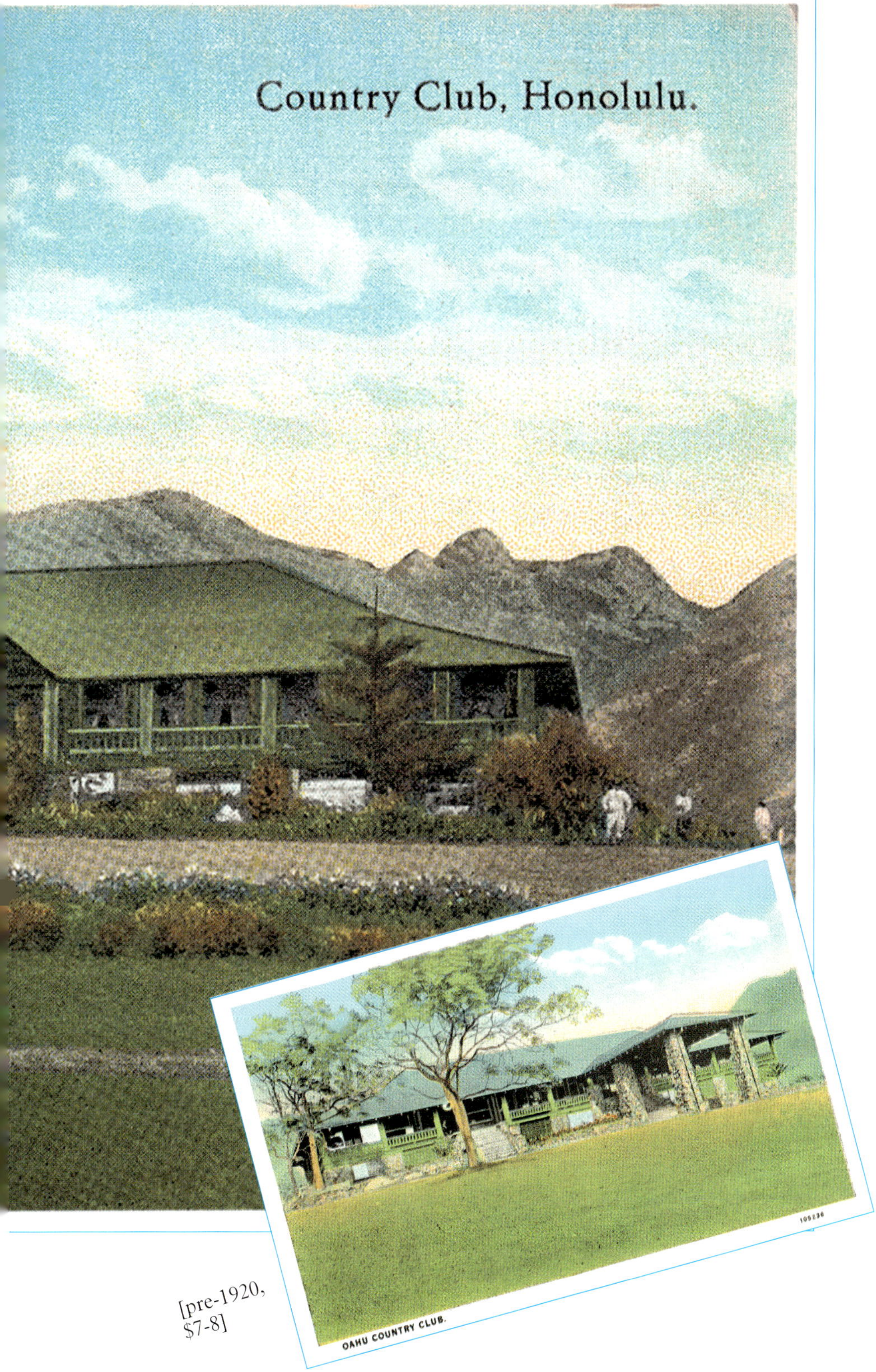

[pre-1920, $7-8]

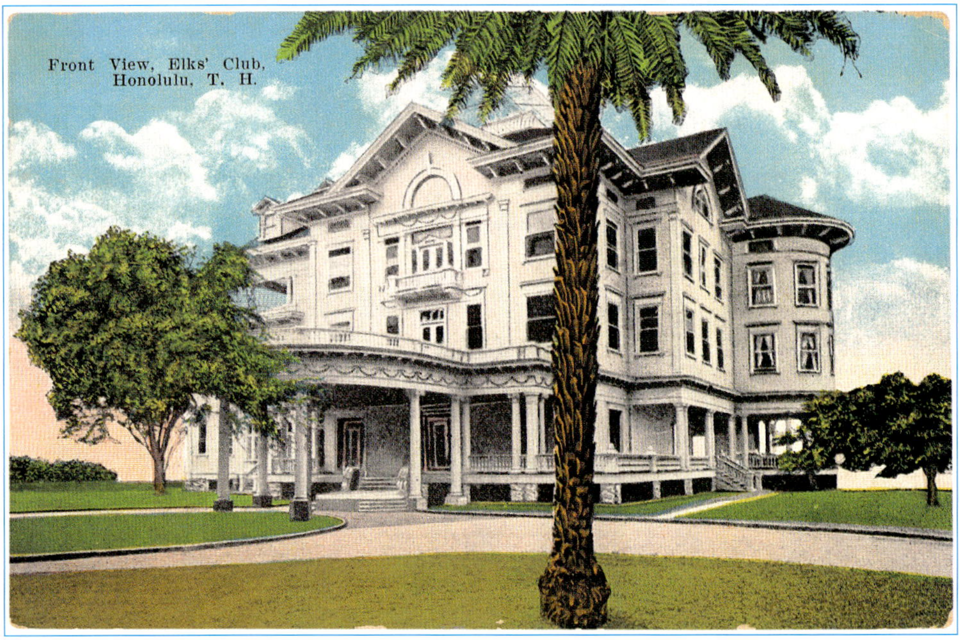

A front view of the Honolulu Elk's Club. [pre-1915, $7-9]

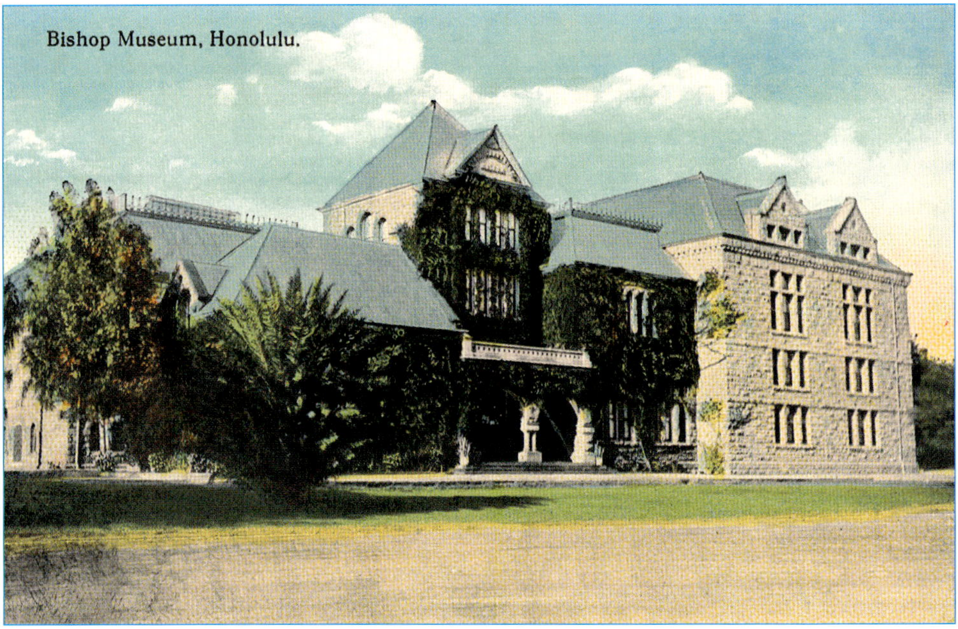

The Bishop Museum was founded in 1889 by Charles Reed Bishop to honor his late wife Princess Bernice Pauahi Bishop. [pre-1915, $7-9]

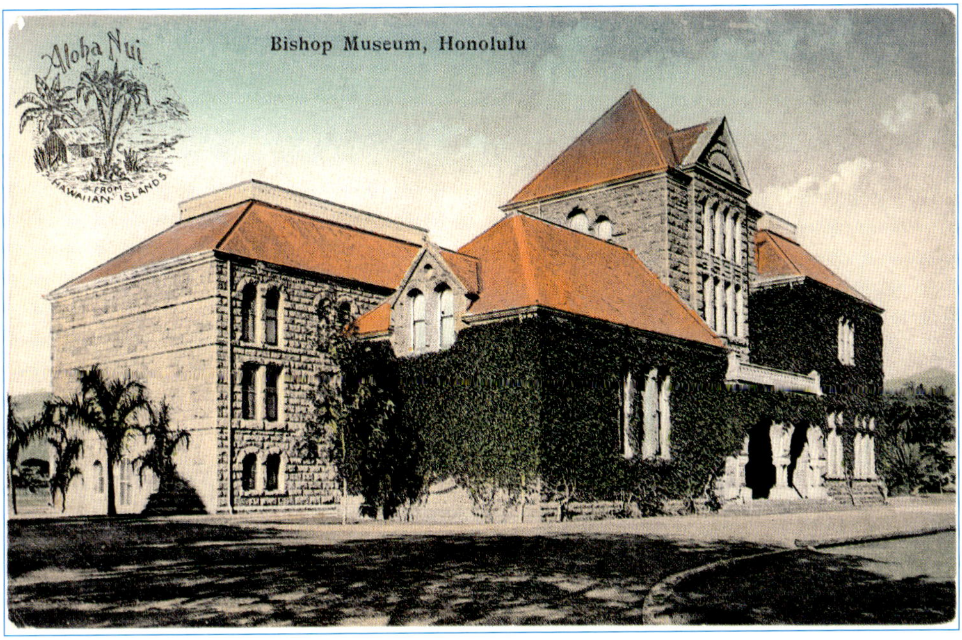

From the back: "The Bishop Museum now houses "the finest ethnological collection of Hawaii and South Sea life of any museum in the world." [pre-1915, $20-35]

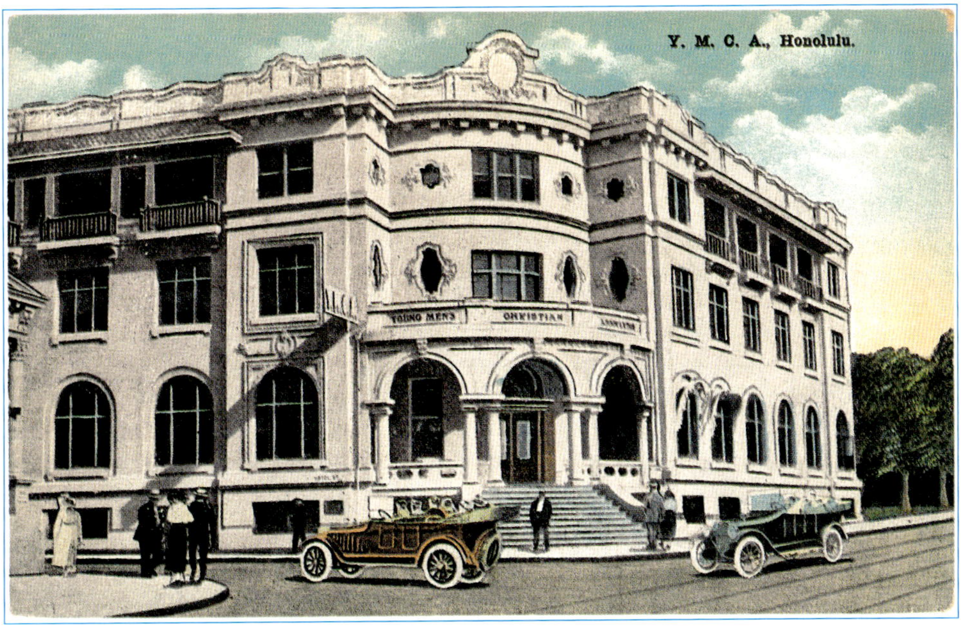

Young missionaries from Boston built the YMCA in Honolulu in 1869. [pre-1915, $8-10]

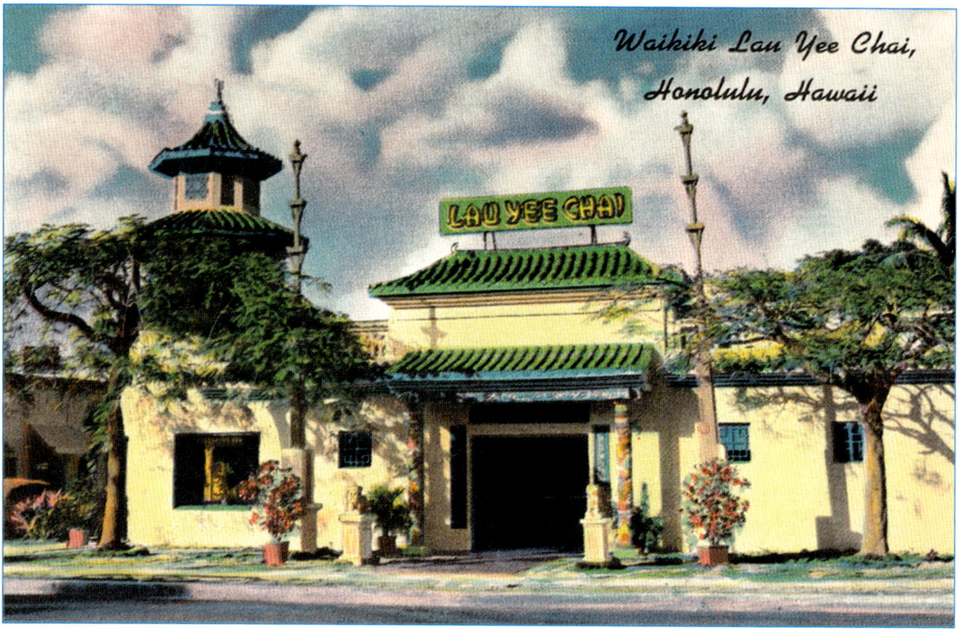

The Waikiki Lau Yee Chai Restaurant, "the world's most beautiful Chinese restaurant." It offered its guests "Chinese cuisine amid authentic Oriental setting." [pre-1940, $3-6]

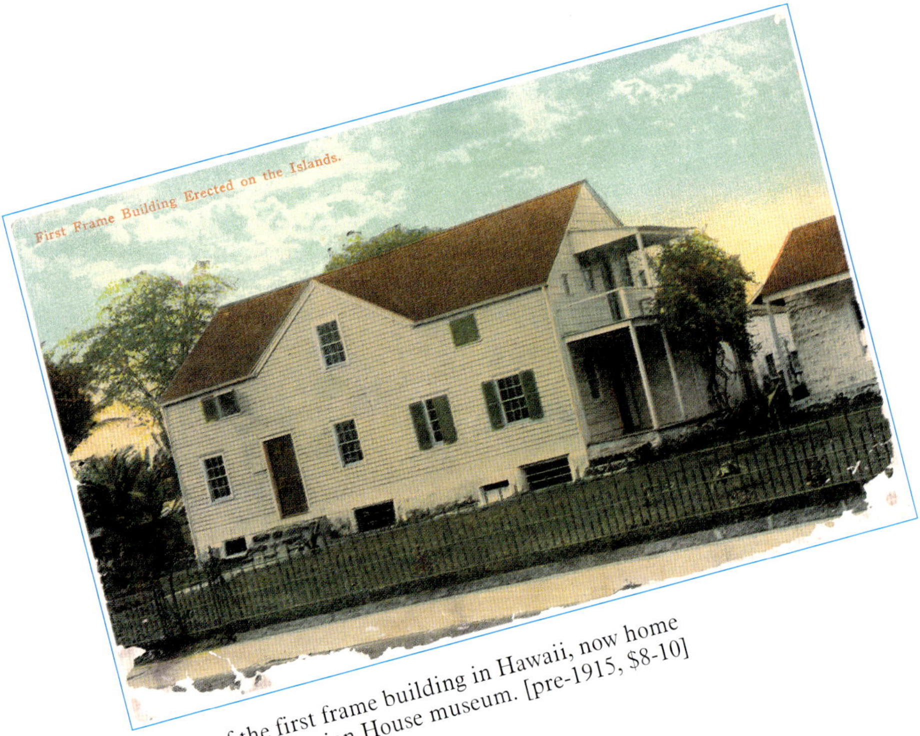

A view of the first frame building in Hawaii, now home to the Cooke Mission House museum. [pre-1915, $8-10]

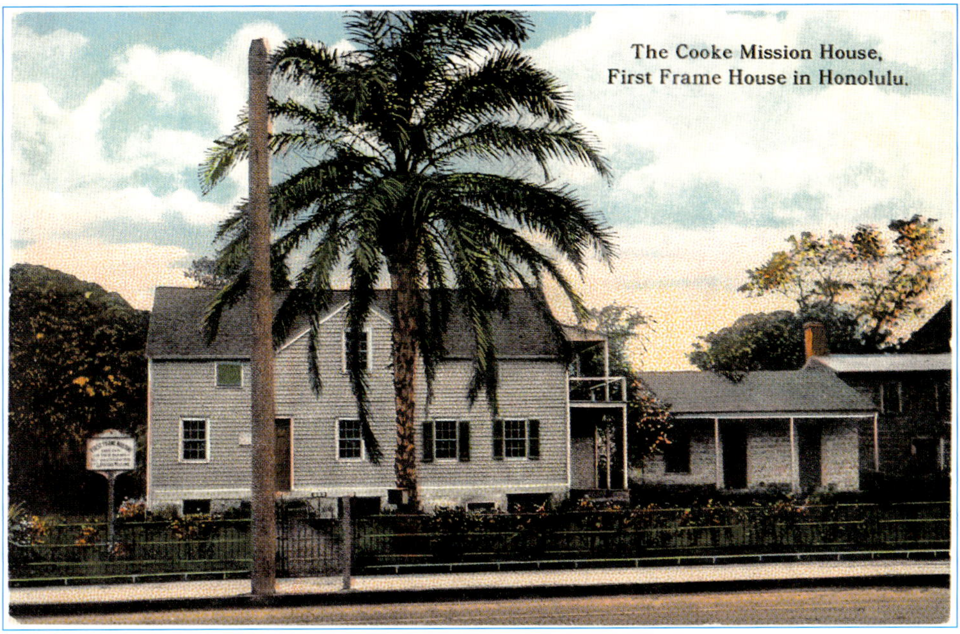

The Cooke family, missionaries from New England, built this house in 1821. [pre-1915, $7-9]

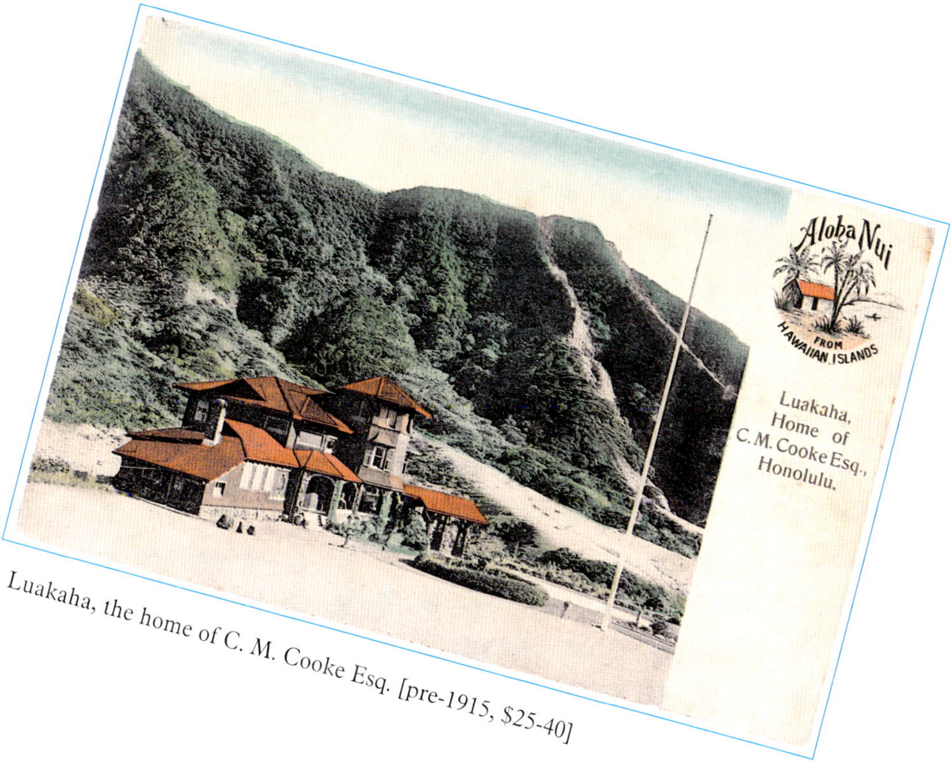

Luakaha, the home of C. M. Cooke Esq. [pre-1915, $25-40]

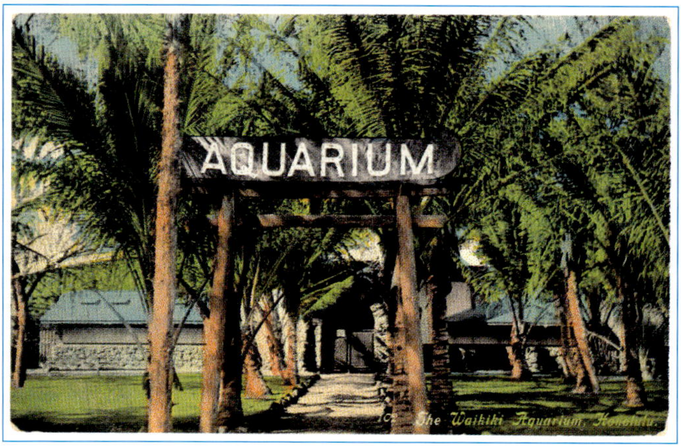

The Honolulu Aquarium, where "From six hundred to one thousand fishes of one hundred varieties are constantly in the aquarium." [pre-1915, $6-9]

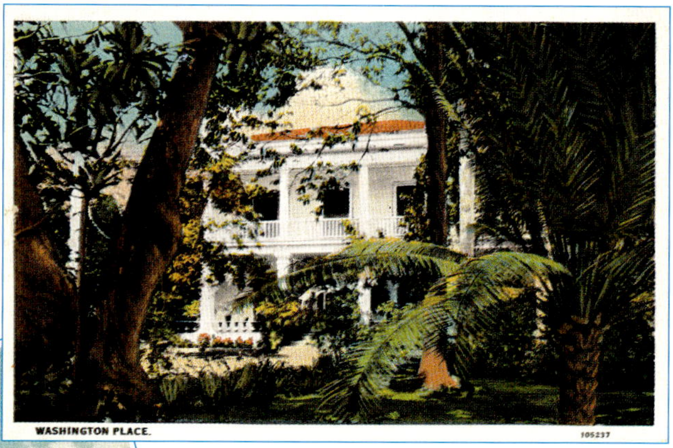

Washington Place used to be the house of former Queen Liliuokalani, now it is the official residence of the Governor of Hawaii. [canceled 1939, $7-9]

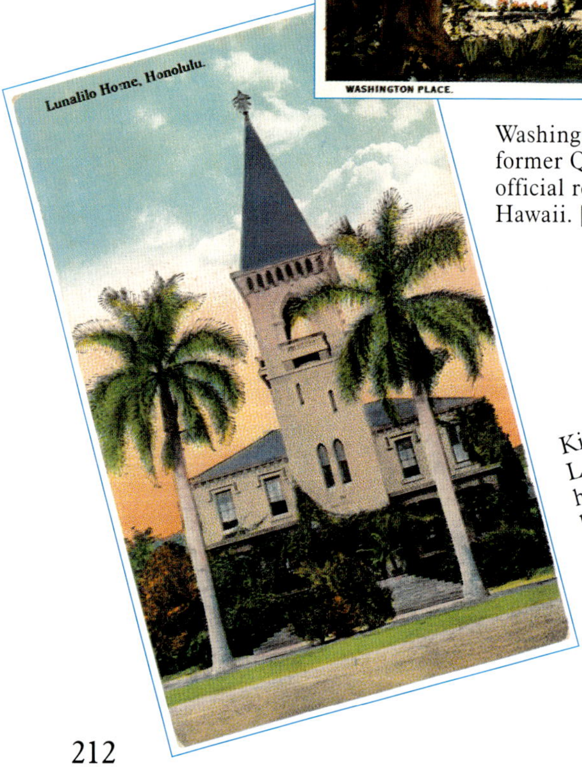

King Lunalilo founded the Lunalilo Home as a retirement home for older Hawaiians. After his death in 1874 he left most of his property to the home, which was opened in 1881. [pre-1915, $7-9]

Churches

The history of religion and education in Hawaii is understandably intertwined. The first missionaries arrived in Hawaii about 1820, to establish churches, schools, and to convert the "heathens." In 1823, Queen Mother Keopuolani became the first Hawaiian to receive a Christian baptism. Missionaries in Hawaii are also credited with establishing a written form of the "Hawaiian" language, which previously had only an oral tradition.

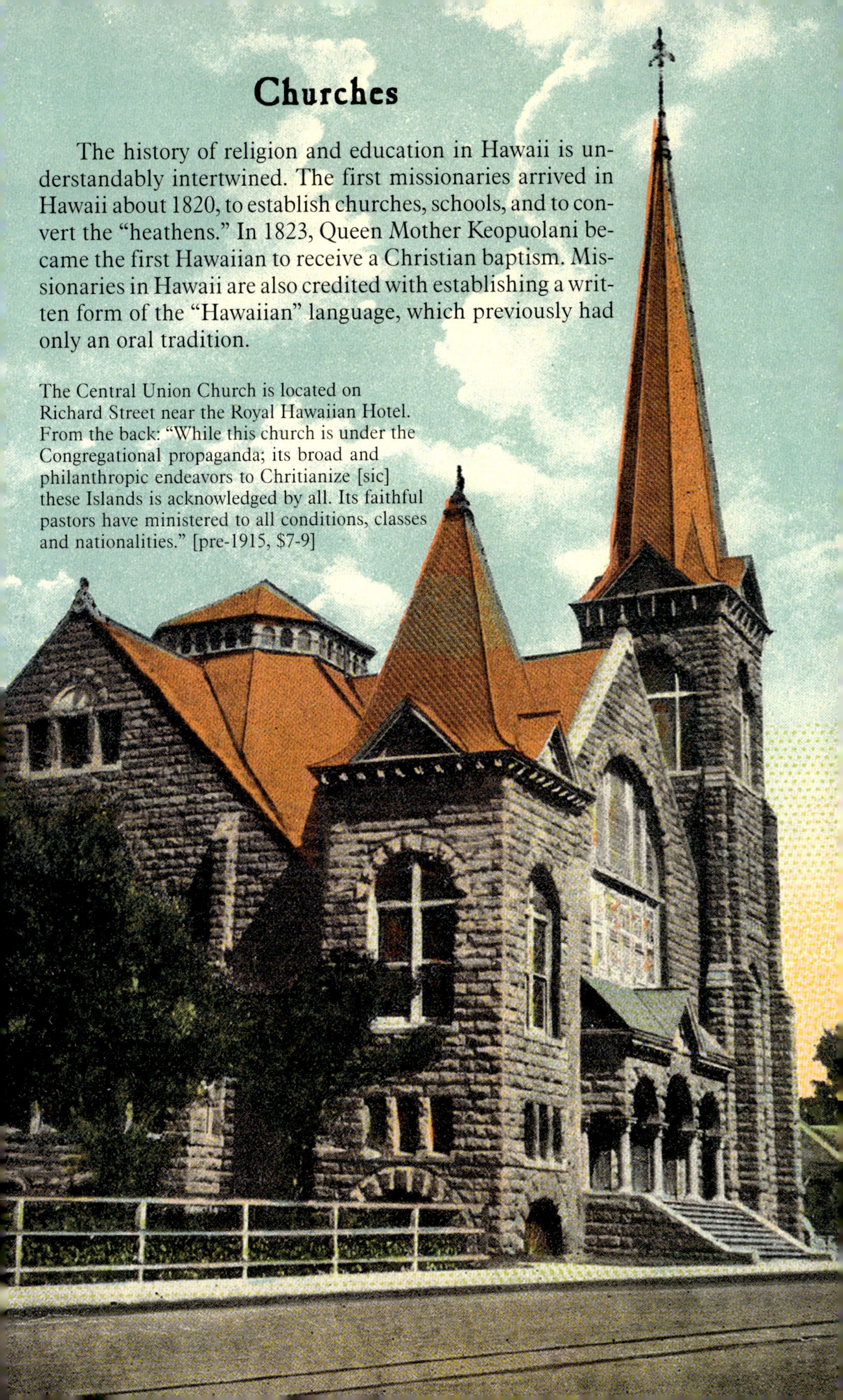

The Central Union Church is located on Richard Street near the Royal Hawaiian Hotel. From the back: "While this church is under the Congregational propaganda; its broad and philanthropic endeavors to Chritianize [sic] these Islands is acknowledged by all. Its faithful pastors have ministered to all conditions, classes and nationalities." [pre-1915, $7-9]

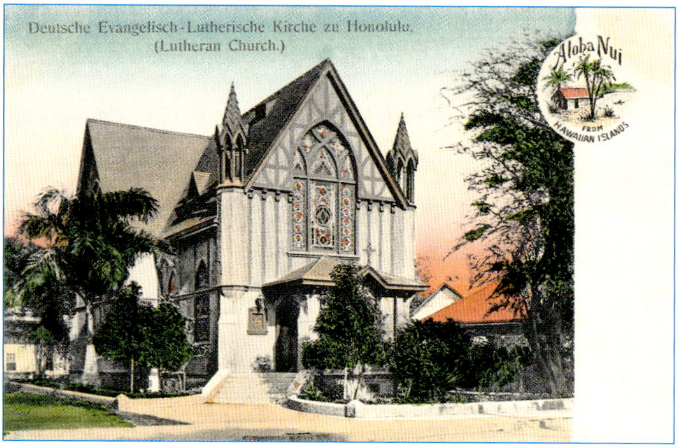

The Deutsche Evangelisch-Lutherische Kirche zu, Honolulu was founded in 1900 by German immigrants. [pre-1915, $20-30]

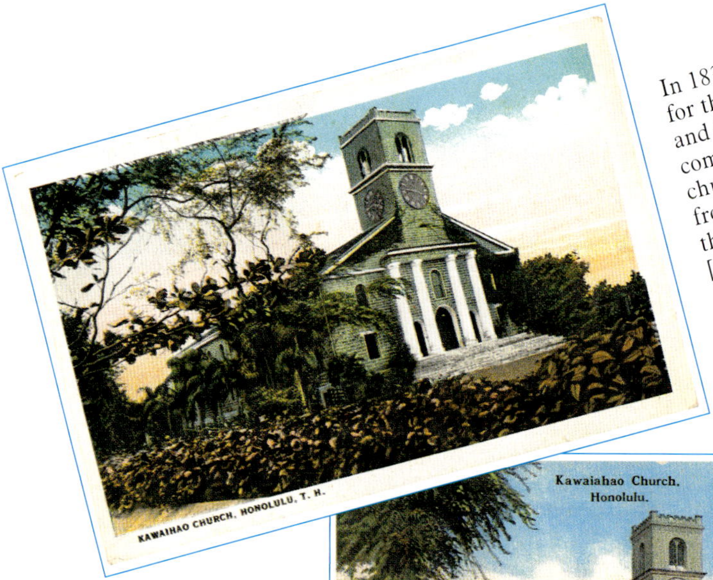

In 1839, the cornerstone for this church was laid and it was finally completed in 1841. The church itself is built from coral taken from the Pacific Ocean. [pre-1915, $6-8]

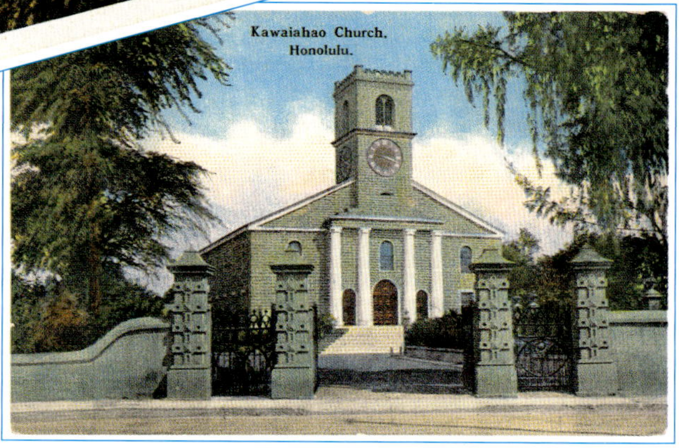

The Kawaiahao Church is the oldest native church in the Hawaiian Islands. From the back: "… the corner stone was laid in 1839, and the edifice completed in 1841. It has been the church of ancient royalty." [pre-1915, $6-8]

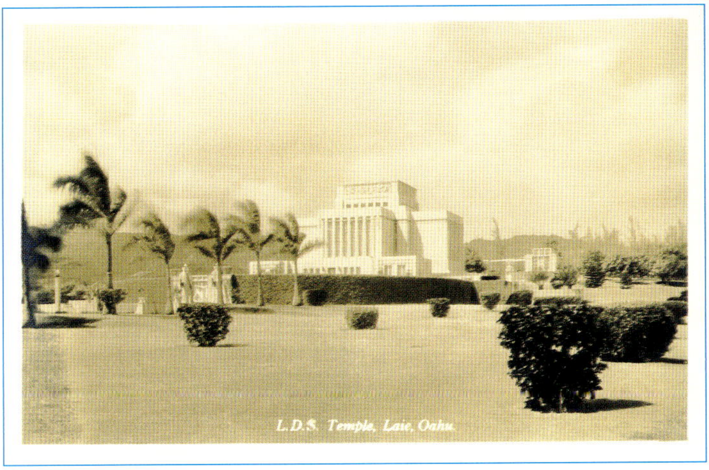

The design of the Mormon Temple is reminiscent of ancient temples found in South America. [pre-1940, $6-9]

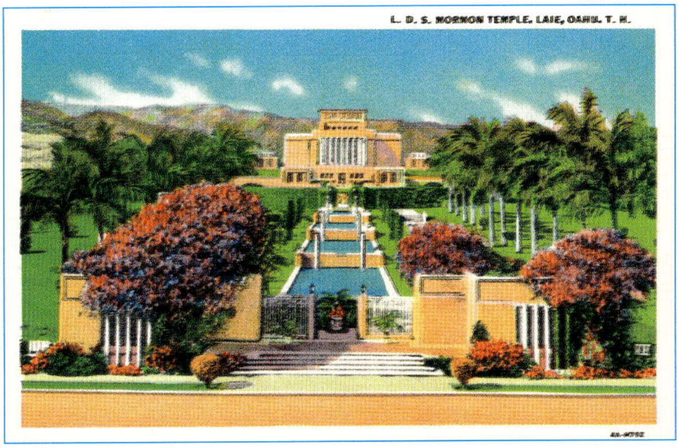

The land on which the L.D.S. Mormon Temple in Laie, Oahu stands is former plantation land purchased by the Mormon Church in 1865. [pre-1940, $2-4]

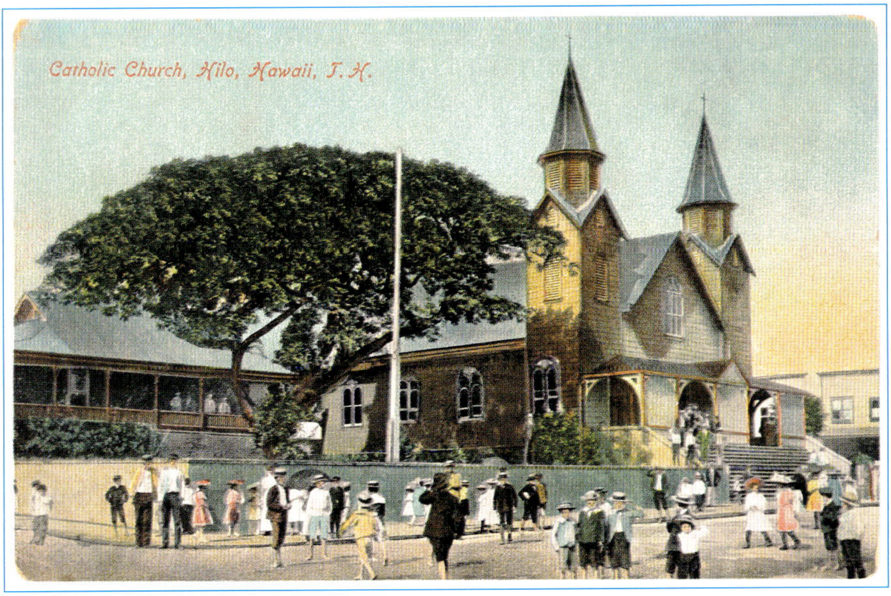

A Catholic Church in Hilo. Catholics first came to Hawaii in 1827. [pre-1915, $8-10]

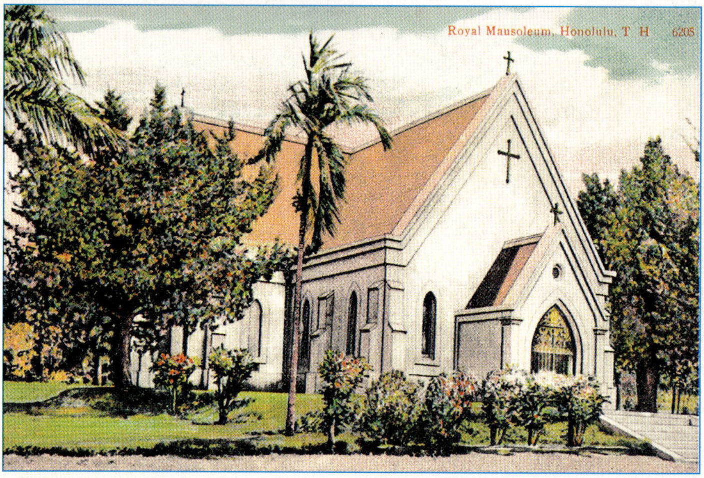

The Royal Mausoleum was constructed in 1865 and the occupants were moved there from the old mausoleum on the grounds of 'Iolani Palace. [pre-1915, $8-10]

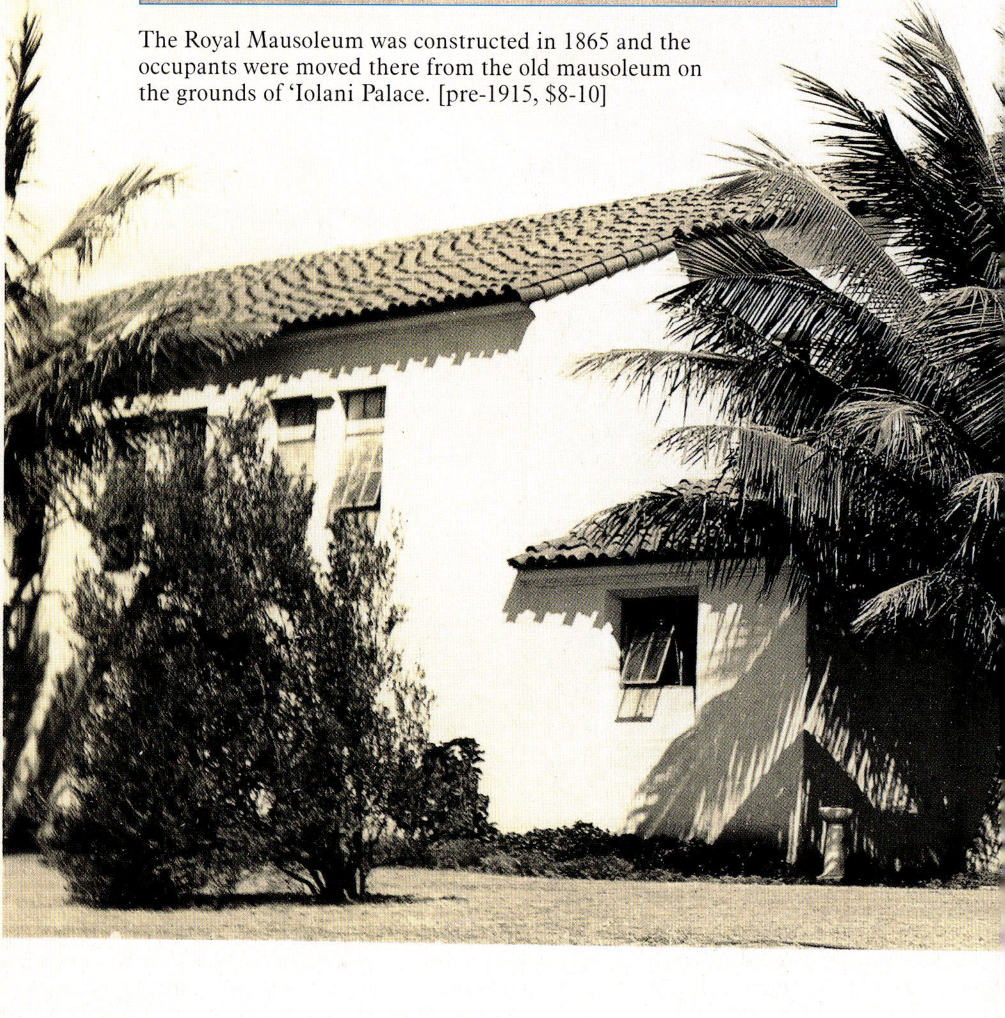

St. Teresa's Church, Kahaluiu, Maui. [pre-1915, $8-9]

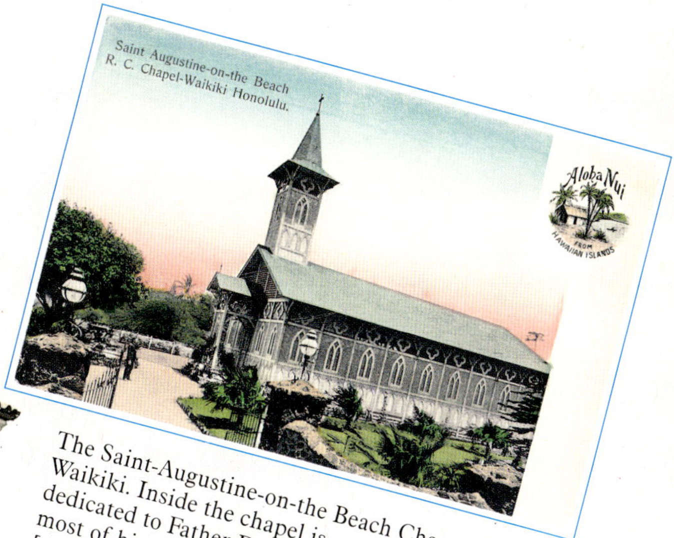

The Saint-Augustine-on-the Beach Chapel in Waikiki. Inside the chapel is a small museum dedicated to Father Damien DeVeuster, who spent most of his life caring for Hawaii's leprosy victims. [pre-1915, $20-30]

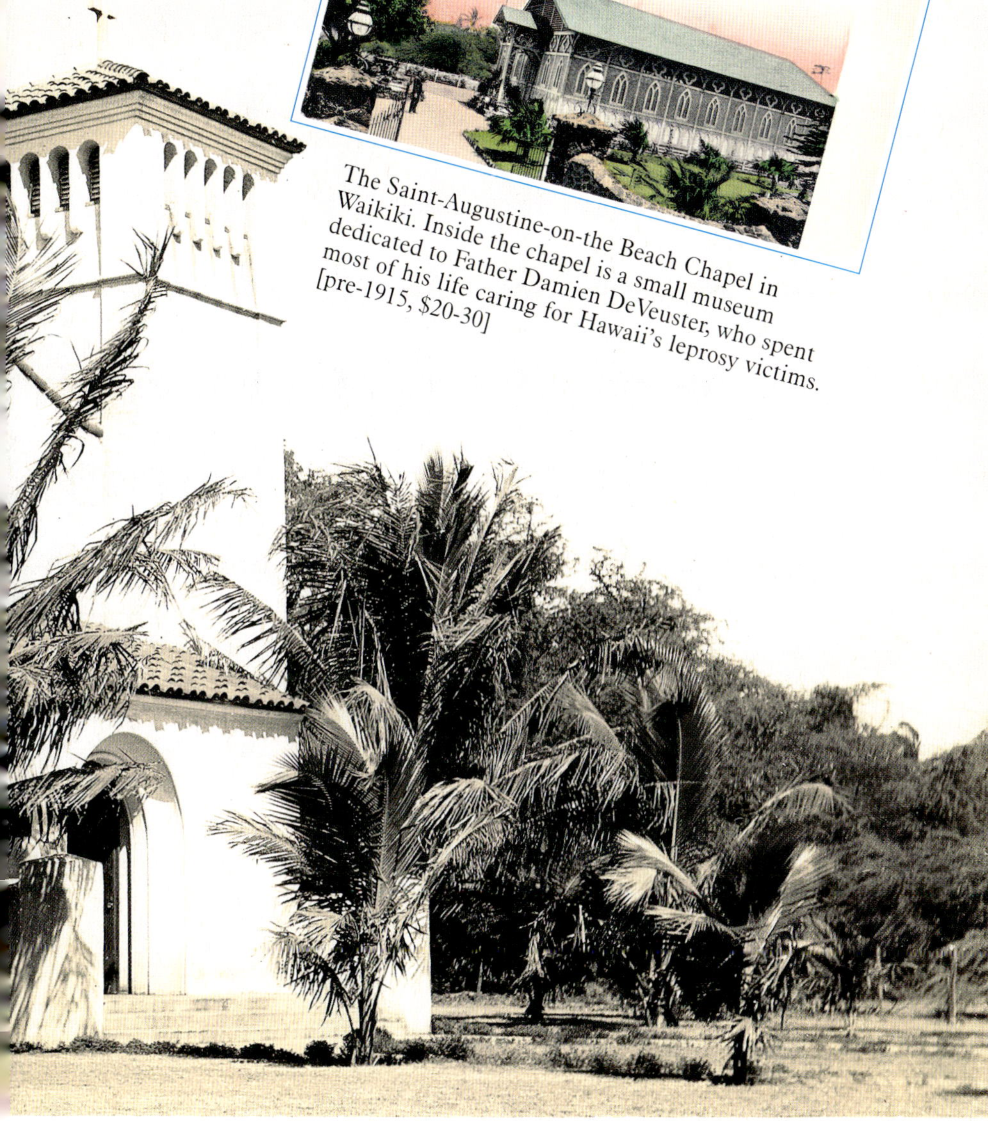

Schools

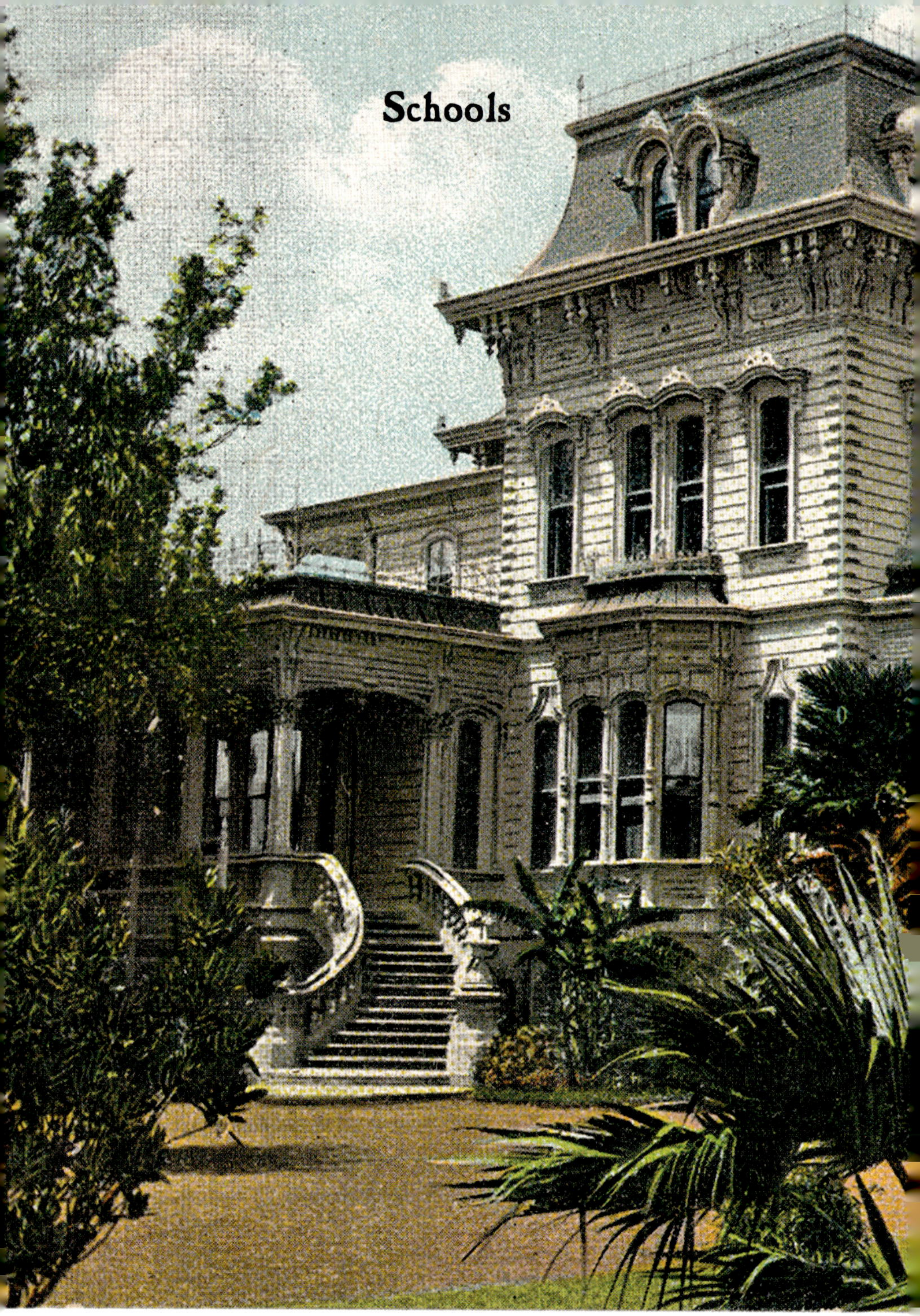

The high school in Honolulu. [canceled 1910, $8-10]

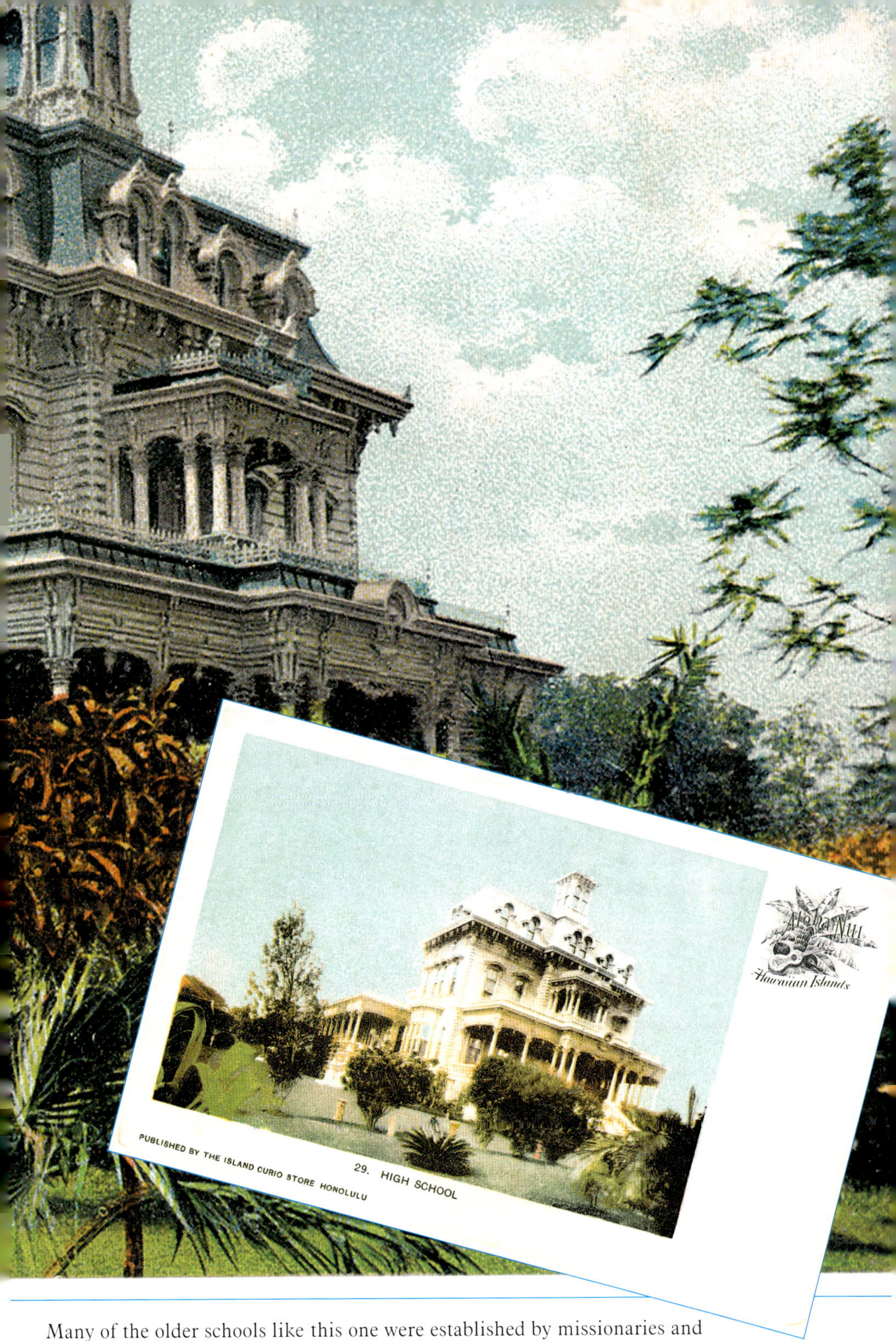

Many of the older schools like this one were established by missionaries and served to educate the children of prominent Hawaiian citizens. [pre-1915, $30-40]

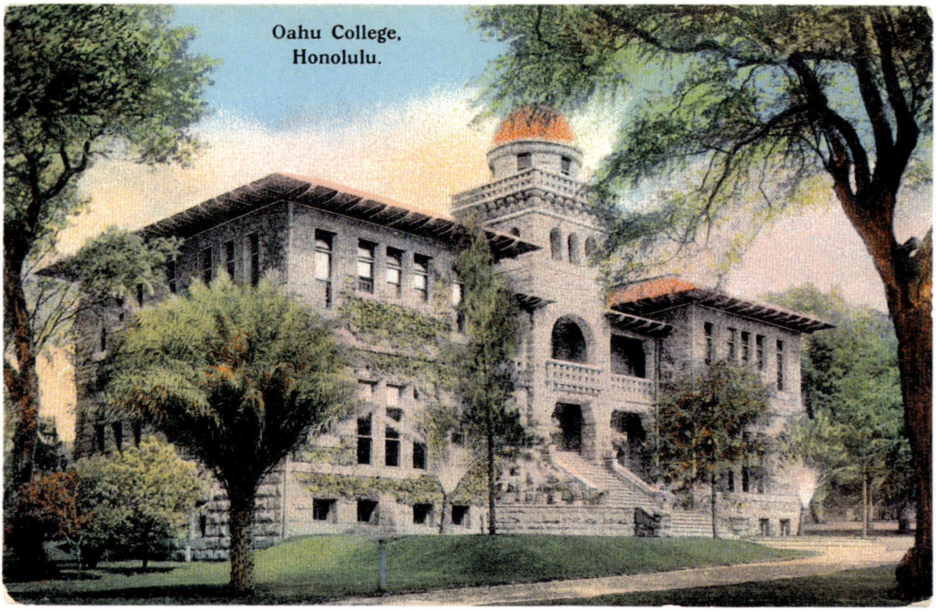

Oahu College was opened in 1854 by Protestant missionaries. [$4-6]

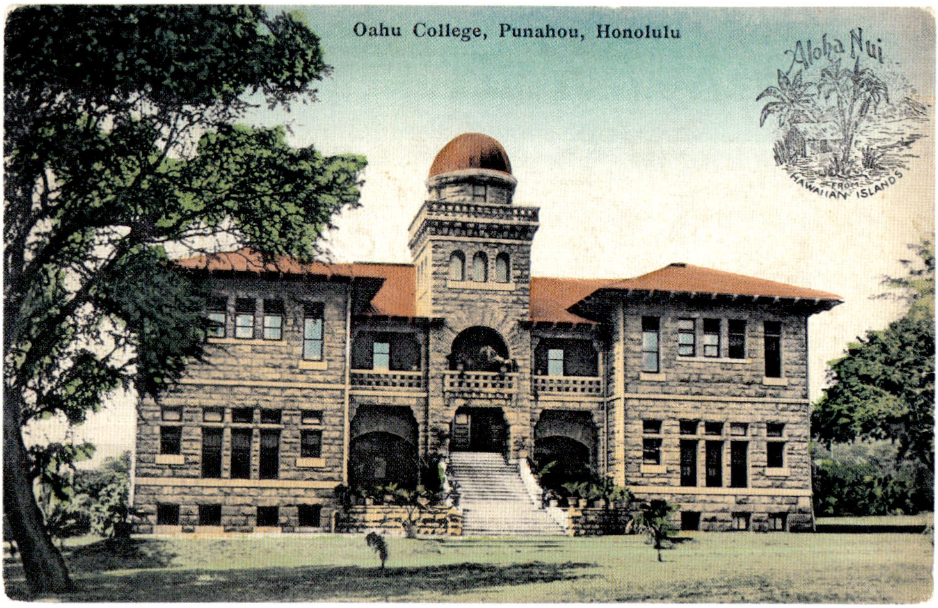

The Oahu College possessed a curriculum "of the highest" standards and "all the modern appliances for the study of the sciences and art." [canceled 1909, $4-6]

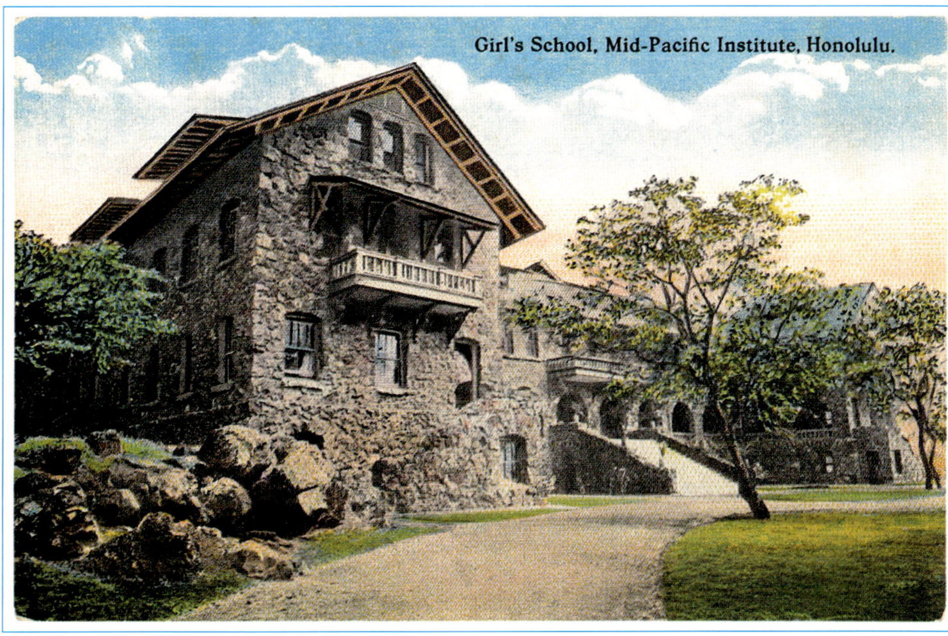

The Girl's School of the Mid-Pacific Institute was one of the premier schools in Hawaii. Many of its teachers were descendents of missionaries. [pre-1915, $8-10]

A Short History of the Postcard in the United States

Pioneer Era (1893-1898)

Although there were earlier scattered issues, most pioneer cards in today's collections begin with the cards placed on sale at the Columbian Exposition in Chicago, Illinois, on May 1, 1893. These were illustrations on government printed postal cards and privately printed souvenir cards. The government postal cards had the printed one-cent stamp, while the souvenir cards required a two-cent adhesive postage stamp to be applied. Writing was not permitted on the address side of the cards.

Private Mailing Card Era (1898-1901)

On May 19, 1898, private printers were granted permission, by an act of Congress, to print and sell cards that bore the inscription "Private Mailing Card." Today, they are called "PMCs." A one-cent adhesive stamp was required. A dozen or more American printers began to take postcards seriously. Writing was still not permitted on the address side.

Postcard Era (1901-1907)

The use of the word "Postcard" was granted by the government to private printers on December 24, 1901. Writing was still not permitted on the address side. In this era, private citizens began to take black-and-white photographs and have them printed on paper with postcard backs.

Divided Back Era (1907-1914)

Postcards with a divided back were permitted March 1, 1907. The address was to be written on the right side and the left side was for writing messages. Many millions of cards were published and printed in this era, most in Germany, where printers were far more advanced in the lithographic processes. With the advent of World War I, the supply of postcards had to come from England and the United States.

White Border Era (1915-1930)

Most domestic-use postcards were printed in the United States during this period. To save ink, a border was left around the view, thus the name "White Border Cards." The high cost of labor, inexperience, and public taste created cards of inferior quality. Competition in a narrowing market caused many publishers to go out of business.

Linen Era (1930-1944)

New printing processes allowed printing on postcards with high rag content that caused a linen-like finish. These cheap cards allowed for the use of gaudy dyes for coloring. Curt Teich's line of linen postcards flourished. Many important historical events are recorded on these cards.

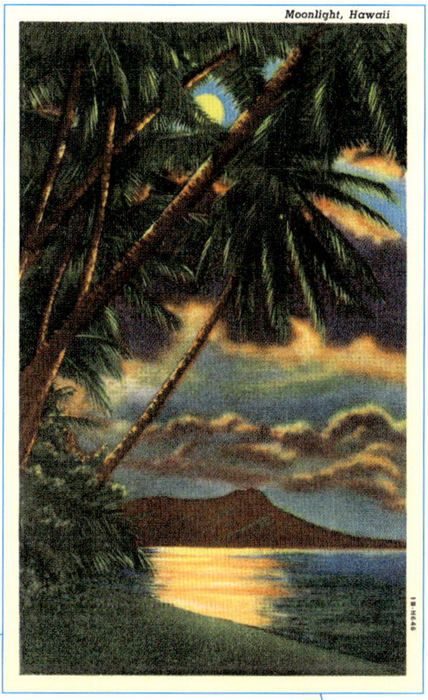

[pre-1940, $1-3]

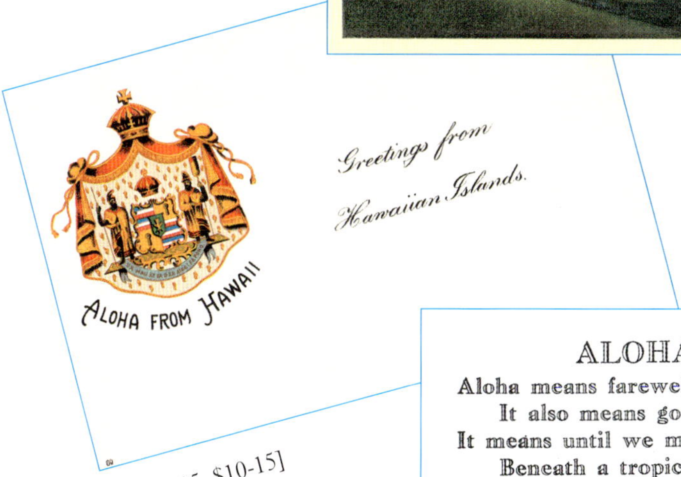

[pre-1915, $10-15]

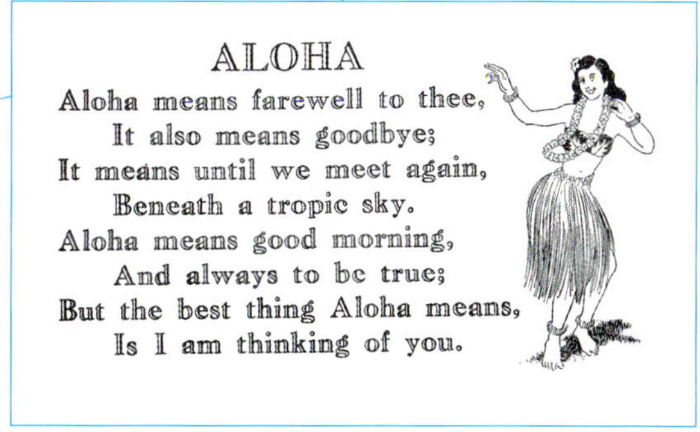

[pre-1940, $1-3]

Bibliography

Brown, De Soto. Hawaii Recalls: Selling Romance to America: Nostalgic Images of the Hawaiian Islands: 1910-1950. Editions Limited, Honolulu. 1982.

"Canoe Plants of Ancient Hawai'i". http://www.canoeplants.com/awa.html. 6/16/04.

"CRFG Publications". http://www.crfg.org/pubs/. 6/17/04.

Durham, Brian N. *Ancient Times in the Islands.* http://www.hawaiischoolreports.com/history/ancient.html. 8/20/04.

"The Food Network." web.foodnetwork.com. 6/17/04.

"Hawaii's Agricultural Gateway". http://www.hawaiig.org/. 6/16/04.

"Hawaii Agriculture Resource Center (HARC)". http://www.hawaiig.org/harc/. 6/17/04.

"The Hawaiian Historical Society". http://www.hawaiianhistory.org. 6/16/04.

Hiroa, Te Rangi (Peter H. Buck). *Arts and Crafts of Hawaii Vol. V: Clothing.* Bishop Museum Press, Honlulu. 1964.

Historical Society Conference, 'Ka'Aina: Rethinking our Kuleana,' October 17, 1998" http://www.hawaiianhistory.org/urls98.html. 6/17/04.

"Internet Sites for Hawai'i Researchers Compiled by Kawika Makanani for Hawaiian

"The Polynesian Cultural Center." http://www.polynesia/islands/hawaii. 6/21/04.

"Queensland Government Department of Primary Industries and Fisheries." http://www.dpi.qld.gov.au/horticulture/5224.html. 6/16/04.

"RiceWeb: A Compendium of Facts and Figures from the World of Rice". http://www.riceworld.org. 6/17/04.

Schweitzer, Sophia. "Taro: Gift of the Ancient Gods." "The Hawaiian Lei." *Coffee Times.* Fall/Winter 1995-96.

Stillman, Amy Ku'uleialoha . International Encyclopedia of Dance, Hula in Hawaii. Oxford University Press, New York. 1998.